Amelia, My Courageous Sister

Biography of Amelia Earhart • True Facts About Her Disappearance

by
Muriel Earhart Morrissey
and
Carol L. Osborne

OSBORNE PUBLISHER, INCORPORATED   1987   Santa Clara, California

Amelia, My Courageous Sister

Biography of AMELIA EARHART

Copyright © 1987, Carol L. Osborne and
Muriel Earhart Morrissey
All rights reserved under International
and Pan-American Copyright conventions.
Published in the United States by
Osborne Publisher, Incorporated, Santa Clara, California

No part of this book may be reproduced by
any means, especially to include electronic
reproduction, without permission in writing
from the publisher, except by a reviewer to
quote brief excerpts in connection with a
review in a magazine or newspaper

Copyrights and Permissions: Every effort has been
made to secure proper permission for use of
copyrighted works and to secure courtesy permissions
as well for all material reproduced in this biography of Amelia

Morrissey, Muriel Earhart, 1899–
Osborne, Carol L., 1946–

Library of Congress Cataloging-in-Publication Data

Morrissey, Muriel Earhart.
    Amelia, my courageous sister.

    Bibliography: p.
    Includes index.
    1. Earhart, Amelia, 1897-1937. 2. Air pilots—United States—
Biography. I. Osborne, Carol L., 1946–   . II. Title.
TL540.E3M66 1987   629.13′092′4 [B]   87-7798

ISBN 0-940997-00-2
    0-940997-02-9 (pbk)

12   11   10   9   8   7   6   5   4   3   2   1

First Edition, 1987

Distributed
by
Aviation Book Company, 1640 Victory Blvd., Glendale, CA 91201

Table of Contents

		Page
Chapter One	Our Heritage	1
Chapter Two	Amelia Mary and Grace Muriel "Meelie" and "Pidge"	7
Chapter Three	The World About Us	19
Chapter Four	Atchison Interlude	23
Chapter Five	Success and Failure	29
Chapter Six	Lean Days	37
Chapter Seven	Changing Backgrounds	41
Chapter Eight	Toronto War Nurse and Columbia Student	49
Chapter Nine	California Girl and Fledgling Flier	59
Chapter Ten	Boston and Beyond	69
Chapter Eleven	20 Hours and 40 Minutes	81
Chapter Twelve	Fame and More	95
Chapter Thirteen	Between Record Flights	109
Chapter Fourteen	Solo Over the Atlantic	123
Chapter Fifteen	Honors Beyond Imagination	131
Chapter Sixteen	Across the Pacific Ocean	151
Chapter Seventeen	Preparing to Circle the Globe	165
Chapter Eighteen	Just One More Long Flight	193
Chapter Nineteen	The Search	249
Chapter Twenty	History Not Mystery	267
Appendix		299
Index		310

Acknowledgments

Without the assistance of the following people this book could not have been written. I would like to offer each of them a very special and heartfelt thank you:

Thomas M. Wilson, for his assistance with the technical analysis used to reconstruct Amelia's flight from Lae to Howland Island.

Carol "Petey" Johnston for her professional preparation of camera ready art work.

Roberta Wainright who helped review and evaluate the thousands of pages of records and reports.

Harvey Christen, Sol London, Bob Ferguson, and Eric Schulzinger of Lockheed Corporation who provided copies of photographs and historic records of Amelia and her airplanes.

Herb Boen, Aviation Historian, who provided outstanding support and technical evaluation of our manuscript prior to publication.

W. H. "Walt" Grosselfinger, F.O. "Fuzz" Furman, R. D. "Bo" McKneely and Commander H. M. Anthony, U.S. Coast Guard Retired, who reviewed parts of the manuscript for technical accuracy.

George Akimoto for his paintings used on the cover of *Just Plane Crazy* and *Amelia, My Courageous Sister*.

Father Angelus Lingenfelser, for his help and kindness giving us access to Atchison County Historical Society's memorabilia.

Willys Peck, Copy Editor, for his editorial reviews, suggestions and support.

Marty Blaker and Louise A. Vernon for their editorial and writing assistance.

Robert Parks, Raymond Teichman, and Frances M. Seeber, archivists of the Franklin D. Roosevelt Library, for providing copies of all documents relating to Amelia and her disappearance.

Eva Mosley of the Schlesinger Library, Radcliffe College for access to many of the personal Earhart and Morrissey family papers.

Don Dwiggins, author of *Hollywood Pilot: The Biography of Paul Mantz*, for information and memorabilia of Amelia's from the start.

Helen Q. Schroyer, Purdue University, for support and sharing Amelia's and George Putnam's personal materials. Amelia had deposited most of her personal medals, awards, certificates, and papers with President Elliott at Purdue when she left on her last flight.

Leonard Grant, Joseph Blanton, and Barbara Shattuck, *National Geographic Magazine*, for permission to reprint Amelia's own story about two of her most important flights.

Thomas J. Ringers, grandson of T.F. "Tommie" O'Dea for the last known photographs taken of Amelia and Fred, and to Joan M. Hill who helped us obtain the copies.

Norma McCormick of Western Electric, for copies of photographs and letters about Amelia's radio equipment.

Phillips Dewey of the *San Francisco Chronicle*, Greg Rohloff of the *Atchison Daily Globe*, the *Boston Globe*, and Roy Grimm and Yae Shinomiga of the *Oakland Tribune* for use of their photographs and newspaper clippings.

Enid Williams, Sam Kahalewai, Kathleen Brooks-Pizmany, Claudia Oakes, Major Susan Neugebauer, Forest M. Johnston, Cleo Hall, U.S. Naval Archives, The National Archives, and The Library of Congress.

Paul Mennen for use of his Great Circle Program to reconstruct Amelia's last flight in "History Not Mystery."

LCDR Frank Lopez, Bud Mitchell, Bob Wallace, Neta Snook Southern, W. M. "Bill" Clough, and other OX5 Aviation Pioneers for loaning their special photographs.

Bonnie Riggins and Bruce Orwoll of Camera Mart, Sunnyvale, California, for much of the photographic reproduction in the book.

Eugene J. Suto, author of History of Classification, who allowed us to quote from his paper.

San Jose Public Library Reference Desk and Periodical Reference Department, who were always willing to answer numerous questions, and

Especially, Charter Ninety-Nine and friend of Amelia's, Bobbi Trout, who devoted hours to the preparation and layout of this book.

Muriel Earhart Morrissey and
Carol L. Osborne

*To all who knew and loved Amelia
and to all who want to know her,
this book is offered gratefully
in her memory*

*Muriel Earhart Morrissey
and Carol L. Osborne*

Foreword

I believe you will find this is an excellent opportunity to come to know Amelia Earhart as a real person by reading this book, *Amelia, My Courageous Sister*. Even ninety years after her birth, many have heard of Amelia as a woman flier who broke many records. However, in 1987 when flying in planes is an accepted method of travel together with automobiles and trains, why should this woman be considered any more important than any of many women pilots who helped develop the aviation industry? Since I came to know Amelia when we were students and found her an unusual person and a wonderful friend, I will include some personal experiences in the story.

It was a happy coincidence that Amelia Earhart and I enrolled at the same time for the biology course taught by Dr. James MacGregor at Columbia University in New York City in 1919. Amelia was taking courses to complete her undergraduate college degree. I had graduated from Smith College but needed more science credits before entering Johns Hopkins Medical School. Amelia and I were assigned desks next to each other and became good friends while working together. We also enrolled together in an inorganic chemistry course at Columbia and an organic chemistry course at Barnard College. It was a great privilege to study with Amelia because she was keen and intelligent and also great fun to be with. Amelia was studying French and enjoyed reading and writing poetry. I was also involved in auditing courses in other parts of the university . . . However, it was not all work and no play.

We occasionally went for hikes and picnics on the Pallisades across the Hudson River near Columbia University. In many ways we were sad to have the school year end in June, 1920. I continued to work at Columbia during summer school and then went to medical school, but Amelia went with her parents to California. We kept in touch through letters for the four years during which I studied and obtained my M.D. degree at Johns Hopkins.

I went to Boston in July, 1924, to serve my internship at the New England Hospital for Women and Children. Much to my joy, Amelia had left California and come to Boston to join her sister and mother. She lived with them in West Medford until she joined the staff at Denison House in Boston. She had her famous Kissel Kar and would drive to my hospital to take me and my husband on expeditions to Marblehead for swimming and picnicking on the beach or to explore other parts of Boston. In July, 1925, Amelia and I had to say goodby again since my husband and I moved to St. Louis and she became involved with her flying career. We did keep in touch through the years. I remember Amelia's writing especially concerning the health of women students while she was teaching at Purdue University.

I did not see Amelia again until about 1934 and then again when she, once more, was to speak to a large assembly at Yale University. My husband and I were then members of the faculty at Yale. Amelia invited us to come to have dinner with her in her room at the hotel for greater privacy before the scheduled lecture. Afterwards we went for a hot fudge sundae for old time's sake, reminiscent of our student days.

I found Amelia unspoiled by all her fame and exploits. She was still a caring person, caring about what was happening to people in need all over the world in sickness and in health. She was interested in what was happening to the United States and how President Roosevelt was handling the problems in this country. Her sense of humor was unspoiled. She gave me her orchid corsage saying, "I will have another one tomorrow when I speak in Massachusetts." The following day I went with her in her car to Massachusetts and returned to New Haven by bus, not realizing that it was the last time I would see her in person. She was a thoughtful person, a private person, unspoiled by her triumphs and always trying further ways to improve aviation. In 1928 when she wrote her first book, *20 Hours and 40 Minutes, Our Flight in the Friendship*, she sent us a gift copy with the inscription, "To Louise and Dan with the promise to read anything they write if they will read this." I was only twenty days younger than Amelia so have had many years to think about her since her last flight. I think in reading this book, you will find inspiration and pleasure in learning more about the development of a fine, sensitive, generous, intelligent and wonderful girl and woman.

Dr. Louise DeSchweinitz Darrow, Director of Pediatrics at the Children's Rehabilitation Unit of the Kansas University Medical Center, now retired.

Foreword

Amelia, My Courageous Sister, is a complete reference book on Amelia Earhart, from her birth, in 1897, through her last flight, July 2, 1937.

It is succinctly written, without embellishments or conjectures. The last chapters of the book are devoted to the documented facts on all facets of the searches for Amelia. The authors present no solutions. They let the readers draw their own conclusions or feel free to follow the well-documented, researched leads in the book to create their own endings.

The biography of Amelia is of course also a partial biography of her sister, Muriel Earhart Morrissey, who shared so fully those early years. Muriel followed her adored, older sister on a wonderful flight of childhood fantasy that sustained them through the roller-coaster adversities of their young lives.

Muriel called Amelia "Meelie" because she couldn't say Amelia, and Amelia called Muriel "Pidge" because she loved whimsy.

Muriel, despite her very busy life these past fifty years as a wife, mother, educator and civic leader, has patiently, happily and with humility lived in the shadow of "Meelie." Muriel's definitive biography of her sister, *Courage Is The Price*, explains why.

Courage and *Amelia* should be side-by-side in the libraries of everyone interested in aviation lore and the flying adventures of Amelia.

Fay Gillis Wells, early aviator and member of the Caterpillar Club for being the first woman to use a parachute when needed, is a charter member of the Ninety-Nines and a long time friend of Amelia's.

Introduction

Amelia Earhart's career as a world-famous flier spanned only a few years. She achieved instant acclaim as the first woman to fly the Atlantic in 1928; she disappeared while on the last leg of a round-the-world flight in 1937. Yet her fame has endured in a remarkable fashion over the past fifty years, assuring her a permanent place in history. Books, magazine articles, films, televised biographies, symposia, memorials, schools and other public buildings named in her honor—all testify to the lasting impression that she made as one who truly embodied the spirit of adventure and the desire to advance human knowledge.

In recent years, the attempt to find a definitive solution to the mystery of her disappearance has tended to overshadow her actual achievements and to obscure the meaning of her life, which is quite independent of the circumstances of her death. In this book I have attempted to bring up to date my earlier biography of my sister, *Courage Is the Price*. I reiterate my belief, expressed in that book, that those who have propounded often sensational theories about Amelia's disappearance have consistently failed to produce convincing, substantial evidence that would incline us to reject the more plausible view that Amelia's aircraft ran out of fuel and crashed in the Pacific when it failed to make its landing at Howland Island.

My closeness to my sister throughout her life gives me an expertise which other biographers lack. As children growing up in Kansas, we were inseparable, sharing many tomboyish activities, riding horses together, loving animals, participating in imaginative games. Throughout our lives we confided in each other, experiencing each other's triumphs and tragedies. We understood each other; each one was there for the other at crucial times such as Amelia's first solo flight or my wedding.

Amelia's childhood and young adulthood provide many clues to understanding the person she became. The persistence that she showed as a child while hunting rats in the barn foreshadowed her determination to make a lasting contribution to the science of aviation. The home-made roller coaster has become the symbol of her early love of adventure which later found its realization in her flying. The influence of her family and her education remained strong throughout her life.

I have missed Amelia, both as a sister and as a friend, during these past fifty years. I wish that she too could have lived to celebrate the fiftieth anniversary of her last great flight. Still, it is a comfort to know that during her short life she touched so many people, and that her story still provides inspiration to all those in whom the spirit of adventure is alive.

Muriel Earhart Morrissey

Chapter One

Our Heritage

OUR great-grandmother, Maria Grace Harres, was two and one-half years old when her father lifted her onto his shoulders to see General George Washington on July 4, 1799. Our grandmother told us about watching Washington pass by on his way to meet President Adams. Amelia and I remembered that story all our lives.

Our great-grandmother lived to be almost one hundred. She died in 1896, one year before Amelia was born. Our mother, who lived to be ninety-five, died in 1962. The lives of these two women nearly spanned the life of our nation.

According to the family Bible, Maria Grace married Gebhard Harres, a young German-born Philadelphia industrialist, in 1818. Gebhard and Maria had seven children. The youngest, Amelia Josephine, was born in 1840. She married Alfred Otis, a young lawyer.

Alfred was a direct descendant of James Otis, who gave the speech that John Adams called "the opening gun of the Revolution."

Our great grandparents, Maria Grace and Gebhard Harres, who married in 1818.

Our grandparents, Amelia Josephine Harres and Alfred Gideon Otis. They married in 1862, and died in 1912, within three months of each other.

An early graduate of the University of Michigan, Alfred was equally devoted to freedom. Four years before the Revolution, he settled in Atchison, Kansas. He built his home on bluffs overlooking the Missouri River. He no doubt had qualms about bringing his bride to live in a community where Indians, even though considered friendly, were still a common sight. The main street became thick mud during the spring and autumn rains. At that time, there were no bridges across the Missouri River.

The Civil War broke out soon after our grandparents arrived in Atchison, bringing many changes. Our grandfather joined a regiment of Kansas soldiers under the command of Colonel John A. Martin, who later became governor of Kansas and a close friend. They were sent as far south as Mississippi, but after a discouraging march through swamps and desolate fields, they found no enemy to fight. The men then boarded several army barges and were hauled back up-river to guard the border along Fort Leavenworth. Our grandfather received his honorable discharge on the day news of President Lincoln's assassination reached Atchison.

In the next few years, Atchison became an important terminus for the Burlington and Santa Fe railroads. A Lutheran college was established on the outskirts of town, streets were paved, and churches built. A successful law practice and wise land investments made our grandfather wealthy. He became a bank president and an elected Judge of the United States District Court.

This 28-page genealogy document was written January, 1907. Page 11 is to the right.

Descendants of Isaac and Caroline Curtiss Otis.

There were thirteen children born to Isaac and Caroline Otis, of whom eleven were living at the time of the father's death in 1853 and survived that time about thirty years. They are here named in their order, with such matters of special interest pertaining to them and their respective families as I have been able to obtain.

I

Alfred Gideon Otis. He was born December 13th, 1827 in Little York, New York, where his boyhood days were passed, as he was left there with his grandfather when his parents came west, and did not join them in their pioneer home until 1841, at which time he returned with his mother who visisted among her eastern relatives that year. He entered the University of Michigan in 1849, taking a classical course, and graduating in 1852. He then studied law in Kalamazoo, Michigan, and in 1853 commenced the practice of his profession as a member of the firm of Gottschalk and Otis in Louisville, Ky. Two years later he took up his residence and professional work in Atchison, Kansas, where he still resides. In 1878 he was elected Circuit Judge on the Democratic ticket in a Circuit theretofore strongly Republican. At the end of his term in 1882 he declined a second nomination and upon retiring from the bench did not again resume law practice, but engaged in the banking business and other financial enterprises, and was president of the Atchison Savings Bank of his home city until he retired from active business in 1891. He was appointed a Regent of the State University of Kansas by Gov. Glick (a Democrat) in 1883, and served through his own term of office. Governor Martin (a Republican) who succeeded Governor Glick re-appointed Judge Otis to the Regency and he continued in such position during the two terms of office of Governor Martin, and during this time it is said of him that he was the only Democrat in the State, (then strongly Republican) holding public office.

--11--

Our grandfather Reverend David Earhart, father of Edwin.

On the other side of the family, our grandfather, the Reverend David Earhart, was a modest, happy man. In his brief autobiography, he told of his achievements as an organizer, author, and preacher. He married Mary Wells Patton in 1841. They had six sons and six daughters. Three died during a scarlet fever plague and one was killed by a bolt of lightning as she lay in her cradle next to an open window during a sudden thunderstorm. Grandfather Earhart wrote:

> In the spring of 1860, I moved my family to Kansas and located in Sumner, a small town about three miles south of Atchison. There I gathered a small congregation, but a severe storm with great winds blew down and destroyed many of the poor wooden houses . . .

Grandfather Earhart studied theology in Wooster, Ohio, and preached in the Evangelical Lutheran Church for five years. While in Kansas, he became regent of the State Agricultural College for six years. He had to travel the one hundred miles to the college by horseback or surrey before the more convenient Kansas Pacific Railroad was laid.

Grandfather encountered many hardships during this time. The year 1860 brought a severe drought. Many of the farmers' crops failed. When the Civil War broke out, nearly all of the men capable of bearing arms went off to war, leaving only women, children, and older men to do the farming. Kansas gave most of its men to the Union Army while it experienced three years of border warfare and two successive years of grasshopper infestation. Grandfather Earhart found it difficult to inspire godly living in his congregation when they had to work so hard to raise only enough food to barely sustain life. He taught school and raised his family despite the hard times.

In his writing he told an interesting story about our father:

> . . . one Sunday when I returned late in the afternoon from a preaching mission to find that my youngest son, Edwin, then seven years old, had been fishing and had caught six large and succulent bull-heads. I immediately asked him how it happened that he had desecrated the Lord's Day by fishing. He replied, "Sir, you know fish always bite better when you are preaching."

Our father, Edwin Stanton Earhart, at the age of six in Atchison, Kansas.

Grandfather found our father's answer ingenious. He could not refuse his family's request for nourishment, so they all ate the fish dinner, although grandfather wrote that his conscience was not entirely clear. Amelia and I never tired of hearing this story as children.

Grandfather Earhart stayed in Kansas for thirteen years before returning to Pennsylvania where he served as pastor. In 1887 he retired and moved back to Atchison where he taught a Bible class and occasionally preached. Grandfather's dream was to inspire our father to become a minister. He sent Dad to Greenville, Pennsylvania, to attend Thiel College, which years later awarded Amelia an honorary doctorate. Dad earned excellent grades and graduated with honors. To grandfather's disappointment, Dad did not feel a calling to the ministry and wanted to become a lawyer. He entered the University of Kansas Law School and earned his tuition as an assistant to the professors and as a tutor.

While our Grandfather Earhart's family struggled with living on the outskirts of Atchison, life for Grandfather Otis' family was easier. One of Grandmother Otis' sisters, Mary, married Dr. Paul Challiss, whose brother, Luther, was one of the town's founders. Dr. Challiss acquired a large expanse of land on the bluff-top and built a tall mansion with fountains and a gazebo overlooking the great bend of the Missouri. He kept several spirited horses in a large stable, as well as two steady cobs to pull the wagon when his wife and children went to church.

Our mother, Amy Otis, was an excellent student and was accepted at Vassar College for the fall of 1889. She had been rather sickly since she was sixteen when a serious case of typhoid fever impaired her hearing. Her long chestnut hair had been cut at that time because it was believed that a woman's hair took strength from the rest of her body. This naturally had no effect on her health, and she was no longer teased by her classmates who would dip her pigtails into inkwells or tie them to the back of her seat.

During the summer of 1889, our mother contracted diphtheria. She was nursed back to health by our great-grandmother, Maria Grace Harres, who was spry at age ninety-two. Night and day, Maria kept the rest of the family away to avoid exposing them to diphtheria. She, however, had no fear of the disease. Thanks to our great-grandmother and an Atchison doctor, our mother was eventually nursed back to health.

Our mother, Amy Otis, circa 1870 in Atchison, Kansas.

Our mother's plans to attend Vassar never materialized because of her long convalescence, but she kept busy with many cultural and social activities. She organized the Dickens Club, which presented literary tableaux, taught Sunday School, and often assisted her father by transcribing his legal opinions. She enjoyed being included in the discussions of public affairs, which took place when Senator John J. Ingalls and Governor John A. Martin visited on the veranda at our grandfather's house.

Our mother and the Senator's daughter, Constance, were the chosen leaders of the young social set. They attended military balls at Fort Leavenworth and cotillions in St. Joseph.

Our mother was an accomplished horsewoman, and she rode daily to rebuild her

Amy Otis at age of fifteen.

PHOTO FROM FAMILY BIBLE

Our Mother's father traveled a lot and considered it educational. With Mother's poor health as an excuse, he often took her with him on trips to investigate western lands offered for investment or security, or when he was called upon to visit and evaluate ministerial prospects. Long trips by stagecoach into the Utah Indian Territory, and later Oklahoma, familiarized her with the West back when buffalo herds still grazed along the tracks. Abandoned wagon wrecks and bleached cattle bones were a constant reminder that the Great Plains exacted their toll before yielding to man's domination.

In the summer of 1890, Grandfather Otis took mother with him to Colorado where he planned to interview a young minister who applied to fill a vacancy in the pulpit of Atchison Trinity Church. While there, they met a congenial group of people who persuaded grandfather and mother to join them on a trip to the top of Pike's Peak.

Mother wrote a letter to her younger sister, Margaret, describing the rugged ride but adding that it was worth it when she considered the challenge and the majestic views. The group reached the house at the half-way point by the first afternoon. At dinner the group talked about the following morning's final climb. Mother was the only woman who wished to continue the trip to the peak. In her letter to Margaret she wrote:

> I was the only female. I felt that several of the gentlemen deplored my presence as a restriction upon their language and possibly a deterrent to their speed . . . We made our last halt at about ten thousand feet. Here we left the burros in charge of the second guide and proceeded on foot for the remainder of the ascent . . . We proceeded slowly because of the rarity of the atmosphere, and three of the gentlemen were soon afflicted with serious nose-bleeding and were forced to turn back . . . I reached the lookout platform below the Meteorological Station, just as the gray light was pierced by the sun's first rays . . . The men [in the group] expressed wonder at my being there and both declared I was the first woman to have made the last hazardous quarter-mile climb.

Our mother was apparently making firsts for women long before Amelia and I were born.

strength. One morning a new horse named Circus was sent from the stable. Unknown to her and the stableman, this horse had been a circus performer. She was riding with Constance and Senator Ingalls when her horse suddenly reared up and began balancing on his hind legs. Mother, riding side-saddle, was nearly thrown, but managed to hang on. The Senator jumped off his horse, dodged the pawing forefeet, and caught her horse's bridle, pulling the horse back down. Our mother later discovered she had signaled the horse to do his dance by twitching the reins slightly. Circus soon became mother's favorite mount. She told Amelia and me that she often made Circus perform but only when safely out of grandmother's sight. This was another favorite bedtime story that Amelia and I heard many times when we were children.

Chapter Two

Amelia Mary and Grace Muriel "Meelie" and "Pidge"

OUR mother, Amy, married our father, Edwin Earhart, on October 16, 1895. More than the two families were joined by this marriage; two distinct ideologies and heritages were fused. Similar strains and character traits, however, were apparent, especially the love of learning and a pioneering spirit.

One of Amelia's and my favorite childhood tales was the story of how our parents first met at her presentation ball in 1890. The garden party was held in the middle of June. Grandfather had a carpenter build a floor around the old wrought-iron Stag-at-Eve in their back yard. The garden was decorated elegantly and Japanese lanterns hung every few feet. They were lighted just as it began to darken. Fortunately there was little breeze; otherwise grandfather would not have allowed the lanterns to be lighted for fear of the candles tipping and causing a fire. Seven musicians from St. Joseph played waltzes and reels. As Mother stood by the porch steps with her parents, greeting all the guests, our Uncle Mark introduced his friend Edwin Earhart. Mother confessed she liked him right away, and she soon knew that he liked her also.

Not all was smooth sailing, however, for our parents' romance. Grandfather Otis discouraged our father's suit, expecting any man

Amy Otis and Edwin Stanton Earhart on their wedding day, October 16, 1895.

marrying his daughter to earn at least fifty dollars a month and to increase that considerably as time went on. At that time a large fowl could be purchased for twenty-five cents, and enough cotton material for a voluminous dress cost about two dollars. Our father worked five years before impressing Grandfather Otis. It was not until the fall of 1895 that his law practice produced sufficient income to support his future wife in the manner expected by our grandfather.

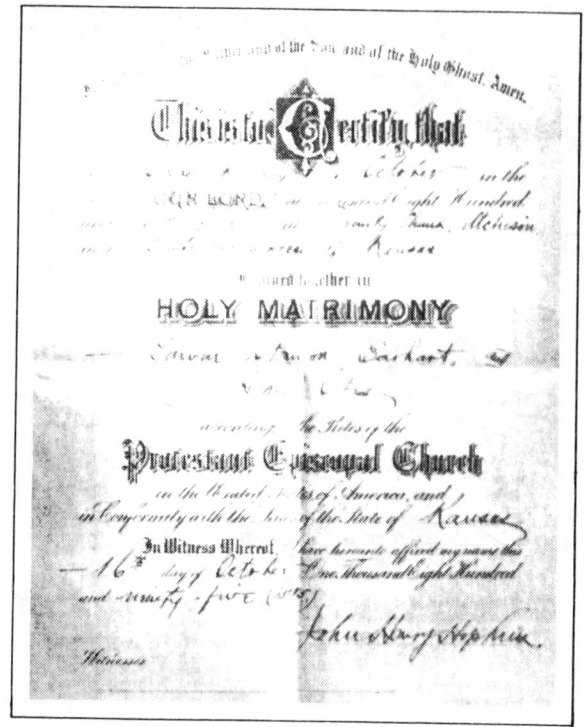

Our parents' marriage license, dated October 16, 1895.

Since a large wedding would be too much of an ordeal for our great-grandmother, who was ninety-seven, our mother and father were quietly married in Trinity Church. Rejecting bridal finery, our mother wore a simple going-away costume of the period. Our father wore a black broadcloth suit with Prince Albert tails that tradition dictated as the proper attire for professional and executive gentlemen. The young couple left Atchison by train for Kansas City, where Grandfather Otis' gift awaited them, a completely furnished home at 1021 Ann Avenue.

Mother's transition from pampered debutante to poor man's wife did not occur without some tears and unhappy hours. Our parents' love and devotion fortunately helped overcome the small disappointments and frustrations. They became a happy married couple, enjoying their own small house on Ann Avenue. Our mother found she was pregnant in the winter of 1896. In the spring, grandmother convinced our mother to come to Atchison for her confinement, which in those days supposedly ensured the birth of a healthy baby.

The house at 1021 Ann Avenue, Kansas City, which Judge Otis gave to our parents as a wedding present. Muriel was born here.

First photograph of Amelia at 4 1/2 months, December 1897.

Earhart Baby Book: Amelia Mary was born Saturday, July 24, 1897, at 11:30 p.m.; Grace Muriel was born Friday, December 29, 1899, at 6:30 a.m.

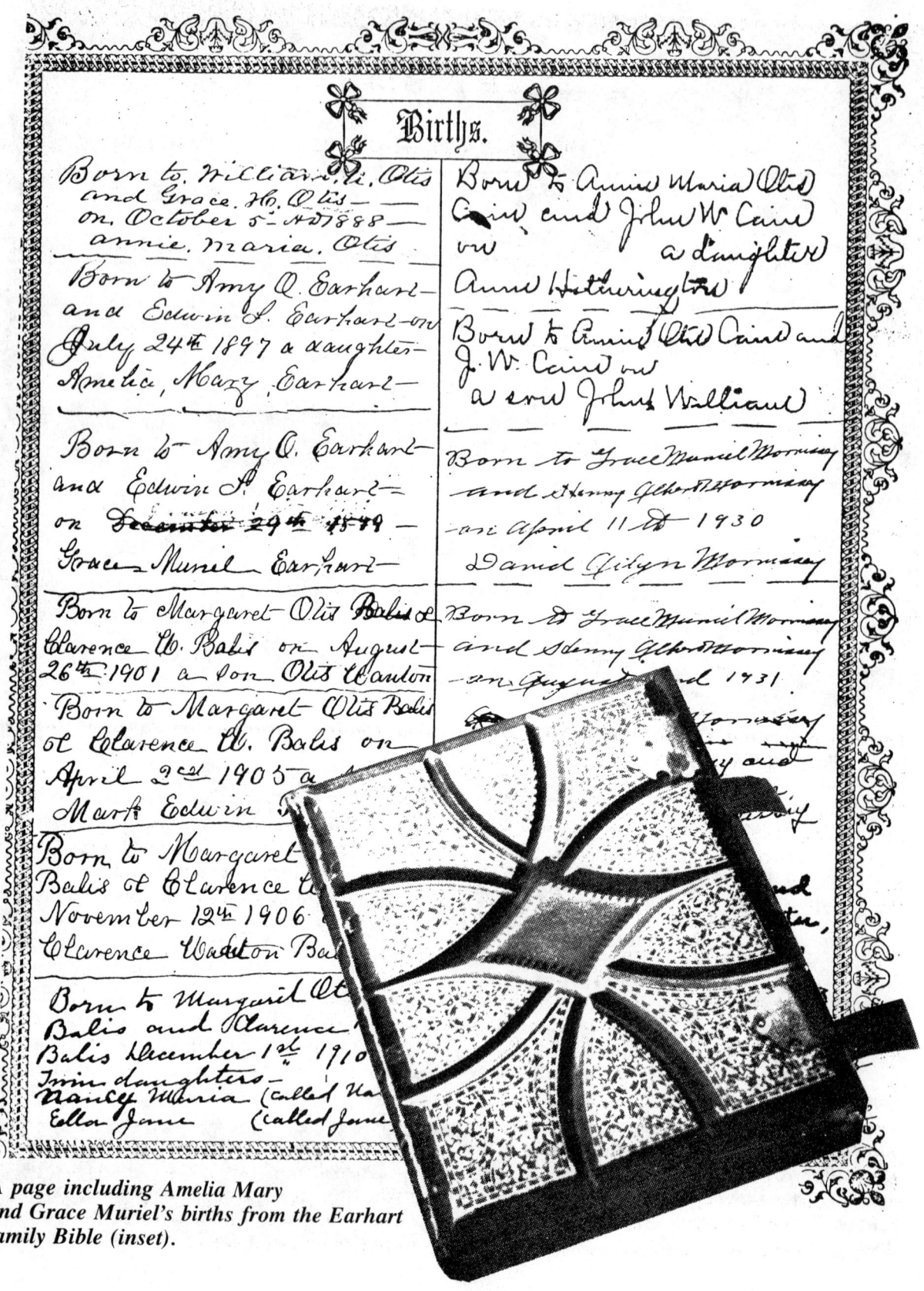

A page including Amelia Mary and Grace Muriel's births from the Earhart family Bible (inset).

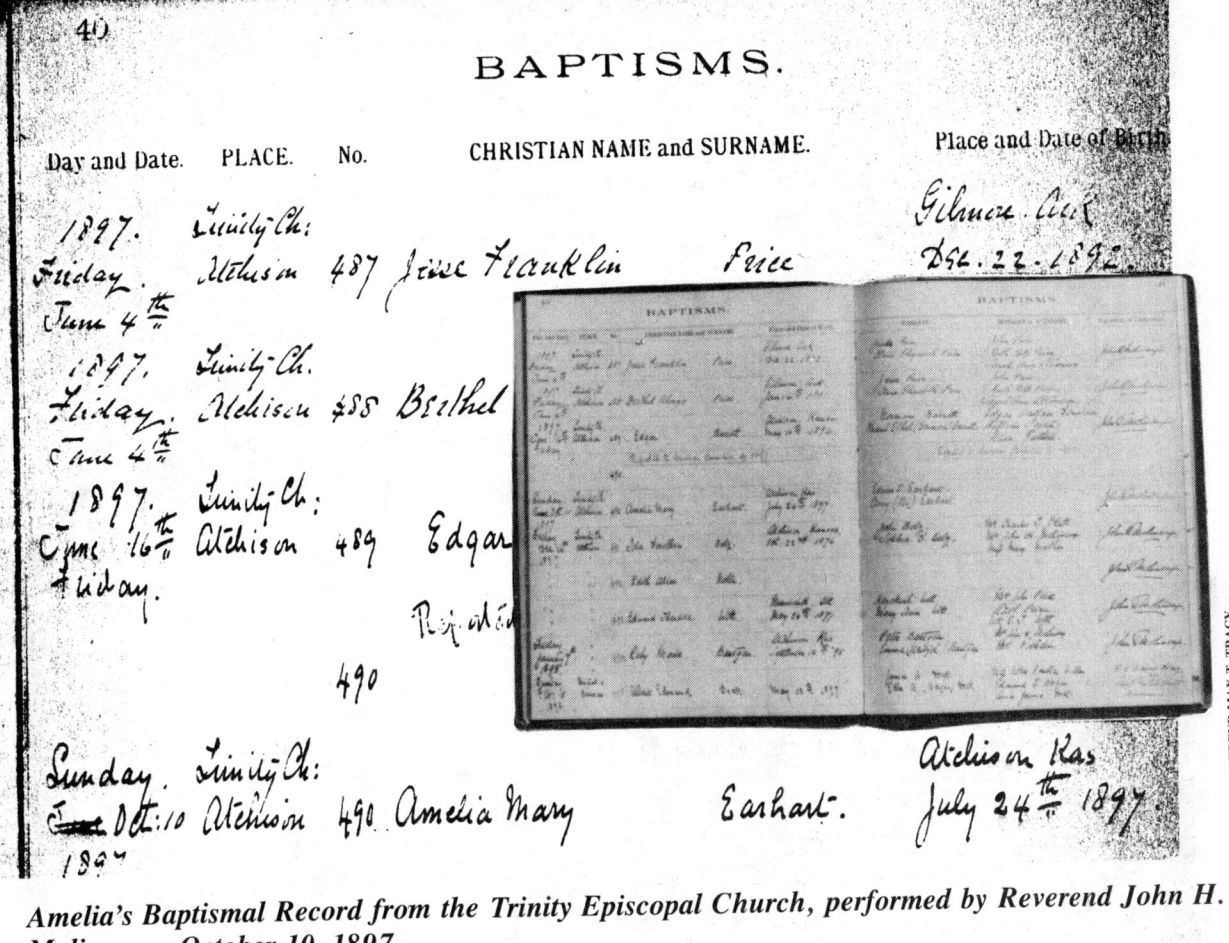

Amelia's Baptismal Record from the Trinity Episcopal Church, performed by Reverend John H. Molineaux, October 10, 1897.

Amelia Mary Earhart was born in Atchison on July 24, 1897. Our parents followed the family custom of naming Amelia Mary for our two grandmothers, Amelia Harres Otis and Mary Wells Earhart.

Two and one-half years later, on December 29, 1899, I was born in Kansas City and named Grace Muriel Earhart. Breaking family tradition this time, my parents named me Grace for our mother's favorite sister-in-law, Grace Hetherington Otis, and Muriel, simply because they liked the name. My birth was only two days before the official turn of the century; it was the same year that President William McKinley became the first president to ride in an automobile. It was also the year the United States annexed Wake Island in the central Pacific for use as a cable station.

When Amelia and I were young, we had pet names for each other. I called her Meelie because I couldn't pronounce her name correctly. She called me Pidge. The names stuck through our childhood and into adulthood.

The hard times of the early twentieth century had little effect on our day-by-day play. Many freedmen came into Kansas during these years after the Civil War expecting to find well-paying jobs in wealthy households. Mother always gave them a few pennies or some bread and bacon before sending them on their way.

In our home in Kansas City, Amelia and I led a rather sheltered life. We had no concept of the economic ills experienced by our country or our family. One of the happiest times of the day was the half-hour after dinner when Amelia and I would sit at the just-cleared dining table and watch Dad tinker with a mysterious invention, which he declared would "bring our ship in."

A page from Amelia and Muriel Earhart's other baby book. Meelie's first word was "Papa." She attempted to repeat any word she heard, however, no matter how long the word. Muriel's first word was "Mama."

Muriel at eight months, Amelia at three years

Later I learned this invention was an ingenious device to hold the required signal flags on the rear of every train. After he had completed three models, he went to Washington to patent it. He had hoped to sell it to the Rock Island Railroad, for which he did legal work during the previous year.

Among the yellowed letters I found in Mother's desk several years ago was one from Washington, D.C., dated May 12, 1903. It is very revealing of our father:

"My dearest Wife,

For two days I did nothing except tramp from one office to another seeking our Kansas member of the House of Representatives, and the various Patent Office clerks who had to establish the classification of my poor little flag holder as mechanical, semi-mechanical, or non-mechanical, and then as to the area of its usefulness: household, farm, factory and so on through seemingly endless categories. All this was necessary, I suppose, to be sure there was no duplication.

When I returned to the main office by appointment about an hour ago, the clerk handed me back my two models with the information that a man from Colorado had filed a patent on an identical holder two years ago. He very kindly gave me the number of this man's patent, so I could look at his drawing in the Patent Office archives.

This news is a terrible blow, because I had been counting on receiving several hundred dollars from the railroad for my flag holder. However, spilled milk and out-dated patents are two things equally useless, so I shall catch the late train tomorrow and may be home almost as soon as this letter reaches you.

I must recount a feeling which I experienced as I walked past the glorious buildings which house our lawmakers and the great legal minds of the Supreme Court. I felt that I shall some day mount those marble steps in an official capacity or never again. Who knows?

Give love to our small daughters, and much to your own sweet self,

Ever thine, Edwin"

The aftermath of not receiving the patent came several months later. Mother received a visit from the city tax collector one afternoon because of a delinquent tax notice. She insisted there was some mistake since the year's taxes had already been paid. She was so positive in her assertion that the collector promised to return after looking through the files for a record of the payment.

That evening, Mother told our father about the tax collector's visit. Father's face told the story even before he said a word. He had used the tax money to get his patent. He had been confident that his idea would make money when the railroad bought it. Mother had never before been involved with bill collectors, and owing money seemed disgraceful to her.

Dad felt he had to find a quick solution. He sold some of the valuable law books that Grandfather Otis had given him and collected two long outstanding fees owed to him. The money was then paid to the tax collector without further embarrassment. The incident would have remained within the family circle, but one of the lawyers to whom father sold the Judge's books bragged about his acquisition. The news soon reached our grandparents. The Judge's feelings were hurt. He was shamed to have an inconsiderate son-in-law and outraged at the thought of having his daughter embarrassed in her marriage to a poor provider. It was the beginning of a rift which was to lead to eventual bitterness and ultimately our parents' divorce.

In the Judge's eyes, this act of irresponsibility was duplicated the following year when Dad took our family to the World's Fair in St. Louis. He received one hundred dollars for legal work defending the railroad's right-of-way and, instead of saving the money, he took us on a week-long vacation to St. Louis. It was the spring of 1904, and I remember watching Amelia, then seven years old, bravely ride an elephant. Amelia was fascinated with the small cars that sped around the aerial track in St. Louis. She later told me that mother insisted that riding on them was too dangerous for little girls, but she compromised on a more dignified and safer Ferris wheel. Amelia rode the Ferris wheel with Dad while Mother and I watched from below.

When we returned to Kansas City, Amelia encouraged our neighbor playmate, Ralphie Martin, to bring over his tool-chest so we could build a roller coaster. Amelia decided that our

"Meelie" and "Pidge" on their Kansas City front porch in the summer of 1902.

A favorite book of Meelie and Pidge, who loved to read. This was a gift from Uncle Mark Otis.

back yard tool-shed, which stood about eight feet high, would be the starting point for our coaster. We pulled several long two-by-fours through the cellar window and put them up against the shed roof.

We used the kitchen stepladder to reach the ridgepole, but we were stymied when we tried to anchor our boards there. We decided to seek adult aid from our much-loved Uncle Carl Otis, the youngest of mother's brothers, who was staying with us while starting in business for himself. We led him to the back yard where Amelia explained our problems. His reaction was practical, and he told us we needed some long nails to secure the slide to the roof, and we'd better nail our track together with boards, like ties.

All the next day Amelia, Ralphie, and I hammered and sawed. We found a wooden packing box and, taking one side which was about fourteen inches square, we nailed two parallel boards on the underside about three inches apart to grip the single track. We soon realized that the pitch would be too great if we used only one fourteen-foot section of track, so we made a trestle about one foot high. This reduced the angle considerably and, as Amelia said, it would give us a longer ride, too. Uncle Carl, whom Amelia and I called "Nicey," brought the long nails, which he obligingly pounded into a stud on the roof. He gave some sturdy blows to our rather shaky trestle and told us it looked fine. All we needed to do was to get some grease on the track and our coaster would be ready.

At dinner that evening Uncle Carl evaded questions about the pounding behind the shed. An obvious wink at Amelia accompanied this remark and evoked spasms of giggles.

The next morning we took a half pail of lard from the icebox and greased the track. We hooked the two lengths of track together and the little car, made from an empty crate, was pushed off on its trial run. We had neglected to provide any kind of a launching platform, but we were all too eager to have a ride to bother with such a convenience. Holding on to the edge of the roof while I held the car from the ladder, Amelia got into the car with her legs doubled up against her chest.

"Let me go!" she shrieked, and I did.

She rode the crate down the track much faster than either of us anticipated. As it careened down the track, we heard the sound of splintering wood. The car and Amelia departed the track when the car hit the trestle. Both tumbled onto the ground. Amelia jumped up, her eyes alight, ignoring a torn dress and bruised lip. She exclaimed happily, "Oh, Pidge, it's just like flying!" Then, ever practical, she added, "We must build more track and a stronger trestle."

The sound of the splintering boards, however, brought Mother running from the house,

Neighborhood children who gathered to play at 1021 Ann Avenue. From left: two unidentified playmates, Muriel, Amelia, and Ralphie.

as well as our next-door neighbor. Mother considered our coaster terribly dangerous and was certain that we would break an arm or a leg if we fell off. Amelia pleaded with Mother to let it stay since we had worked so hard to build it. But Mother insisted it be torn down.

I still believe that if Mother had waited until Dad came home to ask him, we would have been allowed to keep our coaster, as he was in favor of our being as much like boys as we wanted. Our track was soon pulled down, and Sadie, our cook and maid, dragged the boards back to the cellar.

We never played with dolls, but our favorite inanimate companions were our jointed wooden elephant and Amelia's donkey. Ellie and Donk lived rigorous lives which no sawdust-filled, china-headed beauty could have survived. They were made to march through puddles, used to pound nails, or buried alive in the daytime. But, during those early years, we never slept until the two battered but faithful creatures were on guard at the foot of our beds.

To compensate for the loss of our coaster, Mother and Dad got us a lawn swing. A wooden contraption with two seats facing each other suspended from a high frame, it was meant for gentle family swinging, as mother explained, but soon we discovered that it did not have to swing gently all the time. By standing back to back with our hands on the suspending bars, we could get up a momentum that made the whole frame sway and jump. We found it exciting to swing with our knees hooked over the horizontal bar with heads hanging down. Another appropriate means of channeling off surplus energy was devised by Nicey, who built us a flying Dutchman, the primal leg-propelled merry-go-round. Mother and Dad at first objected, but Uncle Carl promised to help construct it, and they reluctantly allowed us to build the device. A long heavy board, twelve feet or so in length, was fastened by a single spike to a stump about four feet high. The spike was loose enough so the board revolved easily. We used to run madly, Amelia pushing on one end and I on the other, until we had worked up momentum. Then we both jumped on the board and whirled round and round until it stopped.

Uncle Carl Otis, born in 1881, whom Amelia and Muriel called "Nicey."

It was this thoroughly delightful, tomboyish activity that led to our emancipation from skirts. Mother, who was in some ways advanced for her day, had a sewing woman make us gym suits for play. This was rare because all nice little girls at the turn of the century wore long, full-skirted dresses with ruffled pinafores over them. However, mother's only sister, our Aunt Margaret, was a trend-setter as a young girl in Atchison. She identified with Amelia Jenks Bloomer, who about 1904 made herself a costume adapted from Turkish trousers and advocated by the pioneer American suffragists, Elizabeth Cady Stanton and Lucy Stone Blackwell. Aunt Margaret was subjected to much teasing and ridicule by her brothers and friends, but she persisted in wearing reform clothes everywhere except to church for several years, until the more sensible shorter walking skirt or rainy-day costume became fashionable. Mother had two dark blue flannel suits made for us with generous pleated bloomers gathered at the knees. We were comfortable, unconventional, and entirely happy tomboys. Thanks to a forward-looking mother who endured the neighbors' raised eyebrows with equanimity, Amelia and I grew up happy with our unconventional lives.

Amelia, on the right on stilts, and Muriel on swing, near their Atchison home. Amelia made the stilts; Uncle Mark was the photographer, circa 1906.

Chapter Three

The World About Us

HOLIDAYS and birthdays were always celebrated by the entire family. We usually had a picnic or birthday party for Amelia's birthday in July. The whole family took turns at the home-made ice cream freezer. We couldn't wait to lick the ice cream off the dasher after it was finished. Amelia and I liked the picnics best because we could run freely through the woods without worries about soiling fussy party dresses.

Amelia at age six in 1903.

Books and animals were always important in our lives. Amelia and I could repeat *Peter Rabbit* word for word long before we could read although both of us read before we were five. Anna Sewell's *Black Beauty* made an indelible impression on us, aroused in us a crusading spirit, and deepened the affection with which we regarded all animals. We lived at a time when stylish turnouts meant horses tortured by check-reins, bobbed tails, and cruel bits. Grocery boys lashed half-starved horses up and down the streets delivering telephone orders. Tired milk-wagon horses were often forced to race to the stables after having been driven on a milk route since four o'clock in the morning. We read and re-read the tale of Beauty and Ginger's sufferings and were fired with anger toward cruel adults. For Amelia, feeling something deeply meant taking action. We began with our next-door neighbor, Mr. Oldham.

Mr. Oldham had a beautiful little mare, Nellie, whom he stabled in a small, low-roofed shed in his back yard. Nellie, driven frantic by the flies and summer heat, always kicked and neighed in torment. Amelia begged Dad to lead Nellie out of the shed and let her graze awhile in our yard. Dad, a humane and gentle person, also thought the horse was being treated poorly and urged Mr. Oldham to build a screened barn.

The summer wore on and Mr. Oldham did nothing about a barn but tried to break Nellie's spirit by whipping her around the legs when she kicked in her vile, cramped stall. Amelia and I constituted ourselves a "Help Nellie" brigade. Whenever we heard the first restless kicks, we dashed over to the shed and climbed onto a box we planted by the tiny window near the horse. We would then reach inside to pat her neck and give her a handful of grass and clover. This calmed her immediately.

One day Mr. Oldham was unharnessing her outside the shed when a piece of newspaper blew across the yard and she reared in fright. Instead of gentling her, he seized the whip from the carriage and gave her a vicious cut. In fright and frenzy, Nellie jumped forward and pulled the loosely tied hitching rein free. She then galloped down the driveway with traces and reins flying, with Mr. Oldham shouting and swearing in pursuit. At the foot of Ann Avenue, there was a wayward branch of the Kaw River, which was sometimes a roaring torrent, but more often a mere trickle of water spanned by a narrow bridge. The cry of "Runaway! Runaway!" brought people running from their houses, and a few volunteer cowboys hurried over to the bridge, hoping to turn the frightened creature back up the hill where her capture would be easy. Desperation drove the little mare to swerve from the waiting posse. She jumped over the wooden railing, plunging to her death into the shallow water below.

Mr. Oldham had turned his ankle and bruised himself in his race after Nellie, so he was confined to his home for several days. In the tradition of neighborliness, Mother planned to send over a generous piece of cake that Sadie, our cook, made. She asked Amelia to take the piece of cake to Mr. Oldham and to see how he was feeling. Amelia came and stood before Mother, put her hands behind her back, and soberly shook her head. Mother looked in amazement at the small rebel, for such insubordination was unknown in our family.

Amelia refused to take cake or anything to

such a horrid man because of the way he treated Nellie. Mother felt more or less the same way, I am sure, and recognizing a martyr to principle, she said no more about Amelia's refusal to make the friendly gesture. Later, after Sadie had returned from the errand, she told Mother that we would not have to worry about Mr. Oldham's keeping another horse in the shed. He decided to get one of the horseless carriages.

Years afterward, Amelia came across the poem by Vachel Lindsay, *The Bronco That Wouldn't Be Broken of Dancing*. She showed it to me and said, "Nellie!" I nodded.

A big black mongrel dog, James Ferocious, was our constant companion. He endured being harnessed to a small cart, decorated with discarded ribbons, and mauled affectionately. Since he tended to be unfriendly toward strangers, he was usually tied to the shed when we were away. One afternoon when we were taking naps, some boys came across the back yard. James jumped up to do battle when the boys began to tease him. One boy would step into the circle of the dog's chain, and then, when James leaped at him, he would jump back to safety. They tried the trick once too often and the chain broke. The boys, terrorized now by the black fury, hoisted themselves to the roof of the shed just in time to escape his jaws. Just then, Amelia was roused from her nap by the dog's frenzied barking and came running down the back steps into the yard. She had never seen James Ferocious act like that.

The boys told Amelia to run, but Amelia stood perfectly still and said calmly, "James Ferocious, you naughty dog, you've tipped over your water dish again." Amelia's voice

A family picture in Atchison, circa 1907. From left: Muriel Earhart, Carl Otis, Amelia Harres Otis, Amelia Earhart, Mrs. Carl Otis, Amy Otis Earhart, and Edwin Earhart.

was loving, firm, and familiar. She put out her hand and James came to her. She smoothed down the hackles of his shoulders and led him into the kitchen. Mother came out just then and ordered the youngsters out of the yard.

James Ferocious was lapping a bowl of water with Amelia beside him when mother came in and told her that she was brave to calm James, but he might have hurt her by mistake if she had run from him. I remember Amelia saying that she wasn't brave; she just didn't have time to be scared.

In later years, people were often to praise Amelia's courage in the face of storms, fire, and flying hazards, but, it seems to me, courage was certainly strong in her young soul that day. "Never run away," was one of Dad's preachments. Amelia instinctively acted on it, doing the only thing which kept the infuriated animal from charging her.

We always liked animals and bugs. Under Mother's intelligent direction we became ardent amateur entomologists at an early age. Mother never was offended by bugs or insects. She taught us about their place in and contributions to nature. Amelia and I collected many different insects. We had a special box with a screen on top where we kept our specimens after we had identified them in Amelia's copy of *Insect Life*.

We were always interested when Mother cleaned and cut up freshly killed chickens for dinner. She always taught us the wonders of God's creation, not the messiness of the task. I doubt that Amelia's interest in biology was fostered by these candid laboratory studies in our kitchen; however, I am sure that this matter-of-fact approach to a fowl's entrails and internal arrangements eliminated her squeamishness in later major dissection assignments in zoology and biology for both of us.

From one of our all-day late summer outings, we brought back a green Luna moth and a Pandorus. We had some goggle-eyed katydids and a tree toad living with a praying mantis.

Mother often invited one or two children from a nearby children's home to accompany us on these expeditions. This home housed from forty to sixty orphans or destitute children, who lived there until they were adopted or reached an age at which they were considered able to support themselves.

I doubt that Mother invited the young guests from the home because she worried about Amelia and my having occasional imaginary companions. She was a Christian woman who dearly loved her own children and hated to think of any child growing up without parental affection. We frequently shared our afternoons with a girl we especially liked named Lily. She had a badly scarred hand. Once when Lily was with us for the day, we were playing on the merry-go-round, and we lay down to rest under the twin maple trees in our front yard. She suddenly spoke with surprise. "Do you know, I have forgotten all about my hand?" The home matron always told her to keep her hand out of sight.

With the kindness which characterized Amelia in many trying situations in her later life, she told Lily to be natural. We had never really paid any attention to her hand. We were more concerned with pushing the merry-go-round. After our rest, we raced to the porch where a tiny chameleon, which Uncle Carl bought for us as a surprise, was waiting. He had told us that the salesman assured him the chameleon would want nothing to eat for three days; then a dozen freshly killed flies would make him happy for another three-day period. We stopped to look at the Pandorus which Lily had helped us catch the week before, but we were greeted by a shocking sight: the Pandorus, the Luna, and the katydids were no more—only a well-fed and sleepy chameleon was basking in the sun at the front of the cage.

Mother lessened our grief somewhat by telling us not to blame the chameleon. He was simply doing what Mother Nature told him to do. He was hungry, so he went hunting for his breakfast. Perhaps it's just as well, because Mother told us we couldn't take our museum to grandmother's house where we were planning to spend some time.

Dad had been transferred to Des Moines, Iowa, and for the first time we were preparing to move far from our Kansas relatives. Thus ended our specimen museum and the years in Kansas City, Kansas. In 1905, our parents moved to Des Moines.

Chapter Four

Atchison Interlude

OUR father was offered a position in the railroad's claim department, headquartered in Des Moines, Iowa. Several times he had done legal work for the Rock Island Railroad, and his well-written, slightly humorous reports came to the attention of the railroad's leading attorney, George MacCaughan. Impressed with Dad's legal background, Mr. MacCaughan called him to Chicago for an interview and hired him.

To Mother, a regular salary meant an end to the penny-pinching days of waiting for income from small legal fees. Although the move from Kansas would sever many girlhood ties for her, it was Dad's first big step up the success ladder, and she was happy with his achievement. Amelia and I thought the move was an adventure. We helped pack while mother filled barrels with her Haviland china and bric-a-brac.

A heavy rain fell as the last bit of furniture was carried out to the moving wagon, and we said our last goodbyes. As we boarded the Kansas City/Atchison Local, the conductor told Dad that there were bad floods along the Missouri, but he felt sure the train would make the trip safely. In the early afternoon, the rain pelted against the coach windows, and the brakeman found it necessary to light kerosene lamps. The flat fields on both sides of the track were shallow lakes, while the farmhouses and

Amelia's report card, 1906–1907.

barns that stood on higher ground appeared as if on small islands. About one-half of the way to Atchison, the train slowed sharply.

The train soon moved no faster than a slow walk. The Missouri River had overflowed and water covered the tracks. The flickering lamps gave out entirely, leaving us in semi-darkness. Heavy logs and floating debris pounded the sides of the coach, and the roar of the main channel's torrent sounded frighteningly near.

A frightened man reached to pull the emergency cord, but Dad stopped him. Dad assured him the engineer knew what he was doing. As long as the water did not put out the train's fire, the passengers were in no danger. As the train inched slowly forward, I asked Amelia if she was afraid.

"Of course not," she insisted. It was just like Amelia, even at eight.

Dad told us the reasons for the engineer's cautious progress and excused the passengers' near-panic as mostly because of ignorance. Amelia and I understood that if we just knew why, we could know whether to be frightened or not.

Amelia remembered this advice. In later years, although she admitted that she was often worried both on the ground and in the air, she never let panic interfere with her course of action.

We finally reached Grandmother's home and sat down to the dinner which had been waiting for us for over three hours. The journey, which usually took an hour and a half, had lasted nearly four hours.

Amelia and I stayed with our grandparents in Atchison while Mother and Dad looked for a house in Des Moines. Our visit, which was planned for two months at the most, extended to almost a year because of difficulties that Mother encountered in finding the kind of home she wanted to rent. We of course missed our parents a great deal, but Atchison was always our second home. We soon became accustomed to the discipline and a more formal household.

Our cousins, Lucy and Katherine Challiss, were always called Toot and Katch. They were our favorite companions when we were in Atchison. We shared many adventures together, real and imaginary. Playing bogey in

Amelia on right, and her cousin, Lucy "Toot" Challiss in Atchison, circa 1912.

the big barn occupied many hours. Although our grandparents sold the horses several years before, the large, two-seated carriage was left standing on the floor of the main barn. We were given permission by the handyman, Charlie, to play in the barn. He held undisputed sway there. The dusty carriage would soon have two imaginary spirited horses harnessed to it and would be taking four adventurers on a perilous journey. In the semi-darkness of the barn we climbed into the carriage and age, sex, time and space magically vanished. Imagination knew no bounds for Amelia and me. Hoarse from screaming, damp with perspiration, and streaked with dust and cobwebs, we were always called home just before we reached our imaginary destination, Cherryville.

One afternoon the four of us climbed up on the fence and looked out onto the stretch of rocky ledges, brambles, and small trees which extended to the river bank. A ten-acre section of the bluff, half way down to the river in front of our homes, was fenced by a solid wooden barrier. Although it was a fairly steep slope, Charlie had planted peach, apple, and plum trees, so we called the enclosure Orchard Park and often played there when the weather was good. Amelia led the three of us out there to look for buried treasure.

We squeezed under the fence where a gully made an ample opening. We ran through the brambles, tearing clothing and scratching arms and legs. On this outing we saw two buffalo [badgers] and four mountain sheep [rabbits]; we discovered an "outlaw's" cave where there were ashes from a small fire and a number of empty flat bottles, but no treasure. Climbing back was much more difficult and time-consuming than we expected. When we wiggled under the fence into the orchard again, we realized that we would be late to dinner and would all doubtless receive a scolding for our thoughtlessness. Grandmother did not scold us for being late. Instead, she scolded us for going beyond the fence and she told us never to go back.

Even Grandfather, who always left matters of domestic discipline in Grandmother's hands, looked serious and somber when Amelia told him about finding the little cave and the bottles. A severe punishment seemed inevitable.

We were not punished for our explorations that time because we had never been told not to go there. There was, however, no misunderstanding the ruling that was then laid down. We knew punishment would be certain and drastic if we disobeyed.

Since the intense summer heat discouraged much physical exertion, we turned our energies to reading. Our grandparents were savers, so ten years of *The Youth's Companion* were collected and bound in large volumes that could best be read while lying on one's stomach on the floor. There were also bound volumes of *Harper's Young People, Harper's Weekly,* and *Puck* in our grandparents' library. On Mother's twelfth birthday, grandfather gave her one of the first complete American editions of Charles Dickens' works. These books kept us occupied for many hours. About twenty-five of Oliver Optic's success stories for boys, such as *Through by Daylight, Learning by Doing, Onward and Upward,* and *The Starry Flag* were on the shelves. We read these avidly although we skipped many pages of the moralizing. Grandfather's shelves also held large complete editions of Victor Hugo and Alexandre Dumas. These two writers introduced us to another world in *Les Misérables, The Count of Monte Cristo, The Three Musketeers* and *The Queen's Necklace.*

Amelia's original water color painting in its original frame of the Atchison Bridge. It was a gift to her grandmother in 1908.

Midsummer evenings always have a mystic quality for the young. The long August twilights exerted their peculiar magic upon Amelia and me when we were little girls in Atchison. We remembered the symphony of summer sounds: the chirping of crickets, the invisible tree-toads, and the shrill sawing notes of the locusts, each one holding the last note until a faraway friend picked up the complaining aria, which we translated as, "Tis hot, tis hot, tis h . . . . .o . . . . . t!" The scolding, "Thief! Thief!" of the vigilant blue jays sounded less frequently as the shadows lengthened across the dusty white road in front of the houses on the top of the bluff. As the last carnation and saffron clouds faded, bats began to dart across the darkening sky, and, as if in defiance of these harbingers of nightfall, fireflies twinkled in the garden and across the way among the peach and pear trees in the orchard.

The thermometer reached the high nineties every day for three weeks, but no Kansan found fault with this high dry heat. Fields of waist-high dark green wheat across the river needed the heat to brown and harden the grain.

One typical breezeless August evening, Amelia and I galloped our imaginary steeds around the garden paths. A row of hollyhocks lined the back wall, but most of the blossoms had fallen. The pungent fragrance of rose geranium and the heavy sweetness of deep blue heliotrope hung in the still air. Mother and our grandparents, fanning spade-shaped woven palm-leaf fans, sat on the wide veranda. We raced through Grandfather's twenty-five foot grape arbor where the Concords hung in small bunches, sprinkled with purple just beginning to show. The sweet Malagas were already in shapely clusters five or six inches long. We were allowed to eat all the Concords we wanted, but the Malagas were always saved to adorn the fruit baskets which Grandmother sent to sick neighbors or to the Rectory family.

"Girls, girls!" grandmother called. "Do stop running around the garden. You make me exhausted just watching you. Be sensible and come sit down here awhile."

"Whoa, Saladin! Stand boy, stand!" Amelia's imaginary beautiful Arabian arched his shining neck as he obeyed his mistress' commands. I drew rein beside her, and with a friendly slap turned free my spirited black Beelzebub. Then we trudged slowly toward the porch steps where we sat down obediently while our imaginary horses galloped off to pasture with Pegasus, perhaps.

When a lull occurred in the adult conversation, Amelia commented in a polite conversational tone that when we are moving fast, we make a breeze, so we really aren't hot until we stop.

Grandmother threw up her hands in mock despair.

We were soon released from idleness. Our favorite Challiss cousins called over the fence, "Meelie, . . . Pidge . . . Can't you come over for a while?"

Grandmother nodded, and we darted off across the lawn. As I was too short to climb over the five-foot paling fence, Amelia bent over and I scrambled up on her back. From there I swung a leg over the top and easily dropped to the ground. Amelia followed close behind, and we were united with Toot and Katch perhaps five seconds sooner than if we had taken the conventional route down the walk and through the yard gate.

Katch pointed out the Second Street light one evening. We turned to look down the shady street where the arc light had just begun to flicker. Atchison, in common with many communities during the first decades of the twentieth century, was in the arc-light era. Suspended from poles, fifteen to twenty feet high, were elongated white glass globes containing two polarized carbon sticks, finger thick and eight to ten inches long. The positive carbon was heated to incandescence by the assaults of the charged electrons leaping across a one-eighth-inch gap from the negative carbon. Regulated by an ingenious mechanical control, the positive carbon could be counted upon to produce a glaring white light for approximately twenty hours. The arc man with a leather pouch for carrying the carbon sticks was an important figure, marking a distinct technological advance from the picturesque lamp-lighter of earlier times. Every three days in the summer, the arc man made his rounds, lowering the light

The home of Judge Alfred and Amelia Otis in Atchison, Kansas, which overlooks the Missouri River. 1937 photo.

globe, removing the carbon stub, and replacing it with a new one. He usually tossed the stubs into the gutters where they were pounced upon by the neighborhood children who used them fleetingly to scrawl letters and pictures on curbstones.

When the town planned to install an arc light beside our grandparents' home, Grandmother objected, saying that having such a garish light so near the corner of their property would attract swarms of insects and make sitting on the veranda unpleasant. In those simpler days the householder was king, so work was halted while a deputation waited upon the Judge. Agreeing that a light was needed on North Terrace, our grandfather promised to maintain a gas light at the corner at his own expense rather than have his family annoyed by the town's lighting arrangements. This seemed a reasonable solution, so an order was given to the gas company to erect there a twelve-foot iron stand topped by an octagonal lantern. This was equipped with a Welsbach burner which diffused a mild yellow glow within a restricted radius.

Grandfather had Charles build four wooden steps against the lamp-pole so he would not need to carry a stepladder from the kitchen to light and extinguish the burner night and morning. So strong was the feeling of civic responsibility that never did the North Terrace light fail to follow the Second Street light by more than a few seconds. If Charles were detained on an errand, our grandfather carried a lighted taper from the house and mounted the steps himself to light the corner gas light. When both men were away, if the twilight came on, Grandmother carried the taper and handed it up to Lottie or Mary from the kitchen. The family's promise to light North Terrace was kept.

By common consent, we four moved toward the orchard gate when we saw Charles coming down the shadowy walk with his hand cupped around a burning taper. As soon as the lamp was lighted, we were expected to be home, and, within a short time afterwards, on the way upstairs to bed. We parted at the gate, with no thought except that a few hours separated us from our cousins.

Looking back, we really were saying goodbye to our sheltered childhood in the gracious surroundings of an era that was bound for extinction as surely as the arc light, the bustle, and the horse-and-carriage.

Amelia and I never forgot that Christmas in Atchison. Dad and Mother, laden with mysterious parcels, arrived on Christmas Eve. Any prying questions about the contents of the packages were answered by the vague remark, "Lay over for meddlers and crutches for lame ducks." In the morning we found that Dad had brought us two boys' sleds. What joy! Now we could belly-flop with our sleds instead of coasting on a light girls' sled upon which one had to sit upright. Grandmother declared that for girls to go coasting like boys was immodest and unladylike, but we promised never to coast unless we had on long leggings and heavy coats.

Another present from Dad provoked more serious opposition—a .22-caliber Hamilton rifle. We had had a Daisy BB air rifle for more than a year and had become fair marksmen, shooting at bottles on the back fence and at targets drawn on the barn doors. In writing to Dad, we openly asked for a real rifle so we could pursue the unfeminine activity of rat hunting—BB's had no effect on a rat's hairy hide except to send him scampering back into his hole. We had read an article in a magazine which told about the disease spread in the Canal Zone by rats and mosquitoes. The old barn was infested with rats, and we reasoned that if rats in Panama spread bubonic plague, the rats in Kansas might do the same thing.

Grandmother opposed Dad's giving Amelia and me, then nine and seven years of age, a gun. Dad rationalized by saying that it was only a small rifle, and his girls knew the firearms regulations and would promise to obey them to the letter. Grandmother finally consented to our having the rifle, but we knew she did not believe that any gun was a suitable gift for a girl.

Amelia's crusade against bubonic plague led to a decimation of the barn's rat population, especially since we adhered scrupulously to the hunters' code, which demanded that no wounded game be left alive to suffer. One day Amelia shot a huge rat, but he managed to get down a hole before she could reload. She sat down to wait for him to reappear, as they invariably did, but it was more than an hour before the wounded rat stuck his head out of the hole and received the final blow. Amelia dropped the dead rat into a solution of quicklime before she left the scene. When she finally arrived at the dining room table in a clean dress, with well scrubbed face and hands, dinner was practically over. Grandmother was annoyed, as were Lottie and Mary in the kitchen, grandmother's cook and maid.

Grandmother carried out her threat to impound the rifle which she made several times before when we were late for meals. We looked to Grandfather, hoping for an appeal to a higher court, but he shook his head. We broke Grandmother's law, we knew the penalty, and we had to accept it gracefully. Later I heard Grandfather telling Charles that the rifle was out of circulation until further notice. Charles agreed it perhaps was just as well; the grain bins and side walls of the harness-room looked like a sieve. Charles made an observation which was repeated many times in different ways as Amelia's life unfolded: "Amelia gets an idea and, by gosh, she stays right with it. Dinner or no dinner, punishment or not, she wanted to get the rats." Grandfather nodded.

Amelia and I were enrolled in a small private elementary school which was directed by two remarkable teachers, Helen Schofield and Sarah Walton. Like the Latin School to which mother went, our school was geared to college preparation and was called the College Preparatory School. Amelia and I were eager to get to school each day.

Breakfast was a rather formal affair. Amelia and I dressed and went down to breakfast together. We ate breakfast, with Grandmother and Grandfather Otis, at the dining room table. Then we set out for our daily twenty-minute walk to school for our education and to see our friends.

As the spring term drew to a close, teachers planned the upper school graduation and the lower school awards and competitions. Amelia and I dressed the last day in our white muslin dresses and tied the ribbon sashes. We were eager for the school year to end and looked forward to seeing our parents.

In the summer of 1908, Mother and Dad came for us, and we moved to our new home in Des Moines. This was the end of our Atchison interlude.

Chapter Five

Success and Failure

IN Des Moines, our lives underwent a radical change. We no longer had an Orchard Park and a big barn for our exclusive use; we had no congenial cousins; and we no longer were known as "the Judge's granddaughters." There was no private school nearby so we attended public school. There were no cooks to prepare breakfast, so Mother fixed it. Amelia and I still walked to school together after breakfast, meeting our friends along the way.

Amelia entered the seventh grade and I the fourth. Even before the Civil War, Iowa was liberal toward its black citizens, so there was nothing unusual in having several black children in our classes. Blacks, however, were still considered by many as second-class citizens and were often poorly paid. One Monday morning Amelia and I set out for school in new dresses made of blue and white patterned gingham which mother bought for us at a sale in one of the downtown department stores. When I entered the schoolroom, I saw that Lulu May, a black classmate, wore a dress identical to mine. I was embarrassed, as the similarity seemed to say that our father could afford nothing better for us than Lulu May's father, who was a porter at the Union Station. I could hardly wait until the noon recess to meet Amelia and rush home to change our dresses. We dashed home together and when inside our front door, we told our mother about the incident.

Mother was perceptive. She told us it was all right to change but asked if we thought how Lulu May would feel when we told her that she was not nice enough to wear the same kind of dresses we did. Amelia and I looked at each other. She closed the door of her closet. She was not going to change her dress, it would be mean. I, too, agreed.

The first Earhart home in Des Moines at 1806 Arlington Street in 1908.

We returned to the playground after lunch and saw Lulu May watching some girls jump rope. Amelia ran up to her and commented that we all three looked alike.

A few days later, Dad received a copy of the Earhart family genealogy compiled by his brother, Joseph. He read us this paragraph:

> Cousin Martha Earhart wrote that Grandmother Catharine Altman's grandmother, Miriah Joseph Altman, was a niece of the King of France, a Bourbon, who had married a German officer, and that to avoid the wrath of the king, they came to Pennsylvania in a Lutheran congregation. Grandmother Altman told her grandchildren that she had seen clothing of her grandmother's, embroidered with a crest, a cock crowing and the motto in Latin.

Amelia and I were excited by the thought that we might have been princesses in the French Court. Dad told us, however, that if we were in a French court, assuming there was one, we would be most unhappy, hedged about by restrictions worse than anything we could imagine. Dad told us that we should remember that good ancestors give one responsibility: "Noblesse oblige." Nobility of birth obligates one to be noble in all his dealings, especially toward those who are less fortunate. Amelia and I exchanged a quick glance, ashamed to think how near we came to behaving in an ignoble manner toward Lulu May.

After a little more than a year, Dad was promoted to head of the Claim Department. His salary almost doubled, and he received special privileges, including the use of a private railroad car for both business and personal trips. We moved into a larger house in an attractive section of Des Moines and mother hired a cook and a maid. Mother said how proud she was of Dad's success, which to a large measure helped ease the memory of his former improvident ways in Grandfather's mind.

Dad arranged for Amelia and me to visit our grandparents in Atchison in the private railroad car. We were in Atchison for a day. Tokimo, the private car's cook, fixed a dinner for us and our grandparents. That night we crawled into our berths, neatly spread up by Tokimo. Dad reached up to dim the hanging lamp and tuck us in. Mother affectionately put her hand through Dad's arm and they stood together in the aisle beside our berths. For the first time in their married life, Dad was able to take a good vacation. We planned to go to Worthington, Minnesota, for the month of August.

Worthington was not a summer resort, but it was on the shores of a small lake which promised fishing, boating, and swimming. Our Uncle Nicey and his recent bride, immediately named Peachie by Amelia and me, was living with us. He discovered Worthington while on a business trip for the railroad. He made arrangements for us to stay with J.P. Mann, the local postmaster, and for us to have our meals at Mrs. Twitchell's boardinghouse.

It was a pleasant summer for Amelia and me. The Manns treated us like members of the family, allowing us to ride their Indian pony, Prince, help with the haying, drive the cows in from pasture, and swim and boat with their daughters, Grace and Genevieve. When Dad and Nicey took a few days away from the office, they joined us.

We celebrated Genevieve's sixteenth birthday by having a picnic at a lake about twenty miles from Worthington. We usually rented a three-seated carryall and took the Manns' buckboard to our picnic, and Amelia and I took turns riding the long-suffering Prince. This time, however, we made the journey in two touring cars, a Reo and a Stoddard Dayton. This was the first time that any of our family rode in an automobile.

We covered the twenty miles in less than two hours because the roads were packed hard and we had no tire punctures to delay us. Clinton Mann, who drove the Reo, took Amelia and me, sitting on the front seat beside him. He said he preferred not having to listen to a lady complain about the noise and smell of the engine. It was a privilege for us. Dad remarked, "An engine still hasn't the sense a horse has about a hole in the road."

Des Moines was one of the first cities whose male electorate chose a woman for Superintendent of Schools, Miss Pearl De Jarnette, my eighth grade teacher at the Hubbell School. Amelia and I became enthusiastic campaigners. We made a large cardboard sign which

Postcard photo of Mann's home, sent to Amy Earhart in Des Moines, postmarked "Sept. 26, 1907."

Postcard from Mrs. Mann to Muriel in Des Moines reporting that "Prince has rested all winter. He ought to be in good condition next summer . . ."

Muriel and Amelia in bathing suits, in Worthington, Minnesota, circa 1910.

screamed: "Down with the man! Up with the lady . . . Miss De Jarnette, of course." This we happily carried in a parade around the school yard on election day.

I never remember a time when problems of local government, national figures, and world events were not explained and discussed at our dinner table. Beloved "Teddy," brave Dr. Gorgas, Governor Pinchot, Elihu Root were names as familiar as those of our neighbors on the street.

The section of Des Moines we moved into adjoined the campus of Drake University. Several of the professors lived near us. For several years we had season subscriptions for a concert series, sponsored by the Department of Music at the University which included performances by many great artists of those days. The concerts were more than just a musical treat for Amelia and me; we saw our parents metamorphosed into beings of another, special adult world.

Dinner on concert nights was quickly prepared so we could have ample time to dress. For Amelia and me there was no problem of what to wear; in the winter months we wore high-necked silk party-dresses; in March and April, white dotted Swiss with pink or blue sashes. We liked Mother best in a dark violet silk dress with velvet bows down the front and a sweep to the skirt behind, which swished and rustled as she walked.

For the half-mile walk from our house to the Congregational Church where the concerts were held, Mother usually wore the seal skin coat and carried the little round muff which had been a part of those worldly luxuries with which Great-Grandfather Harres had liked to shower his erstwhile Quaker wife. The coat had come to mother when her grandmother died. The fur, wonderfully soft and shining, was just slightly rubbed from the years of wearing. Sunday after Sunday, in the chilly churches of Philadelphia, later in Atchison, and now in Des Moines, Mother put a black lace scarf over her head if the weather were not terribly cold. If it were freezing, a practical crocheted fascinator covered her modestly pompadoured dark brown hair. Dad was handsome in white shirt with high stiff collar, dark gray trousers, and Prince Albert coat, which Amelia and I called his "Archie tails."

When we entered the church and took our seats in the first row of the balcony, we were certain to see several of our friends with their impressively unfamiliar parents to whom we waved or spoke with unnatural decorum. Amelia profited more from the concerts than I did. By ten o'clock I was too sleepy to appreciate even the divinest music. It took the brisk walk home to wake me enough to slide out of my clothes and climb into bed, but Amelia and Dad sat up for an hour or more at the piano, playing by ear some of the arias we had heard. Amelia had Dad's uncanny musical ear. Dad could sit down and hum or sing out a tune, and Amelia would pick it right up on the piano.

Semi-annual art exhibits brought a hundred or more canvases to the corridors of the high school for six weeks. Mother always saw to it that Amelia and I participated in the guided tours, and took the appreciation courses so we could vote for the popular choice. If there were a picture of a horse or dog, that one always received my vote, but Amelia, older and more discriminating than I, declared she liked the misty pictures of fields and water.

Although book clubs as we know them today had not yet come into being, we belonged to a neighborhood magazine association. There were few regulations: one read, and passed on, as in the children's game "to the neighbor next to thee" with consideration and courtesy. We were near the end of the line so frequently we waited three weeks or more for our turn at *The Century, Scribner's*, Lyman Abbott's *Outlook* or *The Atlantic Monthly* in its staid brown cover, but the stories and the articles lost nothing by the delay.

I believe there was nothing we missed more than the magazine club when the shadows began to fall on our gifted father, and the amenities of life had to be sacrificed for the necessities of existence.

This happy time of our lives was unfortunately a prelude to a period which saw the loss of our material prosperity and the beginning of the disintegration of our family. I find it difficult to write of the deterioration of Dad's character, yet I know that the hardship and

The Earhart family home in Des Moines, Iowa, 1909–1913.

mental suffering that Amelia and I endured as adolescents made an indelible impression upon us. It serves to help explain some of Amelia's actions and attitudes in her later life.

After we returned to Des Moines from our Worthington vacation, things changed. We always looked forward to Saturday afternoons because Dad came home from the office early to play with us and all the neighborhood boys and girls. After an hour or two of games, we gathered on the front steps of our house for mother's welcome contribution of lemonade and cookies.

One Saturday in the early autumn, ten neighborhood children gathered on our front lawn eagerly awaiting Dad's arrival. At last we saw him getting off the streetcar and raced down the avenue to meet him. As we came near, however, we sensed something was wrong in Dad's behavior. He walked slowly, putting each foot down carefully as if to keep from stumbling. There was no buoyancy in his stride nor in the sickly smile with which he greeted us.

We escorted him home in a curious silence, and he lurched up the steps. Mother opened the door. She sensed the situation, and her face

Amelia at ten years old in 1908.

became frozen. She held the door open, helped Dad inside, and closed the door behind him.

Breakfast the next morning was a silent meal. We hesitated to meet Dad's eyes. Mother passed Dad a cup of black coffee without a word. He drank it quickly and asked for another, ignoring our traditional Sunday breakfast of scrambled eggs and popovers.

"I guess we better go to church this morning," Dad ventured as we rose from the table.

It was evident our family agreed his case required God's forgiveness before he could be assured of ours. Mother came into our room as Amelia and I changed our clothes for church. She explained that every once in a while some of the men in Dad's office asked him to drink with them. Often he couldn't refuse without seeming rude. That's what happened the day before. Mother told us we must try to help him. Amelia and I later learned that Dad's devoted stenographer, Rose, had been covering for him.

Everything seemed normal at church that Sunday morning. Dad looked fine and handsome as he carried the congregation's offering to the chancel steps. Amelia and I almost forgot the disgrace of yesterday. As soon as we were out of earshot of the congregation lingering at the church door, Dad put his arm around Mother's waist and asked her if the three of us would forgive him. He promised to walk the straight and narrow path.

Good intentions and promises soon became less and less meaningful as Amelia and I saw Dad coming home with shuffling steps and a foolish tongue two or three times a week. The worried wrinkle never seemed to leave Mother's forehead. We all became adept at evading Dad's sickness. We learned to joke with him only in the mornings, for sometimes he came home in moods of black temper, inveighing against the household expenses or Mother's family, the railroad, or virtually anything.

Inaccuracies which Rose could not correct began creeping into his reports to the Chicago office. When Dad gave several claimants even more than they asked, a sharp letter was sent him from his boss, Mr. MacCaughan. Dad never endured criticism with good grace but usually admitted his mistakes and learned from them. Had Mr. MacCaughan's letter reached Dad in the morning mail, it would probably have had the salutary effect expected. Dad would not have realized that he was not so deep in the quicksand that he could not turn around and walk out.

Dad had always been on the receiving end of favors from the Otis family, and no doubt he felt an unconscious resentment toward them because of the superiority and assurance which their wealth imparted. Dad was naive in thinking that the men who invited him to drink with them at the hotel bar were true friends, but they applauded his opinions and made him feel he belonged as he had never felt with mother's relatives. Most of the bar acquaintances were social drinkers to whom three or four drinks before going home were routine. Dad could not hold his liquor as they did.

Looking back over this tragic period in our lives, I can see the mistakes we made. As Dad stayed later and later at the bar, mother's treatment of him became more and more scornful and cold, and Amelia and I followed her lead. At eleven and thirteen years old, we could not know the psychological roots of Dad's behavior; we only knew that he did not seem to care for us any more. We lost our adored, companionable Dad. Our attempts to make him stop drinking only made his home uncomfortable and alien; it created a vicious circle.

Mr. MacCaughan's reprimand was delivered to Dad just after lunch when a few drinks had made him irritable and unreasonable. Mr. MacCaughan's advice, "Stay away from that drinking crowd and do your work for the railroad in the creditable manner that you have done it, up until now," was taken as an interference with his personal rights. Dad wrote a scathing letter in reply. When Mr. MacCaughan received Dad's letter, he took the first train to Des Moines, arriving about four o'clock in the afternoon. He found Dad sharing a bottle with a man from another department. Mr. MacCaughan telephoned Mother to say he was sending Dad home in a cab and that he himself would be out for a short visit in the evening.

Mr. MacCaughan greeted us cheerfully and tactfully ignored Dad's flushed face and unsteady steps. After Amelia and I sampled the generous box of chocolates he brought, Mother suggested we should go upstairs to read in our rooms before bedtime. The murmur of voices continued so long that we finally fell asleep.

The next morning Mother told us that Dad was going to a hospital to take a cure for a month. Amelia and I looked forward to having our "old" Dad back again. Breakfast that morning was the happiest we had for more than a year. Dad had at first hesitated at the idea of taking the cure. He said he could stop drinking any time he wanted, but Mr. MacCaughan insisted that his body as well as his will power needed toning up. Dad finally agreed. As he left, he told us that we meant more to him than anything.

We welcomed him back from the Keeley Cure hospital a month later. Mother bought a heavy carpenter's bench, equipped with most of the ordinary tools for light metal and woodworking. Amelia and I picked cherries for our next-door neighbor to earn three dollars with which we bought Dad a jointed fishing rod with a reel on the handle. It was our "old" Dad, bright-eyed and buoyant, who came up the porch steps. Dad was delighted with the bench. He told us we could try out his new fishing rod the following Sunday afternoon.

The obituary of Judge Alfred Gideon Otis in the Atchison Daily Champion, Tuesday, May 7, 1912.

THE END COMES TO JUDGE OTIS

DEATH CLAIMS ONE OF ATCHISON'S PIONEER CITIZENS

For Fifty Years He Lived in the Same House on North Terrace—Found Dead in Bed—Law Firm of Glick & Otis Was Among Most Prominent in Kansas

Judge Alfred G. Otis, 8̄ years old, and one of the oldest citizens of the town, was found dead in his bed at the family home, 232 North Terrace, by his son, Theodore Otis, at 6:30 o'clock this morning. All indications are that he died without a struggle or a pain. Dr. Charles Johnson, who was called in, said death probably came early this morning.

Funeral arrangements have not been completed and will not be until all the children are heard from. It is known, however, that the services will be held from the Episcopal church of which Judge Otis was a member, and that interment will be in Mount Vernon beside Mrs. Otis, who died last February. The Rev. Otis Gray will conduct the services.

While it was sudden, the death of Judge Otis was not unexpected. He was up and around yesterday as usual and was feeling well. He was at church Sunday morning and insisted on walking to and from the edifice.

His comprehension of what was going on in the world was as clear as that of a man fifty years younger.

"Every time I called on him," said J. M. Challiss this morning, "he was able to keep up his end of a conversation on law or politics."

For fifty years Judge Otis had lived in the house in which he died. It was the old homestead. At the time of his death Theodore Otis, Charles Parks, a houseman, and Mary Brashay, the housekeeper, were living in the Otis home.

In 1862 Mr. Otis was married to Amelia Harris of Philadelphia. Two sons, Mark Otis of Chicago, and Theo. Otis, and two daughters, Mrs. E. S. Earhart, Des Moines, and Mrs. C. W. Balis, Philadelphia, survive him. Mrs. Earhart will be here tonight and Mark will arrive in the morning. It is not known whether or not Mrs. Balis will come. Mr. Otis leaves an estate worth upwards of two hundred thousand dollars.

Judge Otis was born in Cortland county, New York, Dec. 13, 1827. When only a small boy his father, Isaac Otis, removed to Barry county, Mich. With other members of the family he was raised on a farm and shared all the hardships of pioneer life. At the age of twenty he determined to acquire a thorough classical education. His first studies in Latin and Greek were commenced on the farm after his day's work was done. He entered Ann Arbor in 1848 and was graduated in 1852. Following his graduation he taught school in Mississippi and studied law at the same time. He was graduated from the Louisville law school in 1854 and for nearly a year practiced in that city.

In October, 1855, Mr. Otis moved to Atchison and engaged at once in the active practice of his profession and for several years was extensively connected with land litigation.

A partnership was formed in 1860 between Judge Otis and George W. Glick. This partnership continued until 1873 and in that time the firm did its share of the big legal business in the state. They were regularly employed as the attorneys for the Central Branch, the Union Pacific, and after the dissolution of the firm Judge Otis retained the same position until he was elected to the district bench in 1876.

During this period, though in full life of actual business, he found time actively to aid the Episcopal church of which he was a member, being a warm and personal friend of Bishop Vail, the Episcopal bishop of the diocese of Kansas.

He was also prominently identified with the business and railroad enterprises of Northern Kansas. Atchison being then as now the commercial center for this section of the state.

Though a prominent Democrat Judge Otis in 1876 was elected judge of the Second judicial district, then largely Republican, his majority over his opponent being several hundred. The closing of his term was made an occasion of especial interest by lawyers generally of the district.

After his retirement from the bench Judge Otis took an active part in the management of the Atchison Savings Bank. He was its president.

For six years he was a regent of the University of Kansas and when Snow Hall was dedicated he took a prominent part of the exercises.

For several days everything was as we had hoped. Dad then began again to drink a little at a time. The doctors at the Cure told him he would be deathly ill if he started to drink in any quantity again. Just at this time Grandmother died, dividing the estate worth several hundred thousand dollars evenly among mother and the other children. Dad regarded the will's instructions of Mother's share to be left in trust for twenty years or until he died as an insult.

Grandmother knew of Dad's drinking and was worried at the possibility of Dad squandering mother's share. All of Dad's old bitterness toward Mother's family became accentuated.

Matters worsened at the office, and Dad was never reinstated. He wrote to railroad claim offices all over the country but soon realized that the reason for his leaving the Rock Island Claim Department was common knowledge. By the spring of 1913, Dad was promised a minor clerkship in the freight office of the Great Northern Railway in St. Paul, so we began packing to move. We all hated to leave Des Moines, but I believe Mother felt the humiliation most keenly. Amelia had two years at West High School and made some friendships which were hard to break, but we were young and optimistic about the future.

As our train pulled out of the Des Moines station, I saw tears rolling slowly down Mother's cheeks. Five years before, we had come into the same station, feeling confident that Dad's next move would be another step up toward the General Claim Office in Chicago. It was no wonder that as I whispered the Lord's Prayer that night in the semi-darkness, I prayed, *"Forgive us our trespasses as we forgive those who trespass against us, except I'll never, never forgive saloon keepers, all of them, everywhere."*

Private car in Atchison yard in 1911–1912. From left: Amelia, Muriel, Edwin Earhart, and Japanese cook, Tokimo.

Chapter Six

Lean Days

WE stayed in a St. Paul hotel while we looked for a house to rent. Dad was eager to move into a house as soon as possible because the hotel expense and the storage of our furniture was eating into our finances. We finally rented a large house which had been vacant for two years but offered us immediate occupancy.

Amelia entered Central High School as a junior; I, as a freshman. Physics fascinated her, and she enjoyed her Latin classes taught by a teacher who required his students to speak classical Latin as if it were a modern language. We attended St. Clement's Episcopal Church near our home, and Amelia soon became a member of the Altar Guild. I joined the junior choir.

After about three months in St. Paul, Dad came home one evening, called to us as soon as he was inside the door and told us to get his traveling bag out. He was going back on the road for the Great Northern Railway.

Dinner was forgotten while we pulled the well-worn bag from the closet. Amelia and I helped him pack as we did many times before in Des Moines.

Dad told us that there was a freight train wreck near Albert Lea. It was not serious, but one of the cars carrying machinery was damaged. Dad's boss, Mr. Mather, wanted Dad to look the damage over and protect the railroad's interest.

I asked Dad if this meant he was getting back into the claim office again. "Could be, Pidge, could be."

Amelia remained strangely silent. While we were clearing the table after our delayed dinner, I learned why. From a corner of the kitchen cabinet she produced an unopened bottle of whiskey and told me she found it when she put Dad's socks in the bag. When he wasn't looking, Amelia took the bottle out. She said she was going to pour the whiskey out.

Quickly, we broke the seal, pried out the cork, and Amelia tipped the bottle over the sink. At that moment Dad appeared in the doorway. The smile on his face vanished as he saw what we were doing. He leaped across the kitchen and raised his voice in anger. He reached for the nearly empty bottle, and I believe he would have struck Amelia if Mother had not come running from the dining room and seized his arm from behind.

Dad's anger subsided. He apologized and told us he did not know what got into him. He nearly hit Amelia, and he had never done such a thing. Dad said he wanted the bottle to warm himself a little after he took care of business along the tracks, but he admitted he would be better off without it.

Soon Amelia and I helped him into his overcoat. He took out his wallet, empty except for his railroad pass and a few coins, and showed us how he couldn't go too far on what he was carrying. Dad satisfactorily concluded his business and was commended. He was not, however, transferred to the Claim Department.

In St. Paul, Amelia and I missed the winter holiday activities. Being unacquainted with the social set, we were not invited to any private parties. Although several ladies from the church called on Mother, that did not, in the caste-conscious society of aristocratic old St. Paul, constitute social acceptance. Mother's prominent uncle and his family paid us one surreptitious duty call. They then ignored us completely. This was a bitter pill for Mother, who was never before treated as an unwelcome poor relation. Mother realized that even if her uncle proposed membership for us in the exclusive skating club or for the sub-debutante Cotillion assemblies, we could not possibly pay the membership fees. It hurt that we were not even approached on the subject.

Amelia and I looked forward to attending a gala Twelfth Night party at church. We were especially urged to attend by two boys whom we knew through church activities. Dad promised to take us and stay to dance once with each of us, for he was a beautiful waltzer. We were not sure we would be asked to dance right away. It was customary for girls to be brought to parties by their fathers, who handed them over to the hostess at the door along with silk bags containing their dancing slippers.

Dad said he would leave the freight office promptly and be home in plenty of time to have dinner, bathe, and dress by eight o'clock. By six o'clock the dinner was in the warming oven; the pail and kettle with his bath water were ready. At seven o'clock things were the same except that the bath water was near boiling, and the dinner was becoming dried in the dishes. Amelia and I, stationed by the front window, hoped that a last-minute conference or a tie-up on the streetcar delayed Dad. When the clock struck half-past seven, and then eight, we were as deep in despair as any self-pitying adolescents could be. About nine o'clock Dad arrived and swept off his hat in an attempted display of gallantry.

This was too much for me to bear, and I rushed upstairs to my room. Amelia scorned to pound her pillow and cry; she went nonchalantly into the living room. This was where we had expected to entertain the last three in the group who came down the street to our house, bringing us home from the party. Amelia took down the bits of holly we left up from our Christmas decorations. She tore up the hand-painted holly napkins, and threw out the marshmallows which were in the cups ready to have hot cocoa poured over them. Then she turned out the light and went upstairs to read in bed until she heard the voices of the boys who would have brought us home as they passed by our house. Our disappointment at missing the party faded, but I added to my prayers a God-bless for Carry Nation in her saloon-haunting and bottle-breaking campaign.

These were lean days. Mother's modest income from her trust fund had to cover all our household expenses except the rent, which Dad paid with his clerk's salary. We literally watched every penny.

I remember one frigid Saturday morning in February when Amelia and I set out to do the marketing. We had two dollars to buy the

Muriel in Saint Paul, 1914.

Amelia in Saint Paul, 1914.

staples and meat Mother had listed. We chose a market some three miles from home since their prices were more reasonable, and we saved ten cents carfare by walking. Lamb was advertised at seventeen cents a pound, so we asked for a five-pound leg of lamb. I still recall the exasperated butcher who weighed piece after piece of lamb until he found one that cost ninety-six cents.

Amelia said she was sure she had a penny in her pocketbook and for me to ride home with the bundles and she would walk. We collected our four pennies change and only then did Amelia discover that the penny turned out to be a Des Moines streetcar token.

Homeward bound, laden with bundles and facing a biting wind, we felt an even more painful experience. Our great-uncle passed us in his car, and although he recognized us with a wave, he did not stop to offer us a ride. Amelia commented that he must think we were walking for exercise. Amelia and I enjoyed the roast lamb more than usual, but we never told Mother that the extra half-pound was the reason we did not have enough money to ride the streetcar home.

Early in March Dad had an accident which might have been serious but fortunately resulted in only cuts and bruises. An automobile knocked him down as he stepped from a streetcar one evening and started unsteadily across to the sidewalk. The hospital bill for treatment and stitches for the long cut across his cheek was only a modest ten dollars. This, added to a staggering coal bill, completely wiped out any funds which might have bought new spring clothes for Amelia and me.

Our entire capital, derived from the sale of rags, old iron, and several dozen wine and champagne bottles which we had unearthed in the cellar of our house, amounted to three dollars and forty cents. One spring day Amelia emerged from the attic with a pleased, mysterious expression on her face. She carried a bulky load of cloth, which I soon recognized as the custom-made curtains Mother ordered for the library of our home in Des Moines. Made of heavy natural silk pongee, they had not been used in any of our St. Paul windows.

Neither Amelia nor I liked to sew. We knew nothing about cutting material from a pattern, but Amelia had an observant eye and an unusual sense of style. She sent me to purchase green dye, matching grosgrain ribbon, and thread for my outfit. Dark brown dye, ribbon, and thread were Amelia's choice. I tended to the dye process, boiling, stirring again and again until, at last, the colors of the pieces matched. Amelia drew her designs and then cut out a pattern from newspaper. Fortunately, the style for skirts was simple. It was the era of the much-ridiculed hobble skirt.

Amelia was an unorthodox seamstress. She simply sewed two lengths of the dyed material together, gathered one end on a narrow belt, and turned the other end up so it cleared the floor eleven inches all around. Shoulder straps were attached to the skirt with large pearl buttons from Mother's button box. Amelia's skirt was the same, but she made herself a short sleeveless bolero jacket to wear over her renovated white blouse. A ten-cent bottle of hat lacquer did wonders for our faded straws. I had a rosette of ribbon on mine while Amelia dyed a feather from our turkey-wing duster and stuck it in the turned up brim of her hat, in the style of T.R.'s Rough Riders. As I left the house early Easter morning to sing in the choir, Amelia called from her window, "If it should begin to rain, for heaven's sakes, take off your hat and get under shelter before you leave a trail of green dye on the sidewalk." Thankfully, the weather was perfect and our costumes passed muster with our friends. We also gained a lasting lesson in "making do with cheerfulness," which was one of Grandfather Earhart's favorite maxims.

Later that spring, Dad was offered a position in a small claim office of the Burlington Railroad in Springfield, Missouri. He was delighted at the opportunity to do legal work again, even though Springfield seemed like only a whistle stop compared to Des Moines. We again packed all our belongings, broke off friendships, and pulled up the roots we had just begun to put down in the last year. Moving hurts more in the heart of a teenager than it does at any other age. The telephone, which had been silent for months, was just beginning to ring for us. We would not be there to answer.

Chapter Seven

Changing Backgrounds

WE arrived in Springfield, Missouri, in the early fall, unheralded and, we soon discovered, unwanted. The train pulled out, leaving us standing in a ring of hand luggage on the splintery wooden platform. Dad told us to go across the street to the little park and wait there until he found out from the claim office about our accommodations for the night.

After our seven-hour journey cramped in a hot and sooty day coach, we found the fresh air, green grass, and trees in the square unusually appealing. After finding a bench in the shade for Mother, Amelia and I began a rapid walk around the four sides of the park. We had just completed our third round when Dad walked toward us and sat down on the bench beside Mother. His face was flushed with anger.

He spoke fiercely, calling the people in the office cheats and liars. Dad found that the man who was supposed to retire and whose job he was promised had changed his mind.

Our indignation could not change the circumstances. The manager at the station promised to wire the main office, explain what had happened, and ask for expense money for our trip from St. Paul. We stayed in a boarding home which was not necessarily clean but was within our budget. The railroad cut across the back yard and came within twenty feet of the porch.

We all went to bed early, and, in spite of the switching and coupling of cars under our window, Amelia and I slept well. The next morning we walked to the park. The boardinghouse owner requested that we linger no longer than necessary in our rooms and that we refrain from talking there—the night workmen could not sleep if there was noise. Evidently the freight train racket was not noise but music to them.

Dad went into the claim office to see what answer had come from the main office. He soon returned with a telegram that said that there was no vacancy in the Springfield office, and they regretted the misunderstanding. The main office requested Dad be reimbursed the eighty-four dollar ticket charge plus freight costs. They suggested Dad work for a month clearing back cases at an adjuster's pay.

This was a welcome, though temporary, respite. From the company's point of view, it was a handsome settlement, but we were nevertheless homeless and, so far as Dad was concerned, jobless.

After a few moments, Mother spoke, weighing her words carefully. She reminded Dad that last year when they were wondering where to turn before Dad heard from the Great

Northern in St. Paul, a friend in Chicago, Mrs. Shedd, wrote Mother and invited all of us to come there and live with them until Dad was established. Mother was sure that invitation still held. Dad helped Mr. Shedd get his present position, and they stayed with us in Des Moines while they were house hunting. Mother felt it would be wise for Amelia and me to go with her to Chicago until the family could be established in a real home again.

We went through with the plan although Dad objected, saying that we were walking out on him in a hard-hearted fashion. The three years of tension and humiliation through which we had just passed were hard on all of us.

Amelia and I liked the idea. The Shedds answered mother's letter with a telegram: "Our home is your home now until next year or longer." We decided that after Dad finished the claim work for the Burlington, he would go on to Kansas City, open a law office and try to do legal work for other railroads. Dad finally agreed it was best for all of us.

The Shedds' hospitality will remain forever in my mind as an example of true friendship. They made us feel like honored guests, not like a homeless, broken family. I entered the small Morgan Park High School which Elizabeth Shedd, who was about my age, attended. Mother let Amelia choose the school she wished to attend. Amelia talked to the principal and declined to go to Morgan. She said the chemistry laboratory was a kitchen sink. She set out to visit several of the high schools which were within commuting distance and based her decision solely on their chemistry laboratory.

We planned to rent a small apartment near the Shedds in Morgan Park, but Mother first looked for a furnished apartment in the Hyde Park district. We found one not far from the campus of the University of Chicago and moved in with two middle-aged sisters. Our agreement said that the small living room was to be available to all of us. We discovered, however, that our landladies pulled down the shades, draped their bedclothes over the furniture, and turned the chairs upside down against the wall in the common living room when they left for work.

While we were attending Hyde Park High School, it was a shock for Amelia and me to face teachers who could not teach. Amelia was assigned to a senior English class with a teacher, who, it was rumored, was an aunt of the mayor's wife. She was so hard of hearing that nothing less than a minor explosion or a loud shout disturbed the tranquility of her expression as she sat at her desk with a book open in front of her. At the beginning of the class period, she always told her pupils to read silently the next four chapters. Near the end of one period she asked, "In what magazine were *The Sir Roger de Coverly Papers* first published?" A boy in the back of the room jumped to his feet and began reciting, "Mary Had a Little Lamb." He concluded with a mocking bow toward the teacher, who nodded absently, "Yes, you are quite right, my boy; they were published in *the Spectator.*"

A few days of this kind of nonsense was enough for Amelia, and she became restive. Her inherent kindness made her resent the ridiculing of a seemingly helpless old person. She also was accustomed to stimulating discussions on the works of standard authors and was bored by the clowning in the classroom. Amelia spoke to two others in the class who agreed that the situation was terrible. They prepared a petition asking that their teacher be replaced by a teacher "who can teach us something." The morning the petition was ready, one of the girls who helped prepare it said her parents had forbidden her to sign it. This frightened the second girl, so Amelia's name stood alone at the top of the signature column. Sitting sideways at her desk near the front of the room, Amelia began to speak above the laughing and talking which characterized the silent reading period. She told her classmates that it was a shame the way they were treating their teacher. Amelia told them that they could not help it if she couldn't hear, but just the same they needed a teacher to teach them. Amelia asked the other students to sign a petition to the principal for a different teacher.

Opposition broke out, and one of the students seized the petition, tore it into little pieces, and scattered it in the aisles. Of course, Amelia was naive to expect a group of teenagers to exchange a fifty-minute period of amusement for a period of work and learning. Perhaps she went about her reform campaign in the wrong way, but it is revealing that she dared to undertake it. The teacher continued to sit with an open volume of Addison's essays while the students wasted their time. Amelia, however, persuaded the school librarian that her English work required her presence in the library. She received her senior English credits for reading four times the books required in the course without attending a single English class after the first two weeks of school. The students branded her a "screwball" and possibly a tattletale. I believe this is why the Year Book caption under her picture says, "The girl in brown who walks alone."

She graduated in June, 1916, but felt no remorse at missing the graduation exercises. It was many years later that she received the diploma and an honorary medal from Chicago Mayor Anton J. Cermak, who said, "I give you this diploma, as of 1916, Miss Earhart, not that you need this small honor you earned sixteen years ago, but that we want you to have it so the world will know that you belong to us."

Mother felt we must return to Dad in Kansas City, and we agreed that this was the wise move to make. We hated leaving our friends in Chicago, but it was also difficult to leave the beautiful, brash metropolis which sheltered us indifferently for ten months. Nevertheless, Amelia and I boarded the train.

In Kansas City we were welcomed by a jubilant Dad who, after living in cramped quarters with his sister and her family, was as eager as we were to have our own home again. We found a small house in a pleasant neighborhood and, after moving our furniture from storage, set up housekeeping. We were once again united and hopeful.

Soon after we were settled, Dad persuaded Mother to go to court to break Grandmother's will. This would allow Mother to deposit her money in a local bank or invest it in real estate. We had watched with dismay the shrinking of the monthly trust income. Uncle Mark foolishly sold some of the gilt-edged bonds which Grandmother held and bought common stock in several questionable enterprises which thereafter collapsed entirely. It was hard for Mother

Amelia in Kansas City, circa 1916.

Amelia with our father, circa 1916.

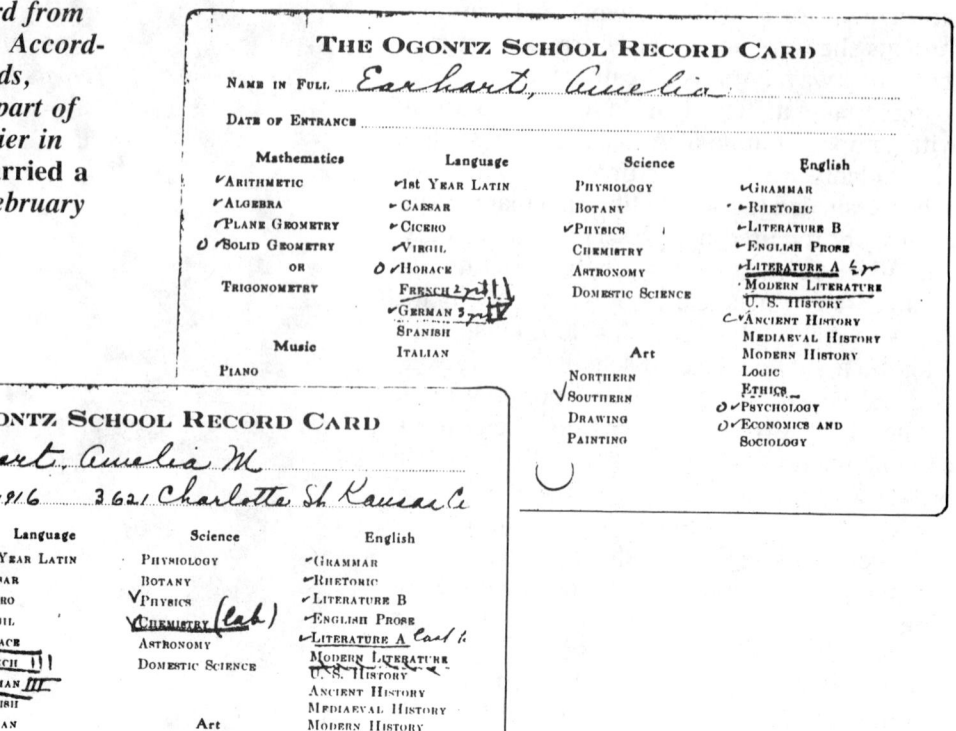

Amelia's report card from the Ogontz School. According to school records, Amelia played the part of Master Jean Maugier in **The Man Who Married a Dumb Wife,** *on February 26, 1917.*

to reconcile herself to litigation.

The airing of family differences in a courtroom was anathema to her, but when it came to a question of protecting the funds set aside for our education, she agreed to act. Sitting in the courtroom with the portrait of her father, Judge Otis, looking benignly down from the wall, Mother listened to the testimony of Dr. Charles Johnson, who attended Grandmother in her last illness. He said:

> I am of the firm belief that my patient, the late Mrs. Alfred Otis, was unduly harassed by worry and illness on the date that this will was altered. I am of the opinion that she was incompetent, and did not understand what was written here when she consented to this codicil which, in substance, places Mrs. Earhart, her eldest daughter, in the same category as Theodore Otis, her son, who has been all his life mentally retarded owing to a cranial injury at birth.

The Court ordered Uncle Mark to turn over all funds and collateral immediately. Since Mother now could draw from the principal for major expenses such as education, she sent Amelia to Ogontz School in Rydal, Pennsylvania. Amelia chose Ogontz because she wanted to transfer to Bryn Mawr College where she could be with her friend Virginia Park from Atchison. Amelia's application was accepted, and she entered Ogontz School in the autumn of 1916. Her letters home told of stimulating classes and pleasant friendships but also of stormy weather when she argued for democratization of sororities and for intellectual freedom.

Amelia was invited to join one of the three secret societies at the school. She enjoyed the carefully guarded ritual and the camaraderie of the members until she found that there were some girls at Ogontz who did not belong to any sorority. She urged the society to take in more

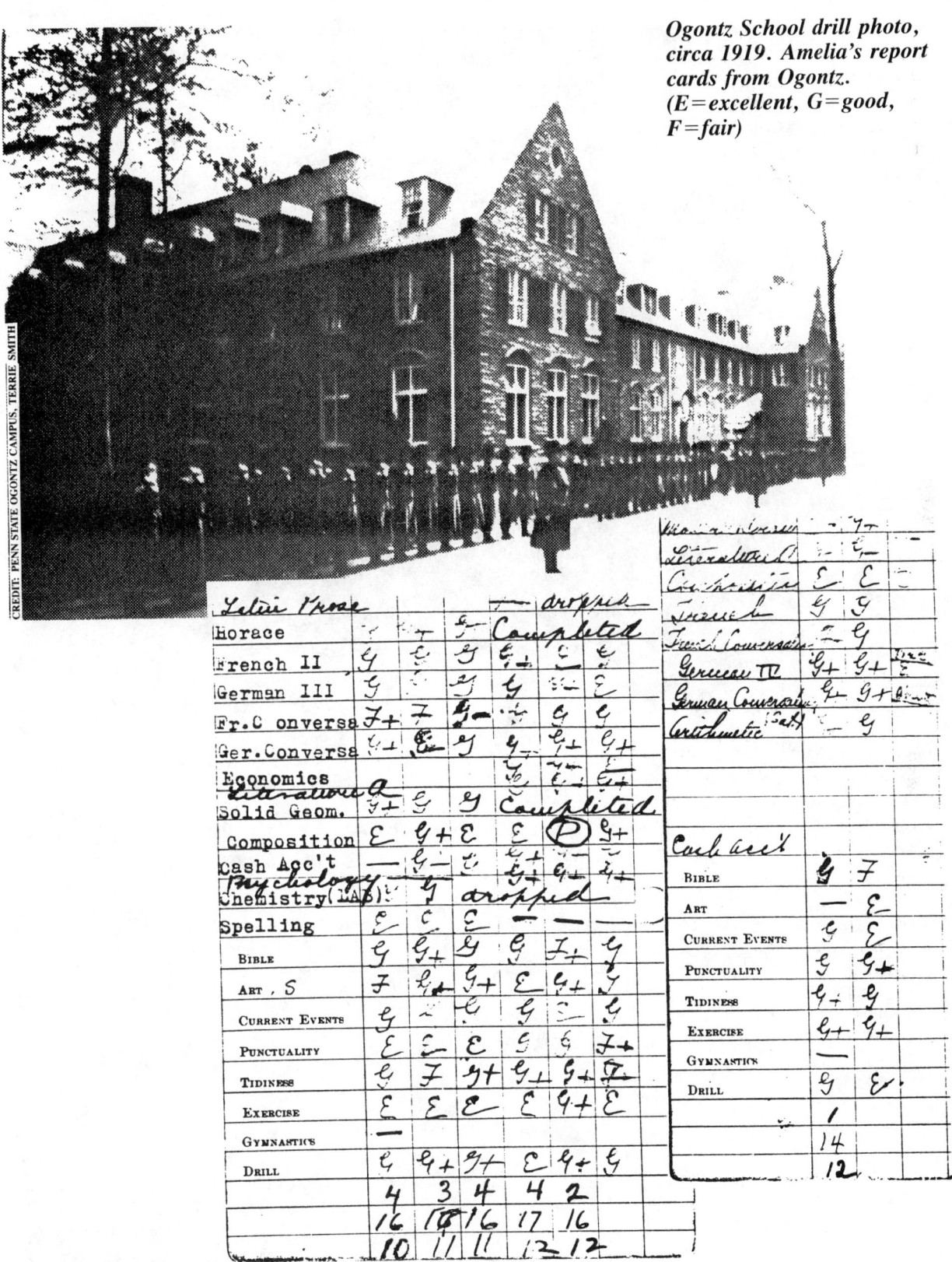

Ogontz School drill photo, circa 1919. Amelia's report cards from Ogontz. (E=excellent, G=good, F=fair)

CHANGING BACKGROUNDS | 47

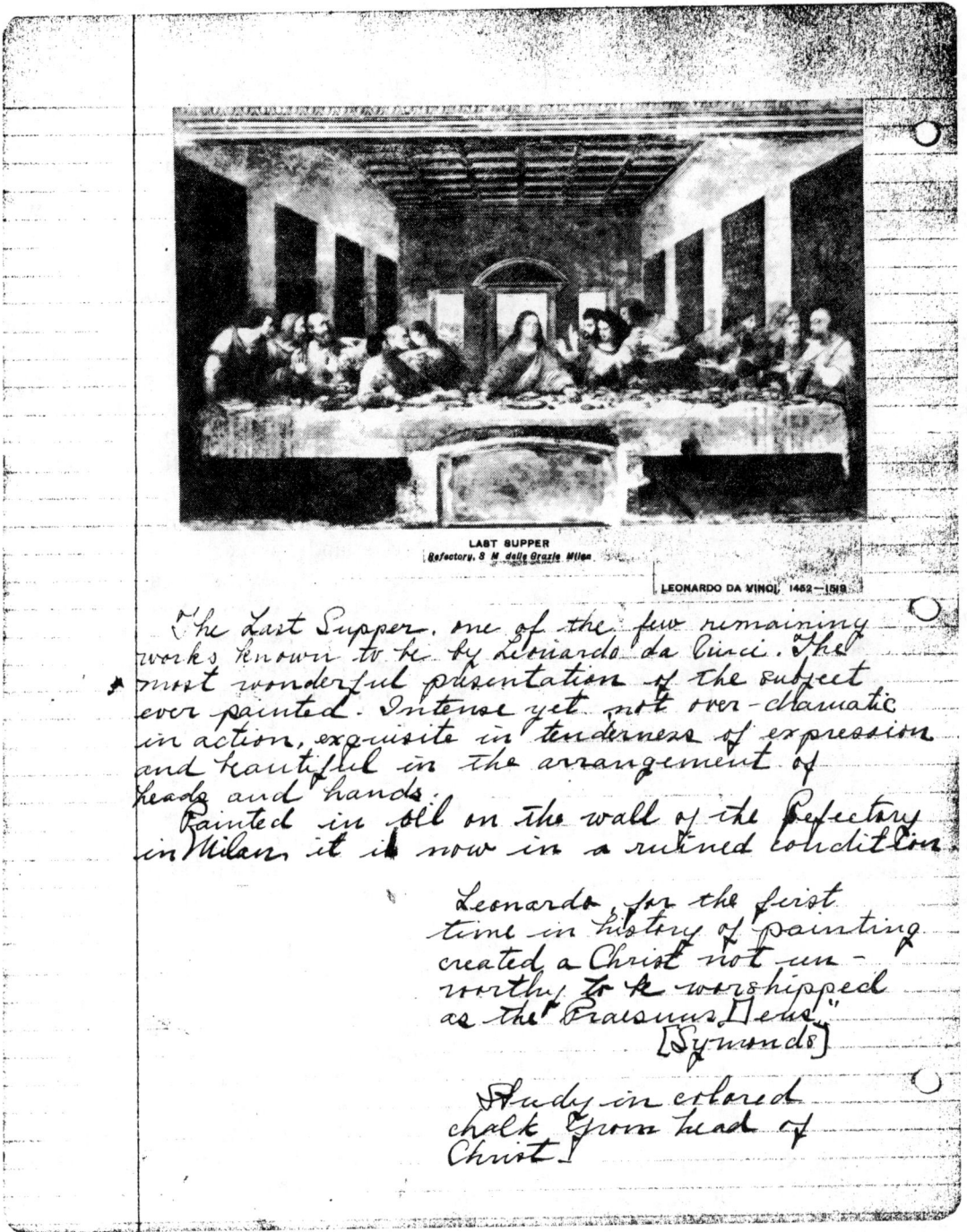

(facing page) Amelia in 1915. (below) Pages from Amelia's chemistry class at Ogontz.

(above) A page from Amelia's notebook from her Southern Art class, circa 1917.

girls, but the idea was not accepted. She then went to the headmistress, Abby A. Sutherland, and asked the faculty to approve four secret societies instead of three. Amelia felt that every girl ought to have the opportunity of belonging to a sorority. I do not know the outcome of this crusade of Amelia's, but her concern for the out-group stemmed from the days at Hyde Park when she too had walked alone, and not from choice.

Amelia maintained that girls should not only be free to join or not join sororities, but that they should also be free to explore any topic through discussion and reading. She rebelled specifically when, in the class reading Ibsen's plays, attention was centered solely upon the problem of the over-protected wife in *A Doll's House*. *Ghosts*, in which attention is focused upon venereal disease, and *Hedda Gabler*, which deals with suicidal insanity, were taboo.

That winter, Sir Rabindranath Tagore, a Hindu poet and mystic, lectured in Philadelphia. Amelia and several girls from Ogontz attended. He read some of his poems, and the students discussed his philosophy. One girl expressed the pious hope that Tagore would become a Christian during his visit to this country. Amelia asked, "Why should he?" This precipitated a school-wide argument. Before it was exhausted, Amelia was accused of being an atheist.

This she stoutly denied. She believed in God, but not in many of the tenets in the catechism we had to learn when we were younger. God, to her, was a power that helped her to be good, and that was really what Tagore meant when he said he believed in "an all-enveloping God." She felt that the way we worship wasn't important.

During the spring of Amelia's freshman year at Ogontz, the United States entered World War I. Because she felt that women traditionally were relegated to a secondary position in the conduct of war, she began her scrapbook on women's careers. She cut items from magazines and newspapers telling of women's achievements in fields usually considered a men's domain. Among the yellowed clippings pasted in a small notebook:

— Mrs. E. E. Abernathy is Oklahoma's only woman bank president.

— Breaking all precedents for this county, the Orange County Medical Association last night elected a woman as president of the organization. She is Dr. Bessica Raiche of Anaheim.*

Amelia included an article dealing with an inquiry on legislation affecting women. The legislators were urged to remove restrictions that prohibited women holding property independently and to grant rights of inheritance. Amelia penciled: "This method is not sound. Women will gain economic justice by proving themselves in all lines of endeavor, not by having laws passed for them."

Writing later about Amelia at Ogontz School in her book *100 Years of Ogontz: A History of Ogontz School*, the headmistress, Mrs. Abby A. Sutherland, wrote, "Amelia was always pushing into unknown seas in her thinking, her reading, and in experiments in science. Her most vivid characteristic was her intellectual curiosity which burned brightly when she was with us and was certainly exemplified by her later career."

Mrs. Sutherland also wrote:

> In the field of aeronautics, Ogontz' bravest and most adventurous pilot was Amelia Earhart. From her first adventure of crossing the Atlantic Ocean, to her last fatal Pacific trip, she was ever given over to the daringly fascinating navigation of the air. As a student, Amelia was always interested in new fields of literature. The last book, whatever it might be, challenged her questioning spirit. She sought out the challenging authors: Shaw, Dreiser, Dostoevski, since for her, reading was an adventure. She stood near her classmates on the field at a final military drill as a judge, but no airplane drone on the farthest horizon failed to claim her attention.

---

*On September 16, 1910, in the Wright plane she and her husband made, Bessica Faith Raiche, a self-taught pilot, soloed and was considered the "FIRST WOMAN AVIATOR OF AMERICA."

Chapter Eight

Toronto War Nurse and Columbia Student

AFTER my graduation from Westport High School in Kansas City, Missouri, I went to St. Margaret's College in Toronto, Ontario, Canada. It was a small Episcopal school with a good academic program which would prepare me to enter Smith College.

During Amelia's holiday visit in Toronto in 1917, she became more involved in the war effort. The staggering numbers of British casualties from the trenches in France in the spring of 1917 had crowded the military hospitals. We met many walking wounded on the streets and in the city parks. One day when we strolled down King Street, three soldiers on crutches approached us. All three had lost a leg. The poignant sight deeply affected Amelia; she had seen nothing like it in our country. Our soldiers were just beginning to see action, and the United States had not yet suffered serious losses.

When Amelia visited me at St. Margaret's College, she took an active part in the war effort instead of playing the passive schoolgirl role of knitting socks and rolling bandages. She made a momentous decision against returning to Ogontz. She wrote letters to both mother and Mrs. Sutherland at Ogontz by the next mail. She took a concentrated course in Red Cross First Aid and enrolled in the Voluntary Aid Detachment. After completing the course, she was assigned to the Spadina Military Hospital.

"Sister Amelia" soon became a favorite among the wounded and discouraged men. Her strong hands were prime for a back massage, and she usually ended her ministrations with a little tattoo on her patient's back, saying, "Shave and a haircut . . . next week!"

Amelia in cap and gown at Ogontz School, December 1917. She never graduated, but instead became a volunteer nurse in Toronto during World War I.

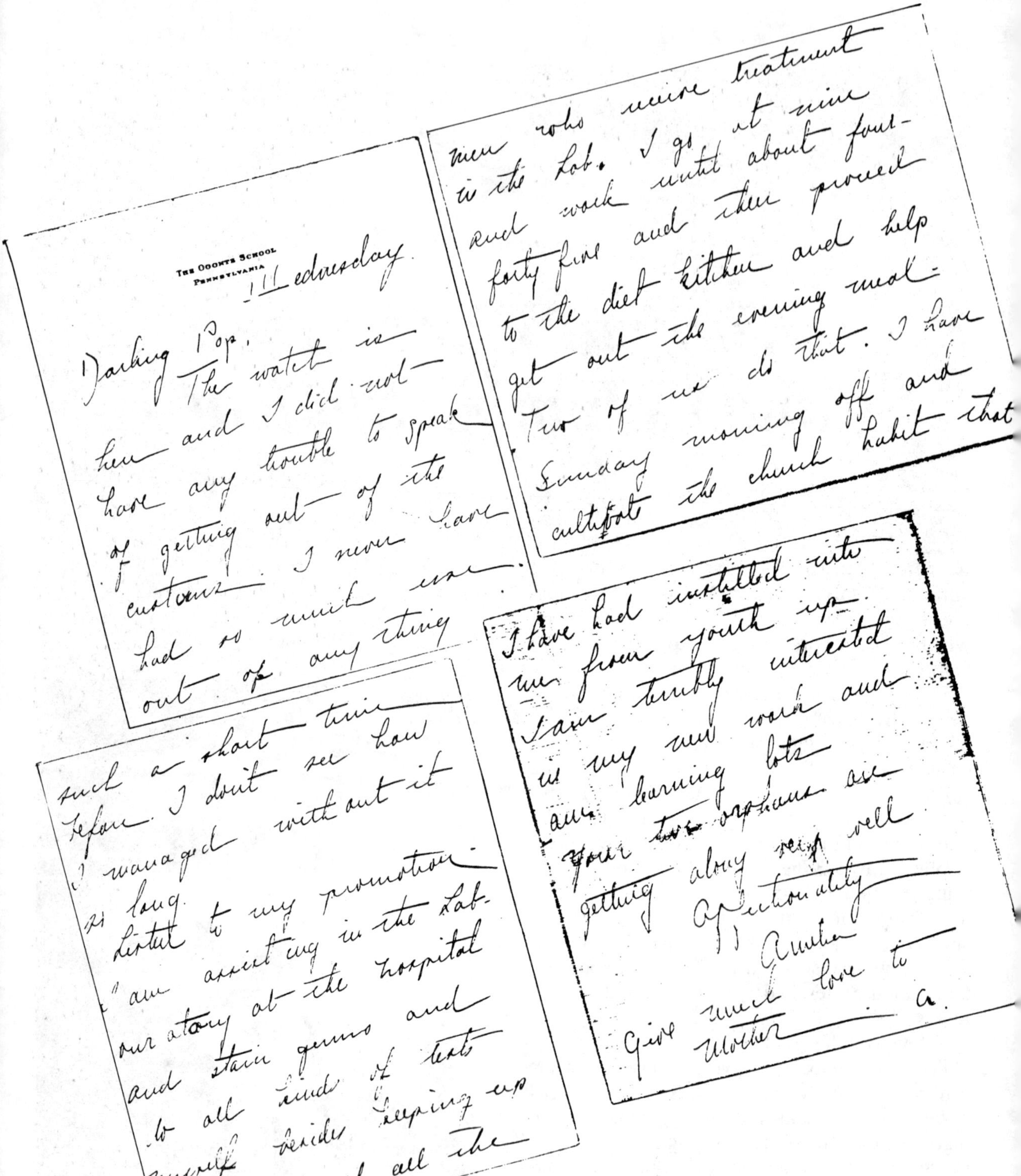

THE OGONTZ SCHOOL
PENNSYLVANIA

Wednesday

Darling Pop,

The watch is here and I did not have any trouble to speak of getting out of the customs. I never have had so much use out of anything in such a short time before. I don't see how I managed without it so long. Listed to my promotion — I am assisting in the Lab. our story at the hospital and stain germs and to all kind of tests myself besides keeping up the records of all the men who receive treatment in the Lab. I go at nine and work until about forty five and then proceed to the diet kitchen and help get out the evening meal. Two of us do that. I have Sunday morning off and cultivate the church habit that I have had instilled into me from youth up. I am terribly interested in my new work and am learning lots. Your two orphans are getting along very well.

Affectionately
Amelia

Give much love to Mother — A.

Letter from Amelia to her father while she worked in the hospital at Toronto, circa 1917–1918.

Amelia as a volunteer nurse in Toronto, Canada, circa 1917–1918.

Amelia on "Dynamite" in Toronto, 1918.

Amelia's knowledge of chemistry impressed the director of nurses, and she was soon promoted to working on diets in the kitchen and dispensary. Amelia felt that hospital life was dreary enough without having unappetizing meals. She approached the head dietitian, a formidable English woman named Mrs. Waldron, and asked to have stewed tomatoes alternated with the turnips and parsnips which regularly served as a second vegetable. She had figures to show that the cost of tomatoes would be less than a cent more per serving, and she ended her plea, "And tomatoes are so much cheerfuller."

The next supply order contained fifty large cans of tomatoes. The turnip war was won, and she was now onto the rice pudding. Some of the long-term men used to groan when they saw it on the trays. Amelia said two men emptied their rice pudding onto the tray one day, heaped the pudding into a grave-like mound, and marked it with bent matches to form the letters, "R.I.P."

Amelia, without identifying the "Rest in Peace" artists, again appealed to Mrs. Waldron for a variation. She said blanc mange was just as nourishing and a little strawberry or cherry flavoring would make it tasty and colorful.

When the extra milk, cornstarch, and flavoring were delivered, Amelia received help from the whole staff to make the first batch. One girl brought some fancy molds from home; another contributed some candied cherries and orange slices, which, owing to wartime restrictions, were highly prized confections. The word somehow got around the wards that the American sister was responsible. The two match-stick artists outdid themselves by printing, "RAY, RAY, U.S.A.," on a noticeably cleared tray.

Amelia recounted this incident to me the next day and said, "I don't know of anything, Pidge, that has warmed my heart as that did." Food surely helps morale everywhere.

When Amelia's day off coincided with my free Saturday from St. Margaret's, we rode horses. Entering the stables on Saturday, we noticed a big, rawboned dappled gray horse that we had not seen before. Amelia asked March, the groom, if she could ride him.

March told her it didn't look like anybody was going to ride the horse, named Dynamite. He belonged to an old-time cavalry colonel who must have been pretty mean to him because the horse was surely like a stick of dynamite now. He tossed off two of the boys who tried to ride him the day before, and he lashed out with his hoofs.

Amelia divided the apple she had brought for the horse she was riding that day and stepped over to Dynamite's stall. As soon as he heard a step beside him, his ears went back and he bared his teeth. Amelia just clucked softly to him and put the piece of apple in his feed box; then she patted his neck lightly and slipped out of the stall. As we rode out of the stable, Amelia told me she was going to stop by every afternoon on the way home from the hospital to try to tame Dynamite.

Little by little her kindness won him. Within a month's time, he had come to accept a brisk canter with an easy bit and a light-handed rider. The owner of the stables never accepted a fee when Amelia rode Dynamite because he said she saved the horse for him.

One of the officers who rode with us several times was an officer in the Royal Flying Corps. He admired the way Amelia managed Dynamite. One day he told Amelia that when he watched her ride that big horse, it reminded him of the way he had to fly his airplane. Sometimes his plane flew as smooth as silk, and then other times it flew contrary and bucked a bit, just to show off, as Dynamite did. The officer invited us to come out to the airfield at Armor Heights the next week and watch him fly.

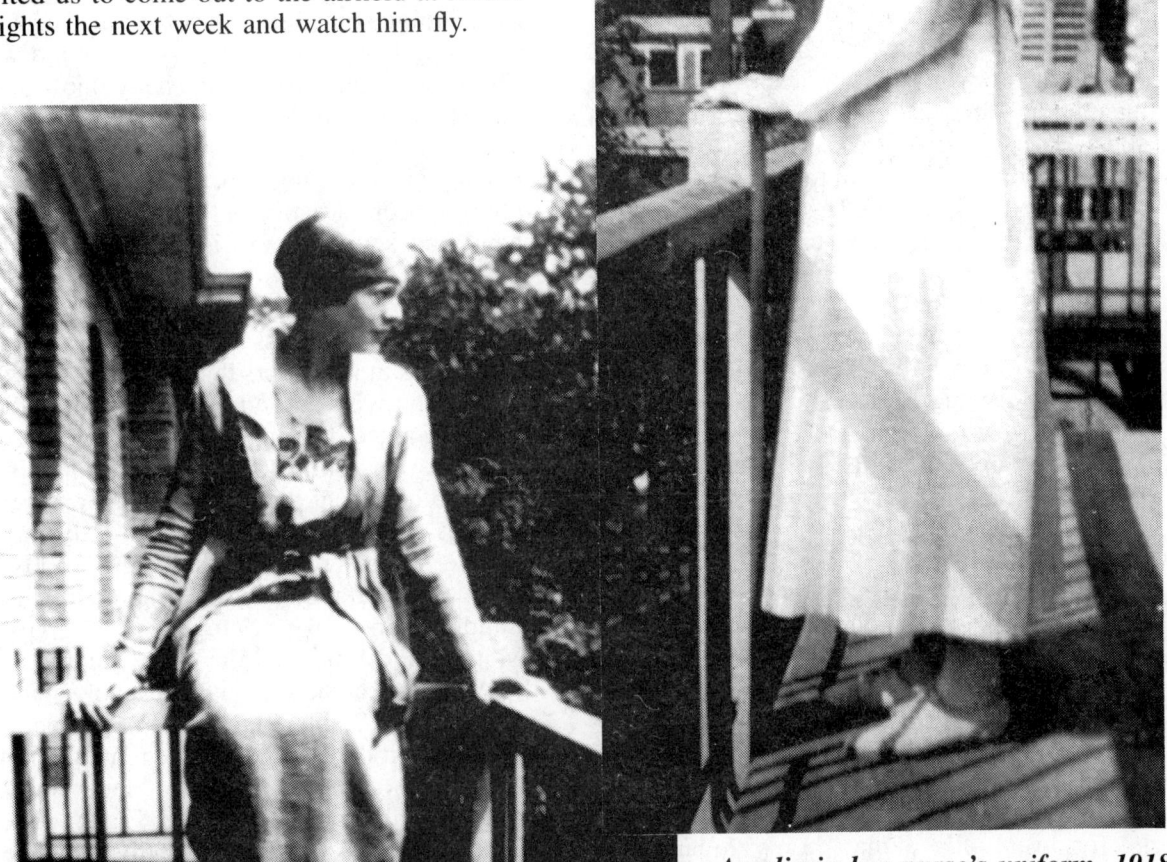

Amelia in her nurse's uniform, 1918.

Amelia in Toronto, 1918.

Amelia knew a number of pilots who were patients at the hospital. Some had been shot down during reconnaissance flights over enemy territory. Others crashed in training maneuvers. Their modesty and reticence about their exploits and their fatalistic attitude toward life appealed to Amelia. At the airfield we admired the planes, especially as they came in for landing. Amelia wanted to fly with our friend, Captain Spaulding, but regulations against civilian passengers were strict, so we had to be content to be spectators.

In the Spring of 1918, I moved to Northampton, Massachusetts. Early in November, Amelia was hospitalized by a serious attack of pneumonia. She missed celebrating the Armistice. When she recovered sufficiently to travel, Amelia came to Northampton to stay with me to recuperate. I had rented a small apartment on Bedford Terrace and took care of her while I studied for the four comprehensive entrance examinations required by Smith College. As Amelia grew stronger, we walked the country roads of Hampshire County. Amelia and I loved to walk and explore, just as in the days when we were children. One day we hiked up Mt. Tom in the Holyoke Range of the Berkshires; another day we walked almost to Hatfield, a village six miles north of Northampton.

When mud or slush prevented our country lane hikes, we explored the byways of Northampton. On one such walk we found a tiny pawnshop displaying a medley of dusty objects in its window. Amelia noticed an unusual five-string banjo, and we went in to find out how much it cost.

The shopkeeper ended up selling the banjo to us for twenty-five dollars, only because not many people were interested in playing such a fine instrument. He said he wanted somebody to have it that would appreciate it.

Amelia loved music and taught herself to read music. She inherited from Dad the ability to play by ear, and she easily picked out many of the familiar opera choruses and arias from hearing them on records. I had taken a few piano lessons in Des Moines but was never able to continue them. Amelia had enjoyed the Mandolin Club at Ogontz and knew the banjo fingering would not be difficult for her to master. She used to practice hours at a time, working out the fingerings and tempos of compositions like Dvorak's *Humoresque,* portions of Rossini's *Stabat Mater,* and Mendelssohn's *Spring Song* and *Hunting Song.*

As in poetry, Amelia's taste in music was catholic. The traditional classical music she loved was always tempered by some of her favorite Gilbert and Sullivan airs, "Tit Willow," and the lovers' duet from *Iolanthe.*

I was delighted to see Amelia show an interest in doing something "just for fun." She was regaining her old *joie de vivre.* Within a week she found a musician to give her banjo lessons, and she also enrolled in a five-week course in automobile mechanics. The incongruity of the two activities did not strike her because she had always been artistic and impractical on one hand and scientific and intensely practical on the other.

In the spring of 1919, Mother came to Northampton from Kansas City. We suspected from hints in her letters that Dad, following the will-o'-the-wisp promises of railroad claim cases, wanted to move to Los Angeles. The furniture was put into storage in Kansas City, and Mother spent the summer in New England with us. Mother saw the move to California as another major ordeal that she did not look forward to. We rented a summer home at Hulett's Landing on Lake George where Amelia, Mother, and I enjoyed the entire summer.

Amelia became especially friendly with the New York Stabler family who owned the cottage next door to the one we rented. Another neighbor was a young poet, Mark Turbyfill. Marian Stabler and her brother Frank, Amelia, and I formed a critical yet friendly audience for Mark. Mark's poetry appealed to us because it broke from traditional poetry both in form and subject.

The harrowing nursing experiences at the Spadina Hospital in Toronto took a heavy toll, but the glorious days by glass-clear Lake George allowed Amelia to recuperate. At the end of the summer of 1919, she enrolled as a pre-medical student at Columbia University, and I began my freshman year at Smith College. Mother, greatly encouraged by the letters

Dad wrote, left to join him in Los Angeles, California.

Amelia took two courses in chemistry, organic and inorganic, and also two biology courses, one of which she took in the university extension program. For fun she audited a course in French poetry.

Amelia's closest friend during these days was Louise DeSchweinitz. After graduating from Smith College in 1918 as a history major, Louise decided to enter the medical profession. She needed two more science courses before being admitted to Johns Hopkins. Amelia and Louise became friends while having biology classes together. It was Louise, now Dr. Louise DeSchweinitz Darrow, who was Amelia's companion on their now famous sightseeing trip to the Columbia Library dome.

One afternoon as they climbed the steps of the Columbia library, Amelia glanced up at the dome and remarked how much fun it would be to climb up there and look out over the city. A few days later, as they tied on their rubber aprons in the biology laboratory, Amelia asked Louise if she was game, after class, to go on a sightseeing trip, all in the name of science.

Upon Louise's ready consent, Amelia told her that the library's custodian, under the promise of secrecy and in the name of science, had shown Amelia the location of the key. One could hardly have found more fitting devotees of the eternal message of spring than these two

Amelia and friend during the summer at Lake George, 1919.

young women just over twenty, who gazed serenely out over the world stretching below them. It was a time and place for confidences and I am sure both spoke more freely of their personal feelings than they would have done under other circumstances.

Amelia broke the silence as they sat back on the dome with their feet propped against the railing. She said that the custodian had asked her, jokingly, whether she planned to commit suicide up there. Amelia could not imagine anybody in her right mind wanting to leave all this, especially in the spring. Louise agreed.

Amelia knew a girl at Ogontz who had killed herself in New York a few months earlier. This girl seemingly had everything to live for, like wealth, looks, and health, but as the papers reported it, she was despondent over an unhappy romance.

Louise commented that she probably didn't have her health.

Amelia remarked how Louise could come up with good common-sense answers, just as she did in biology. She was a remarkable doctor-to-be. Then Amelia added soberly, "Just the same, I certainly haven't met any man yet that I'd want to die for."

Louise wanted Amelia's advice. Louise explained that the last evening, her friend Bert had asked her to marry him. She really cared a lot for him, but not for marriage, at least not right now. Louise wanted to work toward a medical degree and had four more years to reach her goal.

Amelia said Bert had shown wonderful taste in loving her, but she didn't think Louise should give up her career, while he went on with his. Amelia suggested that Louise wait, say two years, and then see how they both felt.

Louise nodded, and said she was really afraid that no one else would ever ask her. More than half of her class in college were married and most of them had babies. Louise was worried that she might never have a chance to have a family. Amelia replied that she could think of a lot of things worse than never getting married, and one of the worst was being married to a man who tied one down. "Of course," Amelia added, "I'm not in love with anybody—yet."

That semester Amelia conducted an experiment testing the nutritive value of certain proteins. Her subjects for experimentation were eight white rats, whom she named after St. Nick's reindeer. One morning when she stopped to feed them and record her observations, she found two of them dead. Two others who ate the low-protein diet could barely crawl. She filled a medicine dropper with chloroform and dropped a little on their noses, killing them painlessly. No one loved animals more than Amelia.

The anti-vivisection propaganda always disturbed Amelia. She felt trained scientists who sought answers to medical problems were not cruel to animals. Ignorant hunters who used vicious traps and circuses that abused wild animals were the people Amelia thought deserved criticism about animal abuse.

Professor James MacGregor, professor of biology at Columbia University in 1920, recognized and appreciated the work Amelia and Louise did in his biology course. He and his assistant frequently invited them to have tea in their office after the afternoon laboratory period. In order that the invitation would not be obvious to the other students, the professor would leave a small piece of paper torn in the shape of a T on their laboratory desk. Amelia and Louise would be purposely slow at cleaning up after the class and, as soon as all the others left, would join them for a cup of tea brewed in a beaker over a Bunsen burner. They talked about biology and discussed the significant experiments being carried out at Columbia and elsewhere.

Dr. MacGregor said of Amelia later:

> She grasped the significance of an experiment, mentally assayed the results, and drew conclusions while I was still lecturing about setting up the experimental machinery. She was a most stimulating student, and when she and Louise DeSchweinitz worked together, they were a remarkable team. I feel that had Amelia not become caught up in the adventure of flying, she would have found equally challenging frontiers to conquer in the laboratory.

Amelia was admitted to the Columbia University Extension Program in 1919 for one year, accumulating 38 points. She filled out the directory card (top right) during registration.

Amelia on the Columbia Library Dome, April 1920.

The year passed. As it has been with students since the first three or four youths gathered to listen to Socrates, Amelia accomplished much serious study but gladly interspersed it with laughter, with friends, and the enjoyment of poetry and music at the close of the day.

I made arrangements to spend the summer vacation with relatives in the east to avoid the expense of two transcontinental trips. Mother and Dad urged Amelia to come to California and continue her studying there. Amelia and I both felt that the relationship between our parents was not a happy one. Amelia said to me, rather bitterly, as I saw her off from New York, "I'll see what I can do to keep Mother and Dad together until you finish college, Pidge, but after that, I'm going to come back here and live my own life."

In 1925 Amelia withdrew from the extension program and registered as a university undergraduate. She wrote her date of birth as 1898, forgetting that she was born in 1897.

Chapter Nine

California Girl and Fledgling Flier

IN the summer of 1920, Amelia went to Los Angeles to be with Mother and Dad who had been there about one year. They rented a large house on Fourth Street, larger than our family needed, so mother agreed to rent two large rooms to three young men who had been sharing a room at the Y.M.C.A. One was a chemical engineer whom Amelia had become friendly with. His name was Samuel Chapman, a Tufts University graduate from Marblehead, Massachusetts.

Both Amelia and Mother wrote me of Dad's complete rehabilitation. Amelia credited Dad's progress to a member of the Christian Science Church, whose office was near Dad's. He saw Dad's problem and cared enough to extend a helping hand. He often invited Dad to his home for dinner before they went together to the Wednesday evening meetings.

The Scientists applied the same techniques used in Alcoholics Anonymous today. Dad wrote of this period of his life in California: "Everybody seemed to care about helping me. I've never seen such unselfish kindness from men, and women, too. I had invitations to meals, to the movies, to go fishing—week after week. I can't begin to tell you the trouble those people took to put me back on my feet."

Dad became deeply involved in Christian Science. He became a member about the time Amelia arrived in California. His church friends helped him by bringing legal business to him on occasion. By the summer of 1921, Dad was again established as a fairly prosperous and respected lawyer within the community.

Amelia's letters to me at Smith College contained more and more mention of Sam Chapman. He was a quiet, well-read New Englander who was attracted to her too. They enjoyed many similar interests: tennis, swimming, books, and plays. They had a common interest in the underdog and were interested in the socialist doctrine of the Industrial Workers of the World (I.W.W).

The Earhart home at 1334 West 4th Street, Los Angeles, California.

Edwin S. Earhart in 1918.

The dynamiting of the *Los Angeles Times* Building killed twenty-one people including the editor, Harrison Gray Otis, who was Grandfather Otis' cousin. The West Coast was still jittery and suspicious of labor activities ten years later. The McNamara brothers, convicted of that multiple murder, were in the federal penitentiary in Leavenworth, but, as with John Brown, some of their anarchic doctrines were still being preached by their followers. California enacted rigorous laws to control the assembling of groups who might again attempt the destruction of property. Many rallies and meetings, however, were held illegally because a license granting permission to assemble was automatically refused to any I.W.W. groups. Some called the association "I Won't Work."

Amelia and Sam once attended an I.W.W. meeting held in a vacant store in the market district. The topic scheduled was, "Pensions for All at Sixty." The I.W.W. was anticipating Social Security laws which were envisioned by Herbert Hoover and enacted under his successor, Franklin Roosevelt, more than a decade later.

Amelia wrote, "Pensions are surely better than poorhouses at sixty. I think the government ought to make people save some of their wages and then give it back to them when they get old. I don't hold with destruction of property, naturally, but I think we should have had the right to talk it out tonight instead of being sent home like naughty children."

Amelia staunchly upheld her ideas of fair play, especially in regard to the rights of those less fortunate than we. I was not surprised by her decision several years later to choose a career in social work.

Early in the spring of 1921, Amelia wrote me that she had begun to take flying lessons. I was not surprised. She took her first flight at Rogers Airport. She quickly became hooked on flying.

Amelia worked in a telephone office to earn money to pay for her lessons. Amelia wanted me to meet her instructor, Neta Snook. Neta was a slim, five foot, five and one-half inch girl. She had bright red hair and always wore her breeches, high shoes with puttees over them, and the black flying coat which she had purchased in 1918.

Sam Chapman in 1922.

Amelia said she was lucky to find another woman in the business. Neta was one of the first women to get a pilot's license in the United States. She owned a Curtiss Canuck, similar to a Curtiss World War I training plane called the Jenny. Amelia felt fortunate because Neta would give lessons on credit. She ended her letter with, "By the time you get out here, I may have soloed and then you can risk your neck with me, yes?"

Amelia wrote in her 1928 book, *20 HRS. 40 MIN., Our Flight In The Friendship:*

> . . . .When I came down I was ready to sign up at any price to have a try at the air myself. Two things deterred me at that moment. One was the tuition fee to be wrung from my father, and the other the determination to look up a woman flyer who, I had heard, had just come to another field. I felt I should be less self conscious taking lessons with her, than with the men who overwhelmed me with their capabilities. Neta Snook, the first woman to be graduated from the Curtiss School of Aviation, had a Canuck . . .

When I came west early in June, 1921, I took a job teaching summer school five days a week in Long Beach. I wanted to learn more about Amelia's hobby so she took me to Kinner Airfield, which was located at the corner of Long Beach Boulevard and Tweedy Road. Amelia dressed in her breeks, the same breeks she wore horseback riding in New York.

We left the house early in the morning and took the streetcar from Fourth Street through Vernon and Huntington Park until we reached the end of the line, which was about one mile from the Kinner Airfield. We started to walk the last mile before a friendly motorist offered us a ride. He could tell where we were going because Amelia was dressed in her flying clothes.

When we arrived, Neta had an oil can in her hand and was squirting oil on the rocker arms of her Canuck. She was an experienced flier and not only knew how to keep the plane in good mechanical condition, but had actually bought and rebuilt the Canuck.

After a short introduction, Amelia showed me the inside of Neta's Canuck. She stood beside the back cockpit and began to explain

Amelia with her first car in 1920.

Amelia with Sam Chapman in Los Angeles.

Amelia, California business girl, 1923.

Amelia on Mount Wilson in 1923.

Muriel Earhart, circa 1923.

Neta Snook gave Amelia her first flying instruction on January 2, 1921.

Rare photo of Amelia with her long hair, circa 1920.

how the controls worked. Soon Neta and a group of boys pushed the Canuck over to Mr. Kinner's gasoline pump. He put the gasoline hose into the Canuck's tank opening, located between the engine and the front cockpit, with the opening on top of the fuselage. Mr. Kinner assured Neta the tank was full, and the boys helped push the plane back onto the field.

Amelia asked me if I wished to take a ride. I liked to try new things just as she did, so naturally I said, "Yes, I'd love to." Since Amelia had not soloed yet, she arranged for Neta to take me up on my first flight. It was not a long flight. We only circled the field and landed, but it was a lot of fun. I could then understand why Amelia was so intrigued by flying.

A few minutes after my flight, Neta took Amelia up for her lesson. I watched the plane take off and thought how beautiful the plane was. Now I knew why Amelia was hooked on flying.

Even though Amelia had not soloed, her next ambition was to own her own airplane. She took lessons from Neta as often as her finances would allow, even taking some on credit.

Neta was the first woman to operate a commercial aviation field where she had an agreement with Mr. Kinner. She instructed at Kinner Airfield and did aerial advertising, as well as some test flying for Mr. Kinner. Amelia liked the Kinner Airster so much that she decided to try to buy it. It took all her savings—and mine. Mother also contributed a few hundred dollars which recently came to her as her share from the sale of the old Atchison homestead.

On July 24, 1921, Amelia's twenty-fourth birthday, she became the proud owner of a new Kinner Airster. She had to dress the part of a pilot now, and this called for a leather jacket —an old leather jacket. Amelia used some money earmarked for a raincoat to buy herself traditional apparel—a coat, helmet, and goggles. Much to the family's amusement, she wore the shiny leather coat around the house and garden for several days to get the "new" look off. She admitted that she slept in it one night to give it some authentic wrinkles too.

Amelia had a harrowing experience with her new Kinner Airster a few days after its purchase. Amelia and Neta took off and landed in a cabbage field two miles beyond. As Neta describes it in her book, *I Taught Amelia To Fly:*

> One day we flew Amelia's Airster to the Goodyear Field about six miles from Kinner Field, to visit with the blimp crew and to admire Donald Douglas' huge "Cloudster" which he was testing. On takeoff to return to Kinner, the Airster wasn't gaining altitude fast enough to clear a grove of eucalyptus trees at the end of the runway. To nose down for more flying speed meant slamming into those trees, and to pull up meant a stall. Amelia pulled up—I would have done the same—and the plane hit the ground. The propeller was broken and the landing gear damaged. This was Amelia's first crash . . .

Amelia never enjoyed cabbage again after that episode.

Neta won my heart by her unstinted praise of Amelia, who she said was a natural and was ready to solo before Neta turned her over to John "Monty" Montijo, Amelia's second instructor. Neta had married and ended her flying career, so Monty finished Amelia's flight instruction and soloed her.

Amelia wrote in her 1928 book, *20 HRS. 40 MIN., Our Flight In The Friendship:*

> Neta sold her plane and I bought one and changed instructors after a few hours' work. John Montijo, an ex-army instructor, took charge of me and soloed me after some strenuous times together. I refused to fly alone until I knew some stunting. It seemed foolhardy to try to go up alone without the ability to recognize and recover quickly from any position the plane might assume, a reaction only possible with practice. In short, to become thoroughly at home in the air, stunting is as necessary as, and comparable to, the ability to drive an automobile in traffic.

One day I was at the field when Amelia and Monty took off and made several takeoffs and landings. Soon I watched Monty get out of the cockpit and motion Amelia on alone. Monty came over to where I stood and we both watched. At last Amelia had soloed; she was a pilot. Monty commmented on what a cautious and qualified pilot she had become.

Amelia, right and Neta at Beverly Hills Speedway on July 16, 1921. The Kinner Airster is behind them.

CREDIT: NETA SNOOK SOUTHERN

When Amelia landed the last time, she pulled the ship up to where we were standing. We gathered around to congratulate her as she climbed out of the airplane. She told us how breathtakingly beautiful the sky was and how she felt comfortable and confident up there alone. Amelia said she would fly whenever she had an opportunity.

I remember Amelia saying more than once that one day we're going to have airplanes with cockpits enclosed, "so a pilot won't have to be blown to pieces." She said that some day we would have airplanes large enough to carry ten or a dozen passengers, and they'd go on regular schedules like trains. And so she talked and continually envisioned flights across the country and around the world in airplanes capable of going as much as two hundred miles an hour.

Air meets were held in those days to try to sell flying to the public. Speed and altitude records were often set at these shows. One afternoon in October, Amelia casually handed Dad and me two tickets to an air meet at Rogers Air Field in Los Angeles. She told us she could not sit with us.

When we arrived at the field, we saw Amelia in the distance. I am sure that no one would have mistaken her for a neophyte, for her helmet was pushed to the back of her head and her jacket appeared convincingly aged. We were not greatly surprised when an announcement stated that a young lady was going to attempt to set an altitude record in her Kinner biplane. We watched her climb into the tiny plane and waved encouragement. The takeoff was smooth and she spiraled out of sight. Dad and I strained to keep our eyes on the tiny speck in the sky. We were not at all interested in the target-hitting contest which was taking place in the field in front of us. We were scanning the sky for the reappearance of the tiny yellow airplane.

Amelia was aloft for nearly an hour, and, though outwardly maintaining a studied calm, both of us became desperately worried.

We then saw Amelia coming in from another direction. She landed, and we watched her climb out. Several officials surrounded the plane, and one handed down an instrument

Amelia in Neta's Canuck.

CREDIT: NETA SNOOK SOUTHERN

which we later learned was a sealed barograph. In a matter of minutes, an announcer shouted through his megaphone that Amelia just set a new altitude record for women. She flew to an altitude of 14,000 feet. Dad and I went down to the rail in front of the bleachers. Amelia soon saw us and came over. We congratulated her, but I reproachfully said, "Why didn't you tell me you planned to do this, Meelie?"

She did not want to say anything about it in case the Fédération Aéronautique Internationale refused to recognize her flight. She really wouldn't have cared about the record except that it would help Bert Kinner sell his airplanes.

The record stood for only a few weeks before Ruth Nichols broke it. Amelia continued to fly whenever she could, always learning and always enjoying the beauty of the world seen from the air although she did had some frightening moments, too.

She once encountered a layer of clouds which proved to be laden with snow. In the open cockpit the snow stung her face and fogged her goggles, so that she lost all sense of direction.

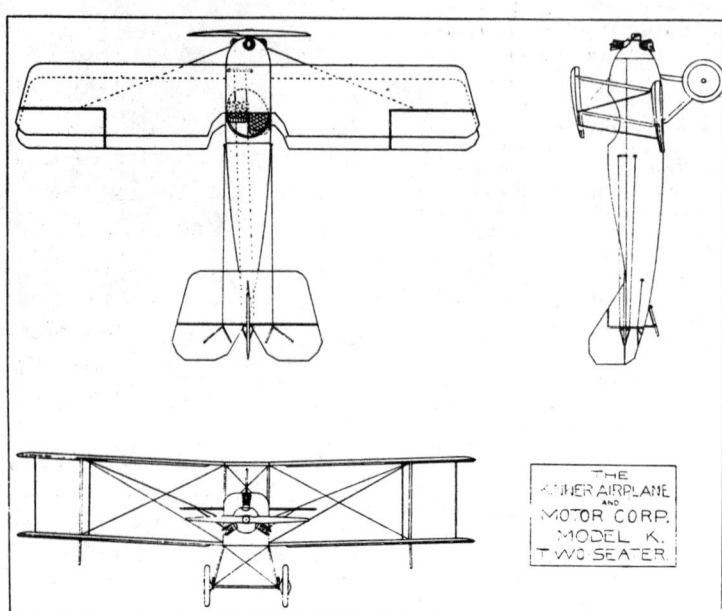

Model "K" Airster - General Utility Plane

SPECIFICATIONS
Number of passengers—One and Two.
Engine:
  Lawrence Model "L"-2 Motor—60 H. P.
Weight:
  Empty—600 pounds.
  Fully loaded—1000 pounds.
  Useful load—400 pounds.
Fuel Weight:
  One Pas., 140 lbs.; Two, 56 lbs.
Range at Full Speed:
  With one passenger, 500 miles.
  With two passengers, 200 miles.
Speed:
  Near ground, 85 M. P. H.
  At 5000 feet, 70 M. P. H.
  Ceiling, 12,000 feet.
Climb:
  To 5000 feet—10 minutes.
  To 12,000 feet, Ceiling—30 minutes.
Loading:
  Per horsepower, 15.25 pounds.
  Per square foot—5 pounds.

Dimensions
Span:
  Upper wing—26.6 feet.
  Lower wing—26.6 feet.
Wing chord, both planes—4 feet.
Overall length—20 feet.
Overall height—7.6 feet.
Gap between wing—54 inches.
Stagger—9 inches.

Areas
Wing areas:
  Upper—106 square feet.
  Lower— 94 square feet.
  Total (with ailerons)—200 sq. ft.
Aileron area—30 square feet.
Vertical area:
  Fin—1.2 square feet.
  Rudder—7 square feet.
Horizontal Areas:
  Stabilizers—20 square feet.
  Elevators—16 square feet.

Main Planes
The R. A. F. No. 6 wing curve is used. Wing chord 4 feet. Span of both upper and lower wings 26 feet 6 inches. Wings are in four main panels in addition to the center panel which is 30 inches wide. Upper and lower panels are interchangeable. Gap between wings, 4 feet 6 inches. Dihedral, upper and lower, 2.5 degrees. Incidence 3.50 degrees at body and 2.50 degrees at wing tips.

Ribs built up with grooved spruce batters and basswood webs lightened between spars. All ribs are identical throughout and are spaced 12 inches apart first 4 foot space and 18 inches apart last 8 foot space. Internal compression members between spars are box-rib. Internal wiring with solid No. 12 wires and turnbuckles. Drift wires doubled in two inner bays and anti-draft wires single.

Leading edge of three ply bass-wood veneer. Spars of spruce channeled to I section between compression and wing struts. Trailing edge of light U-section steel, attached to ribs with copper rivets. Flat head brass nails used throughout. All wood parts coated with two coats of Valspar varnish to protect them from moisture. Metal fittings and wires are enamelled to prevent corrosion.

Special cotton fabric used for wing covering, which from experience has proven as good as linen. Fabric sewed on and bound with protective tape in most approved manner. After five coats of dope, the wings are varnished and enamel applied in any desired color. Yellow wings and maroon body used unless otherwise specified.

Wing Trussing
Interplane struts are all steel tubing fared for streamlining and are similar in shape with the exception of a variation in length to provide for the difference in gap between front and rear spars. Maximum strut section, 1 by 3 inches. Upper ends of center section struts are 30 inches apart. Interplane struts are located 8 feet from center section, leaving an overhang of 4 feet.

Strut fittings consist of an eye-bolt running through the cable plate and a block glued to spar. No bolts piercing spars.

Incidence cables are eliminated in the center section trussing, so that easy access to the front cock-pit is facilitated. One drift cable running from engine mounting to ends of rear interplane struts.

Fuselage
Length of fuselage from back of engine to stern post, 16 feet; maximum depth, 3 feet; width at cock-pit, 30 inches. Centerline of propeller shaft, 6 inches below top of upper longerons to which it is parallel. At the stern, the fuselage terminates in a steel tube stern post.

Longerons are 1 by 1 inch spruce. The top longerons from engine section to rear of cock-pit are laminated 1 by 2 inches. Spruce cross and vertical members cross tied with solid piano wire, No. 10 forward of pilot's seat, No. 12 aft.

All cowls are of aluminum, running on top, from engine to cock-pit and from

Specifications of the Kinner Airster which Amelia purchased in 1921.

engine to cabane on sides—from engine to front chassis members on under side. Elsewhere, special cotton fabric used as covering. All aluminum coverings in region of the engine are provided with inspection doors and are attached with easily removable thumb screws drilled and locked with "safety" wire.

Turtle deck built up of light spruce T section longitudinal members supported on lightened veneer diaphragms. The deck is easily detached for adjustment or inspection of the internal fuselage wiring.

Control cable openings in body protected by heavy pig-skin slots stitched to the cotton fabric.

Seating Arrangement

The two passengers are accommodated side by side except for a slight stagger position. Cockpit and seats upholstered in best grade imitation leather. Seats are made of rattan. Safety belt straps carried down by means of a steel ribbon to one of the heavy longitudinal members near the lower longerons. A continuous aluminum fire wall separates the engine section from the cock-pit. A locker located between top longerons and the curved cowling will hold about 1 cubic foot of contents.

Passengers' floor of three-ply veneer resting directly on lower longerons.

Windshields of transparent celluloid are built up with aluminum frames. Rear shield is designed so as to permit unrestricted vision over the sides in making landings.

Instruments

The instrument board is made of mahogany and is fitted with a tachometer indicating up to at least 2000 r. p. m. The throttle control lever at left side of pilot on upper longeron.

Landing Chassis

Wheel tread 5 feet. Wheels 26 by 3 inches. Axle 1.50 inch diameter; ⅛ inch wall. Axle located in line with lower wing leading edge. Chassis members of all steel tubing, welded and braised, fared for streamline. Shock absorber cord attached to saddle fittings, giving a maximum of impact absorption. A pair of cables brace the forward chassis struts; no cables aft.

One steel tube spaces lower ends of chassis at rear of axle fared for streamline.

Controls

One control stick and foot bars are provided in the cock-pit. Control column and members of square steel tube. The traverse shaft with sheet steel levers for elevators is carried on bronze bearings at either side of the cock-pit. The tandem types have a dual control.

Tail Group

Fin and rudder built up with steel tube and wood frames. Fin stern-post of steel tube which continues down and forms a bearer for tail skid. Stabilizer bolted to upper longerons with O degrees incidence angle. Stabilizer built up like wings, with spruce ribs. Overall span at rear edge, 8 inches; chord, 2 feet 6 inches. It is supported from below by means of four steel tube braces, two at front and two at back of main spar. Elevators are 2 feet wide and measure 8 feet 6 inches from tip to tip.

Tail Skid

The ash tail skid is mounted in the usual manner. Upper ends tied with ⅝ inch rudder cord.

Lower end of skid is shod with a substantial metal shoe.

Because of the difficulties encountered by tail skids, special research was made to obtain a really efficacious skid and this design has proven exceptionally satisfactory in all its details.

Engine Group

The engine is a 3 cylinder Model L-2—Lawrance. developing 60 h. p. at 1800 r. p. m. at sea level. Bore and stroke. 4.25 by 5.25 inches. Weight of engine complete with hub and bolts, carburetor, ignition and one battery but without oil, 149 pounds.

Stromberg Model M-4 carburetor.

Gasoline consumption, 3 gallons per hour at 70 m. p. h. Oil consumption, 3 pints per hour. Fuel tank under cowl has a capacity of 15 gallons in the one passenger type and 6 gallons in the two passenger type. Oil tank on flooring ahead of cock-pit; capacity about 7 quarts.

This plane was in the process of being built from 1918 thru 1921.

The seating arrangement as specified in this article was later changed to two seats one behind the other. The controls were made dual — a stick in each cockpit.

I test flew this plane in 1921 and Amelia Earhart purchased it shortly thereafter.

Neta Snook Southern (test pilot)

Oct. 31, 1981.

1/8/81

I first test flew the Kinner Airster Jan 8, 1921 for 3 minutes. Landing successful and Mr. Kinner very pleased.

July 3, 1921 - first instruction of Amelia Earhart in the "Canary" — Amelia's name for the Airster now owned by Amelia. Flight was 25° duration.

July 23, 1921 the Lawrance engine caused the "Canary" to stall upon take-off from the Goodyear Field. Amelia (A.E.) and I were not injured.

I gave A.E. 5 hours instruction in my Canuck.

I gave A.E. 15 hours instruction in her Canary.

After I retired from aviation Amelia received further instruction from John (Monte) Montijo.

Neta Snook Southern.

The New
Kinner Airster

For 1922. Equipped with the new 3-cylinder air-cooled Kinner Motor, makes an ideal plane for aviation schools and passenger carrying.

25 Miles Per Gallon of Gas
Ceiling 15,500 Feet
Dual Controlled
Standardized Parts

Kinner Airplane and Motor Corp.

Route 3, Box 29,   LOS ANGELES
Factory and Flying Field, Cor. Long Beach Boulevard and Tweedy Road

Amelia knew she must get back on the ground before the sleet weighted down her light fabric wings. The quickest way to set her plane down under control was to spin. So she spun. She came out of her spin with several thousand feet to spare, straightened out, and landed in the warm California sunshine with sleet still clinging to her struts. She realized that she might have crashed, had the clouds been hanging too low for her to pull out of the spin.

The chances to fly did not come too often in those days. It was a hand-to-mouth existence for the group of pilots gathered at the airfield where brave souls could go aloft for ten minutes for ten dollars.

On Sunday mornings, Amelia and I used to bring out to the airfield a market basket with sandwiches and a chocolate cake that mother was always willing to bake for us. The temperature on the field was often above one hundred degrees and the powdered adobe soil rose like a cloud whenever a plane took off or landed, for the paved runway was still in the distant future. There were some tin-roofed shacks for tools and gasoline, but no hangars. I often doped the fabric wings on some of the airplanes or replaced rusted guide wires. If there had been few paying passengers, the pilots saved their gasoline and, sitting in the shade of the shed, let their imaginations soar.

By the summer of 1924, Amelia and I reluctantly faced the fact that there could be no healing of the breach between our parents. Dad filed for divorce, which was uncontested. After two years teaching near Los Angeles, I longed to return to the East to work for my Ed.M Degree. I came to Boston and secured a position teaching in a junior high school in Medford, a historic suburb of Boston. Amelia drove Mother across the country in the yellow Kissel Kar which she had purchased when she sold her Kinner biplane. Sam Chapman, happy at the disposal of the plane, soon followed Amelia east, and her life seemed destined to fall into a conventional and pleasant pattern.

The Airster after failing to climb over the trees. No one was hurt, 1921.

Chapter Ten

Boston and Beyond

SOON after Amelia and Mother arrived in Medford, Amelia was troubled by a recurring sinus infection which dated back to living in Toronto. It flared up in California the previous year, and she went through some painful and ineffective treatments. Upon the advice of our Medford doctor, she had nasal surgery. The surgeon removed a small piece of bone in her nasal passage, allowing her sinuses to drain. Surgery cured the problem completely. Amelia left the hospital after about a week's stay, entirely free from headache and nasal discomfort for the first time in four years.

Amelia began teaching English to foreign students in the Massachusetts University Extension program. She didn't enjoy it too much because the classes were held late in the afternoon and evening and were likely to be scheduled at any location within a thirty-mile radius of Boston. The meager pay and transportation allowance barely allowed her to break even. As a venture, Amelia answered an advertisement in a Boston paper asking for a part-time teacher of English to the foreign-born in a neighborhood settlement called Denison House. Denison House was headquarters to the Harrison Avenue-Tyler Street district which was inhabited mostly by Syrians and Chinese.

Amelia at a picnic with the Stablers at Jones Beach in Los Angeles, winter 1924–1925, before leaving California.

Amelia's registration cards for a job at Denison House in 1926. Her friend Sam wrote a reference for her (facing page).

BOSTON AND BEYOND | 71

Amelia in her Boston training plane, 1926.

Marion Perkins, the head of Denison House, hired Amelia despite her lack of formal social work experience. Miss Perkins employed Amelia at once, and thus began a satisfying and enduring friendship during Amelia's later years. It was obvious to Miss Perkins, as it was to Mother and me, that Amelia had found a consuming vocation. I too was enjoying my own career. In California I had taught fourth grade, but now I enjoyed teaching junior high school.

Amelia found helping her students, many of whom were twice her age, personally satisfying. She enjoyed helping her students with their language hurdles. She watched them attain greater self-confidence almost day by day. She also had charge of the household economics department in Denison House and did some outside social work as a visiting nurse.

Amelia disliked routines, paper work, and dictation, as Miss Perkins soon discovered. Therefore, in an unorthodox procedure, Miss Perkins presented the emotional, economic, or moral problems of the families she planned to assign to Amelia and asked her for suggestions rather than laying down the accepted laws that an inexperienced young social worker would follow. Amelia's wide acquaintance with people of varied backgrounds all her life, along with her common sense and intelligence, kept her from violating too many sociological rules. As Miss Perkins shrewdly conjectured, Amelia, given free rein, entered into the work with boundless enthusiasm, visiting, teaching, comforting, and loving many of the "chronics" of the neighborhood. She often drove her yellow Kissel Kar, with several teen-age girls, to our home in West Medford for picnics in the yard or for storytelling and marshmallow roasts around the living room fireplace.

The neighborhood children loved the low-slung sports car, which was affectionately called the Yellow Peril. She frequently let as many as ten children climb in and stand on the running boards while she drove slowly around the block. For many of them it was their first ride in an automobile. They begged her to drive past their homes where they would wave to their families. Amelia gave of herself as she did at the hospital in Toronto. Her payment was the devotion of the children and the respect and friendship of their parents.

Amelia, however, was never reconciled to the paper work. She hated filling out forms and answering questionnaires. Her reports were often of the "Off again, On again, Gone again —Finnegan" type, but Miss Perkins, understanding Amelia's impatience with records, did not insist that she spend additional time on them. Miss Perkins occasionally reworked some of Amelia's reports before they were submitted to the Board of Directors. She knew Amelia was more engrossed in helping the Denison people solve their problems than in writing about how she did it. Amelia's concept of social work was educative. She believed that intelligent, mature individuals should be able to make adjustments—economic and emotional. Therefore, one should teach skills, enjoy arts, have hobbies, and participate in group activities to prevent boredom and frustration. Every work day she climbed dingy stairways to reach odoriferous tenements.

Amelia's Kissel Kar which she called her "Yellow Peril." She drove it from 1922 to 1929.

AMELIA EARHART, INTREPID FLIER, HAS LYONS FRIEND

Miss Pauline A. Coleman Closely Identified with Spanner of Atlantic in Boston Settlement Work; Admires Young Woman for Lack of Egotism, Courage and Charming Personality. 6/22/28

While all the world is applauding the remarkable feat just accomplished by the charming, modest Miss Amelia Earhart, there is one person here in Lyons who undoubtedly gets more of a thrill out of the young woman flier's achievement, that of spanning the great Atlantic Ocean from America to the British Isles, than any other person in this section, for Miss Pauline A. Coleman, daughter of Mr. and Mrs. S. E. Coleman knows Miss Earhart intimately and for nearly one year has been closely identified with her in settlement work in Boston.

"She is just the most unassuming and retiring, yet sweet and companionable young women one could possibly wish to know" said Miss Coleman when interviewed for the Republican. "Miss Earhart never mentioned the subject of flying to me until this spring and when I asked her if she liked to fly she replied that she was very much interested in it, but she never mentioned to me that she even contemplated flying across the ocean."

Miss Coleman stated that Miss Earhart is not only a licensed flier and that she has carried a pilot's license since 1923, but that she speaks five languages fluently and that her pilot's license is written in the five languages which she speaks. Miss Earhart is a native of Kansas, attended the Kansas State College, later studied at Columbia University and the University of California. While in California Miss Earhart participated in a considerable amount of stunt flying and she subsequently went to Boston where she became interested in settlement work, making her headquarters in the Dennison Settlement House in the Harrison Avenue-Tyler Street district which is inhabited mostly by Chinese and Syrians.

"Miss Earhart had charge of the household economic department in the settlement house" said Miss Coleman, "and I was brought in direct contact with her, having been sent to the settlement house by the Simmons College educational department to do practice teaching in foods and clothing. Miss Earhart by training has become an expert in social service work and one of her duties at the settlement house was to organize classes and superintend the courses of study. The children in the section are from very poor families, mostly Chinese and Syrians, but Miss Earhart worked faithfully to improve their conditions. She also did some outside social work as a visiting nurse."

Miss Coleman also stated that some of the young flier's friends would often joke with her about her flying and that they even went so far as to ask her if she had not thought of trying the hop from America to Europe but that Miss Earhart always remained silent, taking the jests with one of her smiles. This wonderful woman conqueror of the air has been deeply interested in aviation for a long time and at the time she made her successful flight across the Atlantic Ocean she was vice president of the Boston Aeronautical Association.

When asked what she considered Miss Earhart's outstanding characteristics Miss Coleman replied:

"Quietness, lack of egotism, perseverance, remarkable courage and a charming personality".

Miss Coleman further stated that Miss Earhart told her last spring she would attempt to fly alone on some great flight and that she feels there is a big future for the wonderful young woman. As soon as Miss Earhart arrives in the United States Miss Coleman will write her a personal letter of congratulations upon her remarkable feat and she hopes to see the heroine in Boston again this fall. Miss Coleman will return to Simmons College for her senior year at the beginning of the fall term where she is specializing in household economics and clothing.

"Would it not be just bully now that both Lindbergh and Miss Earhart have crossed the great watery divide by air to see them meet and eventually take a life trip together?" Miss Coleman was asked.

"Well, that would be real romantic" she replied, "but I will say that Miss Earhart has the true Lindbergh attitude and she will make a great name for herself. She owns her own airplane in Boston and I feel from the way she talked to me that one of these days she will take the controls of some stoutly built airplane and pilot herself to new honors and further glory".

June 22, 1928 newspaper interview with Pauline Coleman, who worked with Amelia at Denison House.

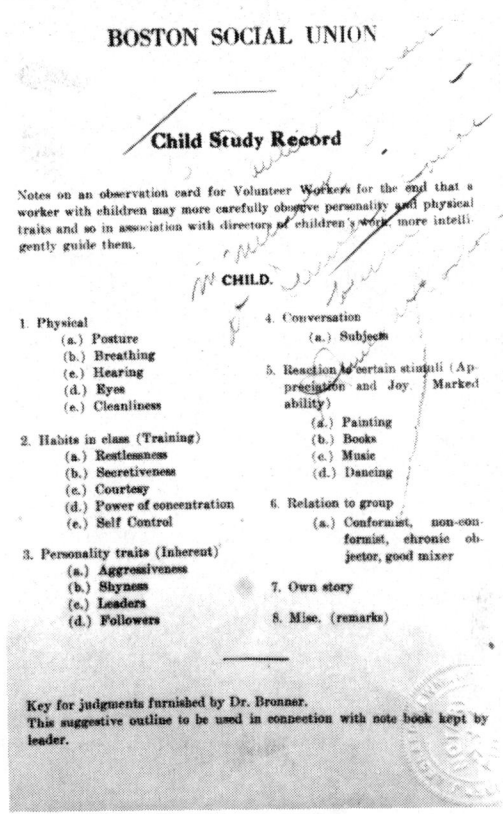

Denison House evaluation page which Amelia and Pauline used.

Mrs. Pauline Coleman Newman in 1986.

Sometimes Amelia took a few yards of bright calico to curtain a bleak window; sometimes, a bright-colored ball to amuse a fretful toddler; sometimes, a single spray of ivy for a beauty-starved Chinese Old One. But with all she left a spark of her own radiant personality. It was the same in dramatic groups and classes she taught. Amelia encouraged participation among the shy and gently suppressed the overly aggressive.

She maintained that the youngsters needed to be pushed into finding and keeping a job. Some economists were predicting a business depression; jobs would be hard to get for the unskilled.

She cast a play while at Denison House called *A House of the Heart*, in which her juniors acted. Miss Perkins soon appointed Amelia to be a full-time resident worker, and she moved from our West Medford home to an apartment on the top floor of Denison House.

Amelia's decision to live at Denison House did not please Sam Chapman. He thought that the fifty Syrian, Irish, and Chinese children took too much of her time and affection and were a poor substitute for the children he would have liked Amelia to bear for him after their hoped-for marriage. However, as her philosophy of social work crystallized, so did her ideas of marriage and family responsibility. The more Sam urged her to marry, the more she shied away from him. Sam mistakenly thought that Amelia objected to his irregular hours as an engineer for the Boston Edison Company. He told her that he would change professions, employers, or whatever she wanted.

Instead of being impressed by his eagerness to please her, Amelia was annoyed. She did not want to tell Sam what he should do. Amelia knew what she wanted and expected to achieve, married or single.

The move into Denison House was her Declaration of Independence. Soon afterward her tenuous engagement with Sam was broken, not the result of her flying, as some have implied. Their relationship was entirely amicable. Sometimes Amelia was affectionate toward him. Sam hoped she would tire of working at Denison House and settle down with him as his wife in his pleasant home in quaint old Marblehead, which they both loved.

It took courage to refuse Sam's marriage offer. She really loved him, and they shared many interests. They seemed ideally suited to one another. However, her reluctance to continue the engagement stemmed from Sam's outspoken disapproval of working wives. His stern Yankee upbringing had impressed upon him the importance of the man's role as breadwinner and protector of his wife; since he was well able to support a wife and family, he expected to do it. Amelia's desire to continue at Denison House seemed unreasonable to Sam, and the thought of living the life of a domestic robot was equally impossible for Amelia.

During this period of emotional conflict, Amelia wrote a poem which she called *Courage*. She wrote it on one of the last Sunday afternoons she spent at our home in West Medford before moving to Denison House. Some have said that the trans-Atlantic flight was its inspiration, but I know it was written several months before Amelia thought of flying the Atlantic.

Courage

Courage is the price which life exacts for granting peace.
The soul that knows it not, knows no release
From little things;

Knows not the livid loneliness of fear
Nor mountain heights, where bitter joy can hear
The sound of wings.

How can life grant us boon of living, compensate
For dull gray ugliness and pregnant hate
Unless we dare

The soul's dominion? Each time we make a choice we pay
With courage to behold resistless day
And count it fair.

Amelia asked my opinion of the rather unusual rhyme scheme and I remember making one or two suggestions. After she had copied it, she wanted to show it to Miss Perkins because at a staff meeting the week before, they had discussed the cowardice of refusing to make decisions.

Amelia was perceptive to beauty as well as to "drab, gray ugliness," and she enjoyed searching for the precise words to convey her impressions. Her love of flying resulted not only from the sensation of power and speed, but even more from enjoyment of the beauty of land and sea seen from above, the tinted clouds, and the star-strewn skies.

It is our loss that so much of Amelia's writing is purely factual prose. I know that she longed for a time when she could write as the spirit moved without regard for deadlines or publishers' limitations.

Her artistic nature was frequently at odds with her practicality, sometimes with embarrassing results. Soon after Amelia became a part-time worker at Denison House, I gave her forty dollars to pay the coal bill. She brought me the receipt for twenty dollars and then triumphantly unwrapped a bird delicately carved from horn which she bought at a Chinese curio shop. She said that she simply could not resist the appeal of its poised-for-flight look.

"So much lovelier than hunks of coal, Pidge, you must admit," she chuckled. "Let me have my hyacinth just this once." This reference was to one of Amelia's favorite quatrains by Moslin Eddiv Saudi:

> If thou hast two coats,
>   Sell one, and with the dole
>   Buy hyacinths
>   To feed thy soul.

Fortunately our credit was good with the coal company, so they were willing to wait for my next pay check to receive the balance of their bill.

Dr. Louise DeSchweinitz and Dr. Daniel Darrow on their wedding day, June 16, 1923.

Albert Morrissey, Chief Quartermaster, U.S.N., World War I.

Plaque in front of the Earhart home in Medford, Massachusetts, where Amelia wrote, "Courage."

During Amelia's first few months at Denison House, we renewed our friendship with Louise deSchweinitz, Amelia's former classmate at Columbia University. Louise had graduated from Johns Hopkins Medical School and was interning at a Boston hospital. In Amelia's yellow Kissel Kar the six of us—Louise and her fiancé, Dr. Daniel Darrow, Amelia and Sam, and a young World War I Navy veteran, Albert Morrissey, and I, often went to Marblehead to swim or clam, followed by a cook-out with a driftwood fire on the gigantic boulders of Marblehead Neck.

Amelia, always interested in new experiences, one day persuaded Louise to pass her off as a visiting intern, so that she could watch the birth of a child. Another time she accompanied Louise through the wards and assisted her in lancing a carbuncle on a patient's neck.

When a little Syrian boy from Denison House was blinded by a kerosene heater explosion, Amelia drove him to the Perkins Institute for the Blind on the outskirts of Boston three times a week. She became fascinated by the techniques used by the teachers, many of whom were blind themselves. She was soon giving several hours a week of her scant free time as a volunteer reader and as assistant to the director of dramatics. She told me that it took so little to make those people forget their handicaps and troubles for a half hour. She could not teach them Braille, but she could make them laugh, and she knew that too was important. Soon, however, she reluctantly resigned from the volunteer aid group at Perkins. She simply could not continue to donate her time.

Amelia joined the American Aeronautical Society when she first came to Boston. She flew a little at Dennison Airport, near what is now Squantum Air Base, during the spring and summer of 1926. Bert Kinner, the designer and manufacturer of the Kinner Canary biplane which she flew in California, had come east in the hopes of establishing a sales agency. He mentioned to some of the pilots during a demonstration of his plane that Amelia had set an altitude record in one like it in California and that she was one of the few women who held a license with the Fédération Aéronautique Internationale. She had never bothered to mention this to anyone in Boston.

She was magnetically drawn to flying again, now that she had the income and the opportunity. She demonstrated the Kinner plane to prospective customers in return for the use of it. On clear Sundays, Amelia picked me up in her car and we drove out to the busy airfield. She changed into her jodhpurs and put on her wrinkled leather jacket and helmet. Fog, muddy runways, and her work cut down her flying hours, but she flew when she could. Amelia became known to most of the free-lance pilots around Boston as a woman who could not only fly well, but who also knew about engine performance, tensile strengths, and something about instrument flying. The mechanics at the field soon learned that she was not averse to getting her hands greasy. She watched, asked questions, and helped service her plane.

One Sunday I went into the hangar where she was watching one of the mechanics tune up her engine; her forehead was wrinkled in concentration as she leaned over the sputtering engine. In a few minutes the mechanic made the right adjustment, and the sputter turned into a steady roar. Amelia clasped both hands over her head, expressing her gratitude and admiration to the grinning, grease-smeared genius. She came over to me and above the deafening sound, she shouted, "Beautiful symphony, what?"

Pilots and mechanics liked and respected Amelia. She admitted to her lack of experience and was eager to learn from anyone. She assumed neither the helpless female role, nor an unwomanly one, in spite of her shapeless coveralls and tousled hair.

Paul Mantz, who became her technical adviser and test pilot for her later flights, once said, ". . . I never knew any man who would try to pull anything with Amelia. If she came into the hangar when someone happened to be telling an off-color story, that person would get a kicked shin or a stepped-on toe . . . ."

Events that catapulted Amelia from an insignificant Sunday amateur to international pilot occurred early in the spring of 1928. It was a year since Colonel Charles Lindbergh had blazed a trail when he soloed across the Atlantic.

The Honorable Mrs. Frederick Guest, for-

November 27, 1927

My dear Mr. Kinner,

It has been a long time since your last letter. I have meant to answer it before but somehow just didn't.

I haven't been out at the field very much of late, as my regular job takes most of my time. However, I get some news, despite my absense.

Since the race at Worcester, there has been much interest in the little ship. Mr. Bourden is crazy about the flying qualities and would use it all the time if he were confident of the motor. Please tell me how the government tests are getting along---the ones that Mrs. Kinner said were to be run at 'Frisco. Even tho the ship itself were O. K., it still couldn't be used for passenger work here on account of the motors not having had a test run.

Now here is a serious question. What is to prevent anyone's taking the dimensions of the Airster and constructing a ship from them and marketing that ship? Such a thing happened to my knowledge, and I wondered whether you are safe in letting your product out here in the East, unless you have a very strong organization to protect it. So many people have tried the little ship and found it so much to their liking, that I am worried lest someone comes along and run it right thru to completion, with no delays in tests delivery etc., and make a killing. I think the time is ripe for that type of plane right now.

The Siemens motor, as written up in a recent Aviation, certainly is rated well. Which Ryan is using Kinners---Ryan himself or Mahoney?

I had a brain storm not long ago, and that of writing to you and asking whether I couldn't come out to the factory and spend next summer in learning the Kinner motor. It seems such a shame that noone here really knows it. If many are to be sold in the East, I think some one should. As things are now, I don't know whether I could get away, however.

Dennison Airport is planning an expansion in the spring which I hope will come to pass. Let me know how you are getting along for I am always interested.

Sincerely yours,

Amelia M Earhart

A business letter Amelia wrote to Mr. Kinner in 1927.

Amelia in 1928.

merly Amy Phipps of Pittsburgh but now of London, purchased a tri-motored Fokker monoplane in which she planned to fly from America to England. Mrs. Guest, a pioneer flier, hoped to further the cause of Anglo-American relations by linking the two continents by flight. Her family vigorously opposed the project, so she reluctantly abandoned the idea of flying the plane herself. She still wished, however, to have a woman fly as an ambassador of good will. So she began her search for a capable, charming, and willing woman pilot in the spring of 1928.

George Palmer Putnam, of G. P. Putnam's Sons Publishing Company, had persuaded Lindbergh to write the story of his flight, *We*. George Putnam, known almost universally as GP, was married to a New York socialite and was living in a Victorian mansion built by his father in Rye, New York. Mrs. Guest requested his aid in finding a woman. GP, thirty-nine years old, tall and distinguished-looking, probably was well acquainted with more celebrities in different fields of endeavor than any other non-political person in New York. GP's first thought was Ruth Nichols, a young flier who lived near him in Rye, but her health at this time prevented her from considering the offer.

GP telephoned Captain Hilton Railey in Boston and suggested he ask Commander Byrd if he knew any possible women fliers. Commander Byrd remembered hearing of a young social worker who possessed a pilot's license, but he could not recall her name. It did not take much detective work to find Amelia.

Captain Railey telephoned Amelia at Denison House. She was rehearsing her dramatic group and disliked interruptions, so her reply was at first was harsh and hasty. Captain Railey first verified that Amelia possessed a pilot's license. He then came directly to the point: "Miss Earhart, would you be willing to do something important for the cause of aviation—such as flying a plane across the Atlantic?"

Amelia's decision was immediate. "Yes," she said, simply. "How could I refuse such a shining adventure?"

Under a promise of secrecy as Captain Railey advised, she told Miss Perkins about the amazing telephone call. Miss Perkins gave her a two-week leave of absence from Denison House. Within a few days after the preliminary phone call, Amelia went to New York to meet the three men who were acting for Mrs. Guest: GP, attorney David T. Layman, and John S. Phipps.

Amelia reported to Miss Perkins on her return. The men were looking for more than a woman with a pilot's license. She thought that they had talked for more than an hour about her education, her work and hobbies, rather than about her flying ability. She had the feeling that they liked her, but, as they did not minimize the hazards of the trip, "maybe that isn't good, because they might not want to put me in a situation where I might be dropped in the cold Atlantic's Davy Jones' locker." Amelia said that they made her talk to see whether she dropped her "g's" or used "ain't," which might have disqualified her.

GP called for a taxi and took her back to Grand Central after the session. He was a fascinating man to Amelia; he had been to the Arctic, and his young son had written a book for other boys about his adventures in Greenland. Amelia wished the ride had been longer because he was so interesting. Once they arrived at the station, Amelia said GP hurried her aboard the Boston train. He didn't even offer to pay her fare home.

Amelia was not kept in suspense long. Two days after her interview, Amelia received a cordial note from Mrs. Guest and a formal agreement from her lawyer, setting forth the aims of the flight. All expenses involving the plane and personnel were paid by Mrs. Guest. Amelia was named captain. Her decisions, once airborne, were to be final. She served without pay and made no income from royalties or advertising contracts, which were to be turned back toward the flight's expenses. The flight was not a commercial venture but rather a voluntary venture.

The wheels began quietly and efficiently to turn behind a curtain of secrecy. Captain Railey was designated public relations officer, and Commander Byrd was the technical consultant.

Commander Byrd selected Wilmer L. Stultz as pilot and Louis Gower as the alternate. Louis

"Slim" Gordon was Bill Stultz's choice of a mechanic. The plane, formerly the property of Commander Byrd, was renamed *Friendship* and equipped with pontoons. Two large gasoline drums were also installed in the tiny cabin just behind the pilot's seat. The work was done at an out-of-the-way East Boston hangar. If any newspaper men or inquisitive pilots appeared, both Bill and Slim would identify the plane as one of several that Commander Byrd was readying for his second voyage to Antarctica. By the middle of April, Bill and Slim had flown the *Friendship* in several shakedown flights.

Since Amelia was known to many fliers around Boston, Captain Railey advised her to stay away from the Fokker. She was scrupulous about following the instructions and neither went aboard nor saw the plane until their take off. She spent much of her spare time with Commander Byrd, Captain Railey, GP, and Bill Stultz, studying flight plans, maps, and weather charts. They held most of the sessions at the Byrds' Brimmer Street home.

Amelia was always grateful to Marie Byrd for her composure and charm, especially as nerves began to fray while waiting for the right take off conditions. She once asked Mrs. Byrd how she literally kept GP and Bill from stomping out of the house. Mrs. Byrd just smiled and told Amelia that she had had much practice.

When Amelia had time, she went to Dennison Airport to take relaxing flights over the Lynn salt marshes and the Nahant and Swampscott beaches. She discussed with Mr. William Chapman of Dennisport on Cape Cod, no relation to Sam Chapman, the value of pontoons for long flights over water. Mr. Chapman, a pioneer flier, designer, and builder, had argued against their use. He had participated in the early air meets sponsored by the *Boston Globe* in 1910, 1911, and 1912 when the great feat of the year was to fly from Squantum around Boston Light.

Mr. Chapman wanted to see Amelia beat out the Diamond Queen, Mabel Boll, a skilled horsewoman. Miss Boll enjoyed being in the news and wanted to be the first woman to fly the Atlantic. The pilot she wanted was a man whom she had known several years before, Bill Stultz. Bill found himself in a difficult position. He stopped by Commander Byrd's home and told him about his dilemma. Commander Byrd advised Bill to stay with Amelia.

The entire group hoped to take off soon because the waiting was wearing them down. Each time the weather report came in and was not good enough to depart, Amelia uttered a heartfelt "Damn" and returned to Denison House.

A week passed, and still the weather was uncooperative. Dr. James H. Kimball of the U.S. Weather Bureau in New York, known affectionately as Doc, called for weather reports from Greenwich and from ships in mid-Atlantic to Halifax. When Boston's weather was favorable, dangerous fog shrouded the coast of Newfoundland; when the fog cleared, Boston's weather deteriorated.

Amelia faced the possibility of not returning and took steps to ease it for those she might leave behind. She rented a safety deposit box in our bank in West Medford and confided to Sam that she had placed her will in it. Amelia listed her debts, about a thousand dollars, and her assets: one United States Treasury bond, the Kissel Kar, and some stock certificates in Kinner Airplane & Motor Corporation and the Dennison Airport. After payment of the debts, mostly for hospital and dental expenses, Mother was to have the balance, if any. She concluded, "My regret is that I leave just now. In a few years I feel I could have laid by something substantial, for many new things were opening for me . . . . Selah!"

Amelia left letters for Mother and Dad in the box which were to be delivered only in case of her "popping off." These were entrusted to GP and were kept secret by him until her death several years later. The first read:

Dear Dad:
  Hooray for the last grand adventure! I wish I had won, but it was worth while anyway. You know that.
  I have no faith that we'll meet anywhere again, but I wish we might.
  Anyway, good-by and good luck to you.
    Affectionately, yr dotor,
    Meel

To Mother she wrote,

> Our family tends to be too secure. My life has really been very happy and I didn't mind contemplating its end in the midst of it.

Late weather reports on June 3 were favorable. Amelia again set the alarm for three-thirty in the morning. Early on June 4 Amelia and the others stopped at an all-night lunch counter and filled their thermos bottles with coffee and cocoa and bought sandwiches.

Amelia wore her brown broadcloth breeks, a white silk blouse and a red necktie. She had on her high laced boots and carried a borrowed, heavy fur-lined flying suit which covered her from head to toe, including her feet. This suit was borrowed from Major Charles H. Woolley of Boston, who had no idea when he lent it what it would be used for.

When they reached T Wharf, Amelia, Bill, Lou Gower, and Slim climbed aboard the tugboat *Sadie Rose* and chugged through the mist to the anchored orange Fokker. Slim balanced on the pontoons and swung the props. Bill soon had the engines running while Slim, after casting off from their mooring, climbed into the cockpit beside Bill. Amelia leaned across the two oil drums behind them. Lou crouched at the extreme end of the cabin to help bring the nose of the plane up by his added weight there.

Muriel Earhart at her desk at the Lincoln Junior High School in Medford, Massachusetts, on June 14, 1928.

Bill could not raise the ship from the waters of Boston Harbor. A five-gallon tank of gasoline was jettisoned, to no avail. Amelia reflected on Mr. Chapman's argument against using pontoons. She later told me that she would never again fly the Atlantic with pontoons although she understood the safety factor represented.

Lou's one hundred sixty-eight pounds might make the difference, so Bill taxied back to the float where GP and Captain Railey were waiting, and Lou jumped out. The next time across the harbor the *Friendship* responded. The plane's pontoons slanted upward and the plane lifted off. They were airborne and headed for Newfoundland.

The shining adventure had begun.

Chapter Eleven

20 Hours and 40 Minutes

IN the plane, next to Amelia, lay a two-inch thick book given to her in Boston by Commander Byrd just before the *Friendship* flight began. The book was inscribed by Byrd on June 16, 1928. Amelia had instructions to give this book to Mrs. Frederick Guest upon her arrival in Ireland.

Later that year, Amelia wrote about this flight in her book, *20 HRS. 40 MIN., Our Flight In The Friendship*:

> The book—perhaps the only one to have crossed the Atlantic by air route—is *Skyward*, written by Commander Richard Evelyn Byrd . . . This copy of his book which I delivered bears the following inscription: "I am sending you this copy of my first book by the first girl to cross the Atlantic Ocean by air—the very brave Miss Earhart. But for circumstances I well know that it would have been you who would have crossed first. I send you my heartiest congratulations and good wishes. I admire your determination and courage."

Even the weight of the book was a critical consideration. Amelia herself took only her toothbrush, a small amount of food, a flying suit, the book, and a small packet of messages from those involved in the flight, addressed to friends on the other side.

Scarcely had the *Friendship* become airborne when headlines screamed from the afternoon editions of the two Boston newspapers: *BOSTON SOCIAL WORKER TO FLY ATLANTIC* and *GIRL PILOT DARES THE ATLANTIC*. Mother and I learned of Amelia's flight from the papers. The secret was well kept. Amelia's former fiancé, Sam, knew of the plans from the beginning and was instructed to break the news to us. However, some reporters picked up on the story, and the papers were on the streets before he got out to our Medford home.

My fiancé, Albert Morrissey, came to help Mother and me deal with that evening's invasion of reporters and officials.

All the newspapers wanted pictures—not only the posed ones of Mother and me reading whatever paper a particular photographer represented, but also baby pictures, school pictures, any pictures of Amelia. With most of our household goods in storage since we had moved to a small apartment near my school, the Lincoln Junior High School in South Medford, I promised to go on the following day to the storage warehouse to look for some early photographs of Amelia which I knew were there.

The next day a neighbor took me, and three cars of reporters followed. I spent nearly two hours rummaging through trunks and drawers but eventually left the vault with a dozen pictures, including Amelia's picture as a senior at Ogontz in her cap and gown, one of her in her Canadian nurse's uniform, and several pictures taken in Atchison.

All the reporters had gone except one young man from the *Boston Post*. He happily set up his camera in the warehouse manager's office and photographed all the pictures without delay. The *Post* reporter asked me to keep the pictures under cover until the first edition of his paper came out. Being naive in the ways of newspapermen, I readily agreed. In the morning the *Post* carried an entire page of pictures and was of course the only paper to have them. Soon after eight o'clock the men from the other papers and the news services arrived at our apartment. I was made to feel as if I had not only thrown these eager young men to the lions but had somehow seriously hampered Amelia's career. As the last camera was packed, one of them said to me reassuringly in a stage whisper, "You don't need to feel too sorry for us, Muriel. We've all scooped each other sometime or other, and we'll get ahead of that fellow at the *Post*, don't worry! It's the fortune of war."

Mother and I were totally unprepared to deal with reporters. Mother's attitude was expressed succinctly, "In my day, nice people had their names in the paper only when they were born, married, and died."

Later she relented, even giving interviews herself, but in this first glare of publicity, I had to mitigate many of Mother's blunt refusals to see not only reporters, but even our local officials. I recall a visit from the mayor of Medford who arrived in formal attire, preceded by the city messenger bearing the traditional staff of office. We had no intimation of his intention to call until he appeared at half-past eight o'clock one evening. Mother failed to grasp the significance of His Honor's visit, and, thinking that he was campaigning for his next term as mayor and had come to ask for our vote, met him at the top of the stairs and said firmly, "Mayor Larkin, you are just wasting your time here. I intend to vote again for Mr. Coolidge, so you really will gain no votes from us. Thank you for coming. Good night."

I reached Mother's side just in time to prevent her from closing the door and leaving the city dignitary on the front steps. Mother, deaf without her hearing aid, had not understood that the messenger was announcing the visit of the mayor to honor Amelia, not to ask for votes. I explained to Mother, apologized to the mayor, and invited him into the living room where he delivered himself of a prepared speech in which the phrase, "Medford's pride in her famous flying daughter" was repeated several times.

Mother's frosty greeting that evening did not rankle Mayor Larkin. He threw himself wholeheartedly into the home-town welcome celebration given Amelia upon her return to Medford in July.

While the calm tenor of our lives here was being temporarily disrupted, Amelia's life was undergoing a major metamorphosis, attended by anguish unsuspected by us.

On June 5, the *Friendship* landed at Halifax, Newfoundland, in thick fog. Amelia sent a telegram to Mother: "Know you will understand why I could not tell plans of flight. Don't worry. No matter what happens it will have been worth the trying. Love, A." Mother had me send a reply to Amelia: "We are not worrying. Wish I were with you. Good luck and cheerio. Love, Mother."

The fliers expected to take off the next day and rented rooms from a local family for one night only. It was soon evident, however, that the weather was going to be bad for several days. Dense fog rolled in and covered the coast; the fog was later blown away by cold north winds. Day after day the plane tossed hopelessly, storm bound in the tiny harbor.

The three fliers felt the long stop-over an anticlimax. Several newspapers were sent from Boston, and Amelia was annoyed to read such statements as, "Amelia hopes to get enough money from making this flight to pay off the mortgage on the family home." She was also angered by the quote from the telegram she sent to Mother in all the news stories. She wrote me a blistering letter about it. I realized that she was under a strain although I did not know the full extent of her problems for several years.

Many of the more kindly Boston papers lost interest during the many delays, and the newspapers that had been critical at the outset became vitriolic in their abuse of the *Friendship* crew, especially Amelia. It was suggested that the sponsors of the flight were disappointed at Amelia's seeming reluctance to

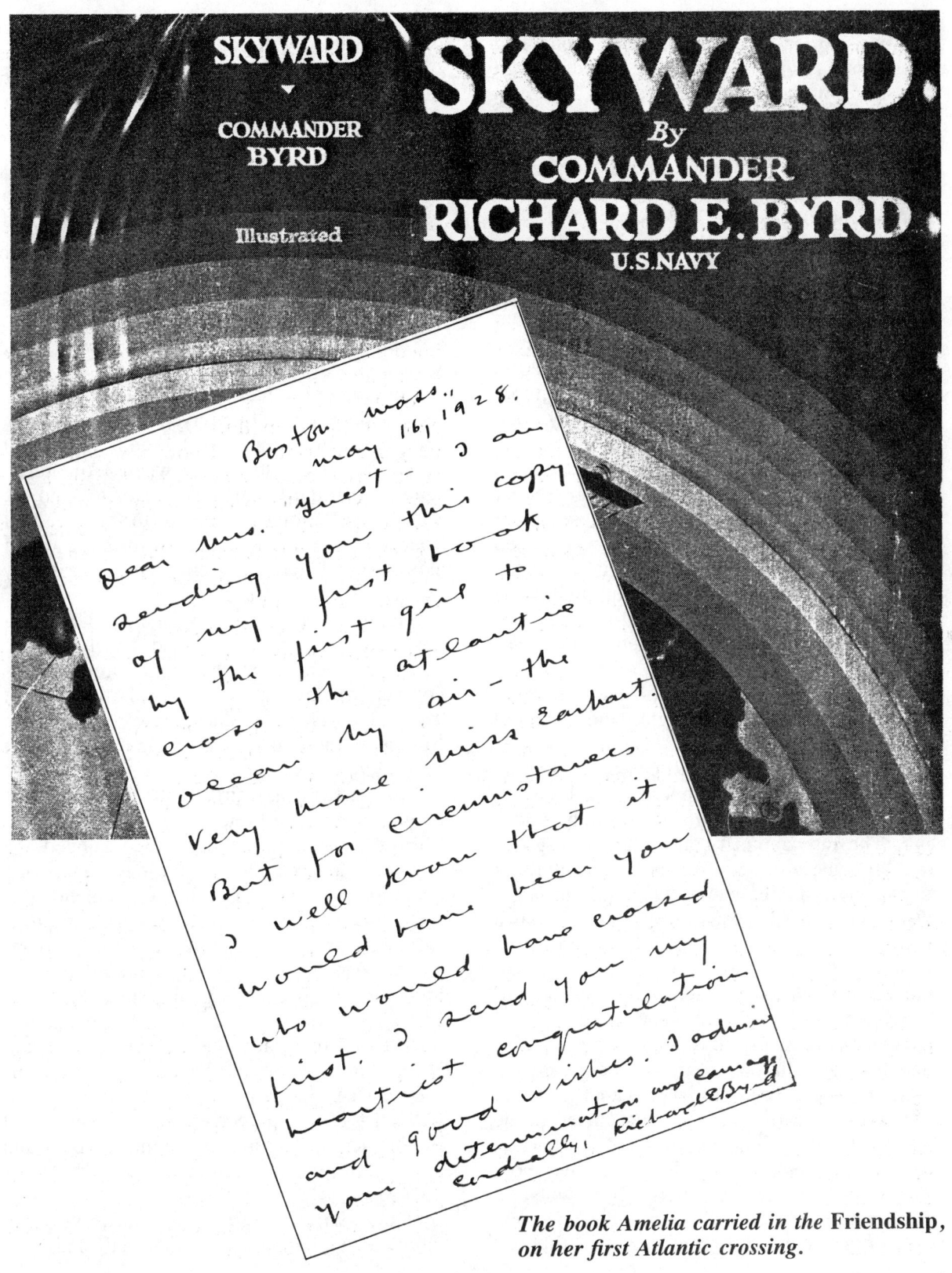

The book Amelia carried in the Friendship, on her first Atlantic crossing.

take to the air again. GP instantly denied it in a strongly-worded letter, but the unjustified criticism was hard to bear. GP wired Amelia reassuringly, ending with the advice: "Suggest you turn in and have your laundering done."

Amelia wired back characteristically, "Thanks fatherly telegram. No washing necessary. Socks underwear worn out. Shirt lost to Slim at rummy. Cheerio, AE"

The wait was almost as it was in Boston, except that the tension, uncertainty, and frustration multiplied. A favorable report, relayed from Dr. Kimball on June 12, sent the fliers out to the plane with high hopes. Bill tried every angle across the bay to get the distance necessary to lift the plane from the water, but without success. On two succeeding days they tried again in vain to take off.

Weight was still a problem for the *Friendship*. It seemed as if all non-essential equipment had been discarded in Boston, but now even a camera and blankets were taken ashore by the trio. Next, Amelia unloaded nearly three hundred pounds of fuel. She realized, as the men did, that this was dangerously lowering the safety factor, but it was necessary.

Annoyance at the gibes of the reporters, frustration from delayed flight, and boredom wore Amelia's morale down. The most serious problem, however, was Bill Stultz's behavior. High-strung and temperamental, Bill sought relief from his own personal Gehenna by drinking. The momentum of adventure was gone, and he could not face the thought of returning to ridicule and failure. Amelia and Slim tried to take him on fishing trips or on hikes. It was a losing battle. Several times Bill agreed to accompany them on such expeditions, only to make an excuse to turn back after about an hour or to produce a bottle from his pocket.

It was the evening on the fourteenth day out, and both Amelia and Slim were close to the breaking point. They sat down to another round of rummy, and Bill stomped and cursed in the room overhead. Amelia considered asking Lou to come to replace Bill. She and Slim both knew that Bill was the superior pilot when he was himself. At eleven o'clock the telegraph operator came by with a message. He held out a torn page from his notebook and told her that he did not wait to write out the formal message.

She thanked him and held the paper under the light. It said that Doc Kimball reported favorable weather off the Grand Banks and out into the mid-Atlantic. It probably would hold for forty-eight hours.

She told Slim, "This is it!" They decided to get some sleep and set the alarm, so they would be out of the bay before the ebb tide.

When Amelia pounded on the men's door the morning of June 17, the sun was shining for the first time since the *Friendship* had anchored in the harbor. Slim and Amelia awakened Bill, who was snoring soundly.

Cold water on the outside and hot black coffee inside eventually revived him. Steadying him between them, Amelia and Slim went down the steep path to the wharf. Amelia arranged with the telegraph operator to send the code word "Violet" to GP in Boston, one-half hour after seeing the plane lift from the water. Word spread that the fliers were going to try again.

Amelia later wrote, "Whatever the harshness and inhospitality of the Newfoundland coast and weather might be, it surely has no counterpart in the hearts of the people of Trepassey. Their kindness toward the three foreigners marooned on their shores will never be forgotten."

It was nearly six-thirty in the morning when they climbed aboard the plane and cast off, and Slim swung the propellers. Bill gunned the engines. He taxied across the bay and swung the ship into the wind at the last moment.

To lift the plane from the water, a speed of from fifty to fifty-five miles per hour was required. Amelia, leaning over the oil drums behind the pilot's seat, saw the speed indicator creep up to forty-five and then fall back. Bill swerved to avoid heading into the open ocean. He turned and looked questioningly over his shoulder at Amelia.

With a nod of agreement from Amelia, Bill headed across the bay, swung the plane around at the farthest point again, and roared for the open sea. The water was thrown out like spreading wings on each side; the whole plane vibrated violently. The airspeed indicator trembled at fifty, and the *Friendship* was again airborne. Bill throttled the engine to cruising speed and set the course east by south at approximately 2,500 feet of altitude.

Amelia turned to the improvised chart table to begin writing the log. She had just made the entry, "Trepassey Harbor, June 17. Airborne at 11:40 a.m.," when she caught sight of a whiskey bottle, three-fourths full, tucked between the ribs of the fuselage and the small bag of Slim's essential tools. She was in a quandary. Her first impulse was to open the hatch a crack and drop the bottle into the Atlantic, just as she had tried to dispose of Dad's whiskey some years before. She decided to leave the liquor where she found it and hoped Bill would not come looking for it.

About three hundred miles offshore they encountered a fog bank. Bill, trying to escape it by climbing to a higher altitude, ran into a freak snowstorm. Fog was less to be feared than ice on the wings. Without warning, Bill nosed down and sent Amelia sliding against the oil drums behind the pilot's seat. He leveled off at a lower altitude, but the driving rain and headwinds still slowed them for more than a hundred miles. Finally they outran the squall and emerged into a belt of clear sunlight over a sparkling ocean. Bill turned the controls over to Slim, eased down in his seat, and in two minutes was asleep. Amelia knelt by the chart table and noted the change of pilots in her log. Two hours later at about seven o'clock, she wrote: "Seven hours out of Trepassey. The greatest sight is the sun splashing into oblivion, showing pink through apertures of the distant fog. I wish the sun would stay longer. We shall soon be gray-sheathed."

An hour later Bill took the controls, and Slim stretched out on the cabin floor. Amelia wrote: "View too vast, too lovely for words. Light of our exhausts is beginning to show as pink as the last glow in the sky. I am kneeling here by the chart table, gulping in beauty. Radio contact *Rexmore*, Britisher bound for New York."

At ten o'clock, she scribbled: "Darkness complete. Bill sits alone, every muscle and nerve alert. Slim sleeps. There are many hours to go."

It was cold in the bare cabin, and she gratefully pulled on the fur-lined suit loaned to her by Major Woolley. It seemed awkward taking it in the warm June weather, but she had yielded to Commander Byrd's advice.

The **Friendship** *at Burry Port, Wales.*

The *Friendship* had been in the air more than sixteen hours now, and there was an estimated four or five hours of fuel left. They should be near some part of the British Isles, but without radio contact, they had to depend solely on Bill's navigational skill. All three searched the endless gray waters when Bill came through the clouds.

Again and again they were certain they saw land, only to have it disappear—a tantalizing mirage. At about half-past six, they sighted a ship, later identified as the *S.S. America*. Hoping to get a bearing, Amelia printed a message and weighted it with two oranges. As Bill circled over the deck, Amelia dropped it, but she missed the target. They did not dare use their fuel to circle again. They were now using their emergency tank and had less than an hour's supply left.

Rain and fog added to their plight. Suddenly a break in the fog bank revealed a cluster of factory chimneys less than a mile away. The three, sighting it simultaneously, shouted, "Land!" Although Amelia knew they were not at Southampton, any port spelled success to a weary crew. Bill dropped down onto the smooth water of a small bay, and Amelia recorded the fact: "20 hrs. 40 mins. out of Trepassey *Friendship* down safely in harbor of _____." The blank was not to be filled in for nearly an hour while the fliers and plane bobbed in a torrential downpour.

The landing at Burry Port, Wales, partook of a comedy scene. Amelia waved and called to longshoremen working on the wharf. The men waved back routinely and continued their work. Eventually a small boat approached. Bill went ashore on the boat and telephoned their friends at Southampton. Slim's back was towards Amelia's as she quietly picked up the whiskey bottle which had worried her so much and dropped it into the water.

Word of the *Friendship's* landing was flashed to Captain Railey, who had been waiting in Southampton for two weeks. He had crossed the ocean by fast steamship as soon as Amelia had taken off from Boston. When he received the coded cable from GP announcing the *Friendship's* successful take off, he alerted the coastal towns of England, Scotland, and Ireland.

Late in the afternoon, Amelia saw a large launch carrying Captain Railey and several easily recognizable town dignitaries, including a *New York Times* photographer. When they reached the Burry Port wharf, they were surrounded by nearly two hundred people, many of whom waved autograph books. Some were so excited that they tried to pull at the fliers' clothes. The crew was escorted a few hundred feet to the Frickers Metal Company office to get some rest and to escape from the crowds.

Twice the crowd asked to see them. Amelia waved but tried to make them realize that all the credit belonged to the men and that she was only a passenger. But of course many people considered that being the first woman to have made the Atlantic flight successfully was an impressive achievement. Amelia longed for a bath and sleep but remained cheerful through the rigors of becoming an instant public figure. With what grace she could muster she agreed to "meet just a few of the citizens and have pictures taken." Finally, a sympathetic woman, the wife of the factory foreman, intervened and took them away from the crowds.

Following a light supper, Amelia sent two identical cables, one to Mother and the other to Miss Perkins at Denison House, saying simply, "Love, Amelia."

After five or six hours of rest, Amelia was ready to start out for Southampton. After the *Friendship* was refueled, the three fliers, Captain Railey, and Mr. Raymond from the *Times* went aboard. The plane lifted easily, circled once over Burry Port in salute, and then began the last leg of the journey that had started in Boston nearly three weeks earlier. Within an hour the plane landed in the harbor at Southampton amid the raucous toots of the tug boat whistles and the deep-throated blasts from the fog horns on several steamers.

A launch put out from the pier to officially greet the *Friendship*. There to greet the crew were Mrs. Guest, her son, Raymond, and Hubert Scott Payne of Imperial Airways. This was the first time Amelia had met Mrs. Guest. On shore they were welcomed by Mrs. Foster Welch, the mayor of Southampton and a cheering, clapping, hat-waving crowd. Autograph

Amelia, left, receiving congratulations from Her Honor, Mayor Welch of Southampton, on arrival.

seekers and hand shakers had to be firmly held back by the mayor's escorting bobbies.

Mrs. Guest invited Amelia to stay at her Park Lane home. Amelia was delighted to accept because in addition to her genuine liking and respect for Mrs. Guest, she felt the need of a woman who could direct her to shops where she could buy some needed feminine clothes and accessories.

Congratulatory messages poured in. Amelia continued to insist that Bill, the pilot-navigator, was the real hero of the flight. Among the messages was one telegram from President and Mrs. Coolidge. Amelia replied in part to the president's cable, "Success was entirely due to great navigational skill of pilot Wilmer Stultz."

At first Amelia had no idea of the furor that her achievement generated, nor did Captain Railey. She was sincere when she said that she expected to return to social service work in Boston. When she shopped with Mrs. Guest, she was amazed to be greeted by Gordon Selfridge, the owner of the Mayfair department stores and even more astounded to have him refuse to allow her to pay for any of her purchases. It was the same everywhere; she was overwhelmed by a shower of gifts. Mrs. Guest gave her a handsome alligator handbag into which she slipped a ten-pound note, saying it was "for incidentals," but Amelia arrived in New York with it still intact.

Amelia was fêted, she believed, beyond her desserts. The days were so crowded with luncheons, teas, and dinners that she was never able to visit any of the hundreds of literary shrines which, as a lover of Shakespeare, Dickens, Scott, and Milton, she would have sought out. Through her meeting with Lady Astor, an American-born Member of Parliament, she had the opportunity to spend several hours at Toynbee Hall, dean of settlement houses, on which Denison House is modeled. Lady Astor was more interested in Amelia's social work than in her aviation exploit. Amelia jotted down several items on the back of an envelope: "Tell Miss P. about Toynbee music groups . . . Toynbee day care for babies . . . Hard to get funds here, too."

Amelia made friends easily. Mrs. Guest was satisfied with the success of her project, *Friendship*. Amelia's behavior did much to counteract many Britons' preconceived notions of American women.

The three days she had planned to stay in London extended to ten. Women's clubs and flying groups vied in honoring her. She felt unhappy about receiving all the attention because she knew that her contribution to the actual flight was practically nil. Again and again she called herself a sack of potatoes, a back-seat driver, a dead-head passenger.

Nearly all the press reactions were favorable. One of the London papers, however, damned her with faint praise by calling her a "pleasant young woman who should be capable of spending her time to better advantage on her own side of the water." She was characterized as a foolhardy female and among the breed of publicity-seeking Americans. At the other end of the scale, she was hailed as a gallant pioneer and a woman of courage and independence.

The women's section of the Air League of the British Empire gave a luncheon for Amelia where she met Lady Mary Heath, Britain's foremost woman pilot. Amelia and Lady Heath, who had recently flown her small Avro from Capetown, South Africa, to London, found that they had had many similar experiences in breaking into aviation. From Croydon Airport in the early morning, Lady Mary and Amelia flew the Avro for a short flight. When Lady Mary mentioned that she planned to sell it, Amelia asked if she would trust her for the price for the plane. Lady Mary agreed and two days later, when Amelia left for home on the *S.S. Roosevelt,* the little plane was lowered to the deck and was carried back to America.

Captain Harry Manning of the *S.S. Roosevelt,* an understanding and considerate person, saw to it that Amelia had privacy and a chance to rest after the strain of her first week as a celebrity. Amelia needed time to ponder her future. She had expected to take a two-week vacation from Denison House, but she now realized it would more likely be a six-month leave of absence. She was under contract to write the story of her flight for G. P. Putnam's Sons publishers, and she had numerous offers to lecture and to advertise products across the United States.

Captain Manning played an important role in Amelia's decision to follow a flying career. He invited her daily to the chart room where he plotted the ship's course. He gave her the practical instruction in navigation which she never had. By the end of the voyage they had developed a warm friendship.

Captain Manning knew of the predicaments which had plagued Amelia during the week in London. Amelia received a radiogram from GP outlining her first week's schedule of welcome-home receptions. She turned to Captain Manning for advice. He promised his aid, directing one of his stewards to make sure Bill Stultz made it off the ship, physically and mentally intact.

It was not only the feeling that she was sailing under false colors in being lionized as a trans-Atlantic flier that made Amelia declare, "The next time I fly anywhere, I shall do it alone!"

First Woman Flies Atlantic; Sails Blindly Through Fog Blanket to Coast of Wales

FUEL BARELY LASTS TO LAND

Only 25 Gallons Were Left in Tanks—Pilots of Earhart Plane Flew by Compass

"HAPPY AS CHILD" OVER HER SUCCESS

Warm Welcome by Welsh —Shuns Publicity, but Will Meet the King

By Arthur E. Mann
Staff Correspondent of The World

BURRY PORT, Wales, June 18.—Flying almost entirely without a glimpse of sea or land for over twenty hours, Wilmer Stultz to-day brought the monoplane Friendship out of an overcast, rainy sky to a landing in the Burry Estuary. He had brought the first seaplane and the first woman to cross the Atlantic by air.

With Lou Gordon, the mechanic who spelled him for a few minutes on several occasions, and Miss Amelia Earhart, he was greeted by a demonstration so ardent that the young

Gas Down to 25 Gallons

Through fog, wet and clouds the Friendship had flown 2,000 miles from Trepassey Bay, N. F., and landed only when a rapidly diminishing gasoline supply showed that it would be impossible to reach her destination, Southampton. She had covered the distance in twenty hours forty-nine minutes, landing here at 12.40 (7.40 New York time.)

Twenty-five gallons of gasoline remained in the tanks, but something had gone wrong with the feeding system and the flyers thought they were completely out when they circled over this little town looking for a quiet stretch of water in which to land.

They had no idea where they were ...t it must be somewhere in

BROOKLINE MAN WAITS IN LONDON

Captain Hilton Howell Railey of 16 Gardner road, Brookline, president of the Fiscal Service Corporation of Boston, a corporation engaged in financing and publicity work, is in London awaiting the arrival of the Fokker plane which left East Boston yesterday, commanded by Miss Emelia Earhart. He was sent to England four weeks ago to handle the publicity attending the arrival of the plane there and the publicity to follow.

Article about Captain Railey's long wait for Amelia's arrival.

Miss Earhart's Own Story; Saw Sea Hour Only in Fog

Did Not Take Control and Was "Only Baggage," She Relates, as She Could Not Fly by Instruments

From World Staff Correspondent

BURRY PORT, Wales, June 18.—Sitting on the edge of her bed in the ... to The World, Wilmer Stultz and Lou Gordon were too tired to receive visitors and were already in bed.

But Miss Earhart seemed to have a great reserve of nervous energy although she was tired too. She jumped up and down on the bed at times and her eyes flashed. She sat with legs tucked under her, wearing high leather boots, black breeches and a gray sweater. On the plane she had worn an overall flying suit which she had removed on shore. This is her story as taken down word for word.

By Amelia Earhart

We were flying over fog practically the whole distance. We saw the sea for just one hour. For most of the rest of the time we could see the sky. Sometimes there were clouds above and below, so land, when we saw it, looked very delightful.

We sighted land shortly after 11. We had passed over the America and tried to communicate with her, but as our wireless was useless we could not get our position from her.

I did not take the control of the plane as I planned. This was because of the clouds it was necessary for a pilot to be at the controls who could fly by the instruments alone, which I could not. I was only baggage last night.

Saw N... Except Ame... ~ 11,000 Feet

Part of an article about Amelia's historic flight.

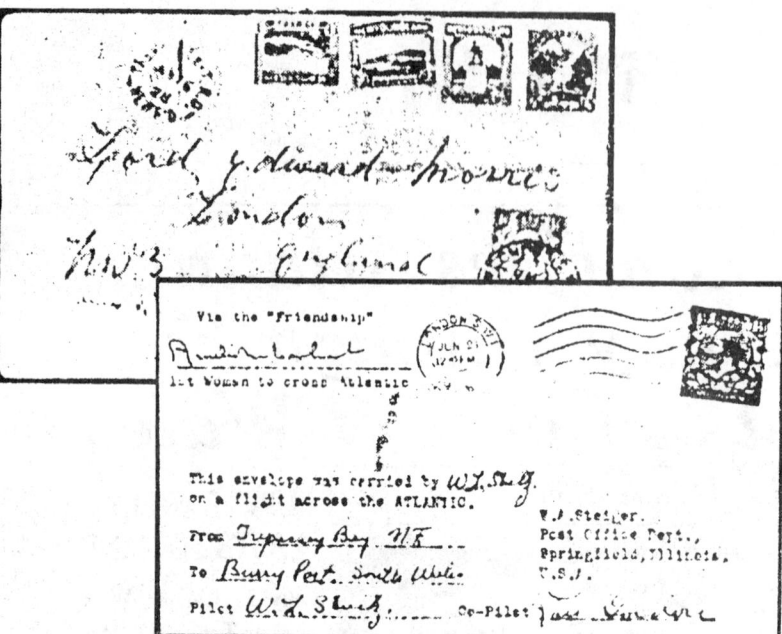

GIRL FLYER'S TUTOR TELLS OF FIRST HOP

Mrs. W. I. Southern at Los Gatos Found Her Pupil "Took to Air Like Duck to Water"

LOS GATOS, June 18.—Nowhere in the country was the progress of the plane carrying Amelia Earhart across the Atlantic followed more intently than on a little farm on the Shannon road here.

It's the home of Mrs. W. I. Southern, who taught the courageous "Lady Lindy" how to fly!

Although she's given up aviation for good, Mrs. Southern's interest in it is just as keen as it ever was, and she recalls vividly her experiences with Miss Earhart. This was in 1921 when Mrs. Southern, then Neta Snook, had leased the airport on Long Beach Boulevard between Southgate and Maywood near Los Angeles.

"It was there I met Miss Earhart," Mrs. Southern said. "She had come to Los Angeles with her father, a Southern Pacific attorney, and was interested in flying. Her father was not in sympathy with her ambitions, and strictly forbade her flying, declaring she shouldn't expose herself to the hazards of the air.

"But apparently Miss Earhart had her mind made up, because she pawned her fur coat, jewelry and other clothing and bought a plane, a three-cylinder Kinner Airster.

"She took to the air like a duck to water and progressed rapidly. We had one narrow escape together. We crashed over Goodyear Field once when we were up in a dual-control ship. But we came out uninjured and a crumpled wing the only damage to the ship.

"Her first 'solo' flight gave us quite a scare. She had taken the ship up before she was really qualified to fly alone. When she landed she headed for the far end of the field. Two telegraph poles were right in front of her. We held our breath—but she flew between the poles and landed safely!

"I hope her luck stays with her—I know it will."

Mrs. Southern herself has a notable record as a flyer. She left Iowa State College in 1917, determined to become an aviatrix. After considerable difficulty she was enrolled in the Curtiss flying school. She made her first flight at Miami, Florida, shortly after the war started, and then did her best to enlist in the flying corps. Finding this impossible, she became inspector at the factory of the British Air Ministry plant opened in Buffalo, New York. Here she remained until the armistice, when she left with a certificate of appreciation from the British government.

MISS EARHART IS 'VETERAN' OF AIR AT 27

Girl Took Up Aviation Study While Student at California University; Altitude Record

NEW YORK, June 18.—(Universal Service.)—Miss Amelia Earhart, who spanned the Atlantic Ocean today in the airplane, Friendship, is 27 years old.

But, in the light of aviation, she is justly called a veteran. She was one of the first women flyers in the world.

Eight years ago this fall, the girl, who so strikingly resembles Colonel Lindbergh, took up aviation. She was a student then at the University of Southern California and her flair for dangerous stunts drove her to flying.

After ten hours of lessons, she started after a woman's world record in the air, and she made it, to the amazement of her instructors. She achieved an altitude of 14,000 feet and that stood unsurpassed for two years.

Then came the accident which checked the birdwoman's fast developing career. This, too, happened in Los Angeles, where her father is a prominent lawyer.

Miss Earhart had just completed the sale of an airplane she had owned to two young Los Angeles men. The youths decided to give their new property an immediate test.

The girl remained on the field to watch them in their solo flight. Her eyes followed the plane as it soared easily toward the clouds. Then something happened. It was never explained, but the plane collapsed, and fell. Both its occupants were killed.

So terrible was the effect this tragedy had upon the girl observer that she announced at once that she would never fly again. And she did not—in an airplane—for some time.

CHICAGO FETES AMELIA TODAY

Her Flight Mechanic to Take Bride Tomorrow

CHICAGO, July 18 (AP)—Amelia Earhart, transatlantic flier, and former Chicago high school student, Wilmer Stultz, and Louis Gordon, will be honored tomorrow by Chicago.

The three who flew the airplane Friendship across the Atlantic will arrive in the morning on the Broadway limited from New York. They will be escorted on a parade of the loop and will be entertained at a public banquet. With the party will be Gordon's fiancee, Miss Ann Bruce, whom he will marry at a wedding ceremony in a public ballroom Friday night. Miss Bruce's mother and George Palmer Putnam, millionaire publisher and backer of the flight, will also be in the party.

Some of the newspaper articles about Amelia's historic flight.

CREDIT: ATCHISON COUNTY HISTORICAL SOCIETY

Amelia returns to America aboard the mayor's reception boat, the Macon, in New York Harbor, 1928.

Captain Manning told Amelia that although he had no crystal globe, he believed that Amelia would have many flights to justify the fame which she alone seemed to feel was undeserved. Perhaps, some day, he would be able to help her plan a solo flight and cheer her when she made it.

The next day the stately liner eased into her berth. Many of the passengers clustered about the gangplank and cheered as they saw the simply-clad Amelia with Lou and Wilmer, who stood on the bridge with the ship's captain. Soon they could distinguish the silk-hatted greeting committee and the tall, young-looking GP who was waving most enthusiastically. If Amelia's heart skipped a beat at the sight, no one would have guessed it, for she squared her shoulders, and firmly linking arms with Bill and Slim, smilingly faced the cameras and the tumultuous welcome of her countrymen.

The **Friendship** *owners letter of authorization to Amelia.*

Boston, Massachusetts
May 18, 1928.

WILMER STULTZ
LOUIS E. GORDON
J. H. LEWES GOWNER
AND TO ANYONE ELSE CONCERNED:

This is to say that on arrival in Treppassy of the tri-motor Fokker plane "FRIENDSHIP" if any questions of policy, procedure, personnel or any other question arises— the decision of Miss Amelia M. Earhart is to be final. That she is to have control of the plane and of the disposal of the services of all employees as fully as if she were the owner. And further, that on the arrival of the plane in London full control of the disposition of the plane and of the time and services of employees shall be hers to the same extent until and unless the owner directs otherwise.

Attorney in fact for the owner

A specimen of Miss Earhart's signature appears below.

CREDIT: PURDUE UNIVERSITY

Amelia visiting Muriel in Utica, New York, circa 1928.

Western Union cablegram Amelia sent to her mother from Wales.

MOTHER SURPRISED TO LEARN OF FLIGHT

The news of her daughter's flight to Europe came as a distinct surprise to her mother, Mrs. Amy Otis Earhart. The aviatrix's sister, Muriel, fearing the reaction, withheld the news till 8 o'clock last night. Then she said simply:

"Mother, Emelia's gone to Europe in an airplane!"

The white-haired mother stared at her a moment, uncomprehending. Then—

"Are you sure?" she asked falteringly.

"Yes, mother."

"Oh, Muriel"—there was a catch in her mother's voice. "Oh, Muriel, I hope she'll be safe!"

Amelia's book, 20 HRS. 40 MIN.: Our Flight In The Friendship. This copy is autographed to Mrs. Ulysses Grant McQueen, Amelia's friend and founder of the Women's Aeronautic Association.

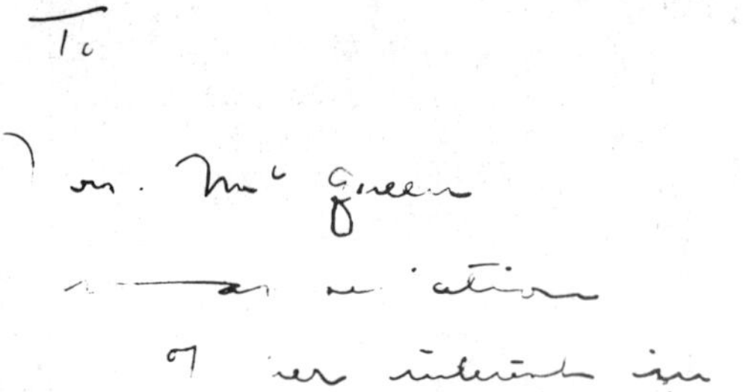

Souvenir button from Amelia's Friendship flight, June 1927.

Chapter Twelve

Fame and More

TO Amelia, the close of the nineteen-twenties meant tumultuous crowds of people and showers of ticker tape along downtown New York streets. Amelia, seated high upon the folded canvas-top of a convertible, rode through downtown New York, smiling and waving. The three fliers were formally greeted by city officials and by a representative of President Coolidge. The mayor of Boston sent an invitation to visit the city, and Medford's Mayor Larkin sent the city's World War I ace pilot, Lieutenant John B. Chevalier, with his personal congratulations to Amelia. There were many invitations, but Amelia, Bill, and Slim declined all except those from Boston, Chicago, and Medford.

Boston's reception was a smaller edition of New York's. It was a personal tribute to a girl who had been headlined across the country as a Boston social worker. Mother, Miss Perkins, and I had a few minutes with Amelia when her plane from New York landed at the unfinished Boston Airport. Soon Amelia was called to take her place with Bill and Slim for the ride to City Hall. She stood for a moment on the steps for the photographers. When she started to get into a waiting limousine, several voices called, "Take off your hat, Amelia." Her short, blonde, windswept hair was a novelty to many. Amelia paused, and with a slight grimace, pulled off her hat. She tossed the small brimmed straw-hat to me, saying, "Here's where I get sixty more freckles on my poor nose, I guess."

Amelia in her Lockheed Vega, 1928.

The hand-clapping and cheering along the route were punctuated by frequent high-pitched, excited yells, "Miss Earhart! Miss Earhart! It's me—Sammy!" or the names of any of the Denison House juniors. They called to her from precarious perches on fire alarm boxes or utility poles and window sills, or as they wriggled between the legs of harassed policemen. All were rewarded by a special smile and "Hi, there!" from the heroine of the day.

After receiving the traditional keys to the city and listening to several different officials' welcoming addresses, the fliers were given a few hours' rest before a formal dinner and an evening of more addresses by well-known figures of the aviation world. Introducing Amelia, Commander Byrd called her "a gallant lady," which was sincere praise from one who had watched her waiting out the frustrating delays in the Boston take offs, and then with honesty and humility, refusing to accept credit for the actual flight. After short speeches by the three fliers, a question and answer period extended far into the night. When Commander Byrd finally called a halt to the questions and the guests dispersed, Amelia and I stood for a moment in the warm July evening outside the hotel, waiting for a taxi to take us out to Medford.

Suddenly, Amelia gave a cry of delight. GP pulled up at the curb in her beloved Yellow Peril. In a few minutes she was behind the wheel, and we were headed along the Charles River, north of Boston.

Lights were dim except in a few sections in the towering Massachusetts General Hospital. As we sped along, Amelia pointed toward the hospital and commented that those were the people doing really worthwhile things. What she had done was important to her, but ninety-nine out of a hundred people who came out to see them did not know or care what contributions were really made to aviation. She felt it was hollow and meaningless.

Amelia hoped that Chicago would be the end of the circus parade for her. She was anxious to begin writing the book and told me she had been invited to write it at GP's home in Rye. GP suggested it as it would be easier there than in Boston. Also GP would have a secretary there to type out what she wrote, and this would expedite matters.

I knew Mother would be disappointed that Amelia was not going to be back at Denison House while writing her book. Amelia was also disappointed, in a way. She was afraid her value as a social worker would be nil until the hullabaloo died down. Trying to help people to realize their abilities and to iron out their own personality problems was work that she loved.

WELCOME Friendship Fliers

Amelia Earhart of Medford, Mass.

Wilmer Stultz - AMELIA EARHART - Louis Gordon

Souvenir Program - July 9th - 10th, 1928

PROGRAM
MONDAY, JULY 9, 1928

Arrival at East Boston Airport 11.30 A. M.

12 Noon
Airport Reception
Welcome by Mayor Nichols

Lieut. Gov. Allen   Commander Richard E. Byrd
Mayor Edward H. Larkin

ROUTE OF PARADE

Maverick street, Maverick square, Meridian street, Saratoga street, Chelsea street, across the bridge to Central street in Chelsea, Central avenue, East street, Chelsea square, Chelsea street, City square, Washington street north through Haymarket and Adams squares, Devonshire street, Congress street through Postoffice squa[re], Franklin and into Federal street where the C[...] located.

12.30 P. M.
Luncheon at Chamber of Comm[erce]
Sponsored by the National Aeronaut[ic...]

2.00 P. M.
Reception at Copley-Plaza
Commander Richard E. Byrd,

4.00 P. M.
State House—Reception in H[...]
Awarding of State Medals by Gov. [...]

5.00 P. M.
City of Boston Official W[elcome]
Boston Common, at Parkman
Band Concert and Addresses [...]

9.00 P. M.
City Reception to Amelia Earhart, Wilm[...]
Boston Arena, Massachusetts Ave.,

11.00 P. M.
Fireworks—Boston Cor[...]

Boston Program (three pages) to welcome the Friendship fliers home.

Souvenir gift given to Amelia

PROGRAM
Reception by City of Medford
TUESDAY, JULY 10, 1928

ROUTE OF PARADE

She will be met by an escort at the Medford-Somerville line near Magoun square and Broadway in South Medford at 12.30 on the afternoon of July 10 and escorted by officials, the National Guard units and delegations of the veteran organizations of the city over Medford and Main streets to Medford square, thence via Forest and Valley streets and Brookview road to the High School athletic field.

2.00 P. M.
Presentation City of Medford Gift
By MAYOR EDWARD H. LARKIN
High School Athletic Field, Fulton Street
Band Concert and Addresses by Officials

LOG OF THE FRIENDSHIP
SUNDAY

*10.51 A. M.—Took off at Trepassey, Newfoundland.
12.20 P. M.—Message from plane said she was passing over Grand Banks, 60 miles to the East.
1.00 P. M.—Steamer Concordia sighted Friendship passing over Grand Banks.
1.30 P. M.—Chatham, Mass., radio station received message from Friendship saying: "Fair weather and going ahead O. K."
2.12 P. M.—Stultz messaged wife at Mineola, N. Y.: "All O. K."
5.45 P. M.—Steamer Rexmore talked to plane 700 miles off Newfoundland.
6.30 P. M.—Rexmore heard further signals from Friendship, "Apparently still going strong."
6.37 P. M.—Steamer Elmworth received message "All's well" from Friendship.
Midnight—Steamer Albertic received message that plane was making 100 miles an hour.

MONDAY

6.00 A. M.—Steamer America reported Friendship circled vessel 75 miles east of Cobh, Ireland..
7.40 A. M.—Plane landed in Burry Estuary off Burry Port, Wales.
*Boston time.

(backside of gift).

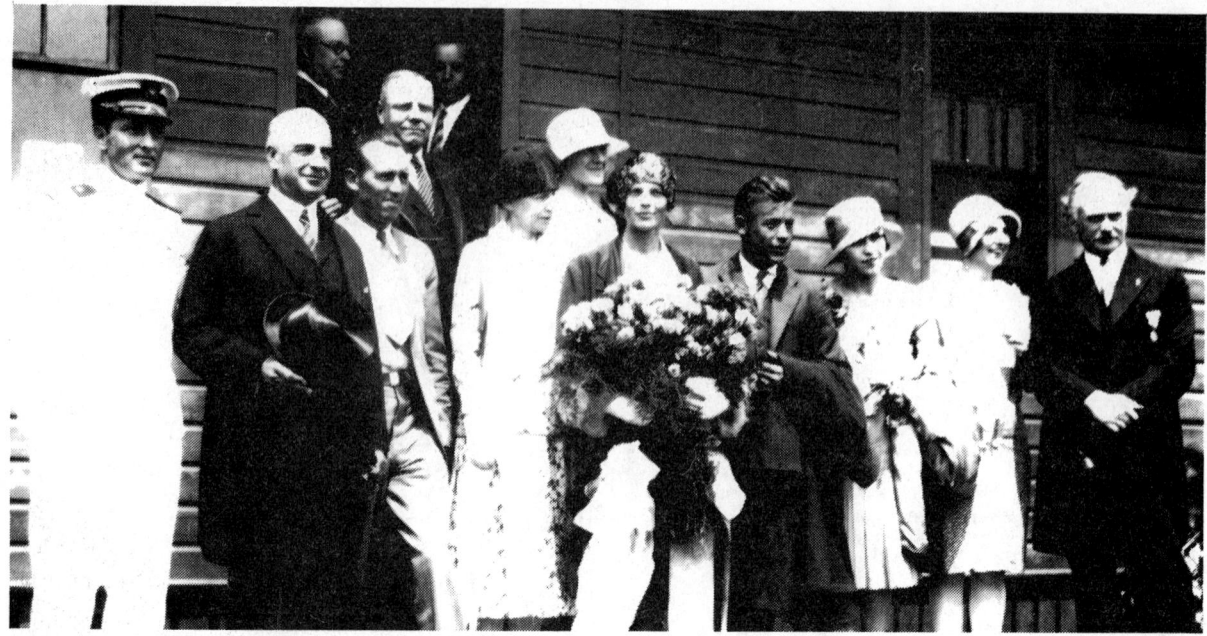

Boston on July 9, 1928. At airport welcome, left to right, Richard E. Byrd, then a Navy commander, Lt. Gov. Allen, Lou Gordon, Mayor Malcolm E. Nichols (rear), Mrs. Amy Earhart, Muriel Earhart (rear), Amelia Earhart, Wilmer Stultz, Anne Bruce and Medford Mayor Larkin.

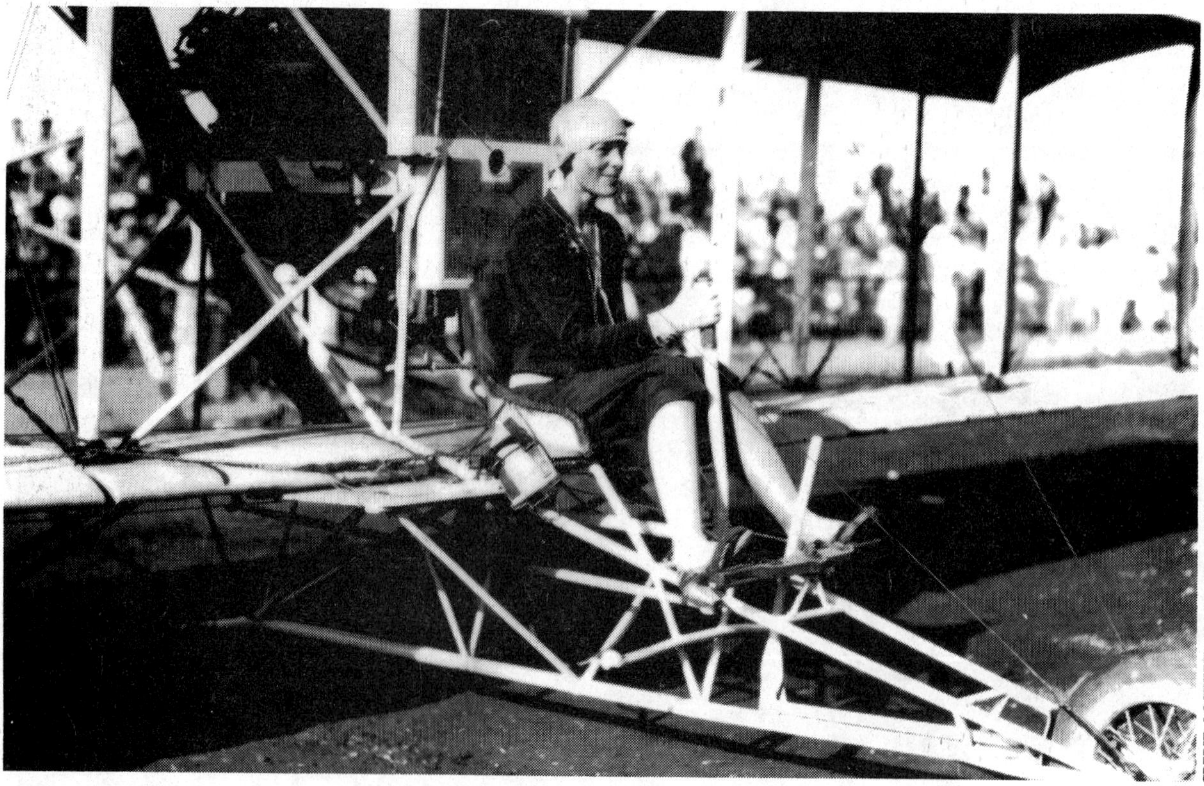

CREDIT: LOCKHEED-CALIFORNIA COMPANY

Amelia on a Curtiss "pusher"

Amelia in her Lockheed Vega, 1928.

GP had said that after the book was out, Amelia could easily earn several thousand dollars lecturing around the country. Why people should want to listen to her talking about being a passenger in the *Friendship,* she could not understand. But the exchequer was low, so she was happy to oblige.

The tentative severing of ties with Denison House, at which Amelia was hinting here, became final within six months. Never again was she to serve as a thirty-five dollar a week social worker; the hobby of her early twenties was to become her career. The times were right for Charles Lindbergh and Amelia.

The flamboyant, prosperous, roaring twenties lionized these two with an ardor unknown before, except for political and military heroes. In spite of the cynicism of the prohibition era, Amelia's modest simplicity of dress and behavior and her avowed abstinence from liquor captivated the imagination of the nation.

Amelia enjoyed the Medford reception. We laughed together over the eagerness of all the reporters to discover Sam Chapman and proclaim him as Amelia's fiancé. They finally decided that Sam was a tall red-haired youth who had ridden on the running board of our automobile for several blocks and had reappeared near the speakers' platform when we entered the athletic field where the welcoming exercises were held. A more positive contrast could hardly be imagined than one between the quiet, intellectual Sam and the broad-shouldered, rough-and-ready "Eric the Red."

Sam, sitting inconspicuously in the fifth row, was impatiently awaiting the conclusion of the ceremonies, so he could spirit Amelia away to a beach in Marblehead for a few hours' relaxation. After a short prayer by the rector of Grace Episcopal Church, the Reverend Dwight Hadley, and a complimentary introduction by Mayor Larkin, Amelia spoke briefly. She paid a gracious tribute to the five aging but still sturdy Grand Army veterans and to Lieutenant Chevalier who, she said, represented "our war." Turning to a large delegation of women's organizations, she told them she especially appreciated their coming out in the July heat to welcome the fliers. She then presented Bill and Slim as the men who made aviation history,

"by flying the *Friendship* and cargo, me, unerringly for two thousand miles in an airway as yet uncharted."

With less than a day's rest, the three fliers departed for Chicago. Bill Stultz disappeared just before starting the drive to City Hall for the official greetings. Amelia and Slim, both tired and overwrought, nearly telephoned the mayor's office to cancel the ceremonies. GP convinced them to see it through, saying it could damage Amelia's reputation as a lecturer and author. GP told her that Chicago had been fooled several times before this, so once more wouldn't hurt—he would be Bill Stultz in the parade.

GP opened Bill's suitcase and took out his worn leather helmet, in those days the insignia of a flier, and put on the helmet.

Amelia need not have worried that the subterfuge would be discovered. The crowd cheered and applauded, and if anybody did wonder at one flier's wearing a helmet on a hot July day far away from his plane, it was not mentioned. At the City Hall, the ceremonies were curtailed because the mayor and his committee were warm and hungry too. It was agreed that because of the necessity of Amelia's making connections for her return to New York, she would speak for the three fliers.

It was not, however, until Amelia was safely settled in her stateroom on the train for New York that she relaxed. GP reported that he had sent an apologetic telegram to the mayor, pleading a sudden seizure of stomach cramps as the reason for his absence from the luncheon. Slim agreed to stay in Chicago until he found Bill and saw him safely aboard the train to his home town. Slim planned to return to his airplane mechanic's job in Louisiana and marry the woman who was waiting for him there. Amelia, to my knowledge, never saw either Bill or Slim again.

After returning to the east coast, Amelia began writing her book at the Putnams' home in Rye. In almost complete seclusion, she completed the book on schedule, without the help of the ghost writer the publishers would have supplied. She titled the book from the last scrawled log entry, made when Bill set the plane down in Burry Port Harbor: "20 hrs.

40 mins., our flight."

She received offers to lecture, many more than she could possibly accept. Nearly two hundred letters per day poured in: requests for autographs, letters of praise and appreciation, a scattering of crank letters, marriage offers, begging letters, and, of course, a few berating letters. Amelia was asked to send a check for one hundred fifty dollars to pay for a woman's divorce because, she wrote, "I know you believe in women's freedom." Amelia also received a letter asking her to send the writer the dress she had worn. "I am just about your size and I know you will not wear an evening dress twice. I will be waiting eagerly for it." The children's letters Amelia tried conscientiously to answer, but requests for autographs were granted, as Amelia said, "by squiggling my name" on a form postal card.

Amelia in Washington, D.C. on November 2, 1928 after a reception by President Coolidge, with Porter Adams of the National Aeronautic Association.

Although Amelia enjoyed meeting people and "talking aviation," the lecture schedule she undertook during the winter of 1928–29 was exhausting. She was delighted, therefore, when the editor of *McCall's* magazine offered her a staff position as the aviation editor. However, Amelia never joined the staff of that magazine because just at this time a cigarette advertisement appeared, featuring a picture of the *Friendship* fliers. The endorsement said, "This is the brand that the crew of the *Friendship* carried." Amelia asked that she be left out as she did not smoke, but the company would not run the advertisement without Amelia's name. By refusing, she would have kept Bill and Slim from a nice bonus, which both of them wanted. Amelia finally agreed to sign the endorsement, with the understanding that her share of the money should be given to Commander Byrd for his second antarctic expedition. Portraying a woman with a cigarette in 1929 was still daring. Amelia's endorsement of a popular tobacco firm caused the publishers of *McCall's* to cancel her contract.

GP took up Amelia's case and eventually the editor of *McCall's* reconsidered. However, by that time the editor of *Cosmopolitan* magazine had asked Amelia to become one of its associate editors. Amelia signed with *Cosmopolitan* and moved into a tiny office. The first thing she did was to circle the fourth day of each of eight months on the calender—her deadline dates. When GP teased her about her long range program, she took it good humoredly, letting him know that writing on a schedule frightened her. She would rather fly than write.

In spite of her avowed preference for doing rather than talking or writing, Amelia's articles were immediately popular. She discussed airport facilities, pilot training, plane design, and similar subjects with a light yet authoritative touch. Although Ray Long and the *Cosmopolitan* staff were completely indifferent to the cigarette advertisement's repercussions, Amelia was disturbed and angry when people unjustly criticized her. One letter concluded with the sentence: "Since you smoke, I suppose you drink also." Another writer declared, "Cigarette smoking is to be expected from any woman who cuts her hair like a man's and who

Routing and publicity for the first "Powder Puff" Derby, August 17, 1929.

wears trousers in public." Amelia was learning that, as a public figure, she must expect unfair censure as well as honest criticism, and amusing or intentional misunderstanding as well as sincere appreciation.

A major milestone for women in aviation was the first Women's Transcontinental Air Derby, to be flown from Santa Monica, California, to Cleveland, Ohio. Amelia bought a Lockheed airplane, which was larger than Lady Mary Heath's Avro, so she could enter the Derby. Twenty women* took off on this historic flight on the morning of Sunday, August 18, 1929.

For the first time in formal competition, women were recognized as pilots capable of long flights without direction from men. Humorist Will Rogers, speaking about the race, coined the name "Powder Puff Derby." Amelia and many other women pilots disliked the designation, feeling it detracted from their desire to demonstrate their flying ability to a skeptical public. Amelia, although she was undoubtedly the best known entrant, placed only third.

---

*Technically—nineteen took off, but one started a day late. Bobbi Trout is the last survivor of the original nineteen women.

Amelia portrait, circa 1931.

Letter from two founders of the Ninety-Nines.

November 16, 1929

Miss Jean D. Hoyt
232 Shotwell Park
Syracuse, N. Y.

Dear Miss Hoyt:

A group of twenty-six women pilots met together at Curtiss Field, Valley Stream, Long Island, November 2nd, to discuss the formation of a club. It was decided at the conference that the organization would be neither strictly frivolous nor entirely serious, that the social side should be emphasized but that problems which arise in connection with women in aviation should also be discussed and acted upon. It was agreed that all licensed women pilots in good standing would be eligible to membership, and that letters be sent to the present Department of Commerce list, giving each the privilege of becoming a charter member.

The name of the club would be taken from the numbers who joined from this first invitation. There are at present one hundred seventeen active licenses. Therefore, if ninety-eight signed up, the name would be "Ninety-Eights." Further increase in membership would have no effect on changing the name.

The organization is to be very loose, possibly governed by a Committee with a Chairman. The committee members to be elected to represent the various sections of the country. The only purpose so far would be the tacit understanding that it is to interest women in aviation, and be a general clearing house of ideas. The club is entirely independent of any commercial organization, as its membership is composed of women employed by many different companies.

It was suggested that meetings be held simultaneously throughout the country, wherever there was a large enough group to do so. Thus, a pilot away from home might attend a meeting in some distant place, and exchange views and ideas with another group of women.

Dues were set tentatively at One Dollar, payable now, with yearly dues to be determined later. For the time being it was decided to meet at each other's homes once a month. No decision as to emblem was made, although it was agreed a bracelet or a ring would be selected. Neva Paris, Kenwood, Great Neck, New York, and Amelia Earhart, 959 Eighth Avenue, New York City, volunteered to act as Corresponding Secretaries pro tem.

We believe that such an organization might become influential and powerful. We hope all licensed pilots will see its possibilities and join at once.

The next meeting is to be held at the home of Opal Kunz, 137 Riverside Drive, New York City, on December 14th, 1929 at 3:00 P.M. Please make an effort to be with us.

Sincerely,

Neva Paris

CREDIT: PURDUE UNIVERSITY

The tragic part of this race was the occurrence of several mysterious mishaps, none of which was ever explained. The most significant was the death of Marvel Crosson on Monday, August 19, in the mesquite jungle in the Gila River valley. Thea Rasche, the German aviatrix, was forced down at Holtville, Arizona, when her engine stalled. Thea soon found the reason. There was sand in her gasoline tank. That same day, Bobbi Trout was forced down near Algodones and her Golden Eagle monoplane was damaged after mysteriously running out of gasoline. Clara Fahy was forced down near Calexico with broken wire braces on her ship; apparently corrosive acid had eaten through the wires.†

Amelia, flying her beautiful Lockheed Vega, was the first to arrive at Yuma. She ran into

---

†*Fully described and documented in* Just Plane Crazy, *biography of Bobbi Trout.*

trouble when her wheels touched the ground. The plane ran into a hummock, a concrete knoll extending about six or eight inches above the dirt, to the side of the regular landing area. The plane nosed over and bent the prop. Within hours a new prop was sent from Burbank, and she was again on her way to Cleveland.

The National Air Races and Aeronautical Exposition in Cleveland, Ohio, ran from August 24 through September 2, 1929. During the first few days several of the women pilots got together for some hangar flying. While standing under the bleachers and talking about the events, they all wondered why there was no organization for women pilots. Amelia, Bobbi Trout, Louise Thaden, Blanche Noyes, Phoebe Omlie, and several other women decided that after the Air Races were over, Amelia and some of the women in the East would make up a set of by-laws and mail them to all women pilots. Because Amelia had a secretary, she agreed to mail out the information and to ask each pilot to mail in her money if she wished to join.

A few months after the conclusion of the first Women's Transcontinental Air Derby, twenty-six women pilots met in a hangar at Curtiss Field, Long Island, New York. There were only one hundred seventeen licensed women pilots in the United States at that time. Although fewer than a quarter of them were present at this informal meeting, nearly all of them signified their interest in forming a club. Various names were suggested—Bird Women, Angels' Club, Sky Larks, but these were all discarded. It was Amelia's suggestion that the group be named for the number of charter members. As requests for memberships came in, the name was changed from Seventy-Sixes to Eighty-Sixes to Ninety-Sevens. With a final tally of ninety-nine, the club officially became incorporated as The Ninety-Nines.

Amelia was elected the first president and served from 1929 to 1933. Their constitution stated: "We propose to assist women in aeronautical research, air racing events, acquisition of aerial experience, administration of aid through aerial means in times of emergency arising from fire, famine, flood, or war." The only requirement for membership was, and still is, an active pilot's license.

Between *Cosmopolitan* deadlines, Amelia flew around the country lecturing. As the aviation editor, she frequently addressed businessmen's groups and chambers of commerce, urging them to support the creation or improvement of air facilities. One of her overnight stops for lecturing was at Utica, New York, where I was teaching at a private school. We were entertained at the home of Mr. and Mrs. Merwin K. Hart, and it was Mr. Hart, a pilot himself, who half in jest said, "Well, Amelia, I suppose you'll be taking off soon to cross the Atlantic solo, won't you?"

Amelia said she would like to do it, but she knew it would be foolhardy for her to attempt it until she had considerably more flying and navigation experience. She suggested he give her eighteen months to two years before she would answer him. Interestingly, Amelia's trans-Atlantic solo flight took place precisely two years to the day later.

Harvey Christen, 16 year old summer hire at Lockheed and friend of Amelia, July 7, 1930.

Amelia's letter to Bert Kinner.

```
Hearst's International
combined with
Cosmopolitan

                           AMELIA EARHART
                           AVIATION EDITOR

INTERNATIONAL MAGAZINE BUILDING
FIFTY-SEVENTH STREET AT EIGHTH AVENUE
         NEW YORK CITY

          March thirty
            1 9 2 9
```

RECEIVED APR 3 - 1929
REFERRED TO Mr. Kinner
ANSD._____ APPD._____

CREDIT: DONNA KINNER HUNTER

Dear Mr. Kinner:

I see various things are happening to Kinner stock. Have you any information to give one of the most ~~anxious~~ subscribers as to what is planned to do with it? Several of my friends are making inquiries, and I thought I would write you and ask what you think the top price will be, if you have any plans.

I have written a letter for a gentleman by the name of Hildesheim to present to you. He is a Dutchman with considerable mechanical knowledge and, from what I understand, a fine ability. He is connected with insurance in some way and finding that I knew you, asked for an introduction. He will be in California shortly.

I talked with your representative, Leslie Bowman, and he gave very rosy accounts of progress. Please remember me to your family, and believe me sincerely interested, as always.

Sincerely yours,

Amelia Earhart

While Amelia was in Utica, we discussed the final plans for my wedding to Albert Morrissey at the end of June, 1929. She promised to be my maid of honor and to fly in from New York to be at the rehearsal and party the evening before the wedding.

Mother and the entire wedding party waited for Amelia. An hour after the scheduled time for the rehearsal, Amelia still had not appeared. I was worried and more than a little cross. As we were leaving to go to the church without her, the telephone rang. In a few seconds I heard Amelia's voice, "Pidge, I'm terribly sorry—I'm fog bound in New Jersey. Don't worry; I'll be down tomorrow morning, even if I have to take—heaven forbid—a train."

The overwhelming feeling of relief in knowing that she was safe banished my earlier resentment. The marriage was duly solemnized the following day with Amelia playing the supporting role perfectly. In speaking later with our minister, the Reverend Dwight Hadley, Amelia said in answer to a question about her feelings during the Atlantic flight, "I think what Pidge has just done today took more courage than my flying did."

Reverend Hadley said with a kindly smile that when Amelia met the man she deeply loved and who felt the same toward her, marriage would be the happiest and most natural thing in the world. Amelia nodded soberly but made no reply.

AMELIA EARHART MAID OF HONOR FOR SISTER

Shares Limelight With Bride at Pretty Church Wedding in Medford—Declines to Talk of Possible Marriage Herself

SISTER OF AVIATRIX MARRIED IN MEDFORD
The bridal party at the Earhart-Morrissey wedding yesterday at Medford is shown above. Left to right: Amelia Earhart, maid of honor; Richard Tadgell, best man; the bride and Henry A. Morrissey, the groom.

Miss Amelia Earhart, the only girl who has crossed the Atlantic by aeroplane, stepped out of her flying togs to act as maid of honor at the marriage of her sister, Grace Muriel Earhart, to Henry Albert Morrissey in the Grace Episcopal Church, High street, Medford, yesterday afternoon.

HONORS SHARED

It was one occasion when a June bride had to share the spotlight with another, and although Amelia sought to efface herself from the picture, she attracted wide attention as she stepped down the aisle behind the bride. A slim girl in green chiffon, demurely bearing a sheaf of yellow roses on her arm, it was difficult for one to think of her as the daring aviatrix who flew the ocean just a year ago.

Attention was focused on Amelia not alone because of her fame as a flyer, but for the reason that Samuel Chapman of Marblehead was one of the ushers at the wedding ceremony. Chapman was spoken of, after Amelia's European flight, as her intended husband and his presence at the wedding yesterday confirmed the fact that they are still friends.

But when approached on the subject of matrimony he begged the reporters "to leave me alone." Amelia likewise would not divulge any information as to a wedding of her own in the future. She passed the question by as she said, "I would make a poor wife, running around the country as I am."

She said it with a wide smile, referring to the fact that she is constantly flying from city to city, lecturing and gathering data for her monthly magazine articles on aviation. While she chatted with the newspapermen, Chapman, making himself as unobtrusive as possible, but always with an eye on Amelia, stood to one side talking to her mother.

Amelia had intended to fly to her sister's wedding, but at the last moment was forced to resort to the train to bring her to the Hub. She was in New York and was about to board her little Moth biplane when she discovered a nick in the propellor, caused she believes by a stone striking it as it was spinning while warming up.

300 Guests Present

Rather than take a chance on having trouble with the damaged propellor and being unable to get a propellor to replace it at once, since the plane is of English make, she took the midnight from New York. She was unable to be present at the pre-nuptial supper at the Hotel Victoria Friday night and was also disappointed because she did not have the opportunity of landing at the new airport at East Boston, which she said she was very anxious to see.

More than 300 guests, chiefly residents of Medford, attended the wedding ceremony at the church. On the lawn and sidewalk outside the church half a hundred people craned their necks to see the bridal party.

The bride wore a simple gown of white chiffon. Her veil was of tulle, caught with orange blossoms and with sprays of the blossoms sprinkled down its length. She carried a bouquet of white roses.

The bridesmaids included Miss Lucile Pollock of Aspinwall, Pa.; Miss Katharyn Trufant of Whitman and Miss Mary Short of Worcester. They wore gowns of yellow chiffon, with skirts of yellow and tan figured chiffon of uneven hem lines, with large natural straw hats. They carried bouquets of spring flowers in yellow and pink tones.

Honeymoon in Bermuda

Richard Tadgell of Somerville was best man. The ushers were Edwin Babbot of Boston and Mr. Chapman. The ceremony, a single ring affair, was performed by the Rev. Dwight W. Hadley, rector of the church. Harold Bridges presided at the organ. A number of the Knights of King Arthur, a boy's organization of the church of which the groom was chief advisor, attended the wedding.

Following the marriage there was a reception at the Women's Clubhouse on Governor's avenue, Medford. The bridal party was assisted in receiving by Mrs. Earhart, mother of the bride, and Miss Rhoda Slate. The couple left on a honeymoon trip to Bermuda. They will be at home at 15 Vine street, Medford, after Aug. 1.

The bridegroom is a resident of Medford, where the bride lived up until last June, when she removed to Utica, N. Y., to teach at a private school. She attended Smith College and for three years was a teacher in the Lincoln Junior High School of Medford. Mr. Morrissey is the son of Mrs. David C. Morrissey and is assistant service manager of the Boston Woven Hose and Rubber Company of Cambridge.

Newspaper account of Muriel's marriage to Albert Morrissey on June 29, 1929.

Amelia modeling for Vanity Fair, November 1931.

Chapter Thirteen

Between Record Flights

DURING her visits to Boston, Amelia never failed to stop for an hour or longer at Denison House. Miss Perkins suggested that she be on the Board of Directors, so, although she could not attend many meetings, her interest and her pocketbook never failed them. Amelia was asked to join the Boston Chapter of Zonta International, an organization of executive women in business and the professions. Her brief biographical sketch in *Who's Who* listed her occupation as: "Aviation lecturer and writer, active pilot and holder of U.S. and international licenses." It was in the aviation classification that Amelia joined the Boston Chapter of Zonta. She had little interest in the usual women's clubs' activities, but she thoroughly believed in the Zontian professional women's code of ethics, and she liked the international scope of their membership. Zonta was the only non-flying organization to which Amelia belonged.

A business venture which brought her pleasure, experience, and two new records was her autogiro flight for the Beech-Nut Packing Company. Amelia accepted the advertising contract not only because of the sizable fee, but because of the irresistible appeal this newly developed type of heavier-than-air craft had for her. After two lessons in the management of the horizontal windmill-powered machine, the forerunner of today's helicopter, she felt competent to start on the leisurely transcontinental journey to proclaim aloft the virtues of Beech-Nut products. At the end of the flight, Amelia set an autogiro altitude record and another record as the first woman to cross the United States in that type of craft.

Amelia, circa 1932.

Amelia joined the Ludington Lines, November, 1930.

Hourly Inspection

FLIGHT FARE

Round trip rate between

New York or Trenton and Washington or Baltimore $20.00

Bus transportation between Newark Airport and Uptown N. Y. C.
75c additional.

Bus transportation between Martin Airport and downtown Baltimore included in above fare.

Other fares listed in Schedule.

For Information and Reservations

NEW YORK: Pennsylvania Station, Pennsylvania 2000; N. Y., P. & W. offices, 122 E. 42nd Street, Caledonia 3080; Newark Airport Mulberry 2970

TRENTON: Pennsylvania R. R., Trenton 2-3101; Mercer Airport, Trenton 2283.

PHILADELPHIA: Broad Street Station, P. R. R., Locust 3030; Public Service Jersey Bus Terminal, Walnut 5050; Central Airport, Camden, Camden 2088.

BALTIMORE: Pennsylvania R. R., Baltimore, Plaza 5430; N. Y., P. & W. A. C. offices, Glen Martin Airport, Essex 300

WASHINGTON: Pennsylvania R. R., 613 Fourteenth St., National 9140; Washington Airport, District 6081; N. Y., P. and W. offices, Washington Bldg., National 7529

also

Pennsylvania Railroad Ticket and Suburban Offices, Western Union Offices, Travel Bureaus, Leading Hotels, Public Service Bus Terminals and all A. A. A. offices

Constant Private Communication

Washington

OFFICERS

C. T. LUDINGTON, *Chairman of Board*
N. S. LUDINGTON, *President*   PAUL COLLINS, *Vice-President in Charge of Operations*
GENE VIDAL, *Executive Vice-President*   AMELIA EARHART, *Vice-President in Charge of Traffic*

General Office
Washington Bldg., Washington, D. C.

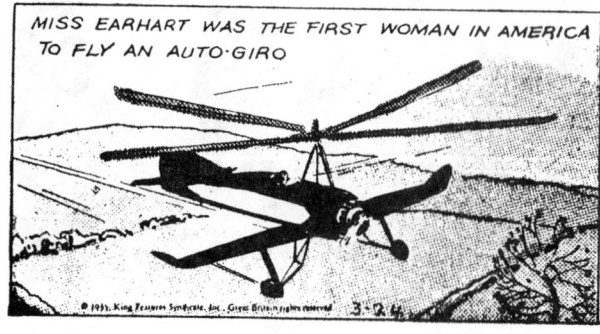

1931 cartoon about Amelia.

Amelia after a hard day's work on her airplane.

Atchison, Kansas, Amelia's real home town, invited her to attend the dedication of the new high school stadium which was named for her. Able to arrange the visit between lecture engagements in Kansas City and Chicago, she accepted gladly. Amelia enjoyed meeting our cousins, the Challisses, and the members of some of the families, the Foxes, Waggoners, and Campbells, whom we had known at Miss Walton's school nearly twenty years before. Amelia rode down Commercial Street with almost the entire population cheering and waving to her. Following the ceremonies, Cousin Jim, Mr. James Challiss, took Amelia past our grandparents' old home, which now boasted a neat white sign informing the public that this was her birthplace. Amelia echoed the feelings of the many small town boys and girls who seek wider horizons with maturity. Amelia told Jim that Atchison was a good place to grow up in. The old barn, the bluffs, the picnics at Deer Creek, and all the rest—she would never forget them. There is something special about a childhood spent in a small town.

At about this time a gift to Dad brought Amelia lasting satisfaction. In the first tier of foothills rising behind Los Angeles and just within the circumference of the old city, there stood almost in the shadow of Old Baldy a monolithic boulder called Eagle Rock. On a pleasant slope near the rock, the novelist Harold Bell Wright had built a cabin where he sought Emersonian seclusion for his last years of writing. After his death the property was offered for sale at a low figure, even for those days, because it was on the wrong side of the city, away from the popular beaches. One small pipe brought water to the cottage, but of other modern conveniences there were none.

After his divorce from Mother became final, Dad made a down payment on this cabin and the five acres of land surrounding it. He married a mature and kindly woman whom he met in the Christian Science congregation and entered upon what was probably the happiest period of his life since the early days in Kansas City, Kansas. After giving up his office in the city, Dad made his wide legal knowledge available to members of the church and his neighbors. Because of the soundness of his opinions, often rendered while leaning on a rake or sitting cross-legged on the rustic bench he had built, he was informally and affectionately given the title of Judge. On one of Amelia's flying trips to the West, she visited Dad and found him worried about meeting the mortgage payments on the property. Helen, Dad's cheerful and understanding wife, had a small but regular income from her work as a saleslady for a jewelry company, but Dad, like many an old time doctor, refused to send bills to the many friends to whom he had given advice, so, as he remarked wryly to Amelia, "I'm long on friends, but short on cash, Meelie."

Amelia paid the outstanding mortgage, about two thousand dollars, and had a lawyer execute a life tenancy freehold which would give the property to Dad, and after his death, to Helen, but would retain the title in Amelia's name.

Amelia and friend in Grand Central Air Terminal, circa 1930.

Amelia in front of Grand Central Air Terminal in Los Angeles. First Transcontinental Autogiro Pilot on June 22, 1931.

She wrote me about what she had done because she had made me ultimate heir. She added, "I'm afraid Dad may not enjoy his little cabin too long, Pidge. He's done wonders in planting trees and vines on the hillside, but he looks thinner than I've ever seen him, and Helen says he has no appetite at all and tires very quickly now." Less than a year later, Dad died of throat cancer and Amelia wired me, "Dad's last big case settled out of court, peacefully and without pain."

Always generous, Amelia quietly paid for a six months' treatment for alcoholism for the husband of one of her friends in the Ninety Nines; she helped to finance a date farm in Arizona for her former California mechanic who had contracted tuberculosis; and she loaned my husband and me money to make the down payment on our first Medford home. She delighted the heart of the youngest little girl in our Chicago rector's large family by sending her three new dresses because, as she wrote, "It's no fun wearing hand-me-downs all the time." There were many other similar "lifts," as Amelia called her deeds of kindness, known only to herself and her checkbook.

Following the successful publication of her book, *20 HRS. 40 MIN., Our Flight In The Friendship,* Amelia had come to depend a great deal upon GP for friendly advice in many matters, literary, financial, and social. GP and his wife had separated in 1929, and in 1930, she obtained a divorce. She moved to Florida with their two sons, then eleven and fourteen years of age. GP was then free to try to persuade Amelia to think of him as more than a mentor and friend. It was a harried courtship because they both were involved in so many projects that they had little time together—a few minutes before a take off at a crowded airport, a twenty minute coffee break in Amelia's *Cosmopolitan* office, or a taxi shared after a lecture or conference.

The family Bible entry of Amelia's marriage.

Amelia's Transport Pilot's License

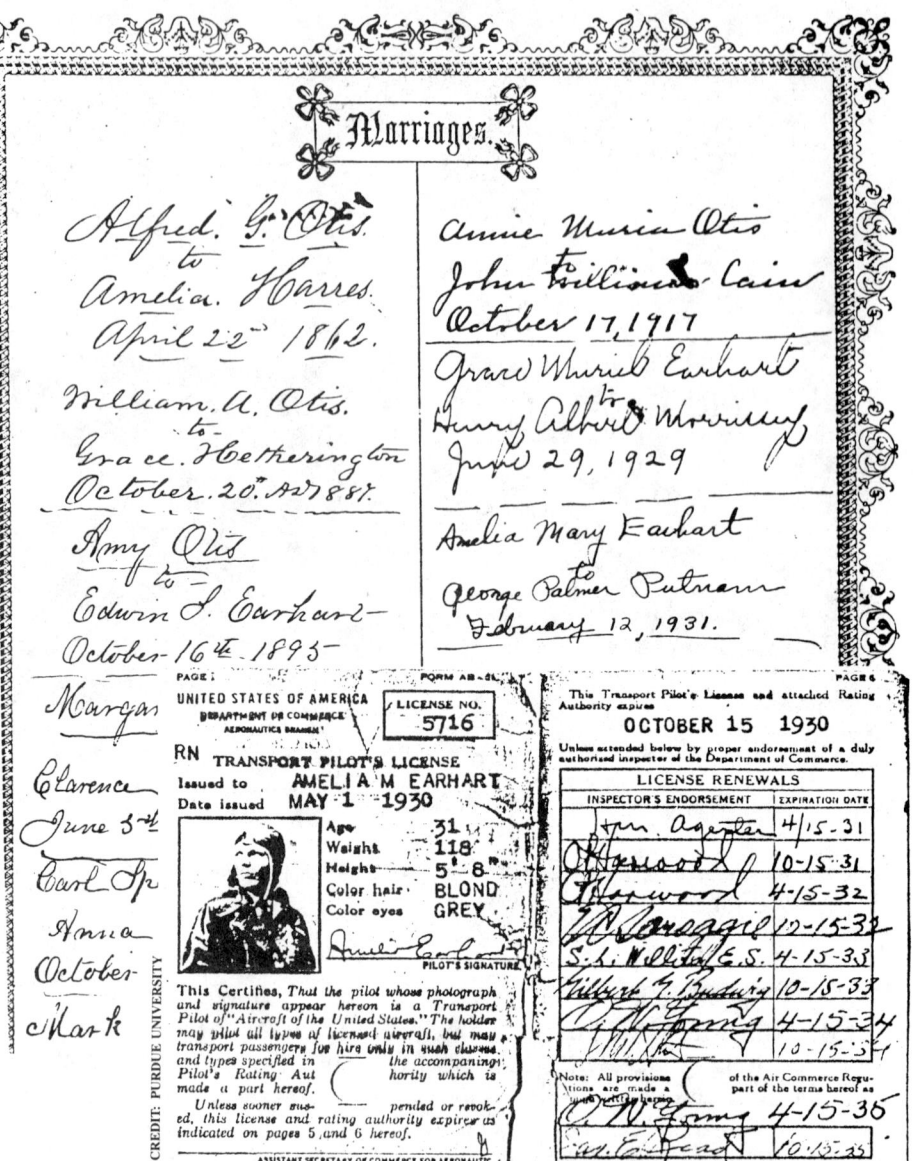

GP said he proposed to Amelia six times, the last time being in the Lockheed hangar while she was waiting for her plane to warm up. Amelia simply nodded, "Yes," then patted his arm and climbed quickly aboard. The deafening noise of many engines running and the presence of several mechanics, resentful of the intrusion of a white-collared civilian in their domain, kept the moment from being romantic, but GP felt as lovers have down through the ages. A wave of her scarf as she entered the plane was the last he saw of his new fianceé for several days.

Mother opposed the marriage upon the dual grounds that GP was twelve years Amelia's senior and a divorced man. Neither of these objections had any weight with Amelia, who recognized in GP a kindred spirit whom she had first respected and then come to love, as the Reverend Hadley had predicted.

Amelia and GP were quietly married at the home of GP's mother in Noank, Connecticut, on February 7, 1931. "Over the broomstick with GP today. Break the news gently to Mother," she wired me in Medford. My husband and I immediately sent them our best wishes, and, carrying out the simile Amelia had used, I added a Gypsy blessing we often heard as children, "May the floods never reach your cooking pots."

AMELIA EARHART WEDS G. P. PUTNAM

But Atlantic Flier Will Remain "Miss Earhart" for Business Purposes and Writing.

BACK TO WORK ON MONDAY

Married in the Home of the Bridegroom's Mother in Fishing Village in Connecticut.

Special to The New York Times.
NOANK, Conn., Feb. 7.—Secure from the eyes of the millions who have acclaimed her America's most famous aviatrix, Miss Amelia Earhart, slender blonde social service worker, who has been the only woman to fly the Atlantic in an airplane, was married here at noon today to George Palmer Putnam, publisher, author and explorer, of New York in his mother's New England home overlooking Long Island Sound.

Noank is a quaint little village, celebrated in Summer time chiefly for the excellence of the lobsters its fishing population brings up from the Sound and for the flavor of the strawberries and the melon-rind preserves served in its lone tea house. In Winter Noank dozes. Nothing as interesting as this has happened there since the big wind and tidal wave of '78. And when something did happen to put Noank on the front pages of New York newspapers, nobody knew about it until the bride and bridegroom had motored away, as they did immediately after the ceremony, for an unknown destination.

The ceremony itself, performed by Probate Judge Arthur Anderson of Groton, Conn., consumed but five minutes. The only witnesses were Mrs. Frances Putnam, Mr. Putnam's mother; Charles Faulkner, his uncle; Robert Anderson, the judge's son, and twin black cats.

Phones Wedding Announcement.

As Mr. Putnam slipped a plain platinum ring on Miss Earhart's finger the cats, coal black and playful, rubbed arched backs against his ankles. Then, while Miss Earhart, who has been said to resemble Colonel Lindbergh, put on a brown fur coat over a brown suit and light brown blouse, Mr. Putnam telephoned his secretary, Miss Josephine Berger, in New York, announcing the wedding.

Immediately afterward he and Mrs. Putnam bade the others goodbye and drove down the winding lane leading from the cream-colored, two-story house to the main Connecticut highway and the outside world.

GEORGE PALMER PUTNAM.

AMELIA EARHART.

"They didn't tell me where they were going, so that I shouldn't be able to tell," said Mrs. Putnam Sr. an hour after the wedding.

Bride and bridegroom—he is 42 and she 32—were extremely happy but undemonstrative, Mrs. Putnam said. Miss Earhart asked to have it known that she will retain her own name for business and writing purposes. Both will be at their desks in New York, on Monday morning—she at the Pan-American Airways Company and he in his publishing firm.

The comfortable old house, said to be about eighty years old, was an ideal setting for a family wedding. With ample grounds, standing next to the local Baptist church, it is the picture of New England charm and simplicity. The ceremony, lighted by the sun's rays, for the day was cold but clear, took place in the low-ceilinged living room on the ground floor facing the southwest. The walls of this room, which is lined with bookcases in which books by Mr. Putnam and his 17-year-old son, David Binney Putnam, stand out, are painted a mustard yellow, adding to the homelike cheerfulness. As the judge performed the ceremony a crackling fire burned in the fireplace.

Got License on Nov. 8.

The house had long been set as the scene of the wedding. As long ago as Nov. 8, the couple obtained a license for marriage here, and thereafter there were rumors that they had already been married. These, however, were denied. Mrs. Putnam Sr. said today that the engagement dated back about three months, and that it was not until last night that she was informed that they were to be married today.

"They telephoned me from New York and told me they would be married here today," she said. Then they motored out last night and made arrangements with Judge Anderson, a friend of the family.

"There was no fuss, no religious ceremony, no demonstration," said Mrs. Putnam, pointing out that the house contained no flowers and that no one in the neighborhood had been informed. Brown shoes and stockings and a close-fitting brown hat were worn by Miss Earhart in addition to her brown traveling suit. Brown, it seems, is her favorite color. Mrs. Putnam Sr. wore a gray Canton crêpe house dress, and Mr. Putnam and the other men wore business attire.

Mrs. Putnam Sr. said she had never flown, but that, although somewhat fearful, she intended to make a flight with Miss Earhart soon.

"I'll take you for a ride the next time I come up here," she quoted her daughter-in-law as remarking.

"I'll not be afraid with her," she said.

So little was known of the Putnams' affairs in the village that when inquiry was made of Miss Gladys Doyle, postoffice clerk, she said: "I don't think there was any marriage in the village today." All she knew of the Putnams was that Mrs. Putnam Sr. had moved there about a year ago.

Miss Earhart did not promise to "obey" her husband, as the word is not included in the civil ceremony.

Couple Met in 1928.

The couple met first in New York in April, 1928, when Mr. Putnam was preparing to manage and direct the famous transatlantic flight which Miss Earhart was to make with the late Wilmer Stultz, pilot, and Lou Gordon, mechanic, in the tri-motored Fokker Friendship. The flight, with Miss Earhart a passenger, was made on June 17-18, 1928, in 20 hours and 49 minutes from Trepassey, N. F., to Burry Port, Wales.

Although an experienced airplanist, who had flown much before and who later distinguished herself as a pilot, Miss Earhart did not handle the controls during the flight. Characteristically modest, she wrote of it for THE NEW YORK TIMES: "I was a passenger on the journey—just a passenger. Everything that was done to bring us across was done by Wilmer Stultz and Slim Gordon. Any praise I can give them they ought to have. You can't pile it on too thick."

The men, however, were eclipsed in the welcomes given Miss Earhart in Europe and this country. From that time on she was famous. Aviation absorbed her thereafter. She had been the first woman to receive a pilot's certificate from the National Aeronautics Association in 1923, and now she flew constantly.

At one time she held the women's altitude record, having reached a height of 14,000 feet in 1920. In 1928 she flew her light Avro Avian plane across the continent and back, being the first woman to make the journey solo. Subsequently she has owned and flown a Lockheed Vega monoplane powered with a Wasp motor, which she has used constantly for business and pleasure.

In a Lockheed last Summer she established the first women's world speed record and for two years she has held a transport license, a pilot's

Newspaper account of Amelia and George Putnam's wedding, February 7, 1931.

(continued on next page)

Amelia and George Putnam, early 1930's.

AMELIA EARHART WEDS G. P. PUTNAM

Continued from Page One.

highest rating. She is the author of "Twenty Hours and Forty Minutes," the story of her transatlantic flight.

She was born in Atchison, Kan. Her father, Edwin S. Earhart, a railroad attorney, died in California last September. Her mother resides in Philadelphia. She attended the Ogontz School and later Columbia University and served in Canada as a "V. A. D." during the war. She did educational extension work for the State of Massachusetts while living in Boston and later was associated with Denison House in Boston, where she became a settlement worker.

In April, 1928, when the transatlantic flight was in preparation, with Mrs. Frederick Guest financing it, Mr. Putnam selected Miss Earhart to make the flight. She had done much flying in the West, having begun to fly in California in 1918. Today she is regarded by many as the foremost woman flier in the country.

Somewhat pale and slight, she does not look the outdoor girl she has always been. Her interest in aviation has not been confined to flying and her book. She was for a time aviation editor of The Cosmopolitan Magazine and formerly was associated with Transcontinental Air Transport. Since Sept. 1, 1930, she has been vice president of the New York-Philadelphia-Washington Airway Corporation, with offices in the Chanin Building.

Mr. Putnam is the grandson of the late George Palmer Putnam and a son of the late John Bishop Putnam, as well as a nephew of the late Major George Haven Putnam. Last August he withdrew from his position as secretary of G. P. Putnam's Sons and the next month became vice president of Brewer & Warren, publishers, 6 East Fifty-third Street.

In publishing he has especially devoted himself to works on exploration and adventure, having been responsible for the books of Colonel Lindbergh, Rear Admiral Byrd, Roy Chapman Andrews, Captain Bob Bartlett, Martin Johnson and others. His elder son, David Binney Putnam, has written three books about his explorations with William Beebe in the tropics and with his father in the North.

Mr. Putnam organized and headed two scientific expeditions, one to Greenland under the auspices of the American Museum of Natural History and the other to Baffin Island for the American Geographical Society. He is the author of four books, his most recent one having been "Andree, the Record of a Tragic Adventure," in which he described the pioneer efforts of the explorer Andree to reach the North Pole by air and the flight's tragic aftermath.

Mr. Putnam's marriage was his second, his first wife, Mrs. Dorothy Binney Putnam, having divorced him in Reno, Nev., in December, 1929, on a formal charge of failure to provide. Under its terms she and their children, David and George Palmer Jr., are provided for under a joint trust. She was married on Jan. 12, 1930, in the West Indies to Captain Frank Monroe Upton of New York, one of the heroes of the steamship Antinoe rescues.

George Palmer Putnam Jr., who is 9 years old, is in Florida with his mother, and David Binney Putnam is a student at the Roxbury School, Cheshire, Conn. The children, it was said, spend part of their time with each parent.

Miss Earhart was at one time engaged to Samuel Chapman, young Boston attorney, but she announced on Nov. 22, 1928, in Cleveland, that the engagement had been broken. "You never can tell what I will do," she said at the time. "If I was sure of the man, I might get married tomorrow. I am very sudden, you know, and make up my mind in a second."

Since living in New York Miss Earhart has resided first at the Greenwich Settlement House and, until now, at the American Women's Association Clubhouse here. Mr. Putnam has a country home at Rye, N. Y., but the couple for the present will occupy an apartment at the Hotel Wyndham, 42 West Fifty-eighth Street.

Mr. Putnam is vice president of the Explorers Club and a member of the Harvard, Wilderness, Century, Campfire, Coffee House and Apawamis Clubs. He attended Harvard University and the University of California

Amelia and GP outside their summer home, Lone Pine, California, in 1935.

Amelia, early 1930's.

I was well aware of Amelia's unwillingness to have her wings clipped by conventional marriage vows. With characteristic honesty she wrote a note to GP which she gave him on their wedding morning. In it she asked that he promise "to let me go in a year if we find no happiness together." She pledged to him, "I will try to do my best in every way."

Many well intentioned friends of both GP and Amelia prophesied a short and rocky voyage on the matrimonial sea. They said that the spoiled, talented son of wealthy parents and the independent, mature young woman who had soared to fame through pure coincidence were certain to become incompatible before long. Possibly it was because both Amelia and GP realized the hazards in their course that they avoided many danger spots by using intelligence and tolerance in their relationships. They both had consuming interests, distinct from each other: Amelia's, writing, lecturing, flying; GP's, publishing books about other people's adventures. They had much in common, too. They shared a love of the world of books, good theatre, music and art. Both enjoyed people.

GP claimed friendship with men and women famous in many fields, and Amelia delighted in knowing those who had done the unusual. Roy Chapman Andrews, explorer of China, Burma, and Tibet, and expert on Far Eastern culture, was a frequent visitor at their Rye home. Rockwell Kent, the artist, a long time friend of GP, readily included Amelia in his friendship.

Another new friendship which Amelia enjoyed was that with the brilliant actress and writer, Cornelia Otis Skinner. These two young women found they had not dissimilar backgrounds: rather insecure and unrooted childhoods and parents whose marriages had been opposed by their parents. Both Amelia and Cornelia had definite and slightly radical ideas regarding their right to independent careers. Both had broken with tradition and were pioneers in their fields. Cornelia's kindly humor, gently ridiculing the weaknesses of men and women, delighted Amelia.

The path of Amelia and GP crossed that of Charles and Anne Lindbergh occasionally at the same aviation functions. Amelia enjoyed comparing notes with Anne on their flights around the country. Amelia and Anne were alike in their determination to have a home life as nearly as possible normal and beyond the reach of the demanding and prying public. Amelia staunchly defended the colonel's brusqueness with crowds of his frenzied admirers when he refused to stop his spinning propellers and leave his plane until the police had dispersed them.

She understood how horrible and frightening it was to have her clothes grabbed and to be pushed and almost smothered. She did not blame the colonel a bit.

The first year of marriage passed and Amelia did not ask GP to release her. They had an intelligent and affectionate comradeship which weathered many unusual stresses. From the first they had an equitable financial agreement. All expenses were divided exactly between them and the surplus put into a mutual savings fund labeled "Quien sabe?" meaning "Who Knows?" Since GP was a perpetual, hard headed promoter, while Amelia was inclined to be impractical and self-effacing, clashes of ideas for money making were inevitable. The affair of the "AE hats" was a case in point. GP entered into a contract with a manufacturer of children's hats to produce a replica of Amelia's small tan cloche worn on her return from the *Friendship* flight. A darker brown ribbon with Amelia's signature reproduced on it was the only trimming. It was to be mass produced and to be sold for three dollars, with Amelia realizing a profit of fifty cents on each one. Negotiations were completed while Amelia was on a trip to California, and upon her return GP proudly showed her the sample. She was horrified and outraged.

Amelia, in the early 1930's.

FLYER DESIGNS SPORTS CLOTHES

Amelia Earhart Tells of Simple, but Smart, Dresses She Prefers

DOES NOT FOLLOW PARISIAN TRENDS

Clothes for active living—that's what Amelia Earhart calls her designs for simple clothes for women, which are on sale and on display exclusively at Jordan Marsh Company, in a new shop that is as trig and modern as an airplane. Miss Earhart herself, dressed in one of her own smart tailored outfits, sat hunched up on the floor of her room at the Hotel Manger, peered up through her tangled curly bang, and talked about her new enterprise—the designing of sports clothes.

"You know, women pilots had a lot of trouble getting practical clothes to wear flying," she said. "We had to buy men's clothes, or special models made up by stylists, and they were seldom really useful or appropriate, besides being too expensive. So we banded together and a committee was appointed by our organization to confer with manufacturers and get something useful in flying togs made."

DESIGNED OWN CLOTHES

"We began to go into the whole subject of clothes for women in sports. I was offered a chance to do some designing and I took it. Way back, years ago in my career, I used to make my own clothes from my own designs. This was like the fire bell to the old fire horse. I was right there, snorting."

Her long arms linked around her knees, her singularly beautiful hands clasped together, her long slim legs stretched out, she looked the typical American girl. Her jacket of punched white suede, with its rabbit-ears bow under the chin, and her plain dark blue woollen skirt were typical, too.

"There is a typical American type," she said. "I try to keep it in mind. I want to make clothes that are well-cut for active living and working, smart and simple, and inexpensive. The middle of the road all along. I don't want to do anything extreme, in the way of gadgets, superfluities that are expensive and likely to look dated in no time, colors that don't suit every one, or prices that are too high. I use mostly tan, brown, blue and green for colors, besides a lot of white, but no very vivid or trying shades."

CUT FOR COMFORT

"And my clothes will be cut for comfort. How I've suffered with sleeves that were too short, or shoulders too tight! For women whose figures don't conform to regular standard, I've made two-piece dresses that can be jumbled—six 16 skirts, with size 14 blouses, or vice versa. And shirt-tails will be long enough in my frocks. Haven't you cursed shirts or blouses that were too short or your skirts? I have, often, and I make my frocks easy to get into."

She is the most utterly natural, unassuming person in the world. No make-up on. Just her shining clean skin, with pink cheeks, and a powdering of golden freckles. Her hair, cut short, is as shock-headed, and as naively curled as a high school girl's. Her frequent laugh is honest, and accompanied by a shoulder hunch that is unconsciously charming.

"Most of us go along in the middle of the road when it comes to dress. The English cut of clothes is nice, but their materials are too stiff, too heavy and water-proofy. We can use softer fabrics and gentler colors.

DOES NOT FOLLOW PARIS

"Of course it's necessary to bow the head a trifle toward Paris. Nobody wants to look 'out of it.' But awfully few of us really go Parisian, you know. You see the Parisian trend is in such expensive clothes that we c[an't afford] them, or in the cheapest o[f] clothes, that we wouldn't [wear].

"I've felt for a long tim[e that the] living of an age dictates pr[ovision] for it. It isn't the other [way round.] We've really got past the [bustles] and sitting-by-the-harpsich[ord eras] that belong properly to th[e last cen]tury. And as for thos[e fluffy] dresses' with ruffles, fussy [little] frills around the neck, thos[e who] have them can still get t[hem if] they always have. I thin[k they're] basically passe."

How Miss Earhart, who [as she] puts it, "a chronic vice-pres[ident con]nected with the new airw[ays, a di]ment of the Boston and M[aine, and] and home-manager for Ge[orge Palmer] Putnam, and still essential[ly an avia]trix, works in dress design[ing, many] minutes, is a problem yet t[o solve.] But there they are, in Jor[dan's,] smartly cut flannels, shet[lands,] silks and tweeds, with the[ir smart] tailoring, their airplane g[adgets,] their look of practical, jolly, [wear]ability, that she works out from sketches, helps cut and supervises the making of.

Such conservatively tailored clothes will continue to gain in popularity, she feels, as women continue to devote themselves to interests outside the home as well as in.

"So you don't believe that woman's place is in the home?"

"I believe both men and women should be in the home some of the time, and out some of the time. Fifty-fifty. It's by no means as co-operative a world as it should be, but it's coming fast. And with it comes a change in what women think is feminine clothing. In time, things that women

Newspaper account of Amelia's latest design.

COAT DESIGNED BY MISS EARHART

Amelia Earhart wears a coat of Shetland cloth, trimmed with tailored stitching on the cuffs and collar. With it is worn one of Miss Earhart's own hat designs, simple and severe, but pert.

CREDIT: ATCHISON COUNTY HISTORICAL SOCIETY

Clothes for Women Who Live Actively!

Distinctive tailored garments made to look well, to wear well, and to give comfort, at medium prices

Amelia Earhart Fashions

are for sale at thirty stores throughout the country

BLOUSES
HATS
SUITS
DRESSES
COATS

Amelia and Carl Squier of Lockheed in front of the Vega she used to fly the Atlantic, fall 1932.

She told GP she could not ever go along with this. It was terrible. She insisted that he cancel whatever contract he made at once. GP was annoyed and bewildered. He told her the hats had already been shown around, and they were a sure money maker with youngsters.

Amelia liked that even less. First, she did not like the idea of everybody who had three dollars advertising her name; and second, she thought that they were not worth three dollars and that lots of children would be cheated. She told GP to call the man up and cancel the contract. Amelia was adamant about this, and GP reluctantly stopped production before the AE hats were on the market.

However, many commercial ventures were longer-lived. Amelia designed colorful sport clothes, suitable for plane travel; she introduced lounging pajamas and light weight airplane luggage, still marketed today. Unusual buttons shaped like bolts or twisted wires trimmed her man-tailored suits and coats. A lack of feminine furbelows characterized Amelia's designs, which were popular with wealthy business and professional women. She enjoyed creating new models but was too extravagant in her use of materials to make any profit on her custom-made clothes, so, after about a year, the label "Amelia Earhart Design" was called home and the pins and shears put away.

Amelia, November 1931.

GP was not surprised when one morning in early April, 1932, over breakfast, Amelia asked if he would mind her flying alone across the Atlantic the next spring. Within a matter of minutes, GP arranged a meeting with Bernt Balchen, a skilled Norwegian flier, who would be the master-mind behind the flight. Eddie Gorski, a Lockheed mechanic, was recruited by Bernt.

As in the *Friendship* adventure, Doc of the U.S. Weather Bureau furnished invaluable data and personally checked and rechecked conditions along the coast toward Newfoundland and as far out over the Atlantic as possible. There is little doubt that Doc Kimball knew the reason for GP's haunting his office and for Amelia's more-than-passing interest in the Atlantic ceiling, but he never gave away their secret.

Had anyone asked Amelia what force impelled her to risk her life alone over the seemingly limitless expanse of water, I imagine she would have said with a shrug and a smile, "Why, for the fun of it, of course!"

In her heart she would have admitted that the real reason for this flight was to wipe out the stigma she felt at being only a passenger on the *Friendship*. Amelia, however, was thoroughly convinced that safe flying was important for the United States and the world; hence, each flight had to open an exciting frontier which eventually would become commonplace.

Amelia in New York, preparing for her next flight, circa 1930.

Chapter Fourteen

Solo Over the Atlantic

"I'LL just have to keep going until I get to land," Amelia jokingly told GP after insisting that pontoons not be installed on her Lockheed Vega high-winged monoplane for her Atlantic flight. "You know I hate to get my hair wet!"

On the morning of Thursday, May 19, 1932, GP telephoned Amelia at the Teterboro Airport where her Vega was hangared. The weather over the Atlantic was finally acceptable for her crossing. Dressed in tan jodhpurs, a white silk blouse, windbreaker, and a bright blue and brown scarf around her neck, Amelia gathered her things and left early that afternoon. Her flying suit was already folded under the Vega's pilot's seat, and two cans of tomato juice were stashed in her knapsack. She had tucked a toothbrush and a comb in her pocket and left the house telling the housekeeper not to prepare dinner that evening. Except for a twenty dollar bill from GP for telegrams back to the United States, she planned to carry nothing else on her crossing.

Amelia, Balchen, and Gorski took off from Hasbrouck Heights, New Jersey, at 3:15 p.m., New York Daylight Savings Time. Amelia slept on the floor, using her suit as a pillow, while they flew to Saint John, New Brunswick, in three and a half hours. Early the next morning they started from Saint John and arrived at Harbour Grace, Newfoundland, about 2:15 p.m. The weather looked good, the plane was refueled, and Amelia was ready to begin.

Aviatrix Makes Perfect Start on Solo Sea Flight

'You'll Hear From Me in 15 Hours.' Her Farewell Message

Carries Only Broth as Food on Long Air Journey

HARBOR GRACE, Newfoundland, May 21 (Saturday) —At 5 o'clock this morning (2 o'clock Pacific Coast time) Amelia Earhart was more than half way to Paris and rapidly approaching the coast of Ireland if she maintained the speed which she had scheduled for her plane when she left here at 4:51 p. m. yesterday. Her plane's normal speed is 140 miles an hour with a maximum of 180 miles, but favoring winds were expected to materially increase these figures. Roughly, Paris is 3000 miles from Harbor Grace by the Great Circle route, which she expected to fly.

Far Over Sea

Amelia Earhart Putnam

CREDIT: SAN FRANCISCO CHRONICLE

Doc reported fair skies but warned her about foul weather south of the regular Atlantic crossing lanes. Before she took off, Amelia received a telegram from GP. It was characteristically unsentimental: "Have booked passage on ship tomorrow night. Will join you in France."

At 7:12, on the evening of Friday, May 20, five years to the day after Lindbergh's flight across the Atlantic, Amelia departed on her historic flight. It was a flight marked by fierce storms, the malfunctioning of mechanical equipment, and the joy of sighting land after long hours of solitary flying. Amelia's own words, first published in *The National Geographic Magazine,* best tell the story.

"Four years ago I went on the *Friendship* and, as has been said, was simply a passenger. In fact, in England I was referred to as 'a sack of potatoes.' That all too-appropriate appellation, probably as much as any other single factor, inspired me to try going alone.

"Some features of the flight I fear have been exaggerated. It made a much better story to say I landed with but one gallon of gasoline left. As a matter of fact, I had more than a hundred. The exact quantity I remember because I had to pay a tax for every gallon imported into Ireland!

"I did *not* land within six feet of a hedge of trees. I taxied to the upper end of a sloping pasture and turned my plane into the shelter of some trees, as a matter of course. It made a much better story the other way, I admit.

"No flames were threatening to burn my plane in the air. I did have some trouble with my exhaust manifold, of which I shall tell you later. There was no extreme hazard from that cause, however.

"I did not kill a cow in landing—unless one died of fright. Of course, I came down in a pasture and I had to circle many other pastures to find the best one. The horses, sheep, and cows in Londonderry were not used to airplanes, and so, as I flew low, they jumped up and down and displayed certain disquiet. I really was afraid that an Irishman would shoot me as I stepped out of the plane, thinking that I was just a 'smart Alec' from some big town come down to scare the cattle.

"To begin at the beginning, I left Harbour Grace at dusk. I preferred to fly all night and land on the other side in daylight rather than leave during the day and run the risk of landing, when daylight was failing, on an unknown shore. I had at least two hours of daylight or two hours when I could still see the glow of the setting sun if I looked back.

"I started to keep a log, but it didn't continue very long. On that log I jotted down '8:30 —two icebergs,' and a little later I recorded the fact that I had seen a small boat a couple of hours out of Harbour Grace. I was flying at 12,000 feet and I blinked my navigation lights, hoping that the vessel would sight me. However, I do not think I was seen because I received no answering signal and probably was too high to be noticed, anyway.

"Two hours after I left the moon came up over a field of little, scattered, woolly clouds. Those little woolly clouds grew compact and finally covered the ocean with their soft whiteness. I flew along with nothing happening until 11:00, when an enormous dark cloud loomed before me, stretching as far as I could see. Behind it I watched the moon finally disappear. It was entirely too high for me to climb over. I could not waste the gasoline, and flying for any length of time at 20,000 feet, which was approximately the height of the cloud, is too hard on the pilot without special apparatus.

"Two things happened before I struck the storm. One was that my altimeter, the instrument which shows height above a level, had failed me for the first time in 12 years of flying; so that I could not know how high I was above the sea. The other, a weld in my exhaust began to burn through. I knew after several hours the sections would become loosened and tend to vibrate. It was a heavy manifold and very rigidly attached to the cylinders, so that excessive vibration might have been more or less serious.

"I plunged at 11:30 into the storm cloud and met the roughest air I have ever encountered while flying completely blind. By blind I mean I could not see out of my cockpit at all. I had light there which, of course, did not cast much illumination beyond the windowpane, any more than a lamp in a house throws its glow far outside. For about an hour I could not keep my course absolutely. I was tossed about to such an

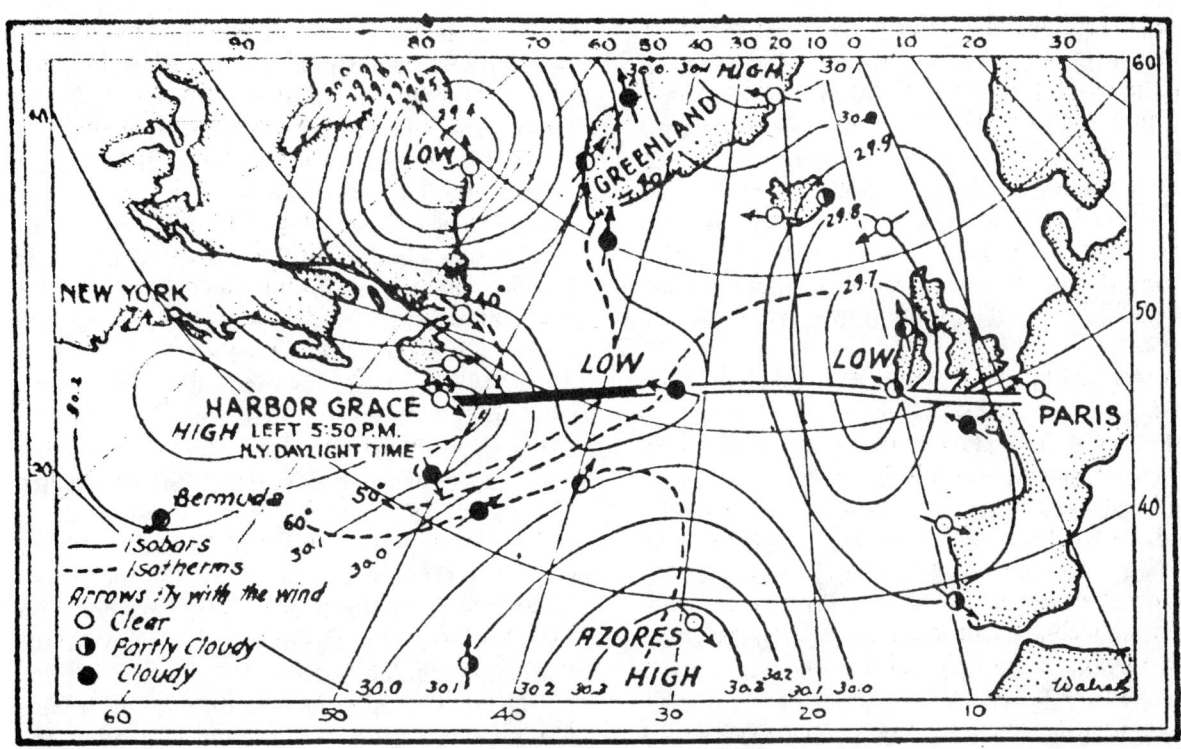

Doc Kimball's weather forecast.

extent that accuracy was impossible.

"I had been told by the Weather Bureau that there were storms south of my course; possibly those storms would come on my course about midnight, but after that I should probably have moonlight and stars.

"I did not get out of the storm area. In fact, I continued in it until daylight came. When I tried to climb out, I picked up considerable ice, and ice is a hazard which all flyers dread.

"In order to get out of the ice area, I came down. Aviators have no other protection, except to get out of the particular temperature zone where ice forms. I went down until I could see the white caps breaking in the darkness. If it had been a smooth sea, I might have gone too far.

"As my altimeter was out of commission, I could not tell whether I was 50 feet off the water or 150. I only knew I was too close; so I tried to climb through again, and again picked up ice, and concluded that I must fly under the altitude, whatever it was, where I collected ice, and over the locality where I thought the water waited.

"When daylight came I could see on my wings traces of the ice which had gathered —droplets of water and very small frozen particles. Probably, if I had been able to see what was happening on the outside during the night, I would have had heart failure then and there; but, as I could not see, I carried on.

"Instrument flying is easier sometimes than trying to see an obscure horizon. By instrument flying I mean that type of flying in which the pilot cannot see a horizon—cannot see outside his cockpit, probably. It is a curious fact that our sense of position in space sometimes depends on our being aware of the horizon. A flyer in a fog is just as blind as if he had a bandage tied over his eyes, and his unaided senses may give him the incorrect impressions. Modern instruments have been invented to help our faulty senses under such conditions.

"The instruments I had for flying were three different types of compasses—one a simple magnetic compass, the other an aperiodic, and a third a directional gyro, which has to be set about every 20 minutes with one of the others as checks. It is, by the way, one of the best blind-flying instruments I know.

"I think that instrument flying will be a significant step in aviation. With it developed, I think the weather will not hinder flying any more than it does any other means of transportation. After all, trains are stalled by washouts and ships by fogs; so their performance isn't perfect either. Probably more weather information, possibly through mid-ocean stations, will add further to aviation's reliability.

"In my opinion, any expedition owes 60 per cent of its success to the preparation beforehand. I was fortunate in having Bernt Balchen, the great Norwegian flyer, who was with Admiral Byrd at the South Pole, to help me with my preparations. In fact, he flew me to Harbour Grace to save me fatigue before the actual take-off.

"The motor I had was a super-charged Pratt and Whitney 'Wasp,' developing about 500 horsepower. I carried 420 gallons of gasoline. I had flown my plane for three years; so I really ought to know it and it ought to know me. Of course, I had the advantage of having crossed once before and of knowing something of the conditions which were inevitable—that no one can expect good weather over the Atlantic for 2,000 miles.

"For food I carried a very simple ration —tomato juice. I think that serves as food and drink, and I used just a few swallows of it. I had no sandwiches or anything of that sort with me. The fact is, one doesn't think much about food on such a journey.

"I have been asked many times whether I was sleepy, and I can say, 'No, indeed,' emphatically. With very concentrated flying, one becomes wider and wider awake. Then, after all, one night is not any particular strain. One can do almost anything for one night; so that I did not have any great fatigue. Possibly, if the night had been a beautiful, clear one, with the moon and stars shining and with nothing for me to do, I might have got somewhat drowsy. Flying in the kind of weather I met, however, made even winking an eye impossible.

"When daylight came I found myself between two layers of clouds. One I should estimate at 20,000 feet and the other a thousand feet over the water. With a glimpse of the water that I had then, which was the first in many hours, I noted that I had a strong northwest wind. I thought then that I must be south of my course, inasmuch as I had run into storms predicted south of my course, and I found myself in a northwest wind. Therefore, instead of following implicitly the course which I had laid out, I tried to allow for what I considered my southward drift. Consequently I hit Ireland farther north than I had expected.

"With my exhaust burned out, as it was by that time, I thought it was common sense to check over the first land available, and I did not want to miss the tip of Ireland. So I corrected too much. After sighting land, I started down toward the southern coast, found thunderstorms in the mountains, and, not knowing the topography of the region, thought it was not very sensible to try to fly through. I then turned north into clearer weather.

"Using United States reasoning in Ireland was not quite effective. I thought if I followed a railroad I should come to a large town, and a large town would have an airport, as they usually do here. I found the railroad, followed it, came to a fair-sized city, but found no port. Consequently I selected the best pasture I could find and settled down in it. I pulled up at the front door of a farmhouse and asked the surprised farmer for a drink of water—an unusual request in Ireland, I found!

"Probably more exciting than actually sighting land was seeing a small fishing vessel about 100 miles off the coast. I was going by, as I wanted to reach land, but then decided to circle, that all might know I had got so far, anyway. I circled and received an answering signal. A whistle and some kind of bomb was sent off. Of course, I could not hear them, but I could see the smoke and the steam from the whistle. It was the first human contact since Newfoundland.

"My flight has added nothing to aviation. After all, literally hundreds have crossed the Atlantic by air, if those who have gone in heavier-than-air and lighter-than-air craft are counted and those who have crossed the North and the South Atlantic. However, I hope that the flight has meant something to women in

Amelia arriving in Culmore, Ireland, May 21, 1932.

aviation. If it has, I shall feel it was justified; but I can't claim anything else."

Amelia had set her red Vega down in James Gallagher's pasture on the outskirts of Londonderry, Ireland, on Saturday morning, May 21, 1932, fourteen hours and fifty-six minutes after taking to the air at Harbour Grace. Her flight would live forever among the great flights made through the years.

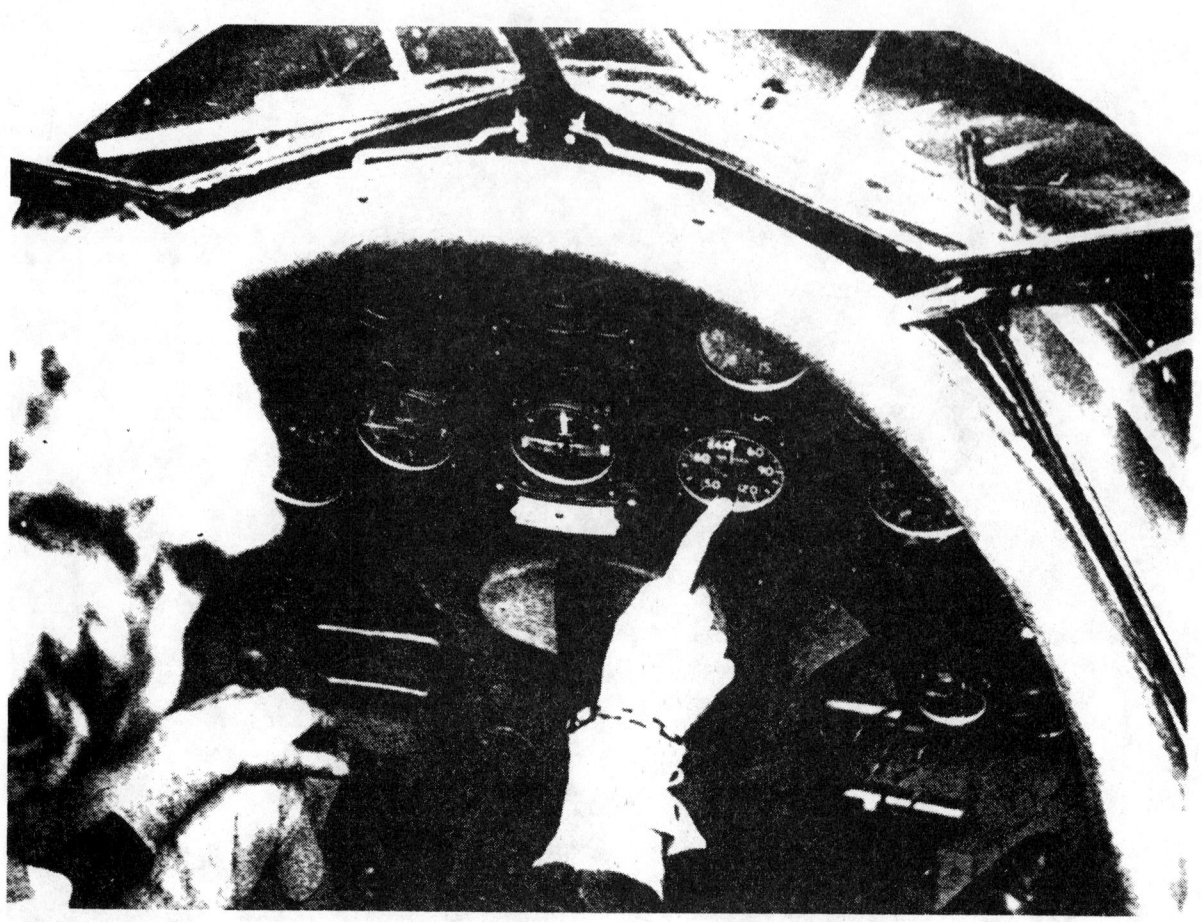

Inside Amelia's Vega. She is pointing to the airspeed indicator on the instrument panel, May 1932.

San Francisco Chronicle
The City's Only Home-Owned Newspaper

SAN FRANCISCO, CAL., SUNDAY, MAY 22, 1932 — DAILY 5 CENTS

Ireland Greets Earhart After Solo Hop Across Sea From Harbor Grace

Motor Exhaust Pipe Burned Out and Leaky Gas Line End Flight

Brings Plane Down in Pasture on Ulster Farm

CULMORE, Ulster, North Ireland, May 21 (P)—Amelia Earhart Putnam, the first woman ever to fly the Atlantic alone, landed this afternoon in a field in this green countryside after a hazardous flight in which she conquered fog and storm and the even more dangerous menace of fire.

Four hours after she put out yesterday afternoon from Harbor Grace, Newfoundland, she saw flames spitting from her exhaust. But she didn't turn back.

"I thought it safer to go ahead," she said.

SLEEPS IN FARMHOUSE

Tonight she slept in the farmhouse of Robert Gallagher, owner

WILL BROADCAST TODAY

NEW YORK, May 21 (P)—Amelia Earhart Putnam will be heard at 8 a.m. (Pacific Coast time) tomorrow in a transatlantic broadcast from London through the Columbia Broadcasting Company network.

of the field in which she landed. Tomorrow she will go to Croydon, England, in a borrowed airplane, having her own red and gold monoplane to be crated up and shipped back home.

Flying on the fifth anniversary of the successful conclusion of Colonel Charles A. Lindbergh's New York-Paris hop, she put her name just under his on the roll of transatlantic honors, for Colonel Lindbergh is the only other person in the world who has made a solo transatlantic flight.

FARM OWNER SURPRISED

ATLANTIC'S FIRST QUEEN

Mrs. Amelia Earhart Putnam, photographed at the start of her flight across the Atlantic.

Skimmed Sea Most of Way, Says Amelia

Rather Drown Than Burn, She Tells Husband in Phone Chat

Special to The Chronicle

NEW YORK, May 21—Amelia Earhart Putnam, only woman to fly the Atlantic alone, only person to fly it twice and second soloist over its northern wastes, told her husband, George Palmer Putnam, over the transatlantic telephone this afternoon a story of a nightmare over the ocean.

DO-X Lands In Azores on Flight Home

Air Liner Makes Hop in Sixteen Hours 55 Minutes

NEW YORK, May 21 (P)—The Do-X, giant of all heavier-than-air craft, tonight completed the third leg of her homeward flight to Lake Constance, Switzerland.

Sixteen hours and 55 minutes after she lifted her bulk from the waters of Holyrood, Newfoundland, the twelve-motored seaplane came to a

Rum Runner Hunted for Lindy Clue

Man Who Told of Murder Two Days Before Body Was Found Evades Search

Jafsie Starts Mystery Auto Trip to Rhode Island

HOPEWELL, N. J., May 21 (P)—The Lindbergh murder investigation turned tonight into a concerted hunt for a Jersey rum runner who, two days before the famous baby's body was found, told how the infant had been killed and where the battered little form had been hidden.

There is a possibility this unnamed character may hold the key to the secrets of what is already one of the world's strangest crime mysteries.

He has boasted, it was disclosed today, that he knows several of the band who perpetrated the fiendish kidnaping and killing.

JAFSIE ON MYSTERY TRIP

As new light was thrown on this mysterious character, "Jafsie," the ransom payer, went dashing through New England on an unexplained mission.

At the same time another of the bills used in paying the $50,000 ransom was reported to have turned up at a New York bank. Direct confirmation of the report was lacking.

The two-day hunt for the man identified by State police only as "a gangster reported in Maryland and thought to be connected with the case" was given real significance by Arthur Mills, identification expert at the Maryland House of Correction.

REFUSES TO NAME MAN

At Baltimore Mills refused to identify the fugitive, but said he is a character long identified with the liquor traffic in New Jersey.

CREDIT: SAN FRANCISCO CHRONICLE

Amelia arriving in Londonderry, May 21, 1932.

Chapter Fifteen

Honors Beyond Imagination

AMELIA'S welcome at the American Embassy in London was that given to a genuinely-loved friend. The many congratulatory telegrams and cables touched Amelia deeply. She enjoyed the message from Phil Cooper, the owner of the dry cleaning business which she and GP patronized. He cabled, "Knew you would do it. I never lose a customer." In the midst of their personal tragedy, Colonel and Mrs. Lindbergh cabled, "We do congratulate you. Your flight is a splendid success." There were the adverse critics too: one columnist characterized the flight as "a useless display of courage;" another called her "unwomanly."

Amelia had an audience with the prince of Wales. Unknowingly, Amelia was signally honored because his royal highness prolonged her visit at the palace by more than a half hour to draw from her the details of her flight. After she left, the prince declared with sincerity that he envied her freedom in flying. He would like to have his own plane and license too, but British tradition was hard to circumvent. He expressed his happiness that her second flight also had a successful termination in the United Kingdom.

Amelia received the Certificate of Honorary Membership of the British Guild of Airpilots and Navigators, an organization as august and selective as its title is impressive. With the exception of Dr. Hugo Eckener, she was at that time the only non-British pilot so honored.

As soon as GP heard of Amelia's safe arrival, he rushed from his New York office where he had spent the night, mentally flying with her. He reached the North River Pier just in time to get aboard the *S.S. Olympic* so he could keep his promised date with his wife in France.

Amelia left London to keep an important appointment in France. She was the guest of the C.R. Faireys aboard their yacht, *Evadne*, for the Channel crossing, and when the *Olympic* docked at Cherbourg, France, GP had an early reunion with Amelia. The French Senate had voted to receive her, the first woman of a foreign country to be invited within those sacred precincts. She was awarded the Cross of the Legion of Honor by the French Minister, M. Painlevé, who, five years before, had similarly decorated Colonel Lindbergh.

Amelia and GP continued to Rome where Amelia had been invited to attend a meeting of world-wide ocean fliers. The sessions were over when they arrived, which undoubtedly prevented Mussolini's government from facing an uncomfortable dilemma: either to accept Amelia as a woman flier who certainly deserved a medal for her achievements, or to ignore her as a flier because she was of the sex whose only glory and duty should be staying at home minding numerous children. Officially Amelia received no awards from Italy, but privately she and GP were entertained by General Italo Balbo of the Italian Air Force. More than a year later in Chicago, a so-called Balbo medal was bestowed upon Amelia by Dr. Giuseppe Castruccio, Italian consul-general. Evidently the consul or the general or both had spoken out of turn, for, scarcely two weeks after the public presentation, Amelia received a letter designed to correct the erroneous impression that the medal was a gift of the Italian government. No, indeed, it was merely "a token of personal esteem for the recipient." The handsome piece of hardware with its red, white, and green ribbon was immediately carefully packed, insured, and sent back to General Balbo with a letter explaining that Amelia could not accept so valuable a decoration as a personal gift. Perhaps Amelia and Dr. Castruccio should be exonerated for their misunderstanding because inscribed on the case were these words: "Conferred on Amelia Earhart by the Italian Government, May 23, 1935."

Amelia and GP were received by the king and queen of the Belgians. They had a delightfully informal luncheon at the summer residence at Laeken, and while Amelia discussed transoceanic air travel with his majesty, GP enlarged upon American rose culture at the request of her majesty, an ardent amateur gardener. At a formal and glittering convocation later in the day, King Albert conferred upon Amelia the Cross of Chevalier of the Order of Leopold. GP was eager to talk with the Belgian stratosphere balloonist, Auguste Piccard, because Piccard soon expected to publish a book describing his many balloon adventures. Amelia and GP greatly enjoyed meeting this sturdy pioneer, who although an avowed "lighter-than-air-craft" man, had words of praise and appreciation for Amelia, an advocate from the other camp.

Amelia in the French Chamber of Deputies with the American Ambassador and French Air Minister M. Paul Painlevé where she received Cross of Legion d'Honneur.

Amelia and Commander Pennoyer, sightseeing in Rome, 1932.

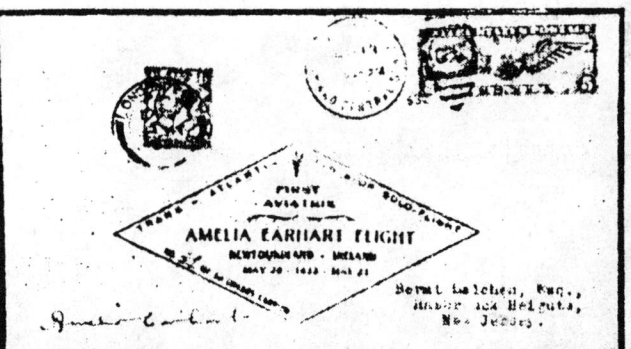

One of about 50 covers carried by Amelia Earhart on her solo transatlantic flight of May 20, 1932.

Library in Miniature

AMELIA EARHART.

1—When did Miss Earhart make her first flight across the Atlantic?
2—What was the name of the airplane that carried her?
3—What was the route of that flight?
4—How long did the trip take?
5—In what time did Miss Earhart made her solo flight?
6—What records did she achieve in her latest flight?

ANSWERS.

1—On June 17-18, 1928, piloted by Wilmer Stultz and Lou Gordon, Miss Earhart made her first transatlantic flight. She was, as she says herself, "strictly a passenger."
2—The Friendship.
3—The plane took off from Trepassy, Newfoundland, and landed at Burry Port, Wales.
4—The 2,137 mile trip was made in 20 hours and 40 minutes.
5—In her latest and solo flight, Miss Earhart, flying from Harbor Grace to Londonderry, Ireland, made the 2,026-mile trip in 14 hours and 56 minutes, an average of 135 miles an hour.
6—She was the first woman to make a transatlantic solo flight; she has established a new record time for linking the old and new worlds by air and she is the first person, man or woman, to fly the Atlantic twice by plane.

John Oliver LaGorce, left and Gilbert Grosvenor, both of the National Geographic Society, greating Amelia.

Amelia welcomed at Washington, D.C. airport as she arrives to receive the National Geographic Medal, June 21, 1932.

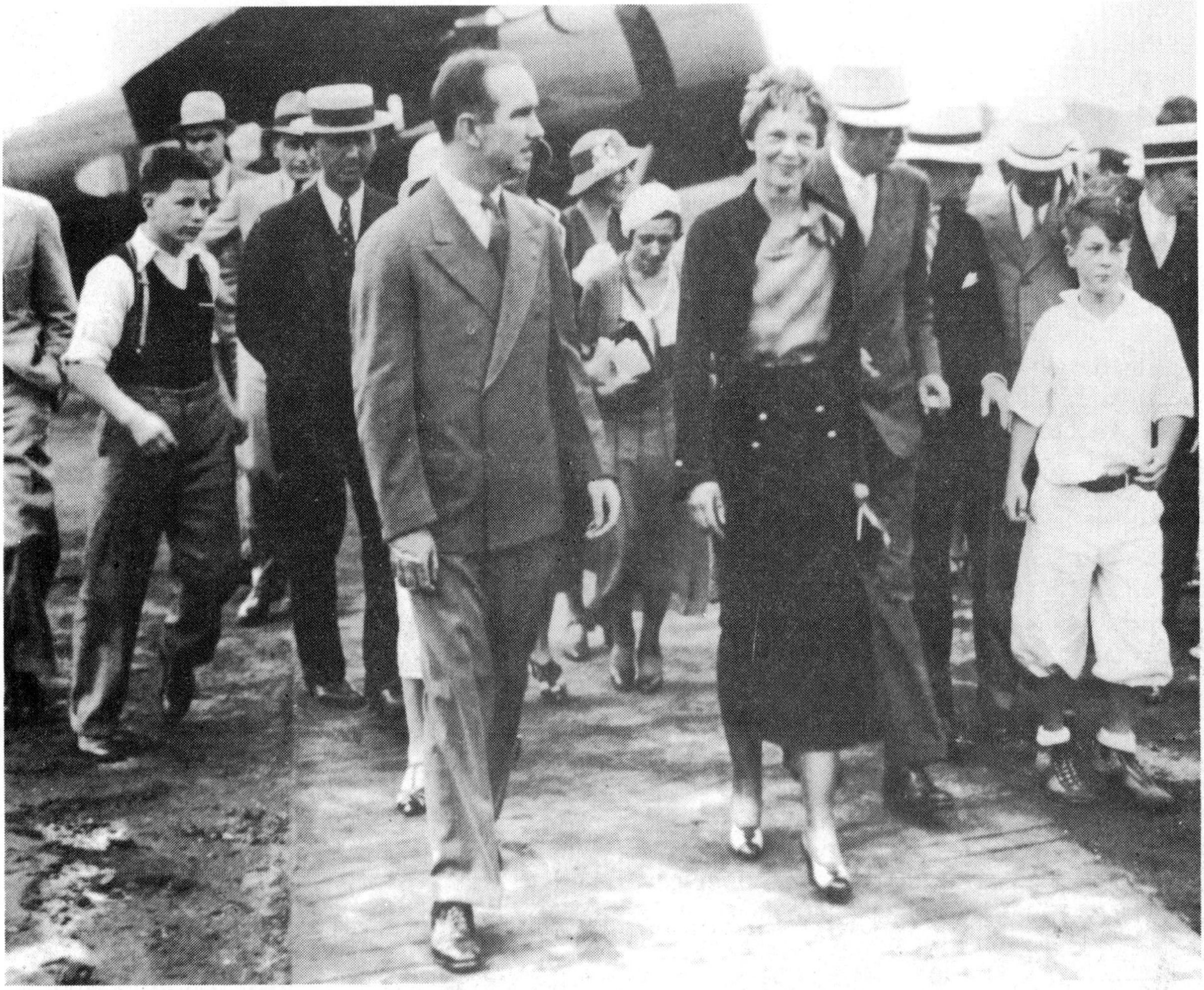

CREDIT: HISTORICAL PICTURES SERVICE, CHICAGO (Harris & Ewing 3-15-435-15)

Amelia in Washington, D.C., June 21, 1932.

CREDIT: NATIONAL GEOGRAPHIC SOCIETY

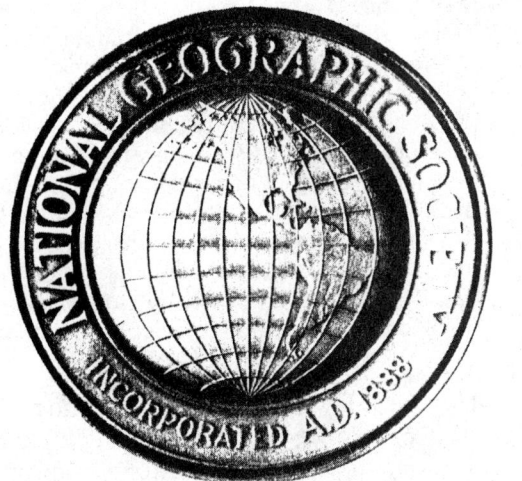

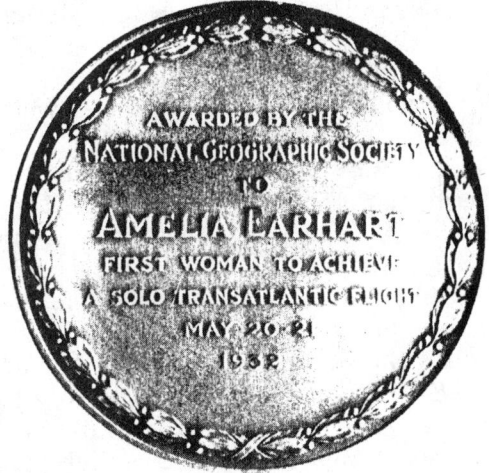

Medal presented to Amelia on June 21, 1932, by President Herbert Hoover.

After a few days of shopping and sightseeing in Paris, she and GP embarked from Cherbourg for the United States on the *Ile de France*. As they stood together at the rail and watched the shore recede, Amelia thanked GP for the wonderful three weeks. Amelia knew that if it hadn't been for his help, she would not have been able to make the flight solo—at least not that time.

Amelia, lightly wearing her fame, returned home again.

Amelia returned to the United States to be honored in scientific circles as few other woman have been. The National Geographic Society voted to present their gold medal to her for her contribution to the science of aviation. According to the society's custom, the president of the United States was to make the presentation. Amelia and GP were invited to the White House to a dinner preceding the ceremony.

In talking with the president at dinner, Amelia said she mentioned her visit with King Albert of the Belgians, who had expressed his undying gratitude to Herbert Hoover for saving thousands of Belgian refugee and orphan children from starvation during the tragic days of World War I.

Amelia said President Hoover was obviously pleased and replied that he thought the incident was one of the most satisfying assignments he ever undertook. He told her that he was frequently frustrated and handicapped by lack of funds and workers, but he believed that this effort showed the world the generous spirit of the American people. President Hoover told her that she had added immeasurably to our country's stature, too, and he concluded with a courtly bow.

After the dinner, the White House party went to Constitution Hall, the beautiful gold and white assembly rooms of the Daughters of the American Revolution. The Marine Band played "Hail to the Chief" as the president mounted the steps to the stage with Amelia on his arm. Dr. Gilbert Grosvenor, president of the Society, presented President Hoover, who gave what Amelia later described as a "mercifully short speech" and then presented the beautiful medal to her.

The president's introduction was gratifying

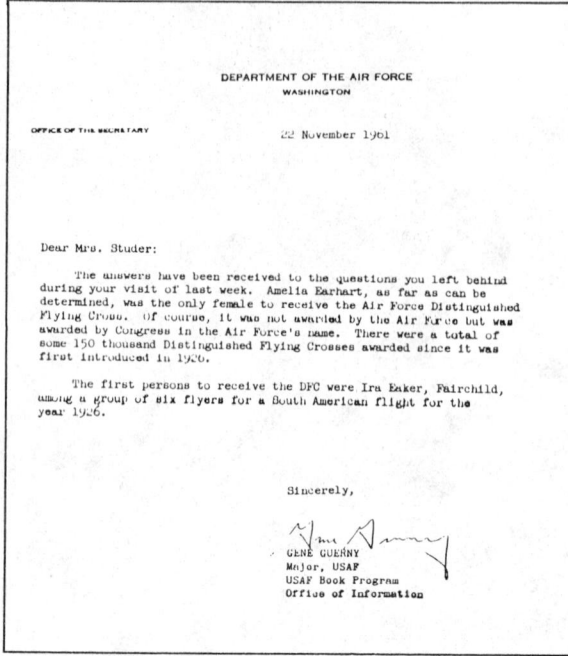

Letter from the Air Force noting Amelia's being one of the few to receive the Air Force Distinguished Flying Cross.

to Amelia, not only because of its brevity, but because of its appraisal of her flight by a man of kindred scientific and engineering interests. He said in part:

> Amelia has a place with the great pioneering women to whom every generation of Americans has looked with admiration for their firmness of will, their strength of character, and their cheerful spirit of comradeship in the work of the world. Her success has not been won by the selfish pursuit of a purely personal ambition, but as part of a career generously animated by a wish to help others to share in the rich opportunities of life, and by a wish to enlarge those opportunities by expanding the powers of women as well as men to their ever-widening limits . . . The nation is proud that an American woman should be the first woman in history to fly an airplane alone across the Atlantic Ocean.

The next day before a joint meeting of the House of Representatives and the Senate, Amelia was awarded the Distinguished Flying Cross, the first woman in our history to be so honored.

President Herbert Hoover and Amelia.

Recognition of another sort came to Amelia from Thiel College of Greenville, Pennsylvania, Dad's beloved Alma Mater. At the 1932 Fall Honors Convocation, Amelia received the honorary degree of Doctor of Science. The citation reads in part:

> To Thiel College has come an opportunity to honor one of the greatest women of our time—Amelia Earhart, not only because she is one of aviation's pioneers, but also because she is a woman whose high character has endowed all her attainments with unusual significance . . . Amelia Earhart is an ideal representative of American womanhood. Aviation is but one of her interests, all of which were motivated by the wish to help others. Despite her choice of a career which kept her continually in the public eye and despite the honors showered upon her, Amelia Earhart has always retained her dignity, her modesty, her preference for a simple mode of life, and the high-mindedness reflected in her every word and deed.

Amelia enjoyed her short visit on the Thiel campus. As she left for the drive back to New York, she looked over the distant hills, the rolling well-kept lawn, and the great trees wearing their golden autumn foliage. It was as beautiful as Dad had always said it was. She wished that he had been able to come back and be honored as an alumnus in her stead.

AMELIA EARHART

Dear Mother,

As usual I got caught and didnt send my Xmas box in time to reach Mudford for the holiday. However it will come.

I had a very interesting time at Thiel. I met several people who were in Dads class and others who knew him. I found his record for scolarship, ie age of graduation has never been equalled. He was fourteen when he entered college and only eighteen when he got his degree. The crowd at the convocation was the greatest ever assembled and a number were turned away. Everyone remembered Dad as so handsome and bright. His nickname was "Kid". I didnt know that slang was popular then. Kid Earhart now sounds like a prize fighter. His best friend and class mate introduced me, a nice old codger who was once president of the college and now lives in N.J. He said he saw him last in Phila. when he came there some years ago and bunked in his rooms. I dont know whether this was before or after you were married.

I stayed all night and then drove to Toronto in a sleet storm.

Well as I started out to say Murry Xmas.

Amelia's letter discussing her return to Thiel College in 1932, where she was awarded an honorary doctorate.

UNION OIL BULLETIN *for* AUGUST, 1932

Amelia Earhart Spans Continent in Record Time

Amelia Earhart (Mrs. George Palmer Putnam in other than aeronautic circles) is seen here supervising loading of her ship with Union aviation gasoline prior to her transcontinental hop last month, when she bettered the former woman's record for a Pacific to Atlantic flight by more than ten hours. Miss Earhart lifted her plane, loaded with 426 gallons of gasoline, from Los Angeles Municipal Airport at 1:11:25 p. m. July 12 and, despite a forced landing at Columbus, Ohio, landed at Newark, N. J., port the following day at noon. The Lockheed Vega which Miss Earhart flew on the transcontinental flight was the same in which she spanned the Atlantic. As in that epochal flight, Miss Earhart flew alone. Her elapsed time for the trip was 19 hours, 14 minutes, and 10 seconds, within an hour of Frank Hawks' record which has stood since 1929.

Amelia with our mother, Amy Earhart, in 1932 in North Hollywood.

1932 celebration with stepson David Putnam, Amelia, Mayor Porter of New York, and George P. Putnam.

Amelia's position at the pinnacle of aviation fame demanded that she follow one of two courses: either vanish into semi-retirement as Colonel Lindbergh chose to do, or else accept the challenge of making more pioneering flights in the as-yet-unexplored skyway. Amelia, if not actually urged by GP, certainly abetted by him, chose the latter course.

During the years of the early nineteen-thirties when I was reveling in the delights of motherhood with my small son and daughter, I was frequently asked, "Doesn't Amelia want children?" In reply, I could only quote what Amelia once said to me during one of her brief visits at our Medford home. Watching my son climb up on a bright rope-tailed rocking horse while my little daughter was engaged in dumping the blocks out of a cart and then reloading it, she said suddenly, "You are lucky, Pidge."

She paused a moment, then continued, whimsically, "If it just didn't take so long to make a baby . . . There are so many exciting flying things to be done. Maybe, next year . . . " But of course that "next year" never came.

Amelia was deeply concerned with GP's two young sons. When they came to visit at the home in Rye, Amelia cancelled all her outside engagements and persuaded GP to do the same, so they could devote their time to the boys, horseback riding, sailing on the Sound, swimming, and picnicking. Amelia's sincere interest in them was repaid by their real affection for their famous, fun-loving stepmother.

Amelia enjoying the National Air Races, July 2, 1933.

WOMAN FLIER OFFERS PRIZE FOR WOMEN

Amelia Earhart, Best-Known Woman Flier, Sponsors Prize for Woman Flier

Amelia Earhart, premier woman flier of the world and the only woman who has ever made a solo flight across the Atlantic ocean, has announced that she will sponsor an Amelia Earhart trophy race to be held for woman fliers at the national air races in Cleveland during the week of August 27-September 5.

First prize of an Essex Terraplane automobile will be awarded by Miss Earhart to the woman winning first place in this race, which will be the biggest women's event in connection with this year's national air races. Numerous entries already have been received.

Miss Earhart recently christened the next Essex Terraplane automobile at Detroit. The car which she christened at a public ceremony later was presented by the Hudson Motor Car company to Orville Wright of Dayton, Ohio, inventor of the airplane.

The Terraplane, because of its high power to weight ratio, has many of the characteristics of the airplane. Hudson engineers have announced that a Terraplane engine, placed in an airplane of the same weight as a Terraplane car, would fly the airplane at a rate of as high as 100 miles per hour.

Amelia Earhart obtained her first practical experience in mechanics with automobile engines at a New England school. Her interest became so great that she soon took up flying, and now is credited with being the world's greatest woman flier.

When the new Essex Terraplane automobile was developed, Miss Earhart took a keen interest in it, and soon following her trans-Atlantic flight she inspected the new car at the Hudson factories in Detroit.

Her christening of the new Terraplane car before a crowd of thousands of Detroiters and the subsequent driveaway of 2000 of the new cars by Hudson-Essex dealers from all parts of the United States, was reported to have been the biggest industrial celebration ever staged in Detroit, which is no novice to automobile demonstrations.

At the christening Miss Earhart publicly stated that the Terraplane car is of particular interest to aviators because of its high power to weight ratio and the steady manner in which it handles at high speeds.

CREDIT: THE OAKLAND TRIBUNE

Amelia sponsors a trophy race at the Cleveland Air Races, August 21, 1932.

Amelia, right, with Cliff Henderson and Margaret Perry at the Cleveland Air Races on July 2, 1933.

CREDIT: DAVID D. HATFIELD AVIATION COLLECTION

Amelia in 1932 at the Lockheed factory. Left to right: Amelia, Allan Lockheed, Carl Squier, and Lloyd Stearman

Vera (Doane) Christen, switchboard operator and later the first woman to be promoted to manager at Lockheed. Vera greeted Amelia and many other customers. July 7, 1933.

Amelia at Robinson's Department Store, Los Angeles, autographing copies of **The Fun Of It**, *which she wrote in 1932.*

In November, 1934, Amelia went to California to have her Lockheed Vega overhauled at the factory. GP planned to join her as they expected to consult with the architect who was drawing plans for their home in North Hollywood. The house in Rye was to be closed since GP stayed at his mother's home in Connecticut when Amelia was away for any length of time. Jim, the trusted houseman, was directed to wait until the water company shut off the water and drained the pipes; then he was to turn off the oil burner and lock the doors. After the water was shut off, Jim locked the doors but forgot to disconnect the heater. The large tank of fuel oil was nearly full, so the heater heated the empty boiler which after several hours became almost red hot. The heavy, uncovered beams over the furnace began to char and smolder. A fire burned through the floor of the dining room. As the house was tightly closed, there was no circulation of air, and the fire did not blaze until more than twelve hours after Jim had locked the front door and left for his home in New Jersey. Eventually the pressure of the hot air within the building forced out two panes of glass, and then the interior became an inferno. Firefighters, summoned at four o'clock in the morning by a passing motorist who heard the explosion and saw the leaping flames, arrived in time to save most of the second floor and the rooms on the first floor in the front of the house. GP, notified by neighbors, reached the scene as the firemen were preparing to seal off the water-soaked and still smoking ruins from the undamaged front portion of the house. He made a quick inventory and then sadly sought a telephone to tell Amelia of the fire's havoc.

When he reached Amelia in Los Angeles and broke the news to her, GP said that it was characteristic of Amelia to first think of his grief and loss, not her own. Her first words to GP were about, "How are your father's books?"

GP told Amelia that most of the books were not damaged because the heavy built-in bookcases protected them from smoke and water. But he told her the Rockwell Kent paintings were gone. Everything in the dining room was destroyed and the silver was a shapeless mass in a pile of ashes which had been their rosewood buffet.

GP also told Amelia that her beautiful teak wood trophy chest bearing the carved records of her flights was miraculously saved, but she did not ask about that. The chest contained her medals and decorations and had been pushed into a closet under the stairs in front of the house. Much as Amelia appreciated receiving the medals, awards, and citations, they never were placed on display or even mentioned by her.

Wright Honored Here On 30th Anniversary Of Pioneer Air Flight

Noted Inventor Guest, Amelia Earhart Speaker, as Dedication Service Is Held for Aviation Section of Franklin Memorial

Orville Wright and Amelia in December, 1933.

Orville Wright, who thirty years ago yesterday flew 540 feet, remaining aloft twelve seconds, was guest of honor yesterday afternoon when the thirtieth anniversary of this epoch-making first flight by a power-propelled airplane carrying a man was celebrated by exercises at the Benjamin Franklin Memorial and the Franklin Institute, on the Parkway at Twentieth Street.

Amelia Earhart, who a year and a half ago was the first woman to fly alone across the Atlantic, was there to pay honor to the distinguished pioneer.

Standing beneath the plane in which she not only flew across the Atlantic but also achieved the longest nonstop flight yet made by a woman, Miss Earhart dedicated the aviation section of the Franklin Institute, where her famous Lockheed-Vega now has been permanently installed.

Picture shows Orville Wright, guest of honor at a celebration yesterday at the Benjamin Franklin Memorial and the Franklin Institute of the thirtieth anniversary of the first flights ever made by man in a power-propelled airplane—the achievement of himself and his brother, Wilbur Wright. With him is Amelia Earhart, who yesterday dedicated the new aviation section of the Institute standing beneath the monoplane in which Miss Earhart was the first woman to fly alone across the Atlantic

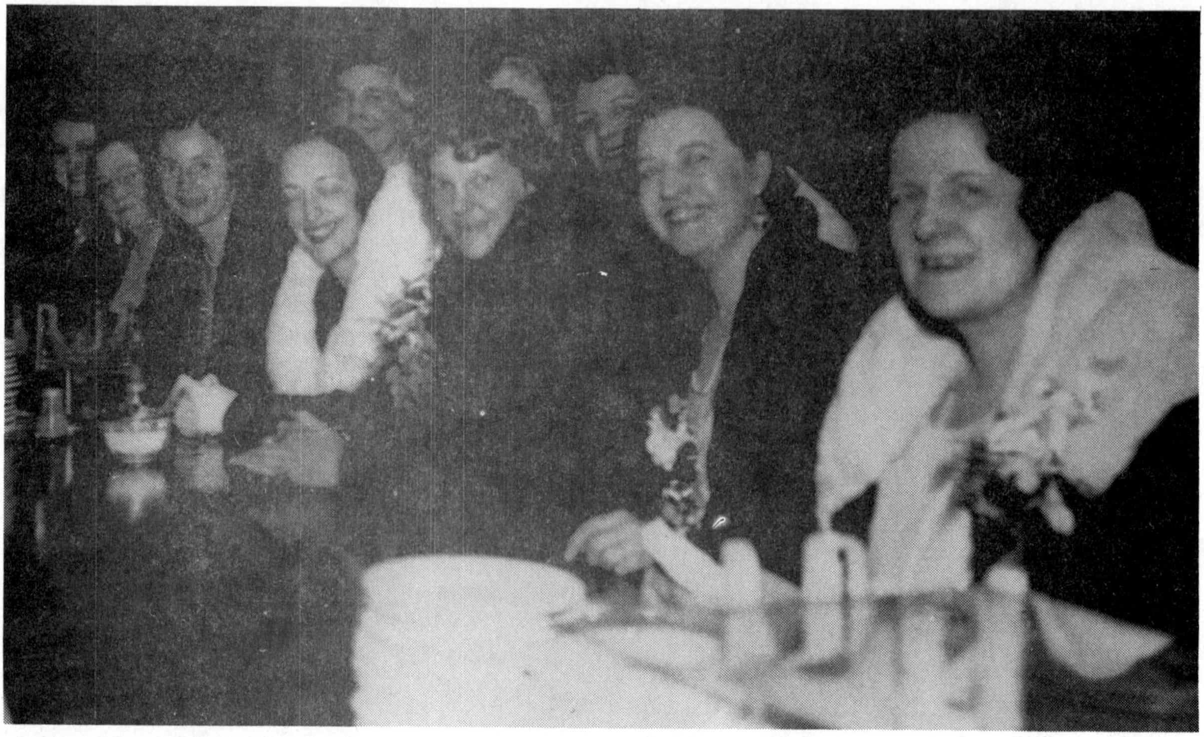

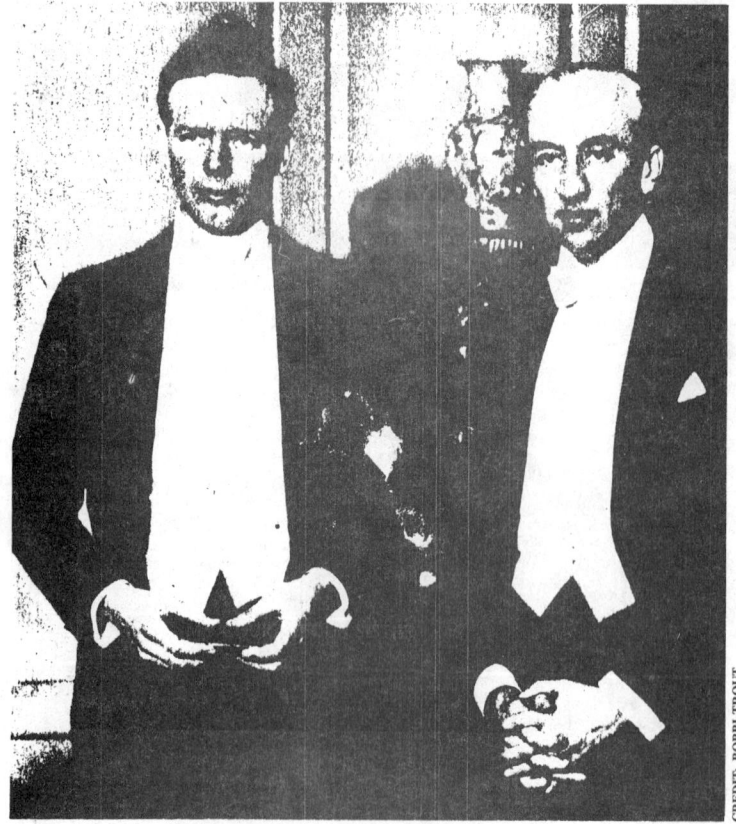

After a formal banquet, Amelia and several Zonta members went across the street to a sandwich shop where they enjoyed a snack. 1934, Springfield, MA.

CREDIT: BOBBI TROUT

King Carol of Rumania minted a gold cross medal to recognize outstanding feats in aviation. Charles Lindbergh, left, receives this medal from Charles A. Davila, the Rumanian Minister to the United States. Amelia and Bobbi Trout (facing page) were the only other Americans to receive this honor from King Carol.

CREDIT: BOBBI TROUT

Amelia, circa 1936, at Mission Inn, Riverside, California.

DRIVER'S LICENSE

It was decided the other day in Los Angeles that Amelia Earhart was fit to drive an automobile. But she was forced first through a rigamarole of starting and stopping, signaling and parking, that must have seemed a peck of nonsense to her. Taking off and landing are for Miss Earhart, not usually confined to the limits of bumpers and tail lights.

But what hero is not required at some time in the course of events to step down to the mere pedestrian status? The stock exchange president must occasionally walk to work, and great actresses ride on street cars. The pity is, they do not always accept the come down gracefully.

The more credit to Miss Earhart that she took *hers* with a smile. Even common folks have been known to boil under the overhauling of a motor vehicle bureau inspector.

CREDIT: THE OAKLAND TRIBUNE

Amelia and Husband Buy Hollywood Home

LOS ANGELES, Sept. 10.—(*P*)—Amelia Earhart turned architect-builder today.

With her publisher - husband, George Palmer Putnam, the noted aviatrix has purchased a home in North Hollywood. They plan to add a second story and make a few other changes.

It isn't likely, however, that Miss Earhart is deserting the sky lanes. The new home is located a short distance from Union Air Terminal, where she keeps her plane.

CREDIT: OAKLAND TRIBUNE

The medal awarded to Amelia by King Carol of Rumania.

CREDIT: CLAUDIA OAKES, SMITHSONIAN INSTITUTION

George Putnam and Amelia at their Rye home, circa 1936.

Amelia Earhart's Honolulu-to-Oakland Flight Branded Stunt That May Turn Into Costly Tragedy

Nothing to Be Gained, Much May Be Lost, Say Aviation Experts

Aviation experts of the Bay Region protested today the proposed Honolulu - to - Oakland flight of Amelia Earhart-Putman as extremely hazardous, valueless to aviation if it succeeds and a costly setback if it fails.

Heralded as a scientific adventure, the flight which the world's foremost woman flyer is making is in reality a publicity stunt, The News learned today. She has entered into $10,000 contract with the Pan-Pacific Press Bureau of San Francisco, which already has paid $5000 to George Palmer Putman, her husband and manager.

For this Miss Earhart is not only risking her life in a plane which, if it maintains almost maximum speed and flies under ideal conditions, will have less than 50 gallons of gasoline left when it lands at Oakland, according to aviation experts, but the Federal Government might be compelled to expend $100,000 or more searching for her.

Ulm Tragedy Is Example

Fresh in the minds of the Army, Navy, Coast Guard and airport officials is the ill-fated flight last month of Charles T. P. Ulm, which cost the lives of the Australian flyer and his two companions. Forty-two craft, including 20 Navy planes and several Coast Guard vessels, joined in the search for Ulm's Star of Australia.

Already charted by Sir Charles Kingsford-Smith, Australian air ace, nothing can be gained by Miss Earhart in flying the west-east route, officials declared. Such authorities as Capt. Eugene Blake, Commander F. C. Connell, Maj. Donald P. Hughes, Lieut. Commander Clarence H. Schildauer and others point out transocean flights should be attempted only in large planes equipped to stay afloat several days.

Since the contract between the Pan-Pacific Association and Miss Earhart, which calls for the final $5000 payment before she takes off from Honolulu, was signed several months ago, they have attempted to throw a veil of secrecy about the flight. Even as late as Dec. 22, when she sailed from Los Angeles for Hawaii, Miss Earhart declined to verify reports she would try to make the flight.

Lectures in Islands

She is now engaged in flying to the various islands, lecturing at the University of Hawaii, and if the jaunt is successful, has entered into a contract to exploit the flight and Hawaii in two magazine articles. The flight is a part of a publicity campaign of the Hawaiian Sugar Planters' Association to defeat the Jones-Costigan Sugar Control Act, adopted by Congress last May.

Since passage of the Jones-Costigan Act, by which domestic sugar quotas and territorial possession quotas are limited under the AAA, the Sugar Planters' Association entered into a contract with Bowman, Deute, Cummings, Inc., San Francisco advertising agency, for an educational and advertising campaign to change public opinion in the United States against the act as it applied to Hawaii.

Sydney Bowman, president of the advertising firm, formed the Pan-Pacific Press Bureau for the purpose of carrying on the $125,000 campaign. He reached an agreement with Miss Earhart whereby the flight, coming while Congress is in session, would climax the extensive propaganda campaign.

May Mean Costly Search

With her limited supply of fuel, Miss Earhart's life will be in grave danger if she encounters stormy weather or loses her course. She has only a little more than enough gasoline to remain in the air if the flight is completed in the 14-hour schedule, according to Municipal Airport officials. Search for her would compel the Government to expend thousands of dollars badly needed in Army and Navy work, besides endangering the lives of aviators who would make the search.

In spite of his opposition to the flight, Capt. Eugene Blake, commander of the Western Coast Guard, San Francisco, stated Coast Guard vessels would be sent out along the route for a distance of 150 miles from the Golden Gate in the event Miss Earhart leaves Honolulu.

"I see no reason for the flight," he declared. "The search for Ulm proved costly and another large expenditure looms if Miss Earhart fails to reach Oakland. It is only a stunt flight."

Commander F. C. Connell, in charge of the Oakland Reserve Air Base since 1928 and veteran of several searches for lost aviators, commented:

"I wish she wouldn't leave. There is nothing to gain by her flight, for the route has been charted. I thought the Ulm flight showed the fallacy of attempting trans-Pacific jaunts in planes not equipped for ocean flying."

Maj. Donald P. Hughes, acting air officer of the Ninth Corps Area, San Francisco, declared:

"Such flights do not prove anything. They are harmful to aviation when they fail."

Joining with the Bay Region experts in condemning the flight, Lieut. Commander Clarence H. Schildauer, U. S. N. R., who recently arrived in Los Angeles from Hawaii, declared:

"Army and Navy pilots are agreed the flight is dangerous and would serve no purpose to aviation."

Ten aviators have lost their lives attempting to span the Pacific between Oakland and Honolulu. Seven went down when the Dole flight was staged in 1927 and Ulm carried two more to their deaths with him.

Sir Kingsford-Smith is the only aviator to make the west-east hop. He flew off the 2400 miles in 15 hours, arriving in Oakland last Nov. 5.

AMELIA EARHART.
The first lady of the air with a tiny hula maiden who welcomed her to the islands where she is lecturing and planning a flight to the mainland for $10,000, it is claimed, to publicize the campaign against the sugar quota for Hawaii. She plans the flight—declared futile and hazardous—in the plane being lifted from the liner Lurline.

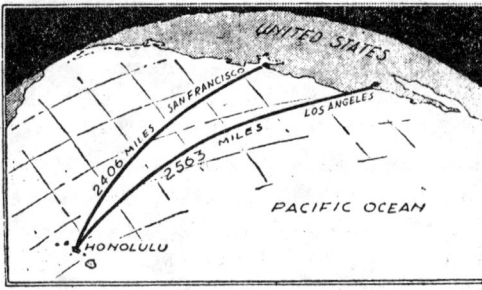

Aerial routes to the mainland.

CREDIT: OAKLAND TRIBUNE

Chapter Sixteen

Across the Pacific Ocean

IN 1934, Amelia made preparations to fly 2,400 miles from Wheeler Field, Honolulu, to Oakland, California. This was in response to a ten-thousand dollar purse offered by a group of Hawaiian sugar and pineapple growers, hotel owners, and business men to focus attention upon their beautiful islands. Amelia successfully completed this flight, the first from Hawaii to the mainland, on January 11–12, 1935. It was a story of setbacks, perseverance, and accomplishment, one that can best be told in Amelia's own words. In May, 1935, *The National Geographic Magazine* published her firsthand account of the trip from beginning to end.

"The story of my flight from Honolulu to San Francisco begins several months before the date of the crossing. Paul Mantz, my technical adviser, Ernie Tissot, mechanic, and others had worked for some time getting the plane and motor in readiness. On December 22, 1934, these two, with Mrs. Mantz, Mr. Putnam and me, set off from Los Angeles for Honolulu. The airplane, intact, rode with us on the *Lurline*, secured as only sailors could do it, on the aft tennis deck.

"During the five days of the voyage we ran the motor up several times, lest it swallow too much corroding salt moisture, and tested the radio. After midnight, as far as 1,000 miles from shore, we picked up the familiar airway

Amelia studying her charts, 1934.

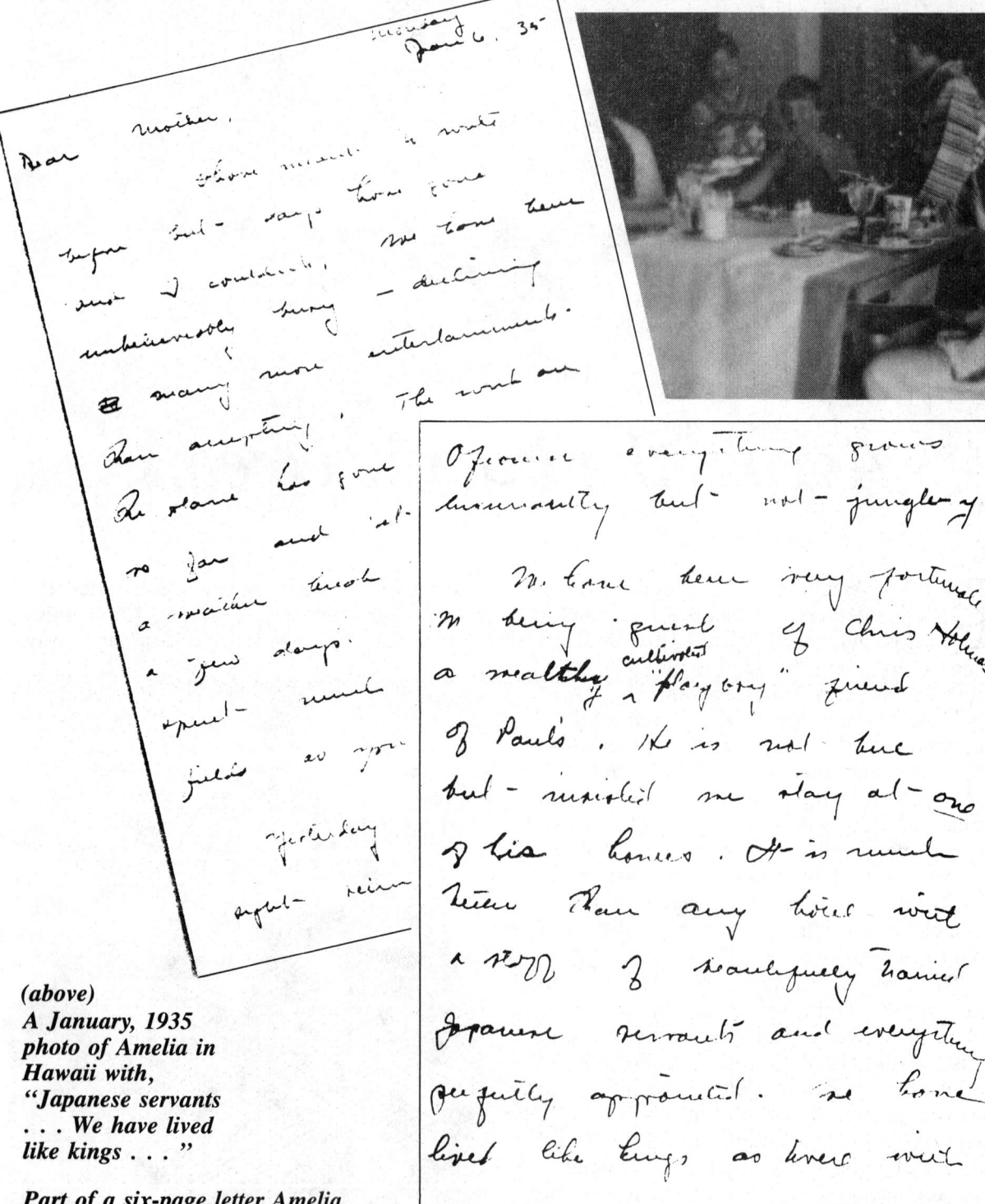

(above)
A January, 1935 photo of Amelia in Hawaii with, "Japanese servants . . . We have lived like kings . . ."

Part of a six-page letter Amelia wrote to her mother from Hawaii. The letter is postmarked January 8, 1935, six days before she began her flight back to California.

station signals. 'Sparks,' the *Lurline's* radio operator, was much interested in our set and was extremely helpful.

"Two weeks in Honolulu were necessary for final testing and checking. Paul and Ernie, with United States Army helpers, worked day and night. I stayed away except for special tests I had to make. This was partly because I could not help the competent gentlemen in any way and partly because I believe it is better for the flyer's peace of mind to back away from the project in hand, occasionally, and get perspective.

"By January 11, Paul had completed to his satisfaction final mechanical details on the plane. I was fit as could be and weather was favorable.

"I had intended to try taking off about 1:30 or 2 o'clock in the afternoon, but late in the morning light rain began to fall. Before 1 o'clock it had turned into a tropical downpour. The wind, instead of blowing from the northeast as it had been doing, came perversely from the southwest.

"Wheeler Field, the Army airport which I planned to use, has no hard-surface runways, and I knew the ground would be fairly soft for a heavily loaded plane. I was carrying more than 500 gallons of gasoline, and this, combined with other extras, weighted my plane more than ever before.

"However, the field is 6,000 feet long and slopes into the direction of the prevailing winds. A plane takes off against the wind as does a small boy's kite. Even with unfavorable surface conditions and without the usual help from the wind, I still felt I could lift my plane in a 3,000-foot run, perhaps less. The Army authorities had kindly mowed a pathway for me in the smoothest part of the reservation and had planted small white flags along the edge to guide me.

Amelia, left, and Mrs. Paul Mantz stand on the aft tennis deck of the **Lurline**, *on the way to Honolulu, December, 1934.*

"As lunch time approached with no improvement in weather, a small group of those intimately connected with the flight had luncheon at the home of Lieutenant and Mrs. George Sparhawk. The invaluable aid Lieutenant Sparhawk rendered in connection with radio tests was equaled only by his wife's ability and willingness to turn her home into a temporary boarding house for Putnams, Mantzes, and their associates.

"Intermittently someone at the window reported weather changes. I went to sleep for a while and awoke about 2:30—to the continued patter of rain.

"About 3:30 the rain slackened. The wind died down and the clouds gave promise of breaking at last. So I drove to the hangar where my plane was housed. Weather forecasts over the Pacific were satisfactory, but would not remain so the next day. Unless I took off, despite the local meteorological upset, I might be held indefinitely.

"I found the field wet, the plane wet, and certainly the spirits of the faithful few who were standing by were damp, indeed. However, I asked that the motor be warmed and my few belongings stowed. At 4:30 I climbed into the cockpit and tested the motor. It sounded crisp and lusty.

"There were about two hundred people standing silent on the apron, somber weather having discouraged more of the curious. I saw several women with handkerchiefs obviously ready for any emergency.

"Out of the corner of my eye I sighted three fire engines and an ambulance posted down the field where 'X' might be expected to mark the spot if an accident occurred. The Army to a man seemed to have portable fire extinguishers in their hands.

"Such precautions were wise enough, for the take off, with excess load, is considered by many flyers the most hazardous moment.

"My loaded plane weighted more than 6,000 pounds. Three tons is considerable weight for a comparatively small type like mine to get into the air, even from a smooth, paved runway under favorable conditions. Here I had no runway, and the weather was definitely unhelpful.

"At 4:45 I taxied to the end of the marked pathway. Paul Mantz freed a ball of mud and

Amelia relaxes at Chris Homes' estate before she takes off across the Pacific.

grass my tail skid had rolled up. My last human contact was a fleeting glimpse of Ernie, my mechanic, trotting along beside the plane, mud sloshing over his shoe tops at each step. His cigarette drooped forlornly from the corner of his mouth; his face was as white as paper. I hope he saw me smile.

"I looked ahead between the marker flags, checked again the spot at which I was to begin to stop in case I was not off the ground by the time I passed it, and pushed the throttle ahead.

"The plane did exactly as expected. The tail came up as it gathered speed, throwing up a cataract of red-brown mud. It grew lighter, as the 550 harnessed horses of the Wasp motor gobbled gas. Then a final bounce and it took to the air, holding it easily as I slowly turned to the right toward Honolulu and Diamond Head. The take off, I am told, was accomplished well within 3,000 feet—less than half the length of the field.

"Skirting Honolulu, I could see the human ants, far below, going home after their day's work. I rounded Makapuu Point, the last island outpost on my course. To my right I could see the long sloping side of Molokai, the next island, blue in the hazy distance. Clouds were all about me from the start, and to get on top of them I climbed 6,000 feet, whence I could look down on their fluffy contours moving against the dark sea.

"On three over-ocean air voyages, totalling about 6,500 miles, I have seen little more than a thousand miles of water. On these flights I have been above clouds, between two layers, or actually in the formation most of the time. Certainly, in covering similar distances on ships one gets a much better idea of how mighty oceans really appear.

"The night I found over the Pacific was a night of stars. They seemed to rise from the sea and hang outside my cockpit window, near enough to touch, until hours later they slipped away into the dawn.

"But shortly before midnight I spied a star that differed from the others. It was too pink and it flashed as no star could. I realized I was seeing a ship, with its searchlights turned into the heavens as a lamppost to guide me on my way. I snapped on my landing lights, which are on the leading edge of the wings midway to their tips, and had them bravely blink a greeting to whoever might be watching.

"I was wearing my radio earphones, and after a moment the spattering buckshot of code wiped out everything else on the air, as the radio operator on that ship broadcast to shore stations that I had been sighted. Though we could not converse directly, it was comforting to hear the crackle he produced and to realize that at least thus far I was on the course. Later I learned the vessel passed was the Matson ship *Maliko,* 900 miles from Honolulu.

"An interesting data sheet in my 'chartroom' (a tiny space in the wing beside my shoulder, where reposed maps, tools, etc.) was a blueprint showing the position of every vessel on or near the course, and the exact time I should be over it, reckoned on an average flying speed and a predetermined hour of starting.

"But before starting I thought it unlikely that I would sight a ship. The chance of two specks, one on the surface of a very large ocean, the other thousands of feet above it, passing near enough to see each other seemed slim.

"About midway the *Ramapo,* Navy tanker, reported me, but I missed seeing her.

"Mine was the first civilian long-distance flight made with two-way radio telephone. This equipment, of course, is regularly used on the air-transport lines in the United States, but hitherto has been perhaps too heavy, costly, and complex to find a place in record flying.

"My outfit, in addition to the usual set for beam reception, included a 50-watt transmitter with a possible sending range of more than 2,000 miles. My call letters are KHABQ (a mouthful indeed!), assigned by the Federal Communications Commission under a special license for communication at sea, with frequencies of 6,210 and 3,105 kilocycles. On the Pacific voyage I received certain commercial broadcasting stations, tuning the programs low except when the stations 'talked' to me.

"I was scheduled to transmit at a quarter to and a quarter past the hour. The radio itself was operated by remote control and was situated in the rear of the plane, behind the fuselage gas tanks. In the cockpit I had a dial for tone and sensitivity control and volume, a selector switch, and a handheld microphone.

"To broadcast, I rolled out the antenna through a hole in the floor by means of a reel under my seat. The antenna was weighted with a small lead ball, and streamed out in an arc below the plane in flight—adding another thing for a pilot to think about when taking off or landing, for it had to be reeled in then.

"Commercial stations which generously cooperated with me before and during the flight were KGU in Honolulu, KPO in San Francisco, and KFI of Los Angeles. The latter put on a special all-night program, relayed information, and otherwise kept in touch with me every half hour. The Department of Commerce short-wave airway stations on the coast and at Kingman, Arizona, also stood by for the duration of the flight. They, and the amateurs who cooperated, can never know how much they helped a lone pilot.

"Only a few hours after the start, I happened to hear the KGU announcer say: 'We are interrupting our musical program so that Mr. Putnam may try to communicate with his wife.'

"And then, some hundreds of miles out over the Pacific, I heard my husband's voice as though he were in the next room.

"A.E.," he said, "the noise of your motor interferes with your messages. Please speak a little louder.

"A few minutes later I talked back to him, through the little cup microphone—louder, as requested.

"Crossing the Atlantic, I saw no actual sunrise, because of clouds. This time, with more than half of the Pacific stretched behind me, the rising sun ushered in a new day in orderly fashion. Since I was coming from 'down under,' the sun flared over the horizon not straight ahead but somewhat to my right, fortunately for my eyes. Flying full into the glare at high altitudes is very trying, even with dark glasses.

"All the way I had flown at 8,000 feet, because best winds had been predicted there. From dawn until 10:30 I was over a solid pack of fog in a world utterly remote and quite my own. Once, on the quarter hour, I confided to my microphone, 'I am getting tired of this fog.'

Subsequently I discovered that all of the message which filtered through the static to mainland listeners were the words, 'I am getting tired.' So shore radio announcers, bless them, had fresh ammunition for their word pictures of the little girl battling exhaustion as well as the elements.

"After I had been flying for about 15 hours, the formation began to break up. Large holes appeared, through which I could see the crinkled blue surface of the sea flecked with morning sunlight.

"A larger opening appeared on my left and framed in the middle was another ship. Down through the hole in the clouds I went, happy for the company of that toy steamer and exceedingly pleased because its presence proved I still was on my course.

"Only 150 to 200 feet above the sea I circled the steamer, which proved to be the Dollar liner *President Pierce*. And then I 'lined up' on the wake, which from the air I could see stretching astern for perhaps a mile. The line of that wake checked exactly with the compass course I had been following. So I continued on my way.

"Within a few minutes KPO, in answer to my query, radioed me the position of the *President Pierce* as 300 miles out from San Francisco. I did not pull up again to 8,000 feet, but flew at about 1,500 the rest of the way to shore.

"The last hour or two of any flight is always the hardest. If there are clouds the pilot, straining his eyes, is likely to see illusions of land. In my opinion California is letting slip many a sightly acre in the Pacific just off her coast. I saw them, islands and distant shores almost indistinguishable from clouds. Were they only clouds, after all? I did not let myself turn from my course to explore.

"If there is any time when experience counts it is in putting down the temptation to wander from that course which instruments declare is true to that which the human mind would like to try. A pilot's maxim should be, 'Usually the instruments are right and you are wrong.'

"I *was* glad to see land—but not in a state to 'scream for joy,' as reported in one fervid account. My faithful plane, I believe, would fall apart under me if its pilot grew so senselessly emotional.

"The first land I sighted was the outjutting of Pillar Point, about 21 miles south of the Golden Gate, and Pigeon Point, some 43 miles. I did not recognize the territory at all. As there was a little rain squall directly in my way, I went around to the right. Thus I appeared five miles or so south of where I otherwise would have been—but anyway on the continent I aimed for!

"Pulling up over a notch in the hills, directly on my course, I beheld San Francisco Bay before me. Over San Mateo I sailed and six minutes later NR-965-Y and I sat down on the runway of Oakland Airport, approximately 18 hours from Honolulu.

"My landing was in marked contrast to that of the solo Atlantic flight. At that time a farmer's best pasture had been my journey's end, and there three Irishmen had come out to see what manner of creature the airplane held. My announcement that I was from America was accepted in dubious silence. At Oakland I did not have to explain whence I came to the thousands of people who waited. Cameras clicked as soon as I opened the cockpit and microphones were raised to catch my important (?) first utterances.

"I have said little about the precautions taken in case something went wrong.

"Mine is a land plane, equipped with wheels. Occasionally such a one has come down safely on water, through the landing is generally dangerous.

"There are a number of factors which affect the result. Among them are the roughness of the water, the buoyancy of the craft itself, and its position when it strikes. I had dump valves in the two largest fuselage tanks, which permitted almost instant evacuation of the contents. Empty, these alone had considerable buoyancy—added to that of any wing tanks from which fuel had been used. I felt there was every likelihood the plane would remain afloat for some time.

"Paul Mantz, my technical adviser, who in his flying for motion pictures makes airplanes do unbelievable things, helped me plan the best way to bring a high-wing monoplane down on water without somersaulting. The feat has been accomplished and a craft of that type has been known to float for eight days before the crew were rescued. Of course, a steep dive into the sea would so damage any plane that it would tend to sink at once. Similarly, high waves would demolish either unfortunate land or water craft forced down on their merciless surface.

"Over my warm flying clothes I wore an inflatable rubber vest, divided into two compartments. Each would blow up instantly when I released the compressed carbon dioxide contained in two little metal capsules at the waist.

Amelia in a rubber raft, photographed by W. Stanley Hicks, Paul Mantz's personal photographer.

"Strung to my belt I had a hatchet and a sheath knife. Once down and out of the plane, I was to crawl back along the fuselage. Because of the weight of the motor, the tail surfaces presumably would be sticking out of the water. Immediately behind the gas tanks was a rubber raft. I was to hack my way through the light fabric-covered wood of the plane to reach it. It, too, was instantly inflatable from a carbon dioxide container. The sealed compartments of the raft held tomato juice, chocolate, malted-milk tablets, and a container of water.

"For distress signals I carried a Very pistol which shot regulation red and green rockets. Small flares which burn on contact with water and several small balloons completed my attention-attracting equipment. The balloons were to be let up on stout fish line and bear aloft a very red silk flag.

Amelia tries out her rubber raft before the take-off.

"The raft, once in action, was to be moored beside the plane, as long as the latter kept afloat. Then, as a last resource, I was to abandon ship.

"What did I eat? My standard ration—plain tomato juice, one hard-boiled egg, and the most memorable cup of hot chocolate I have ever had. Drinking hot chocolate alone over the Pacific at 8,000 feet is a unique experience I shall not soon forget. At that, my larder was overstocked. Katherine Sparhawk, at Wheeler Field, put up sandwiches which I did not consume but know were good.

"One seems to require very little nourishment on a long pull of this kind. Though I had had the lightest sort of lunch at noon in Honolulu, when I reached Oakland I was in no hurry for food. Actually my first meal was postponed until evening, 24 hours after taking off. But I vanquished a roast chicken then, with ease.

"The plane I used is at least three years old. It is a high-wing monoplane capable, normally, of carrying six passengers and a pilot. It is closed—like a closed car. I like comfort in flying. More important, I believe comfort decreases fatigue on long flights, and fatigue is a factor to be considered.

"The passenger seats in the fuselage were removed to make room for four tanks, which with five in the wing were required to carry fuel for at least twenty hours aloft. The cruising speed with moderate load is 150 to 160 miles per hour; with a top speed, at higher altitudes, about 200 miles.

"The Wasp motor used is the same one which performed so well on the Atlantic flight three years ago. It is in the prime of life and, after complete rebuilding and mechanical facelifting, better than new. Pacific Airmotive Corporation, Ltd., at Burbank, did the job and I believe no engine of mine ever sang a sweeter song.

"Both motor and plane were checked and double-checked by competent inspectors of the Department of Commerce, and specially licensed for long-distance flying by the Government before I left for Honolulu.

"My cockpit contains every instrument, I think, the practicality of which has been proved for all-weather flying, except a robot pilot. On my solo Atlantic flight the altimeter failed, the first failure of the kind I had ever encountered. Over the Pacific my instrument board carried two altimeters, as well as three compasses and other duplications. Also, metal gasoline lines were encased throughout their length in rubber tubing—double insurance against fuel leaks. Live and learn.

"I have long preached that two-thirds of the success of any expedition is in the preparation. Few know the time and patience expended through weeks or months of testing before even so simple a flight as that between Honolulu and Oakland—and simple it was compared to flights such as Wiley Post's round-the-world.

"For example, every one of my nine tanks had to be filled, run dry, and checked at different altitudes for various characteristics. In one, difficulty was experienced with the venting (necessary to allow air to enter the top of a gas tank as the gasoline is consumed from the bottom); so changes in the venting arrangements had to be made.

"It took hours of work to determine how many gallons of gasoline the motor consumed. If it used more than estimated, the pilot might face a serious predicament. My calculations were about 24 gallons an hour for 150 miles an hour speed. These worked out reasonably well, except that my speed on the actual flight dropped to between 130 and 140 because of head winds.

"Oil consumption is as important as that of fuel. I carried 35 gallons of oil, after carefully determining the quantity used each hour. Load and speed tests had to be made with the controllable pitch propeller to find the most efficient setting. Such a propeller works as does the high and low gearshift in an automobile. The pilot takes off in the 'low,' climbs to the altitude at which he wishes to fly, then shifts into 'high,' for speed in level flight, or moderate climb. And so it goes through all the intricate phases of getting ready a flight.

"Under preparation, in addition to mechanical detail should be considered personnel. Pilots and mechanics and all others concerned should be experienced and physically and mentally fit. Worry and fatigue are relentless enemies of good judgment.

"The subject of navigation looms large on long flights. To keep going is useless unless one knows how to get where he wishes to be. My navigation charts were prepared by Lieut. Comdr. Clarence S. Williams, of the U.S. Naval Reserve, of Los Angeles. On them were worked out alternate courses, one to San Francisco, a second to Los Angeles, and a third providing a shift from the northerly route to the southerly, should Pacific coast weather conditions make a midocean change of destination desirable.

"The charts called for fourteen changes in compass course, each to be made at intervals slightly over one hour. To facilitate time calculations, I had three clocks in the cockpit, one set on Honolulu time, another San Francisco time. The third was set at *zero* when I started and thereafter recorded the exact elapsed time of the trip. All of which is another answer to the question, 'What does a transocean flyer think about?'

"For the last I have left an aspect of the Pacific flight—or of any aerial expedition— whose conduct can spell the difference between success and failure. That is the forecasting of weather to be encountered, a science which, as regards flying conditions over oceans, is yet in its infancy.

"When the *Friendship* flew from Newfoundland to Wales in 1928, only the sketchiest weather data were available regarding Atlantic upper-air conditions. During a fortnight prior to our flight, reports were obtained at considerable expense by those immediately interested in the project from a dozen ships at sea. These reports supplemented the limited material then available to the Weather Bureau. From all of this Dr. James Kimball, meteorological dean of Atlantic flying, constructed the weather maps used. At best the basic information was incomplete and stale.

"The situation was much improved four years later, in 1932, when I flew solo to Ireland. The Weather Bureau was then securing reasonably comprehensive reports from ships every four hours. Dr. Kimball's maps were correspondingly fuller and fresher. However, they still concerned *mariners'* weather. Nautical observers are not equipped or trained to give information exactly as *flyers* wish it. What does a sailor care about the height of clouds or how the winds blow at 10,000 feet?

"The meteorological assistance rendered me on the Pacific flight indicated the accuracy that can be attained in the science with trained personnel and a new theory of forecasting.

Navy Veteran

Capt. Williams is majoring in international relations at SC and is preparing himself for further naval service. During his 30 years in the Navy he took part in World War I aboard a convoy carrying AEF troops to France.

Later he became a navigation consultant and laid out a series of transoceanic courses for such pilots as Amelia Earhart, Harry Richman and Dick Merrill, the latter two having been the first to fly round-trip from New York to England.

During World War II the captain was appointed head of the navigation department of the Navy's midshipman's school at Northwestern University. Later he served as convoy commander in directing fleets of merchant ships in the Pacific.

Won Decoration

His promotion to the rank of captain gave him command of the world's largest floating dry dock, ABSD-I, 827 feet in length and capable of lifting a battleship.

He was awarded the Bronze Star Medal for outstanding service at the time of his retirement.

When not attending classes at SC, Williams lives on his ranch Harmony Hill, in Elsinore.

Captain Clarence Williams. He charted Amelia's course across the Pacific (below).

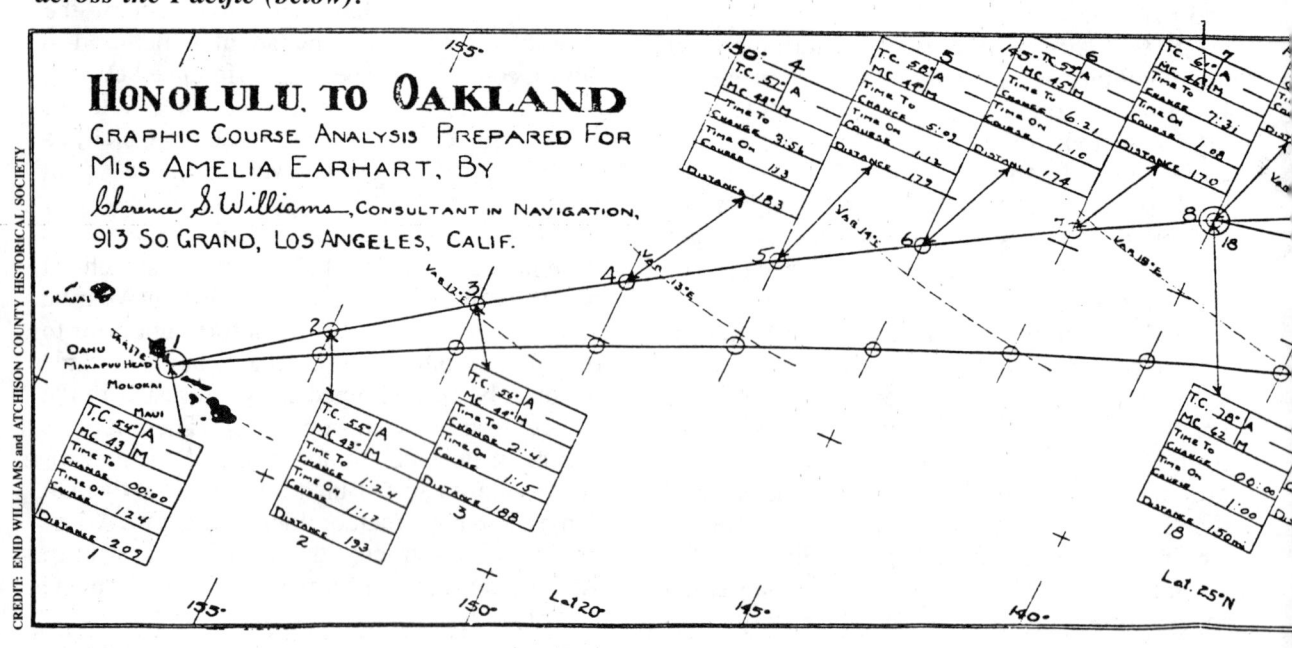

AMELIA EARHART

Locust Avenue,
Rye, New York.
September 6, 1932.

My dear Commander Williams:

Enclosed is my check for $53.05 for your work in laying out my course for the last trans-continental trip.

My last attempt was certainly the hardest. I was sorry not to be able to make better time but I had some return of my fuel trouble and worse than that again had no lights in my cockpit. With thunder-storms all the way to Kansas, I was compelled to waste time following the airways where I planned to cut. I was determined to get through no matter whether the time was slow or not, so kept plugging away. Some time I hope to do a better job.

Shoot the Cooperative Story along as soon as you get it in rough shape for suggestions. Mr. Putnam thinks he can find a place for it.

Sincerely yours,

Amelia E.

"In Honolulu I was fortunate in obtaining the cooperation of Lieutenant E. W. Stephens, U.S. Navy, aerological officer at Pearl Harbor. Lieutenant Stephens, who was responsible for plotting the weather for the Navy's successful flight to Hawaii a year previously, worked with us early and late. Ten days before the take off he constructed a hypothetical weather map embracing much of the Pacific Ocean and western America. That chart—a thing of highs and lows, swirling isobars, barometer and temperature readings, wind directions and velocities —he made as he felt it *should be when I started.*

"Then we waited for the gods of weather to adjust their caprices throughout this far-flung territory so that their handiwork would at least approximately match our ideal.

"After digesting the data that came in by radio from vessels, from tiny islands scattered eastward of Hawaii, from Pacific-coast stations, Lieutenant Stephens on Wednesday remarked: 'It looks like Friday. I think things will work out by then.'

"They did. And because of his satisfaction with the outlook when Friday came, I decided to start, even though that was against advice

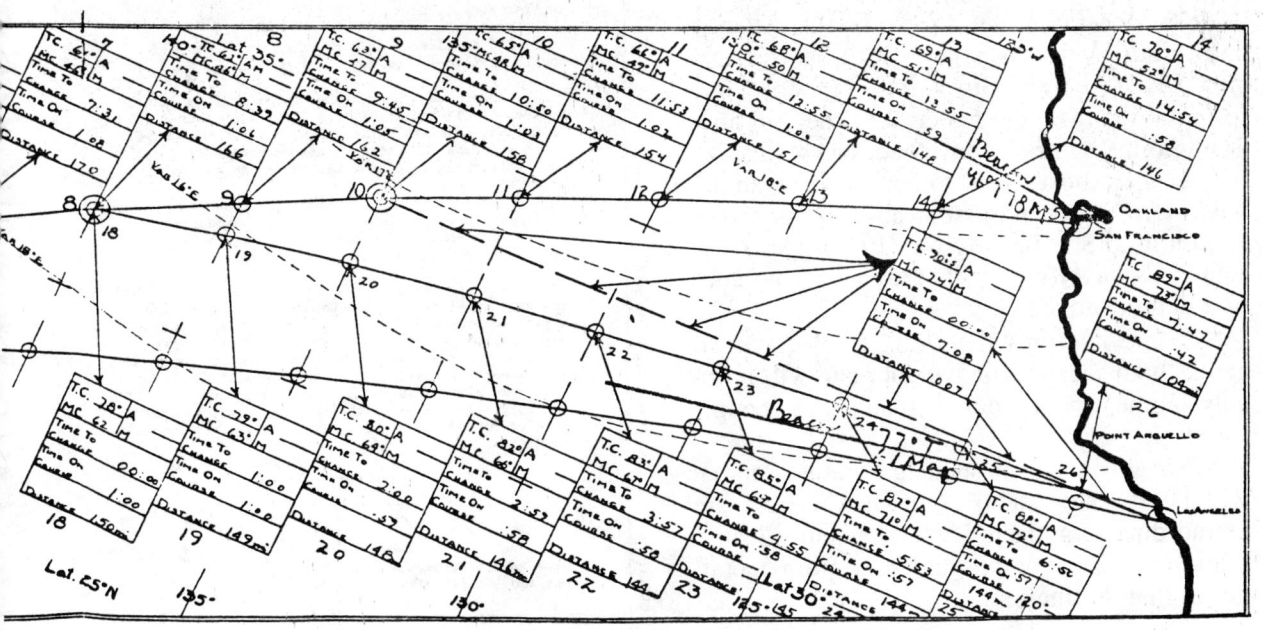

received from California. The consoling fact is that I found conditions substantially as predicted by Lieutenant Stephens, even on the California coast.

"Just now much attention is being directed to the pending possibilities of airlines operating across the Pacific. Momentarily the center of interest has shifted from the Atlantic. But over whatever ocean scheduled air transport may pioneer, a vital factor in its establishment will be the development of meterological data. With what we now know about weather and with the instant communication of radio, it is not at all impossible, with proper preparation, to command a picture of upper-air conditions prevailing at any given hour over even extended routes. One can also forecast what will 'come in' during the time elapsed in the making of a flight.

"The western frontier of the United States lies 2,400 miles from the mainland. Though this stretch of water is several hundred miles greater than the shortest land-to-land distance of the North Atlantic, it probably presents less formidable hazards for the flyer. Of course, no definite statements on this score can be made until after considerable research on weather and more actual flight data are recorded. Further, what is applicable to an individual flight such as mine does not necessarily hold true for transport operation.

"For general comparisons North Atlantic and mid-Pacific weather disturbances are similarly severe at times, but probably ice-formation danger is greater over the Atlantic. The shortest course from America to Europe, followed by most flyers so far, has been somewhat north of the normal steamer lands. From Honolulu to San Francisco or Los Angeles the route lies directly over that traversed by ships —a definite advantage.

"To me it seems that regular air transport across both oceans is inevitable, and will probably come about sooner than most people suspect.

"Probably used in such long-range service will be the new radio compasses. These are extraordinary 'gadgets,' which actually lead a pilot to a selected point, guided by radio operating at that destination.

"This uncanny 'homing' device is gradually emerging from the realms of experimentation into that of proved practicality. One, the Kruesi compass, after Army testing ashore, has recently been tried out over the pacific in flights instigated by Eugene L. Vidal, Director of Air Commerce.

"Another variety of the new instrument, the Lear compass, is being installed in my own plane. With this latest addition to my already generously populated instrument board, I anticipate instructive experience in this most modern means of finding one's way in the air."

* * *

Compared to the flight across the Atlantic, Amelia's Pacific crossing seemed far less monumental. Yet, once again, she forged a new trail in aviation by flying the tremendous distance over the Pacific. Her flight represented a personal accomplishment, but it was not undertaken solely for personal recognition. She believed that her flight advanced the science of aviation. It was also evidence of her personal commitment and fortitude. I was proud of Amelia, and so was the rest of the world.

THE WHITE HOUSE
WASHINGTON

January 13, 1935

My dear Miss Earhart:

I am pleased to send you this message of congratulations. You have scored again.

By successfully spanning the ocean stretches between Hawaii and California, following your triumphant trans-Atlantic flight of 1928, you have shown even the "doubting Thomases" that aviation is a science which cannot be limited to men only.

Because of swift advances in this science of flight, made possible by Government and private enterprise, scheduled ocean transportation by air is a distinct and definite future prospect.

The trail-blazers who opened to civilization the vast stretches of this Continent of ours, who moved our boundary from the Atlantic to the Pacific, were inspired and helped by women of courage and skill. From the days of these pioneers to the present era, women have marched step in step with men. And now, when air trails between our shores and those of our neighbors are being charted, you, as a woman, have preserved and carried forward this precious tradition.

Very sincerely yours,

Franklin D. Roosevelt

Miss Amelia Earhart,
Oakland, California.

Amelia's arrival at Oakland Airport.

CREDIT: U.S.A.F.

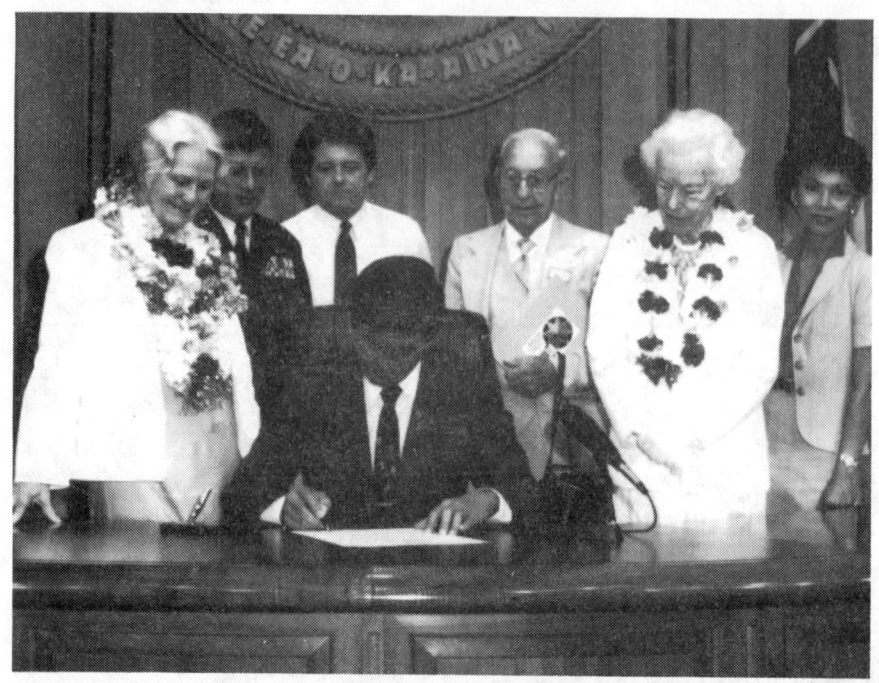

Hawaiian Governor George R. Ariyoshi signs a proclamation declaring January 11, 1985, Amelia Earhart Day in Hawaii. Witnessing are, left to right, Fay Gillis Wells, Brigadier General Thomas A. La Plante, Robert W. Abraham, Martin Jensen, who won second place in the 1927 Dole Race, Muriel Morrissey and Nelwyn Choy.

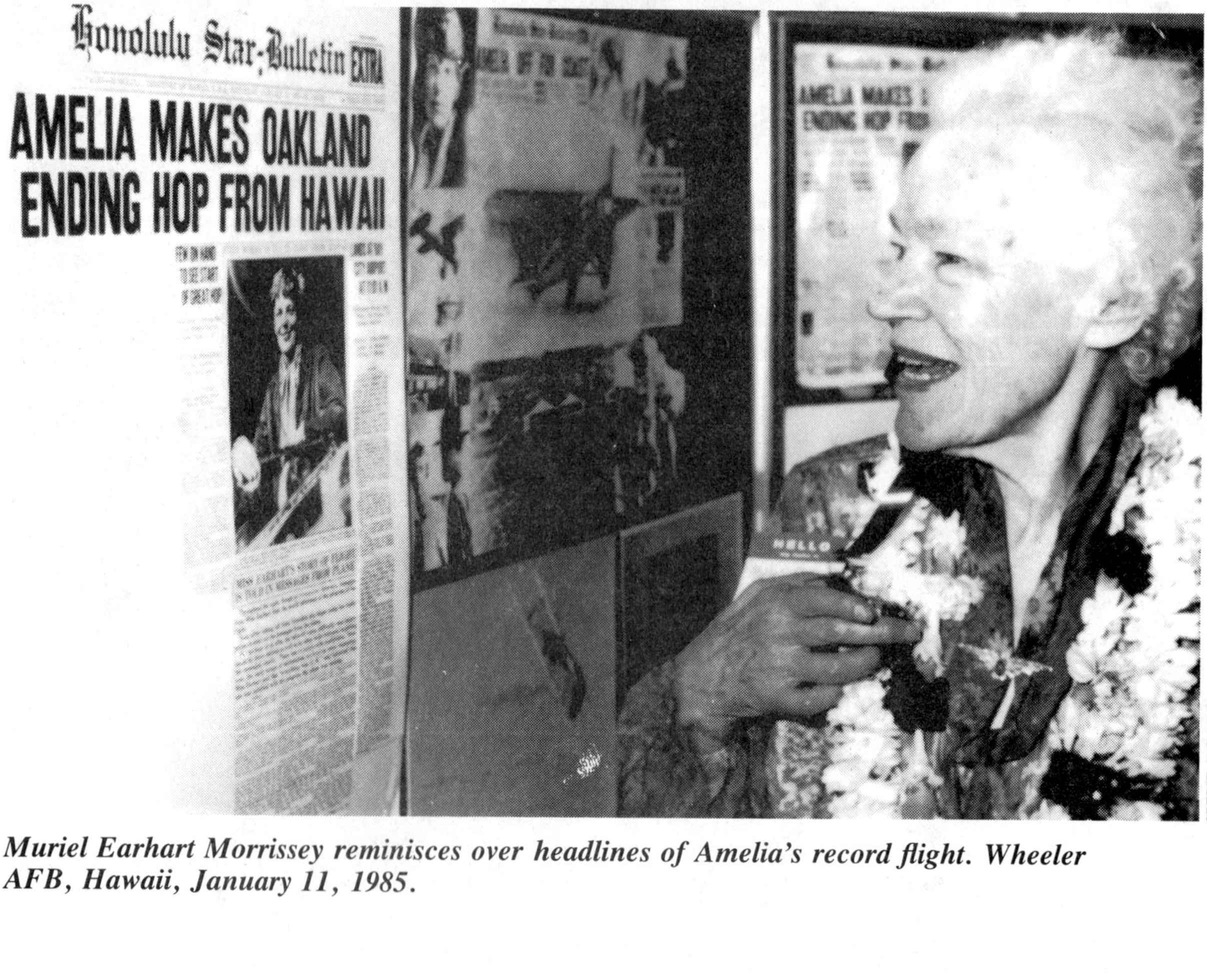

CREDIT: U.S.A.F.

Muriel Earhart Morrissey reminisces over headlines of Amelia's record flight. Wheeler AFB, Hawaii, January 11, 1985.

Chapter Seventeen

Preparing to Circle the Globe

IN the seven years from 1929 to 1936, Amelia flew thousands of miles and logged several thousand flight hours in her Lockheed Vega. It was in March, 1935, while Amelia was in New York, that she met with the Consul General for Mexico, Eduardo Vellasenor. It was the Consul General who suggested that Amelia make a "good will" flight. GP departed for Mexico City to make the necessary arrangements while Amelia continued with her prior engagements.

On April 20, 1935, Amelia flew her red Vega, NR-965-Y, from Burbank to Mexico City's Valbuena Airport in 13 hours, 32 minutes, setting a record. GP met her there and they spent several delightful days in Mexico. Amelia met some "typical" Mexican women and discussed their life's ambitions with them. Señora Cardenas of the Mexican Geographic Society presented her with a medal. Among others, she met Lazaro Cardenas, President of Mexico.

Amelia in Mexico, 1935.

The Mexican Government overprinted the statement, *Amelia Earhart, Vuelo de buena voluntad Mexico 1935* [flight of good faith] on 780 stamps. Amelia took them with her when she left Mexico City. Three hundred were placed on public sale, to be used on correspondence which Amelia carried back with her on her return flight. Today these stamps are rare collector's items.

After two weeks in Mexico, including a May Day celebration, Amelia took off for Newark, New Jersey, setting a record of 14 hours, 18 minutes. Carrying the stamps and some first day covers, she began the flight on May 9, 1935, at 8:06 a.m. local time, and arrived 2,125 miles later in Newark at 11:24 p.m., Eastern time. Amelia had made the first solo flight into Mexico by a woman and was the first to fly non-stop from Mexico City to Newark airport.

Document that initiated the Mexican Amelia Earhart stamp.

Mexico honored the goodwill flight of Amelia with this 20c overprint in 1935.

Newspaper account of Amelia's record flight.

This eventful year of 1935 had its share of sadness, too. Will Rogers, one of Amelia's close friends and supporters, was killed with Wiley Post in a plane crash in Alaska. The death of this kindly and witty philosopher was a loss to her, as it was to the many thousands who knew him through his widely-read newspaper column. Amelia felt that Will had done more to advance the cause of non-military aviation than any other man except Lindbergh.

MEXICO–N. Y. RECORD SET BY MISS EARHART

Woman Flier First to Make Non-Stop Hop Between Cities; Time Is 14 Hours

(Picture on Page 19)

NEW YORK, May 9. — (U.P.) — Tousled haired Amelia Earhart slept late today while the country acclaimed her latest feat—a nonstop flight from Mexico City to New York.

It was the first non-stop flight between the two cities.

Miss Earhart, who has flown solo over the Atlantic from Newfoundland to Ireland, and over the Pacific from Hawaii to California, brought her red Lockheed Vega monoplane down at Newark Airport at 10:28:50 p. m. (E. D. T.) last night, 14 hours, 18 minutes and 50 seconds after she took off alone from the dry bed of old Lake Texcoco, near Mexico City. The distance is 2100 miles.

Tired but happy, she retired at 2 a. m., today, leaving orders that she was not to be disturbed before 11 a. m.

TRIUMPHAL LANDING

More exhausting than her flight, it seemed, was the reception she received on landing. A crowd estimated at 10,000 to 15,000 persons welcomed her in scenes reminiscent of the transatlantic flying days of 1927. Sweeping aside the 45 policemen who had been assigned to maintain order, the crowd swarmed over the field.

Efforts to take her to the New Jersey National Guard hangar in a police car were balked by the wildly cheering mob. Four policemen placed her on their shoulders, and surrounded by the good-natured throng, slowly made their way to the hangar.

She seemed to be the only calm person on the field. Smilingly she complied with the commands of photographers to look this way and that.

CROWD ROILS HUSBAND

But her husband, George Palmer Putnam, former publisher, who had awaited her at the field since dusk, was annoyed by the vehemence of the demonstration.

"Mexico," he said, "is four times as civilized as Newark. This is the most disgraceful scene I ever witnessed."

The speed record for flight with stops between the two cities is credited to the late James R. Wedell who flew from Ottawa to Washington to Mexico City with an elapsed time of 11 hours and 43 minutes in 1932. Colonel Roberto Fierro, ace of the Mexican Army air force, and a mechanic flew from New York to Mexico City in 1930 in 16 hours and 35 minutes.

CREDIT: THE OAKLAND TRIBUNE

Amelia Earhart Here, Mourns Death of Rogers, Post; Will Fly to Funeral

Noted Woman Pilot to Speed West to Attend Rites for Comedian

"The death of Will Rogers and Wiley Post is an irreparable loss. Will was aviation's greatest friend. Wiley was aviation's leading pioneer."

Thus did Amelia Earhart Putnam express herself when she arrived in Cleveland today for a short visit.

After speaking at Lakeside Hospital tonight, the famous woman flyer plans to leave immediately for the west coast, where she expects to attend Will Rogers' funeral.

"It is hard to believe those two are gone," she said. "They have been a part of our life so long."

Mrs. Putnam told how she visited with Will Rogers at his ranch, and Wiley Post at the Union Air Terminal in Burbank, Cal., shortly before the two started off on their ill-fated journey.

Post discussed with her some of his plans for the future. He intended to continue his experimental flying in the stratosphere, she said.

"Wiley left a great deal of work undone," she said. "In flying the stratosphere he was trying to conquer the new frontier in aviaton. He took a plane similar to mine, which will do 170 miles an hour in normal flying, and traveled 300 miles an hour in the stratosphere. It seems remarkable that this was done with practically the same plane and the same motor.

"Wiley had remarkable endurance. He should have been studied as an exceptional human being."

Mrs. Putnam said she knew Will Rogers off the flying field better than she did in aviation. She never had flown with him. But the humorist had entertained her on many occasions. And the two had grown to know each other well.

"His death," she said, "is not only a loss to aviation, but to the entire world."

Amelia Earhart Putnam

Amelia was in Cleveland when she heard about the death of Will Rogers and Wiley Post.

Among the many panels and discussion groups in which Amelia participated was one sponsored by the *New York Herald-Tribune* on the subject, "Women and the Changing World." Amelia, now 37 years old, disavowed membership in the so-called "lost generation," but she earnestly defended their right to stage pacifist demonstrations, to play their new dissonant music called Jazz, to extol cubism in art, or to fly in preference to using more traditional transportation, if they so desired.

By coincidence, Dr. Edward Elliott, President of Purdue University, was in the audience. After hearing Amelia's portion of the program, Dr. Elliott said decisively to his companion that she was the woman he was looking for. He called on Amelia the next day at her office and arranged a luncheon meeting with her and GP. Dr. Elliott told her he was impressed by her insightful discussion of young people's ideas, and that it made him realize that Purdue University needed just such a person. He explained that they had about 800 women students who comprised one-fifth of the University's total student body. They had a Dean of Women, but the women students needed someone to help them direct their school experience and to integrate them into the predominately male school. He asked her if she would consider coming to the Purdue campus, even if only part time.

Amelia joined the faculty as a Consultant in Careers for Women on September 1, 1935. She planned to be on the campus about one week in every four, but her many appointments and career lectures kept her there more often than not. She was pleased when about 20 women students expressed interest in learning to fly. She told them it was doubtful, however, that they would be able to earn a living flying. She encouraged them to fly for fun, and said there was no reason that women should not fly, despite objections from men. To encourage aeronautics at Purdue, the Trustees of the University decided to establish a fund for aeronautical research, and, within a year the goal of $50,000 was reached.

Soon after Amelia had her first flight in an Electra, she made up her mind that she could now accept the challenge of an around-the-world flight, but she kept her plans secret.

When suspicious newsmen queried her about future flights, she admitted that she was interested in circumnavigating the globe near the equator but insisted that she had no intention of making such a flight for a long time.

Amelia with two Purdue students, 1936.

Two members of the Purdue Research Foundation Board of Directors, who wished to remain anonymous, donated $40,000 for Amelia to purchase a Lockheed Electra. In her brief acceptance speech to the President of Purdue and trustees, Amelia said:

> "My ambition is to have this wonderful gift produce practical results for the future of commercial flying and for the women who may want to fly tomorrow's planes."

She subsequently used this airplane for her around-the-world flight. However, according to Frederick L. Hovde, President of Purdue University in 1970:

> "Purdue University was not involved in any way with Miss Earhart's last flight."

Amelia posed with this welcoming committee at Memorial hall in Atchison the evening of June 7, 1935, prior to her address (below). Sheffield Ingalls, former lieutenant governor of Kansas on extreme left. To right of Amelia, Governor Alf M. Landon of Kansas, Robert P. Snowden, aide to governor; unidentified; A.W. Seng, Atchison City Manager; Oscar May and his son, John.

ATCHISON GLOBE—11B
Sunday, July 21, 1963

"Millie" Was A Nickname

When Amelia Earhart was growing up here, she was known by her playmates and friends as "Millie."

After she had become famous, and on her visit here in 1935, she met a former employe of the Otis family who had known her as a little girl.

Having called her Millie when she was a child, the former housekeeper asked her what she should call her now that she was a world famous person.

"Call me Millie as you have always done," Amelia said.

"She was always the most lovable girl imaginable," the woman said, "and her fame had not changed her in the least."

Amelia Earhart To Seek New Firsts

Miss Earhart is shown with President Edward C. Elliott of Purdue University inspecting a model of her Flying Laboratory. Below she is shown with the finished plane.

AMELIA EARHART is adding another "first" to her long record.

First to fly alone from Honolulu to California, first to solo from Mexico City to New York, first woman to accomplish many feats in the air, now America's No. 1 Woman pilot becomes the first to practice aeronautical research with a "flying laboratory" of her own.

The purchase of the new plane, a 210-mile-an-hour twin-engine Lockheed Electra, was made possible by the Purdue Research Foundation of Lafayette, Ind. The "flying laboratory's" scientific activities will be carried on in cooperation with the Foundation and with Purdue University, at which Miss Earhart is a Consultant in Aeronautics. Incidentally, Purdue is the only educational institution in the country owning a fully equipped airport. Recently the Foundation has established the "Amelia Earhart Fund for Aeronautical Research", offering permanent machinery for the conduct of aeronautical experimentation and scientific research along such lines as the Foundation, the University and the aviatrix may elect.

The new plane, just completed in California, is a monoplane, normally equipped to carry ten passengers and two pilots. Built to fit Miss Earhart's requirements, its passenger seats have been replaced by extra fuselage tanks, giving a total fuel capacity of 1250 gallons of gasoline. This provides a cruising range of 4500 miles. The plane is powered by two Pratt & Whitney Wasp motors, developing 1100 horse power. The cruising speed is 180 miles, top speed in excess of 210. The total weight of the plane loaded is about 16,000 pounds.

Among those who cooperated in the project of the new aviation laboratory is Vincent Bendix, sponsor of many aeronautical activities including the annual Bendix transcontinental race. The plane is equipped with Bendix instruments and parts.

Outstanding among the modern instruments to be used by Miss Earhart is the Sperry Gyro-Pilot, a mechanical device replacing the pilot at the controls so that the ship actually can be flown without human guidance.

Additionally there will be a new radio homing device recently perfected by the Bendix aviation interests. This may be set upon any commercial radio station and once so adjusted will point the exact course to that station. Further, this radio path-finder may be hitched up with the Gyro Pilot. The almost uncanny result of combining the functions of the two would be that the ship would fly without human piloting to the designed broadcast station. Indeed, once arrived, it would automatically circle the radio masts, presumably until its fuel is exhausted!

Elaborate two-way Western Electric radio telephone apparatus has been installed, for both voice and telegraph code communication.

Among the flying problems of particular interest to Miss Earhart are those of navigation. To facilitate observations, a special hatch will be cut in the after-part of the fuselage. A Bausch & Lomb bubble sextant and newly designed lightweight binoculars will be among the navigational equipment.

Study of the "human reactions of flying" offer a particularly fruitful field for research, the aviatrix believes.

"The psychological factor has been largely neglected," Miss Earhart declares, "and I want to conduct a sort of clinical survey to determine the effects, upon varying individuals of speed, altitude, pressure, fatigue, mechanical aids and other conditions of flying."

The problems of diet for passenger and pilot are of particular interest. For long flights, emergency rations concentrated in volume and weight are important. In the past Miss Earhart's own stand-bys have been tomato juice, as a beverage, with Horlick's Malted Milk tablets as concentrated sustenance.

Headquarters for the plane's research activities will be the Purdue Airport at Lafayette. The first major aeronautical expedition contemplated is a shake-down flight, in the late autumn. George Palmer Putnam (in private life Miss Earhart is Mrs. Putnam) announces a probable itinerary for that tour of Los Angeles, Mexico City, Panama, Havana, New York, Lafayette and back to Los Angeles.

CREDIT: ATCHISON COUNTY HISTORICAL MUSEUM

Newspaper account of Amelia's plan to purchase her "flying laboratory."

Amelia enjoying an ice cream cone at the Washington Airport, May 2, 1936.

Royal S. Copeland questioning Amelia before the Senate Air Safety Committee, May 1, 1936.

Amelia Advises Senate Hearers

WASHINGTON, Aug. 7.—(A)— Amelia Earhart Putnam strode into a Senate committee hearing today, crushed her brown felt hat on a table and expressed approval of further Federal regulation of aviation—with reservations.

Earlier Mrs. Putnam had resigned her dollar-a-year job as a Commerce Department aeronautical expert.

Giving her views on a bill by Senator McCarran (D., Nev.) to place aviation largely under control of the Interstate Commerce Commission, she told the committee:

"Railroads had 50 years to sow their wild oats before regulation was applied."

She said legislation should tend toward coordination of all transportation, but that to require certificates of convenience and necessity for schedule air line operations at this time might retard development. She recommended an interval of five years.

CREDIT: THE OAKLAND TRIBUNE

Amelia at the typewriter in her North Hollywood home, circa 1936.

Amelia taking off for a flight over Washington D.C., May 1, 1936.

Senator Pat McCarran, Senator Vic Donahey (standing), and Amelia as she resigned her $1-a-year job as a Commerce Department aeronautical expert. August 6, 1936.

Amelia Earhart Gets $1 Year Job

WASHINGTON, March 13.—(P)—Amelia Earhart, noted woman flier, has been engaged at $1 a year by the Commerce Department to test a new radio direction finder for airplanes. The finder is described as a new form of radio compass which would greatly facilitate directional flying.

GEORGE PALMER PUTNAM

November 29, 1938

Dear Mrs. Roosevelt:

I am just completing a biography of Amelia, which will be published by Harcourt Brace next year. Among the files that I have delved through in compiling the material, I found a Student's Pilot Permit which you took out in January 1933, when you were examined by our friend Dr. Henry Templeton Smith.

You sent this Student's Permit to A.E. in a letter you wrote her a few days later, in which you said that having made this start you would now see if you could proceed with the project of learning to fly. And then subsequently you wrote that it wasn't possible. So plans regarding her hoped-for star pupil were shelved!

The incident is really most interesting and I am making brief mention of it in the book. But the purpose of this letter is to send you the original of that Student's Permit. I think you might like to have it. Later, of course, I shall send you a copy of the book, but that will be many months away.

Sincerely yours,

G. P. Putnam

Mrs. Franklin D. Roosevelt,
The White House,
Washington, D. C.

Story of First Lady Eleanor Roosevelt's efforts to learn to fly.

First Lady Goes Sky-Larking

Amelia Earhart In Evening Gown, Pilots Plane

Takeoff Bumpy, But Worth It

TRIB B APR 21 1933

By BESS FURMAN
Associated Press Staff Writer

WASHINGTON, April 21.—(AP)—
The first lady of the land and the first woman to fly the ocean went sky-larking together last night in a big Condor plane.

It was eleven months to the night after Amelia Earhart started off across the Atlantic alone that she flew Mrs. Roosevelt almost all the way from Washington to Baltimore without even removing her white evening gloves.

"It's amusing to think of a girl in a white evening dress and high-heeled shoes flying a plane," said Mrs. Roosevelt.

As for the President's wife, she got her first taste of high life from a control cabin by sitting up there with pilot E. H. Parker almost all the way from Baltimore to Washington.

"It was like being on top of the world," she exclaimed.

IN EVENING CLOAK

Mrs. Roosevelt, evening-cloaked in brocaded black and gold, was accompanied by her brother, Hall Roosevelt. Miss Earhart, in long-lined gown of white with short black coat, was accompanied by her husband, George Palmer Putnam.

The take-off was so bumpy that even Mrs. Roosevelt admitted she'd like it lots better aloft. But once up there—

Miss Earhart turned out all the lights in the plane, explaining the lights below would look more beautiful that way.

Mrs. Roosevelt and the plane full of women reporters and a photographer, sat with their eyes glued upon a Potomac picked out in sparkles, a monument light-drenched, an opalescent conservatory top and a glowing capitol dome while Amelia slipped absolutely unnoticed into the control cabin and took charge of the ship.

FEELS QUITE SAFE

After a while the reporters woke up, and one asked Mrs. Roosevelt, "do you feel just as safe out here, knowing a girl may be flying this ship?"

"Just as safe!" she answered. "I'd give a lot to do it myself!"

That was when George Palmer Putnam got the idea of arranging for Mrs. Roosevelt to go up there, and right above a jeweled Baltimore she made the shift, Amelia returning to the passenger list.

"Oh, Mrs. Roosevelt's flying the plane!" laughed Amelia.

GUESS IS WRONG

But she guessed wrong. When Mrs. Roosevelt returned to her place, just before landing in Washington, she said she didn't have her hand on the controls even once.

"The pilot was just showing me how he did it," was the way she explained the swerve.

And to show she'd learned something up there, she added:

"The board showed 130 miles an hour, but there was a tail wind and we were really going 160. Coming up from Miami the other day they averaged 167 miles an hour the whole way."

CREDIT: THE OAKLAND TRIBUNE and ACME

AMELIA EARHART

April 23, 1933

My dear Mrs. Roosevelt;

It was good of you to invite Mr. Putnam and me to stay at the White House. We enjoyed everything connected with our visit, from sampling Dolly Madison's (?) crab chowder, to flying to Baltimore to see the "silly lights."

Of course much of our pleasure came from being with our hostess. Thank you for giving us so much of your gracious self in addition to all else.

Sincerely yours,
Amelia Earhart

Rye. N.Y.

CREDIT: FRANKLIN D. ROOSEVELT LIBRARY

ORIGINAL RETIRED FOR PRESERVATION

As early as November 26, 1935, via Paul Mantz, Amelia and GP had obtained a quotation from Lockheed Aircraft Corporation in Burbank, California, for a Model 10E Electra at $36,089.70. The Model 10 was an all-metal, low-winged, twin engine, ten-passenger aircraft. It was one of the most modern airplanes of its time. Since this plane was intended for the around-the-world flight that Amelia contemplated, it was to be drastically modified.

Some of the modifications included special instrumentation and tankage to hold an additional 950 gallons of fuel. The standard Electras came as Model 10A's and 10B's which were fitted with Pratt & Whitney WASP SB Junior and Wright Whirlwind R-975-E3 engines, respectively, each capable of 450 hp maximum. Amelia, at the suggestion of Robert Gross, President of Lockheed, opted to purchase the Model 10E, which came with two Pratt & Whitney WASP S3H-1 engines, each capable of producing 550 hp. She had to have as much horsepower as possible due to the overload take off requirements. The additional fuel increased the gross weight of the airplane by more than 50 percent.

> BY DIRECT WIRE FROM
> **WESTERN UNION**
>
> SH7 135 DL=FI NEWYORK NY MAR 16 1936 1037A
> ROBERT GROSS=LOCKHEED AIRCRAFT BURBANK CALIF=
>
> :FINANCIAL ARRANGEMENTS JUST COMPLETED SATISFACTORILY STOP
> SENDING THIS WIRE SO NO TIME LOST STOP THIS WEEK CAN SEND
> INITIAL PAYMENT BASED ON PRICE AND PERFORMANCE GUARANTEES
> QUOTED IN YOUR LETTERS STOP HOWEVER HOPE AS WE PROGRESS
> SOME PRICE REDUCTION CAN BE ARRANGED FEELING OF THOSE
> ASSOCIATED WITH PROJECT BEING THAT UNDER CIRCUMSTANCES
> ALL CONCERNED WOULD BE WILLING DELIVER PRODUCTS AT ACTUAL
> COST WITHOUT PROFIT STOP FOR INSTANCE ENGINES PROPS
> INSTRUMENTS FUEL ALL BEING CONTRIBUTED OUTRIGHT STOP FOR
> YOUR CONFIDENTIAL INFORMATION AE AND MYSELF RECEIVING NO
> FINANCIAL COMPENSATION ANY REMAINING MONEY RESULTING FROM
> FLIGHT PROCEED GO TO PERMANENT FUND FOR AERONAUTICAL
> RESEARCH AT PURDUE UNIVERSITY STOP ANYWAY SUBJECT FURTHER
> DISCUSSION PLEASE WIRE WHAT AMOUNT NEEDED NOW AND WHETHER
> CAN MEET JUNE FIFTEENTH DELIVERY DATE AM REQUESTING ENGINE
> DELIVERY BY MAY TWENTIETH PLEASE STEP ON IT REGARDS=
> :GEORGE PALMER PUTNAM.849AM..

```
           LOCKHEED ELECTRA ENGINES
              AS OF 15 APRIL 1935

ELECTRA                       ENGINE
 MODEL                        MODEL

  10A      PRATT & WHITNEY, WASP JR., R-985-SB
             450 hp @ 2300 rpm @ 36.5" Hg takeoff
             400 hp @ 2200 rpm @ 34.5" Hg maximum
             300 hp @ 2000 rpm @ 28" Hg maximum recommended

  10B      WRIGHT AERONAUTICAL DIV., WHIRLWIND R-975-E3
             450 hp @ 2250 rpm @ 36.5" Hg takeoff
             420 hp @ 2200 rpm @ 34.5" Hg maximum
             325 hp @ 2000 rpm @ 30" Hg maximum recommended

  10C      PRATT & WHITNEY, WASP R-985-SC1
             450 hp @ 2100 rpm @ 34" Hg takeoff
             440 hp @ 2000 rpm @ 30.5" Hg maximum
             325 hp @ 1900 rpm @ 26" Hg maximum recommended

  10E      PRATT & WHITNEY, WASP R-1340-S3 H1 civil
                             (R-1340-AN-1 military)
             550 hp @ 2200 rpm @ 34.5" Hg takeoff
             450 hp @ 2200 rpm @ 29" Hg maximum
             412 hp @ 2000 rpm @ 26.5" Hg maximum recommended

  N.B.  All engines are nine cylinder, air-cooled, radials; all propellers
        are nine-foot, Hamilton Standard controllable (constant-speed
        propellers were available by 1937).
```

Electra engine specifications.

> AIRCRAFT CORPORATION
> DEPARTMENTAL COMMUNICATION
>
> Date March 20, 1936.
>
> Purchasing Dept.:
> Accounting Dept.:
> Mr. Von Hake:
>
> ...mer, Livingston - Sales Dept. Order #1.
>
> ...nd fabricate #1055 Electra as a special 10E
> ...y, in accordance with the following data:
>
> ...following material not later than May 20:
>
> ...ngines, including oil temperature control units
> 2 - Hamilton Standard constant speed propellers
> 2 - Governors for constant speed propellers
> 2 - Eclipse starters
> 1 - Eclipse generator with control box
> 2 - Romec F4RB fuel pumps
> 2 - Eclipse AF5 vacuum pumps
> 2 - Solar exhaust manifolds
> 2 - United Aircraft Products 7" oil radiators

PREPARING TO CIRCLE THE GLOBE | 177

FAA records show that Amelia's Lockheed Electra had two Pratt & Whitney S3H-1 Wasp engines, s/n 6149 and s/n 6150. They were rated at 550 Hp at take off and 450 Hp at altitudes around 4,000 feet. She had two constant speed Hamilton Standard propellers.

GP, from Lockheed's New York office, sent the following message to Lockheed:

"Please be sure that the entire matter is held confidentially. For your information, we expect to make announcement about April 15th."

Lockheed immediately commenced production of Electra serial number 1055 about March 20, 1936, and in an effort to keep the new purchaser confidential, identified the customer as "Livingston." The purchase price was $42,000.00. During construction Paul Mantz, Amelia's advisor, acted as technical coordinator and her representative. On her birthday, July 24, 1936, Amelia took possession of her new Lockheed Electra. Fifteen years earlier, on her twenty-fourth birthday, she had purchased her first airplane, the Kinner Airster.

GP telling Lockheed to keep the purchase of the airplane confidential.

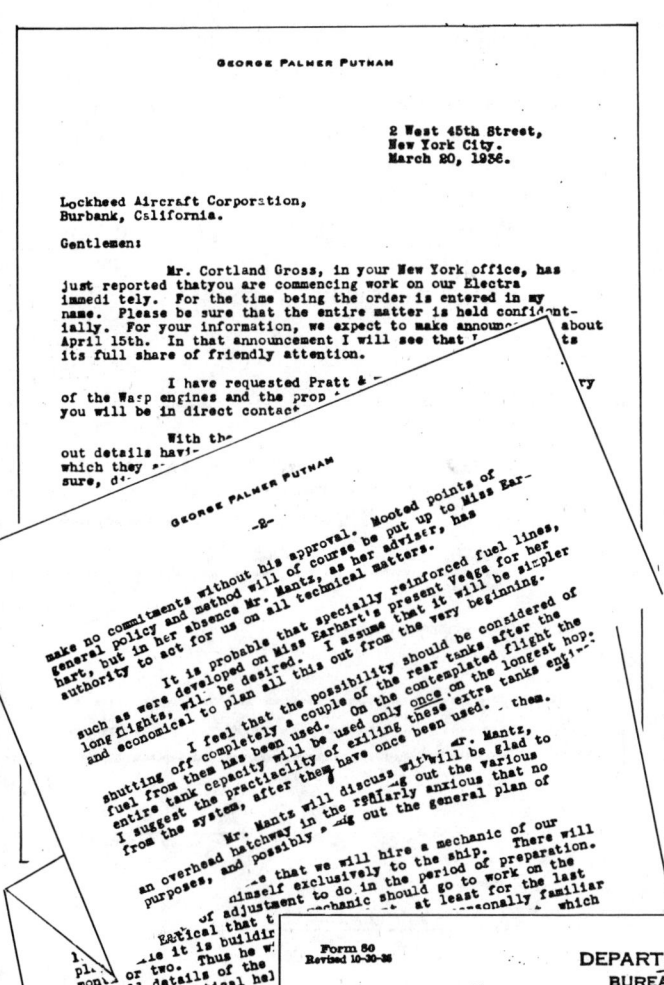

(facing page) Telegram from GP purchasing Amelia's Electra.

Lockheed begins production on Amelia's Electra Model 10E under the purchaser name of "Livingston."

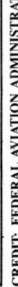

CREDIT: FEDERAL AVIATION ADMINISTRATION

A Western Electric Memo to File dated May 6, 1936, reads as follows:

> " . . . the requirements to be met by radio equipment for use in international and overseas flying are somewhat different than those prevailing in domestic operations, particularly in regard to the matter of flexibility of adjustment, crystal control in both transmitter and receiver being the rule for domestic use while continuously adjustable transmitter and receiver tuning are desirable in foreign operations. It was also pointed out that telegraphy offered some advantages in overseas flying in that contact could be effected with radio telegraphy stations aboard marine vessels and also with the many commercial and government shore stations available in most countries. It was also suggested that considerable weight could be saved by using a low power telegraph equipment such as the Lindberghs have employed on some of their overseas flights rather than carrying telephone apparatus. Miss Earhart said that she had not practiced telegraphy for a number of years and that therefore telegraph operation would involve some difficulty.
>
> "Mr. Putnam indicated that, in any event, the two-way telephone installation would be desired for local operation and also questioned whether the increased weight would be a serious factor due to the exceptional performance of the Electra plane."

The memo concluded:

> " . . . a satisfactory set-up could be furnished Miss Earhart employing our standard transport 50-watt radio transmitter (13A) and new continuously adjustable four-band receiver (20A) with suitable power and remote control apparatus."

W. H. "Walt" Grosselfinger, former engineer for Western Electric, stated that Bell Telephone Laboratories, a subsidiary of Western Electric, provided the design of the radio equipment. He further said that the Westinghouse type (13A) transmitter and (20A) receiver contained frequencies: 6210 for daytime use and 3105 for nighttime use. The crystal-controlled transmitter frequencies are similar to television VHF channels in that they cannot be "mistuned." These frequencies were standard commercial aircraft frequencies of that time.

This equipment was modified by Bell Laboratories to include 500 KC in order to provide emergency communications. A telegraph key was mounted in the cockpit to allow Amelia to communicate with radio telegraphy stations abroad and more important, with ships at sea. She could talk over the 500 KC frequencies by using her microphone. Although she never utilized this telegraphic capability, it was available.

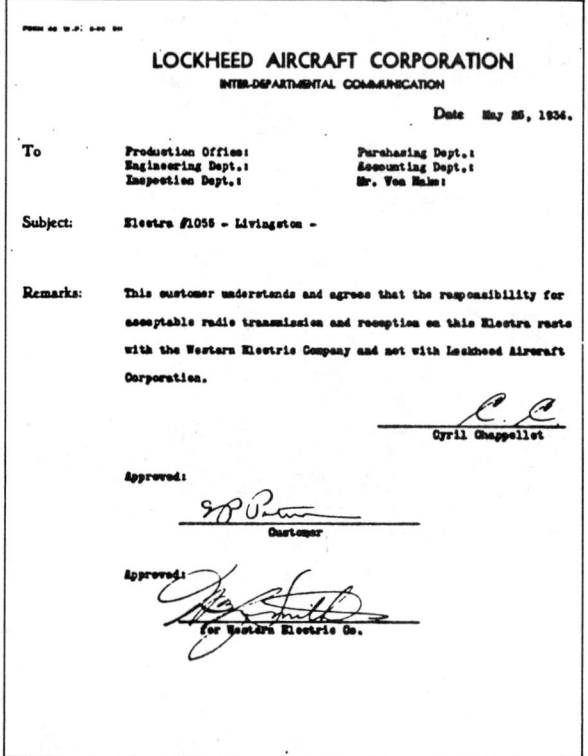

Agreement for purchase of the Electra's radio equipment.

GP arranged the purchase of the radio gear from Western Electric. On May 25, 1936, Lockheed, Western Electric and GP signed an agreement that stipulated, "This customer understands and agrees that the responsibility for acceptable radio transmission and reception on this Electra rests with the Western Electric Company and not with Lockheed Aircraft Corporation."

(above) Amelia looking over her Lockheed Model 10, circa 1936.

Amelia inside her flying laboratory, prior to installation of fuel tanks, circa 1936.

LOCKHEED AIRCRAFT CORPORATION
INTER-DEPARTMENTAL COMMUNICATION

Date May 21, 1936

To   Mr. Chappellet

Subject: Western Electric radio equipment for Number 1055, installation of:

Remarks: The following Western Electric units are to be installed in the respective locations as noted.

    4 B power unit under pilot seat.
  27 A control unit in control box lid.
  20 B receiver on top of gas tank (cabin).
  13 C transmitter in cabinet behind tanks.
   2   transmitting keys with brackets in cock pit.

The equipment as shown above requires a Cannon tuning unit to function $30 properly and is not to be furnished by Western Electric.

Any additional radio equipment desired by customer, such as Kruesi, Lear, etc., will require additional installation work.

Customer desires extra battery-to be furnished by him- installed in $98 nose department. Will require extra switch in cock pit to allow either battery to be charged.

                                    J. W. Cross

LOCKHEED AIRCRAFT CORPORATION
INTER-DEPARTMENTAL COMMUNICATION

Date February 26, 1937

To   Production Office: Mr. Dake: Purchasing Dept.:
      Engineering Dept.:   Mr. Von Hake:
      Accounting Dept.:   Mr. Gaudette:

Subject: Amelia Earhart Electra #1055

Remarks:
1. Install jack box and key (both of which will be furnished by customer) on navigating table in rear of ship. Have electrician who will make the installation talk to Paul Mantz for detailed instructions.   CHARGE

2. Install round control wheel, in accordance with engineering instructions (see Jimmy Gerschler).

                        Accounting: Charge for new wheel and give credit for old one if it can be used by us on another ship.

Western Electric and Lockheed Aircraft Corporation planning correspondence about the radio equipment to be installed in Amelia's airplane.

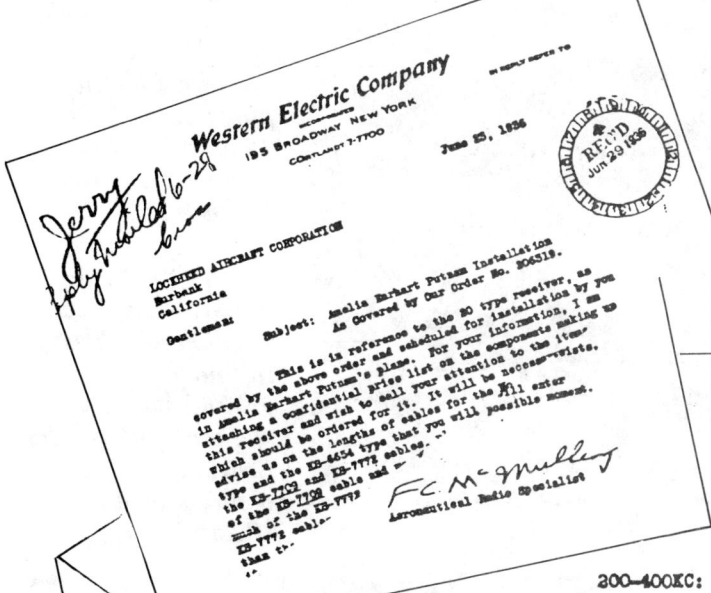

TRANSPORT LIST #16
June 1, 1936

WESTERN ELECTRIC

20-B REMOTE CONTROL RECEIVER
4 BANDS
200-400KC; 550-1500KC; 1500-4000 KC; 4000-10,000 KC

Weight		List	Transport
14 - 11	1 - #20-B Radio Receiver and Tubes	$344.00	$222.60
0 - 3	1 - #297-A Plug (SS12CCT)	3.60	2.35
0 - 2	1 - #6-A-7)		
0 - 2	1 - #6-B-7) included in		
0 - 2	1 - #6-F-7) Receiver price		
0 - 2	1 - #41)		
0 - 3	4 - T2 Magda Lamps	1.28	.80
10 - 12	1 - KS7543 Power Unit	40.00	27.00
- - -	1 - 5S8CCT Socket	.95	.60
0 - 12	1 - 1011-A Headset	12.65	8.20
0 - 6	1 - #1-C Jack Box	11.50	7.50
2 - 5	1 - #27-A Control Unit	92.50	60.00
29 - 10		$506.48	$329.05
2 oz/ft	1 - KS 7709 Flex shaft and casing (Specify exact length including bends from left end of 27 A Control to right end of 20 B Receiver) Price Per Foot		
2 oz/ft	2 - KS 7772 Control cables - per foot		

Amelia Earhart Putnam was reported in trouble today soon after taking off in her Lockheed Electra in the Bendix Trophy race from here to the coast. Photo shows Miss Earhart and her passenger, Miss Helen Richey, at start of race, Floyd Bennett Field.

Western Electric photo dated Sept 1936 . . . Floyd Bennett Airport, Newark, N.J.

Amelia "wearing her Western Electric headphones, keeps in touch with ground stations as she manipulates the instrument-board controls of her 'flying laboratory'."

Jacobson Falls Amid Wreckage—Amelia Earhart Battles for Her Life.

By the United Press.
KANSAS CITY, Sept. 4.—Joe Jacobson, Kansas City aviator flying in the Bendix air derby from New York to Los Angeles, was blown out of his airplane today when it exploded 5,000 feet in the air near Stafford, Kan. He descended safely in his parachute after an exciting few moments in which it ap-

MECHANIC IS TALISMAN FOR AMELIA EARHART

Just before her near-mishap in the Bendix air race today Amelia Earhart told about her special good luck charm, on which she counted in the flight. The charm's name is R. B. McKneeley, of Burbank, Cal., and he's a mechanic.

"I'm all out of superstitions," said Miss Earhart. "The good luck charm which seems to me most important is a good mechanic—that and a good engine. I'm fortunate in having both."

Miss Earhart, at the wheel of her Flying Laboratory just before the racing take-off today, faces an impressive battery of blind flying instruments.   Rudy Arnold Photos.

CREDIT: RUDY ARNOLD PHOTOS. CREDIT WESTERN ELECTRIC

Amelia's Electra 10E in Sept. 1936, just prior to the Bendix Air Race.

PREPARING TO CIRCLE THE GLOBE | 183

AMELIA—FROM VEGA TO ELECTRA

This photo, supplied through the courtesy of the Los Angeles "Times," shows Amelia Earhart standing on the wing of her recently delivered Lockheed Electra and looking, perhaps a bit ruefully, at her Wasp-powered Vega which proved her faithful steed for so many years.

In her new Electra, a "flying laboratory" with nearly every known safety device and mechanical aid, Miss Earhart plans a research which will delve into the physical and psychological factors of flying. A new venture, this program is to be carried on under the auspices and with the assistance of Purdue University, where Miss Earhart is consultant in aeronautics.

The experiments will be conducted either in Southern California or Indiana.

Woman Pilot Guides $75,000 Flying 'La Sees Inventions

TRIB D AUG 3 - 1935

ALAMEDA, Aug. 3.—Amelia Earhart Putnam, America's premier aviatrix, lately turned test pilot under the auspices of a Mid-western university, arrived at San Francisco Bay Airdrome this morning in the $75,000 Lockheed Electra she will use as a flying laboratory.

The woman who has conquered the air lanes over both of the oceans expressed keen interest in the new plane parachute recently developed by a San Francisco aircraft safety corporation and said she "might try one of them out a little later."

E. H. Dimity, president of the company which developed the chute, was at the port. One of the chutes he presented for the aviatrix's examination was 90 feet in diameter, made of 1000 square yards of treated silk and had a total of three miles of cross wires. Dimity said engineers have perfected a spring system which, instead of merely releasing the chute when it is to be brought into play, "kicks" its sides out 10 feet from the plane, thus tending to eliminate possibilities of fouling with the wing tips. Dimity said one company, Consolidated Airlines, will begin using the chutes on all of its planes within about six months.

INSTRUMENTS GALORE

The pilot's compartment of the trim low-wing ship was literally lined with instruments of all sorts, and "they're not all in yet," Miss Earhart assured those who met her.

With E. C. McLeod, test pilot for Lockheed Aircraft, she flew up from Burbank last night in 1 hour and 55 minutes. They landed Mills Field, spent the night incognito at San Francisco and cruised on across the bay today. They left this afternoon. But Amelia will be back.

"I'm going to wear a groove in the airlines between here and Southern California," she said.

FOG DISPELLER INTERESTS

The famous flyer expressed interest in a chemical compound called "no fog" developed during the past four years by C. R. Pleasants, a Bay region engineer who claims that it will dispel fog or "raise" a low ceiling. Its vapors, issuing from heaters ringed around an airport, will clear the air, or pilot desiring to land in fog may throw it in powder form from his ship with the same results, the inventor says.

Lockheed Aircraftsman publication showing Amelia's two airplanes.

Amelia had developed a friendship with President and Mrs. Franklin D. Roosevelt and in fact was planning to teach Mrs. Roosevelt to fly. This plan never materialized, however, because the President discouraged it. In June, 1936, GP wrote to Mrs. Roosevelt:

> "On her [Amelia's] behalf I am venturing this letter to avail ourselves of the help which you kindly offered when we last saw you. Our wish is to be put in touch with the proper person in the State Department whose aid can be enlisted in connection with A.E.'s proposed world flight. We want appropriate guidance in securing the required permissions, etc."

GP ended his letter:

> "Do please emphasize that the project is for the present confidential. As you know, A.E. likes to avoid advance discussion of flights—their realization depends upon so many factors."

Amelia and Eleanor Roosevelt

Mrs. Roosevelt conveyed GP's request for confidentiality in a note to Mr. Richard Southgate, Chief of Division of Protocol in the State Department.

On November 10, 1936, Amelia wrote to the President and reminded him of her plan to attempt a flight around the world at the equator, traveling from east to west. Amelia was most concerned about the leg of her flight from Honolulu to Tokyo. In her letter she pointed out the difficulty of flying the 3,900 miles from Honolulu to Tokyo, and stated:

> "I want to reduce as much as possible the hazard of the take-off at Honolulu with the excessive over-load. With that in view, I am discussing with the Navy a possible refueling in the air over Midway Island. If this can be arranged, I need to take much less gas from Honolulu, and with the Midway refueling will have ample gasoline to reach Tokio*. As mine is a land plane, the seaplane facilities at Wake, Guam, etc. are useless."

Toward that end Amelia remarked:

> "Knowing your own enthusiasm for voyaging, and your affectionate interest in Navy matters, I am asking you to help me secure Navy cooperation—that is, if you think well of the project."

She ended the letter to the President:

> "P.S.—My plans are for the moment entirely confidential—no announcement has been made."

From February, 1936, until public announcement of the flight one year later, Amelia and GP worked constantly with a small corps of devoted experts. Paul Mantz, technical adviser and pilot par excellence, dealt with every phase of the engines' performance and fuel storage; Jacques de Sibour, a British pilot and friend from the *Friendship* flight days, proved invaluable as he worked out the best locations to cache the fuel supplies overseas. He was able to give Amelia first-hand information about the flying conditions over much of the British Empire in Asia and Africa. GP took charge of

*"Tokio" was the accepted Romaji spelling for Japan's capitol city prior to 1940.

(above) One of several reminders for confidentiality.

(below) A letter to Chief of Naval Operations expressing the President's desire to support Amelia's flight.

Two page "Feasibility Study" letter regarding the feasibility of in-flight refueling.

Letter from Chief of Naval Operations to the Commander-in-Chief of the U.S. Fleet, directing him to take necessary action to support the Earhart flight.

Amelia's two loves—her Cord and her Electra, circa 1937.

President Roosevelt answered Amelia's request for help with Howland Island.

```
                        THE WHITE HOUSE
                          WASHINGTON

                         January 11, 1937

My dear Miss Earhart:

     The President has requested me to reply to your tele-
gram of January 8, 1937 advising him that the plan arranged
by Admiral Standley to refuel your plane west of Hawaii on
the proposed round the world flight this spring has been
abandoned and that you intend to land, instead, on Howland
Island, if the construction of an emergency landing field
on that Island is completed by that time.

     An allocation of Federal funds has been made by the
President to the Works Progress Administration to enable
the Bureau of Air Commerce to carry out the construction
of such a field.

     I understand that the necessary equipment and labor
for this work will be transported to Howland Island by
the Coast Guard Service on a boat scheduled to leave
Honolulu on Tuesday, January 12, 1937.

                              Sincerely yours,


                              Assistant Secretary
                              to the President.

Miss Amelia Earhart
Union Air Terminal
Burbank, California
```

procuring credentials and visas. He spent one entire month in Washington, D. C., visiting the embassies of every government within whose boundaries Amelia planned to land or over which she might fly. Captain Harry Manning, of the *U. S. S. President Roosevelt*, was Amelia's choice as her navigator. He agreed to take a six months leave of absence from his ship as he had promised he would nine years before when Amelia returned with him from her "passenger flight" across the Atlantic. Fred Noonan, a veteran Pan American Airways pilot and navigator, was to accompany Amelia and Captain Manning on the first leg of the flight to relieve them of the heavy piloting and navigating tasks westward from Hawaii. Amelia expected to fly the last 4,000 miles alone—from Natal, Brazil, and on to Oakland.

GP discussed the feasibility of midair refueling over Midway Island. In a letter dated October 16, 1936, to the Secretary of the Navy, GP wrote:

> "It is our understanding that some new Navy [flying] boats, now reaching completion in San Diego, will after the first of the year be ferried out to Honolulu. An ideal situation, of course, would be created if one of these boats, with the crew that will man it at Honolulu, could undertake the refueling practise [sic] before departure from California. Thereby the two planes and the same crews will be used both in practise [sic] and in the actual refueling, so that the technique of operation will be mutually coordinated."†

The Chief of Bureau of Aeronautics wrote to the Chief of Naval Operations in an endorsement letter dated October 27, 1936:

> ". . . the attitude of the Department toward pioneering aeronautical ventures should, in general, be cooperative. In this case the amount of effort required to accede to Mr. Putnam's request would be considerable, although some benefit might accrue to the Navy in the line of development of fueling from the air."

---

†*A flight of 12 Consolodated PBY-1's arrived at Honolulu on April 13, 1937. On April 28, 1937, a Pan Am Sikorsky S-42 arrived at Hongkong via Midway Island and Honolulu, utilizing midair refueling at each station.*

Plans proceeded for Amelia to fly from Honolulu to Tokyo and to be refuelled midair over Midway. She received the President's good wishes, and he asked the Navy to assist where possible. Soon GP received a letter which contained the following:

> "The Department [Navy] is willing to render the assistance requested, subject however to the successful completion of preliminary preparations and trials.
>
> The matter of expenses it is believed can be arranged satisfactorily. The Department feels that actual tangible costs, such as that for gasoline and oil to be used in her own plane, and for the expenses of personnel engaged in this work, over and above those normally incurred by the personnel concerned, should be borne by Miss Earhart."

GEORGE PALMER PUTNAM

2 West 45th Street,
New York City.
July 21, 1936.

Dear Mr. Chappelet:

When I was west you kindly equipped me with a memorandum listing in detail the items purchased from Goodyear for Miss Earhart's ship, together with their prices. Will you please send me by air mail a duplicate of this list. I find immediate need for it.

Also kindly let me have a similar list of all purchases from Goodrich in connection with the de-icing equipment, together with prices to you.

Confidentially, I expect, through certain banking connections, to arrange for gratis contribution from both these companies. This, however, please do not mention there. If and when I succeed, Lockheed will simply get a credit from the two companies, which credit can be passed on to us in the final settlement of our account with you.

Sincerely,

GPPutnam

Cyril Chappelet, Esq.,
Lockheed Aircraft Corporation,
Burbank, California.

Dan—Want to airmail this today
RK

Letter from GP discussing delivery and financing of Amelia's Electra. GP "confidentially" transmits information to Lockheed's Cyril Chappellet.

After some time and discussion, Amelia and GP changed the route. She decided to fly from Honolulu to Lae, New Guinea, with a stop at Howland Island for refueling.

In a Western Union telegram Amelia sent to President Roosevelt on January 8, 1937, Amelia wrote:

" . . . I HOPE TO LAND ON TINY HOWLAND ISLAND WHERE THE GOVERNMENT IS ABOUT TO ESTABLISH AN EMERGENCY FIELD STOP COMMERCE APPROVES MY PLAN INTERIOR VERY COOPERATIVE COAST GUARD DITTO ALL DETAILS ARRANGED STOP CONSTRUCTION PARTY WITH EQUIPMENT DUE TO SAIL FROM HONOLULU NEXT WEEK STOP AM NOW INFORMED APPARENTLY SOME QUESTION REGARDING WPA APPROPRIATION IN AMOUNT THREE THOUSAND DOLLARS WHICH COVERS ALL COSTS OTHER THAN THOSE BORN BY ME FOR THIS MID PACIFIC PIONEER LANDING FIELD WHICH PERMANENTLY USEFUL AND VALUABLE AERONAUTICALLY AND NATIONALLY . . ."

Apparently these costs were much more affordable than the refueling over Midway. The White House answered Amelia's telegram, January 11, three days later:

"An allocation of Federal funds has been made by the President to the Works Progress Administration to enable the Bureau of Air Commerce to carry out the construction of such a field.

Scenes on Howland Island, Ocean Airport Amelia Will Use

No. 1—Kuu home alanuinani, meaning "Entrance to our beautiful home." The above sign was displayed at the entrance to a camp on Howland Island.
No. 2—Tent fly and fresh water drums on the island.
No. 3—Dressed for comfort.
No. 4—Food supply tent.

CREDIT: ATCHISON COUNTY HISTORICAL MUSEUM

"I understand that the necessary equipment and labor for this work will be transported to Howland Island by the Coast Guard Service on a boat scheduled to leave Honolulu on Tuesday, January 12, 1937."

When the time came for the many vaccinations and inoculations, Amelia revealed her plans about the globe-circling flight to a group of reporters. To the inevitable question, "Why are you making this flight?" Amelia answered sincerely:

"I hope that this flight will yield some valuable knowledge about human reactions and mechanical performance at high altitudes and high temperatures for long intervals. I am racing nobody, but I do have a time schedule which I shall endeavor to follow. I am not interested in setting any records; I hope the data we shall bring back on fuel consumption and other mechanical details, as well as airport facilities and conditions, may hasten and encourage world-wide civilian plane travel. The flight has been carefully plotted to cover the maximum distance with the minimum number of stops. We expect to log about twenty-seven thousand miles from Oakland back to Oakland."

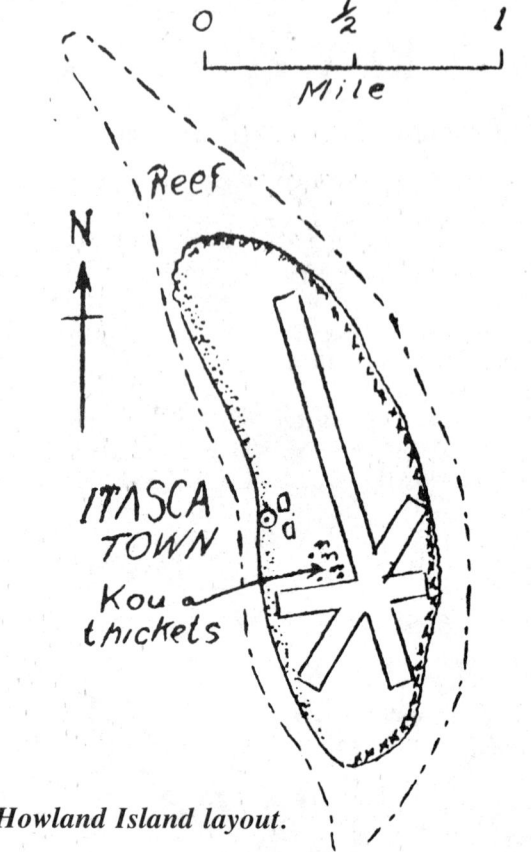

Howland Island layout.

History. Howland was first reported as discovered by Captain George E. Netcher of New Bedford, Massachussets, the discovery having been made on September 9, 1842. On February 5, 1857 it was taken possession of in the name of the American Guano Company by Alfred G. Benson of New York and Charles H. Judd of Honolulu. From 1860 to 1880 colonies of guano diggers were maintained on it and other guano islands in the central Pacific. Supplies reached them by regular quarterly trips of schooners from Honolulu. A large number of schooners, barks, clippers, etc. called and carried away thousands of tons of guano. Anchorage was uncertain, loading was difficult through the surf, and many vessels were wrecked. When the best of the guano had been removed, the American guano colonies were withdrawn. During the period from 1883 to 1890, Howland, Baker, and other islands were occupied by the John T. Arundel Company, a British firm, which removed some guano, and in turn abandoned the islands. A party of American colonists was established on Howland March 30, 1935 from the USS ITASCA, C.G. The natural surface of the island was developed into airplane runways, as shown on the map Amelia Earhart was to have first used them on July 2, 1937; they still remain unused. A lighthouse was established on Howland and dedicated November 16, 1937 by an official party from the TANEY. It is known as Amelia Earhart Light.

NEW YORK HERALD TRIBUNE, SUNDAY, MARCH 7, 1937

Learn How Vidal's Successor Will Treat His Policies

As Amelia Earhart Makes Preparations for Her Round-the-World Flight

Above, left, in the chart room of the Electra, "The Flying Laboratory," with Navigator Harry Manning. Above, right, her complete baggage for the flight. The suitcase in her hand contains her clothing, while the case beside her holds charts arranged for quick reference. Right, the pilot smiles through a Bendix direction finder

Complete Navigation Room Ready to Guide Miss Earhart

Countless Last Details on Plane and Over World Route Being Checked to Await Take-Off; Supplies 'Spotted' Along Her Course

Special to the Herald Tribune

BURBANK, Calif., March 6.—"What does a round-the-world flyer think about?"

When asked that question, Amelia Earhart, poised in California for a hop across the Pacific to Australia and beyond, just grinned.

"If, as and when I get back," she countered good-naturedly, "perhaps I'll be able to answer—although probably I wouldn't even if I could." "But," she added, "if you want to discuss what one who plans a 27,000-mile flight has to think about, it's not an uninteresting subject—to me, at least."

Miss Earhart added that even before the inquiring reporter indulged in much inquiry he'd do well to look around a bit. He did.

These days the Lockheed Electra plane alternates between preparation in the hangar of Paul Mantz, who is Miss Earhart's technical adviser, and periodic test flights. On the ground or in the air the big ship fairly swarms with technicians and mechanics, tinkering with the thousand and one details of its complex equipment.

both cockpit and cabin. On her previous Pacific flight, Miss Earhart's voice messages carried over 2,000 miles.

A few days ago Commander Clarence Williams brought to the field a bevy of aeronautical students using them for man power to move the big Electra about on the compass rose until all its compasses—there are three of them—were properly swung. Which means checked exactly and co-ordinated.

"And just what are you yourself doing?" Miss Earhart was asked.

"Plenty!" Illustrating that answer the aviatrix offered an informal pre

Incidentally, typhoid injections and smallpox inoculations are among the personal requisites of long-range flying.

Takes Walking Boots

"Speaking of personal matters, what about your own equipment? And your food?"

for vital mechanical parts is important. Also, ropes to tie the ship down, and stakes to tie it to. A parachute already waits at Port Darwin—it would be wasted weight over the Pacific. Preparation of the extra-long runway at Oakland.

Two-Way Electric Voice

An arrangement has been devised to open the cabin door about four inches, where it is held rigidly in place. A Pioneer drift indicator is mounted for use looking down through this aperture, to check wind drift on the earth or sea below. For this work flares are used at night over water, smoke bombs in daylight.

Beside the chart table are mounted three chronometers, altimeter, air speed indicator and temperature gauge. All of which gives a skilled navigator about all he could wish to work with for determining course and location aloft.

A last-minute addition to navigational equipment is a Bendix direction finder, installed during the last week. Its "loop," carried on the outside of the ship just above the cockpit, is adjustable by the pilot so that it may be turned in any desired direction. In effect this uncanny device does with man-made radio emissions what a routine compass accomplishes with magnetic forces, in determining position and direction to a desired location.

Both navigator and pilot may utilize the two-way Western Electric voice and telegraph radio communication system with which the ship is equipped. Code transmitting is from both cockpit and cabin. On her previous Pacific flight, Miss Earhart's voice messages carried over 2,000 miles.

A few days ago Commander Clarence Williams brought to the field a bevy of aeronautical students using them for man power to move the big Electra about on the compass rose until all its compasses—there are three of them—were properly swung Which means checked exactly and co-ordinated.

"And just what are you yourself doing?" Miss Earhart was asked.

"Plenty!" Illustrating that answer the aviatrix offered an informal preview of her maps—dozens of them. "Merely assembling these, getting information on fields, weather conditions, servicing facilities, has taken months. And now Commander Williams has just finished another month's work laying out the courses. It's really a very lovely job."

On previous long-distance flights, the woman flyer has developed her own technique of maps for use in the air. Clearness and simplicity are the key requisites. For each flight the compass course, with its hourly or periodic changes, is set down. The distances also are shown, and the estimated elapsed time between specific points, based on a predetermined minimum cruising speed.

In addition to the charts themselves, (one of them is always spread out on the pilot's knees), the "vital statistics" of each portion of the flight are recorded in compact memoranda for easy reference. One of several clocks, by the way, is set at "zero" at the start, so that it records the elapsed time in the air for that particular flight.

Husband Helps Expedition

"What about fuel and supplies at stopping points?"

"We've tried to cover all that," Miss Earhart replied. "Mr. Putnam [George Palmer Putnam, her husband] has had much experience in expedition organization. I think he has had a lot of fun—and some grief! —in working out the arrangements."

Specified amounts of gasoline and oil are now on hand at over thirty points on the 27,000 mile course, with a representative in charge at each Extra engine parts are "spotted" at strategic places, and expert mechanical aid arranged.

"Doubtless there are many places on the existing itinerary at which I actually will not stop," Miss Earhart explained. "But, it's sensible to be prepared all the way. Which of them I will 'leap frog' depends upon weather, on mechanical matters and even on the feelings of the pilot.

"By the way," she continued, "in all this preparation we've been fortunate in having the help of an old friend of ours, the Viscount Jacques de Sibour. He and his wife, the former Violette Selfridge, have cruised in their own planes over much of the territory I hope to traverse. He is connected with the Standard Oil Company of New Jersey, which has generously co-operated in 'spotting' our supplies."

Another matter to be thought about, it developed, is governmental permissions. Even a lone woman flyer—or perhaps especially one—has to have all sorts of permits and official advance arrangements, particularly in these troubled times. Incidentally, typhoid injections and smallpox inoculations are among the personal requisites of long-range flying.

Takes Walking Boots

"Speaking of personal matters, what about your own equipment? And your food?"

"If you mean clothes, one of my own small light suitcases will carry all I'll take," Miss Earhart replied. "Once I crossed the Atlantic with only a toothbrush. This time there'll be a few luxuries like spare slacks and clean linen."

The woman pilot's usual flying togs comprise twill slacks, sport shirt and scarf, plus a leather windbreaker, their color almost always some tone of brown. She will carry a light over-all flying suit—never a hat. In the plane she'll wear light, low shoes. And this time she's taking along a pair of heavy, high walking boots, "just in case," as she puts it.

Other emergency items include a light land compass, waterproof match box, knife, small ax and canteen. In the fuselage will be a two-man rubber lifeboat, instantly inflatable from capsules of carbon dioxide. Likewise a Very pistol for firing distress signals, flares that ignite on the surface of the water, and, as she says, "a very orange" orange kite.

"If we sit down somewhere in the Pacific and stay afloat, I'd like to be noticed," says Miss Earhart.

Tomato Juice a Standby

As another safety precaution—or at least an aid in case of forced landing at sea or in jungle or desert—the top of the plane's wings are having stripes of black, orange and red painted on them to increase visibility for possible searching aircraft. The blue-gray of the Electra's unpainted metal is difficult to see against neutral backgrounds.

Miss Earhart will carry her usual food supplies. Tomato juice is her favorite standby. Her technique is to punch a hole in a can with an abbreviated ice-pick gadget, insert a straw and, as she says, "let nature take its course."

There will be thermos bottles of hot cocoa and a reserve emergency supply of concentrated food, its mainstay malted milk tablets. Raisins and chocolate complete the larder. Two desert water bags will carry water, plus a canteen.

A unique item in the pilot's equipment is a "battery" of sun glasses that have been made up especially for her. Miss Earhart reckons fatigue as a pilot's greatest problem on any long flight, and especially one sustained for many days. A vital aspect of physical and mental fatigue, she has found, is eye strain.

Other items? There are plenty of them.

As, for instance, specially made covers of Grenfell cloth for propellers and engines; there there are no hangars dust and weather protection for vital mechanical parts is important. Also, ropes to tie the ship down, and stakes to tie it to. parachute already waits at Port Darwin. It would be wasted weight over the Pacific. Preparation of the extra long runway at Oakland, and last minute word about the emergency landing field just created at Howland Island.

With most of this accomplished, so far as such things can be arranged in advance, these last days will be devoted to shakedown flights and final testing; also to co-ordinating all arrangements at flight headquarters at Oakland Airport. There W. T. Miller, of the Department of Commerce, is working with Pan American Airways, the Navy and the Coast Guard, all of whom are co-operating.

For a fortnight complete "weather maps" of the Pacific have been compiled daily. When plane and pilot are ready, one such map that is satisfactory—or at least acceptable—will come through. Then the pioneer air adventure will start—after Lockheed inspectors have made one final, painstaking check of the ship from engines to ailerons.

Amelia, left, and Anita King Lee, one of the singing King sisters, in Oakland. Anita was taking flying lessons the day she met Amelia at the airfield.

Chapter Eighteen

"*Just One More Long Flight*"

"I think I have just one more long flight in my system," Amelia told a group of New York reporters in February, 1937. "After that? My lovely home in North Hollywood —California sunshine—books—friends —leisurely travel—many things."

Having planned every facet of her flight carefully, Amelia had fuel consumption tests run on her Electra under the direction of C.L. "Kelly" Johnson, Project Engineer, Lockheed Aircraft Corporation. The test flight results were wired back to Kelly and after careful analysis, he sent his final flight analysis:

> "REVISED FLIGHT DATA FOR EIGHT THOUSAND FEET AT BEGINNING OF FLIGHT AS FOLLOWS . . . AFTER SIX HOURS USE DATA GIVEN IN PREVIOUS LETTER OR WIRE STOP GALLONS PER HOUR SHOULD RUN LITTLE UNDER FIGURES GIVEN."

In the beginning there was a real concern for Amelia's carrying up to 1,151 gallons of gasoline, at six pounds per gallon. Lockheed was particularly concerned with the center of gravity, or balance, as the plane consumed the fuel. To ensure proper distribution of weight, the fuel feed was modified to maintain longitudinal balance but to allow insignificant nose or tail heaviness. This would guard against accidental spinning.

Amelia and C.L. "Kelly" Johnson, January, 1937.

Telegrams discussing fuel consumption and general preparations before the world flight.

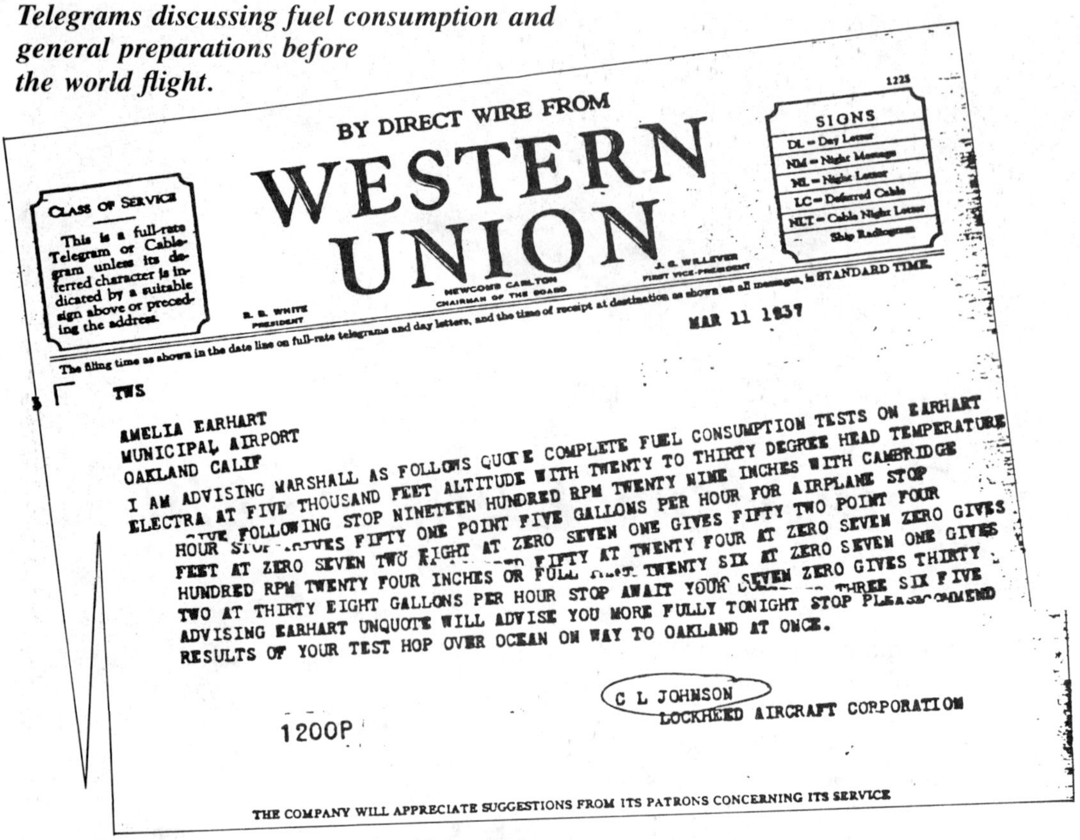

BY DIRECT WIRE FROM
WESTERN UNION

CLASS OF SERVICE: This is a full-rate Telegram or Cablegram unless its deferred character is indicated by a suitable sign above or preceding the address.

SIGNS: DL = Day Letter; NM = Night Message; NL = Night Letter; LC = Deferred Cable; NLT = Cable Night Letter; Ship Radiogram

R. B. WHITE, PRESIDENT — NEWCOMB CARLTON, CHAIRMAN OF THE BOARD — J. C. WILLEVER, FIRST VICE-PRESIDENT

The filing time as shown in the date line on full-rate telegrams and day letters, and the time of receipt at destination as shown on all messages, is STANDARD TIME.

MAR 11 1937

TWS

AMELIA EARHART
MUNICIPAL AIRPORT
OAKLAND CALIF

I AM ADVISING MARSHALL AS FOLLOWS QUOTE COMPLETE FUEL CONSUMPTION TESTS ON EARHART ELECTRA AT FIVE THOUSAND FEET ALTITUDE WITH TWENTY TO THIRTY DEGREE HEAD TEMPERATURE [illegible] FOLLOWING STOP NINETEEN HUNDRED RPM TWENTY NINE INCHES WITH CAMBRIDGE HOUR STOP [illegible]GIVES FIFTY ONE POINT FIVE GALLONS PER HOUR FOR AIRPLANE STOP FEET AT ZERO SEVEN TWO EIGHT AT ZERO SEVEN ONE GIVES FIFTY TWO POINT FOUR HUNDRED RPM TWENTY FOUR INCHES OR FULL [illegible] FIFTY AT TWENTY FOUR AT ZERO SEVEN ZERO GIVES TWO AT THIRTY EIGHT GALLONS PER HOUR STOP AWAIT YOUR [illegible] TWENTY SIX AT ZERO SEVEN ONE GIVES ADVISING EARHART UNQUOTE WILL ADVISE YOU MORE FULLY TONIGHT STOP PLEASE [illegible] SEVEN ZERO GIVES THIRTY [illegible] THREE SIX FIVE RESULTS OF YOUR TEST HOP OVER OCEAN ON WAY TO OAKLAND AT ONCE.

C L JOHNSON
LOCKHEED AIRCRAFT CORPORATION

1200P

THE COMPANY WILL APPRECIATE SUGGESTIONS FROM ITS PATRONS CONCERNING ITS SERVICE

CREDIT: D.D. HATFIELD AVIATION COLLECTION

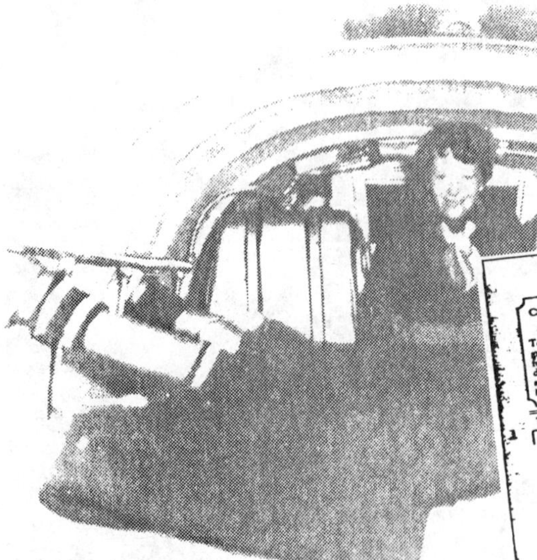

Amelia in cockpit doorway looking aft over the fuel tanks. Note the filler pipes which connect to the outside, where the passenger windows were located.

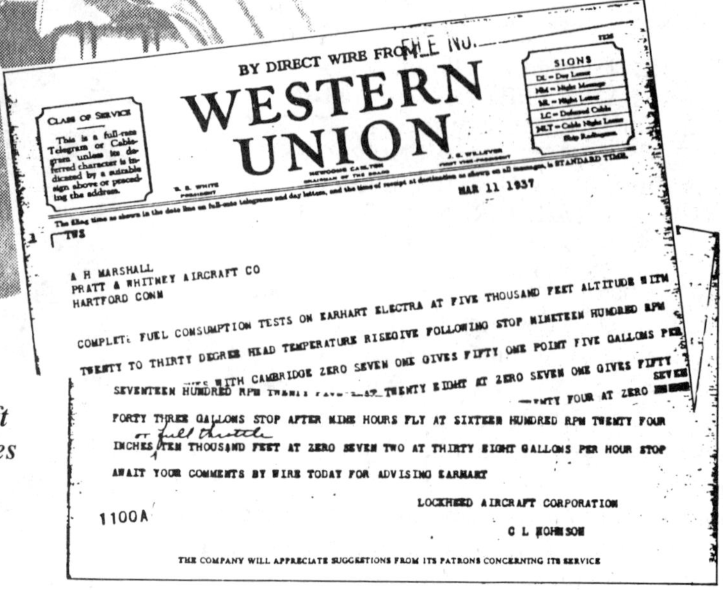

BY DIRECT WIRE FROM
WESTERN UNION

FILE NO.

MAR 11 1937

TWS

A H MARSHALL
PRATT & WHITNEY AIRCRAFT CO
HARTFORD CONN

COMPLETE FUEL CONSUMPTION TESTS ON EARHART ELECTRA AT FIVE THOUSAND FEET ALTITUDE WITH TWENTY TO THIRTY DEGREE HEAD TEMPERATURE RISEGIVE FOLLOWING STOP NINETEEN HUNDRED RPM [illegible] WITH CAMBRIDGE ZERO SEVEN ONE GIVES FIFTY ONE POINT FIVE GALLONS PER SEVENTEEN HUNDRED RPM [illegible] TWENTY EIGHT AT ZERO SEVEN ONE GIVES FIFTY SEVEN [illegible] FOUR AT ZERO [illegible] FORTY THREE GALLONS STOP AFTER NINE HOURS FLY AT SIXTEEN HUNDRED RPM TWENTY FOUR INCHES *or full throttle* TEN THOUSAND FEET AT ZERO SEVEN TWO AT THIRTY EIGHT GALLONS PER HOUR STOP AWAIT YOUR COMMENTS BY WIRE TODAY FOR ADVISING EARHART

LOCKHEED AIRCRAFT CORPORATION
C L JOHNSON

1100A

THE COMPANY WILL APPRECIATE SUGGESTIONS FROM ITS PATRONS CONCERNING ITS SERVICE

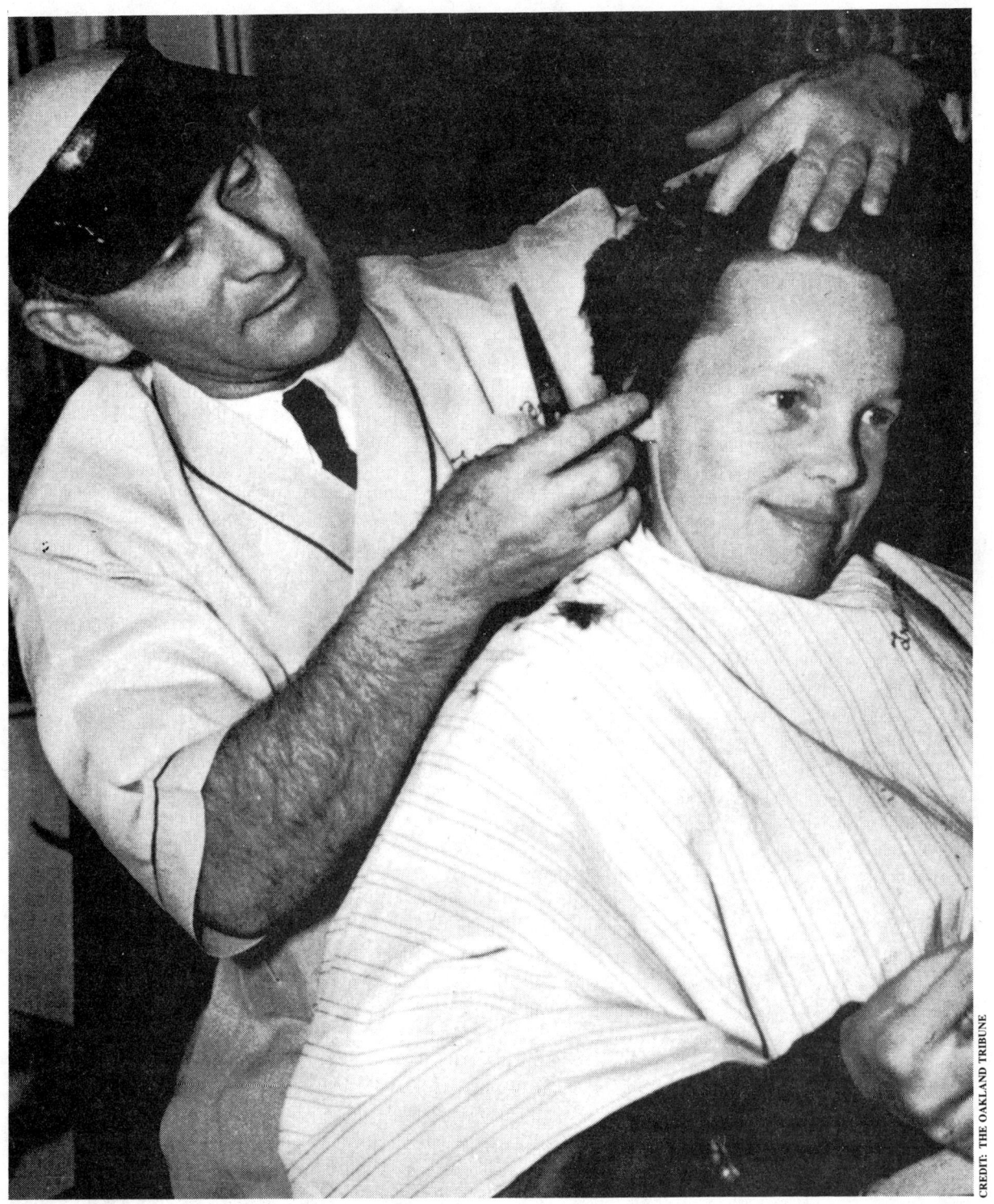

Amelia receives a haircut in the Oakland Tribune barber shop, March 15, 1937. Walter Grieben is the barber.

Previously unpublished photographs by W. Stanley Hicks, Paul Mantz's photographer, prior to the world flight.

Amelia and Fred Noonan

Amelia Earhart shows all the luggage needed for an around-the-world flight. She will c— only two lightweight suitcases with her when she hops off from the Oakland Airport Sunday or M— day evening. One suitcase will contain a few articles of clothing—no dresses—the other maps. An— the maps weigh twice as much as the clothing. —*Tribune* phot—

CREDIT: BUD MITCHELL

CREDIT: BUD MITCHELL

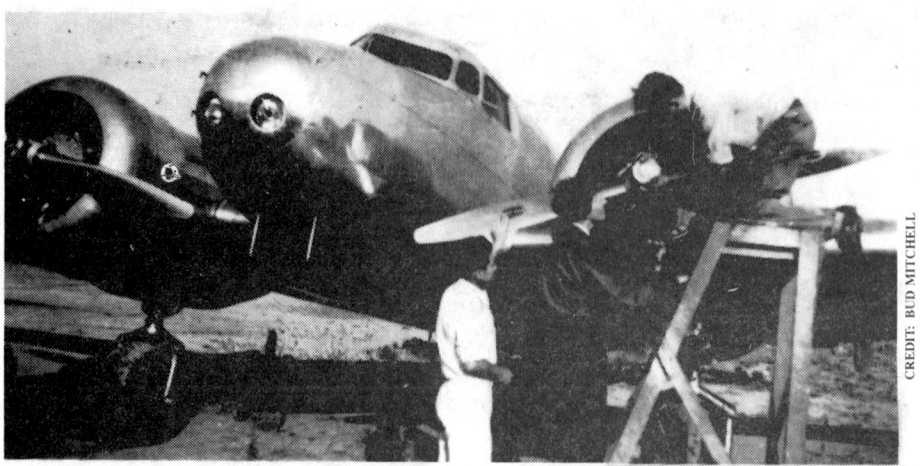

(below left) Margot DeCarrie, Amelia's secretary, Paul Mantz and Amelia.

CREDIT: BUD MITCHELL

CREDIT: BUD MITCHELL

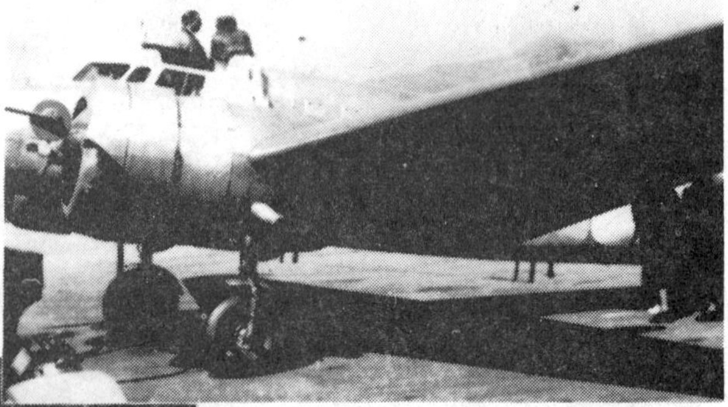

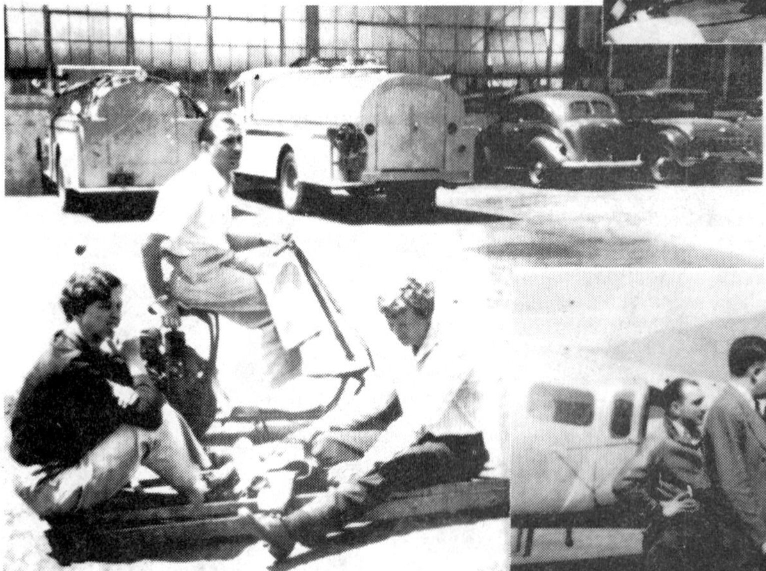

From left: Paul, GP, Harry Manning, unidentified, Amelia and unidentified.

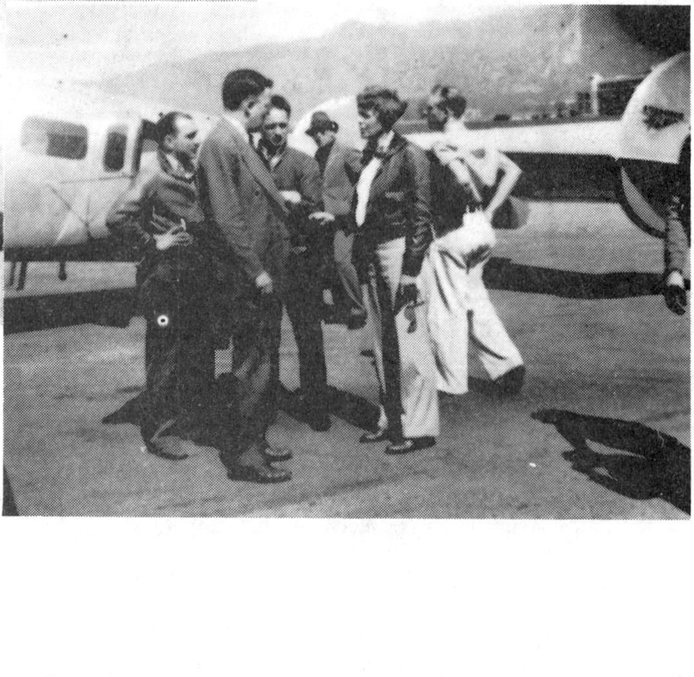

On March 13, 1937, the Navy received a message stating:

" . . . SPEED OF TRANSMISSIONS TO PLANE NOT TO EXCEED FIFTEEN WORDS PER MINUTE . . . "

Captain Manning, being a ship's captain, knew Morse code and could receive at an average rate of 15 words per minute. According to the Society of Airway Pioneers:

" . . . Acceptable transmission speed for the "CW" Morse code was 30 words per minute, but 40 to 45 words was not uncommon . . . "

The Electra was equipped to send and receive in Morse code on 500 KC [kilocycles].

On March 18, 1937, a U. S. Coast Guard telegram from the Commander, San Francisco Division, stated:

"AMELIA EARHART PLANE RADIO CALL KHAQQ WILL TRANSMIT ON 500 COMMA 3105 COMMA AND 6210 KCS USING CONTINUOUS WAVE TELEGRAPHY [Morse code] AND VOICE."

It went on to explain that the plane had a radio direction finder covering, " . . . 200 to 1430 KCS WITH ALL WAVE RECEIVER FOR TELEGRAPHY PERIOD . . . "

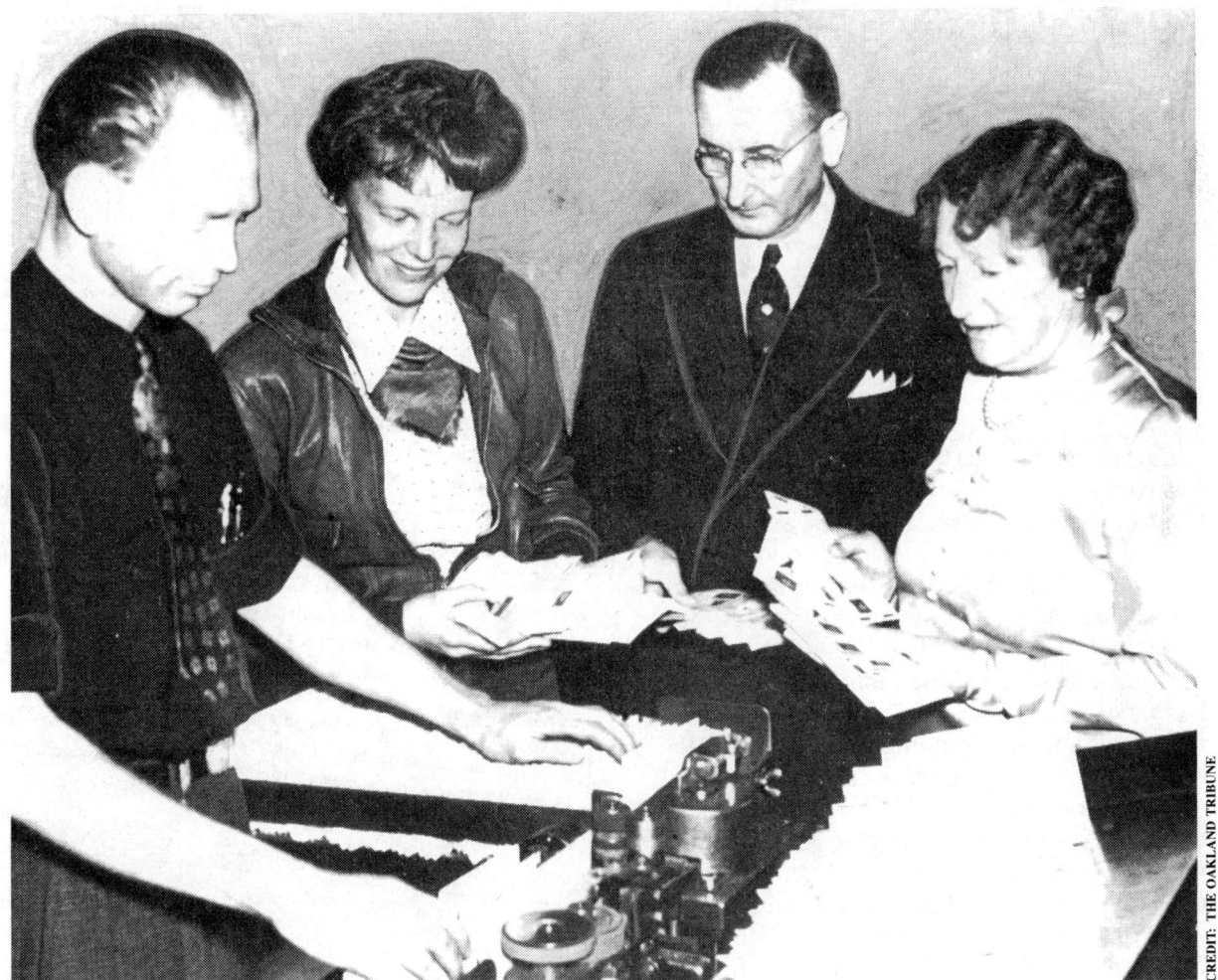

Amelia Earhart inspects the cancelling machine at the Oakland Postoffice, which will handle the 8000 special cachet envelopes to be carried with her around the world. Left to right, **Larry Flemming**, operator of the cancelling machine; **Amelia Earhart, E. H. Dimity**, who is assisting Miss Earhart in her preparations here, and **Postmaster Nellie G. Donohoe**.

CREDIT: THE OAKLAND TRIBUNE

Why Should We Make It Any Tougher?

Thus spoke Amelia Earhart, second from left, when she postponed her scheduled 'round-the-world flight on learning that heavy gales over the Pacific had forced the Hawaiian Clipper to turn back to Alameda. Her crew shown with her here are (left to right): Paul Mantz, Harry Manning and Fred Noonan. Story on Page 1.

CHECK BY RADIO

Short wave radio fans last night watched Amelia Earhart. She carried two 50-watt transmitters on her speedy laboratory plane, capable of working thousands of miles.

For ordinary work she was to use radiophone, working on the 6210 kilocycle band in the daytime and the 3105 kilocycle band at night. Her "CW," or continuous wave telegraph rig, which both she and her crew can operate, works on 5000 kilocycles.

The call letters are KHAQQ.

Earlier on February 23, 1937, Amelia had received an Aircraft Radio Station License. The license identified her call letters as KHAQQ and indicated that the radio was modified. It was to be used on aircraft serial number NR-16020 and had the following frequencies: 500, 3105 and 6210 KC. The manufacturer was Western Electric, and the radio type was 13-C. No serial number was given. This license was issued for a term beginning February 23, 1937 and ending April 1, 1937.

The world flight began at 4:37 p.m. Pacific time, March 17, 1937. Amelia, Captain Manning, Fred Noonan, and Paul Mantz took off from Oakland, into a 14-mile head-wind, utilizing 1,897 feet of runway on the 2,400 mile flight to Wheeler Field, Oahu, Hawaii. The official dispatch from W. T. Miller, Airways Superintendent of the Bureau of Air Commerce commented, "EXCELLENT TAKEOFF ON A MUDDY FIELD."

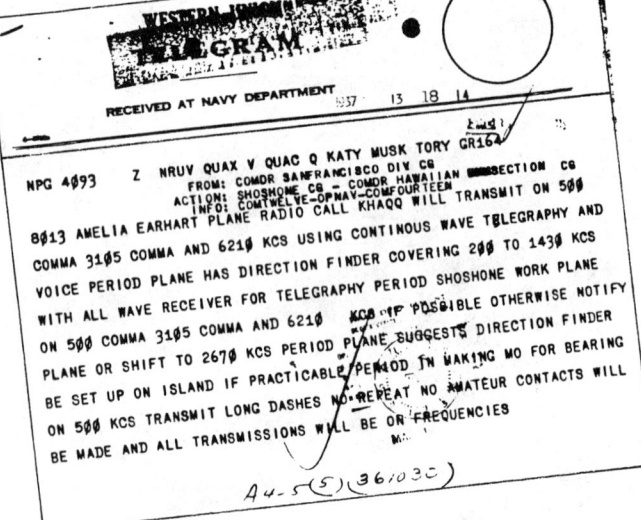

Navy Telegram discussing frequency transmissions to be used for the Earhart flight.

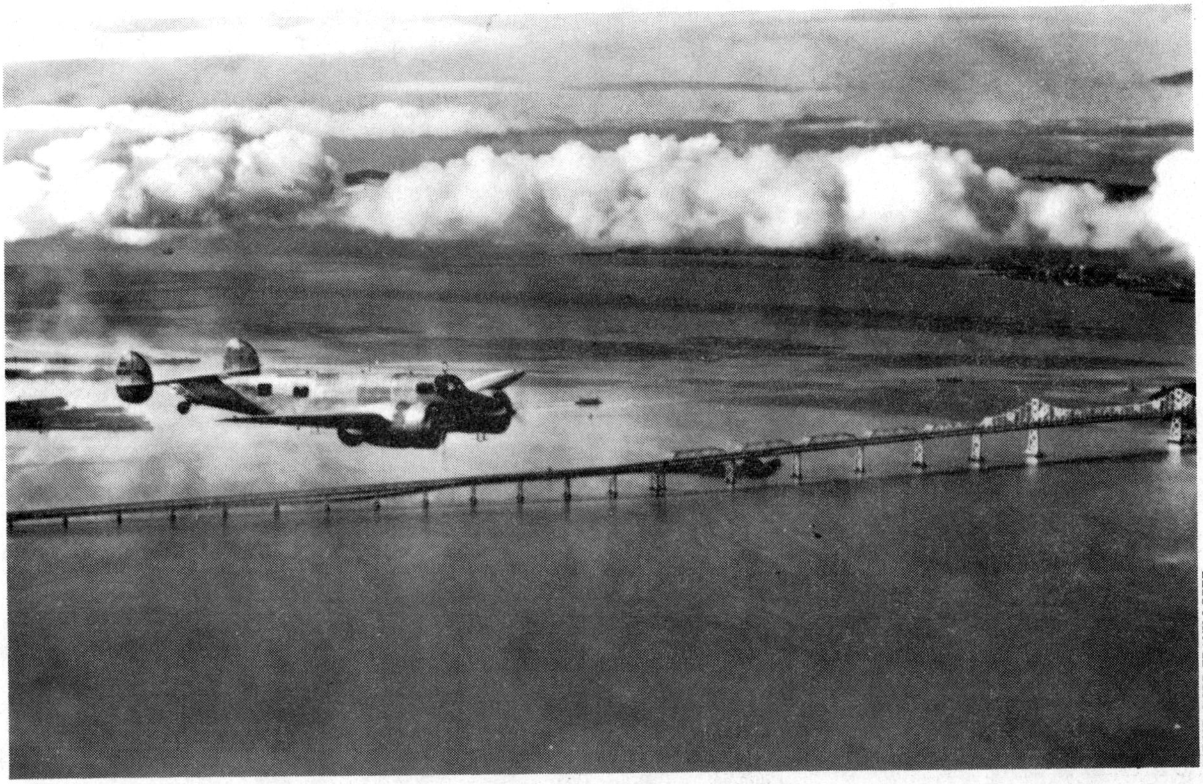

CREDIT: LCDR FRANK LOPEZ

Official Naval Photograph of Amelia's Round-the-world beginning. Here they fly over the Bay Bridge.

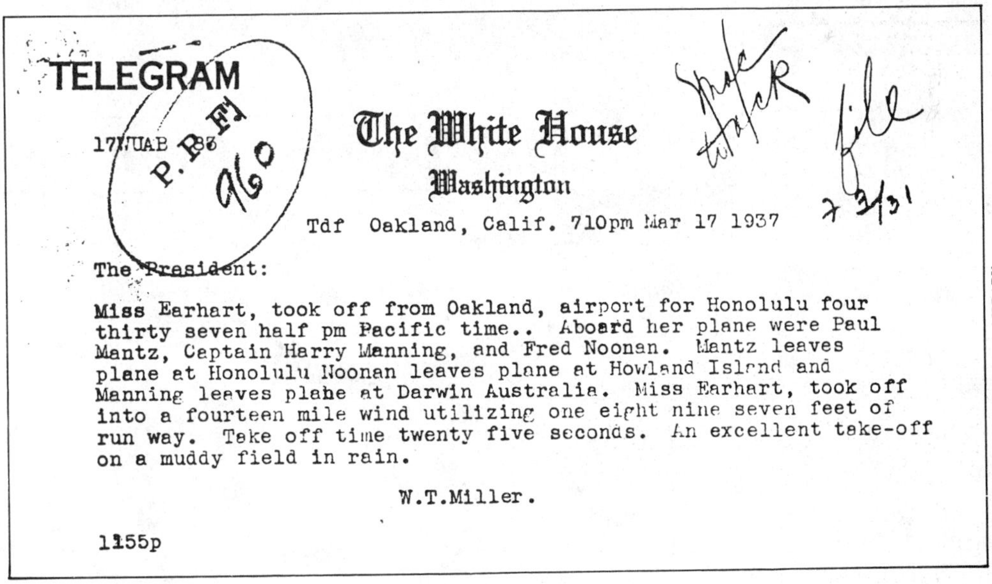

TELEGRAM

P. P. F. 960

17WUAB 33

The White House
Washington

Tdf Oakland, Calif. 710pm Mar 17 1937

The President:

Miss Earhart, took off from Oakland, airport for Honolulu four thirty seven half pm Pacific time.. Aboard her plane were Paul Mantz, Captain Harry Manning, and Fred Noonan. Mantz leaves plane at Honolulu Noonan leaves plane at Howland Island and Manning leaves plane at Darwin Australia. Miss Earhart, took off into a fourteen mile wind utilizing one eight nine seven feet of run way. Take off time twenty five seconds. An excellent take-off on a muddy field in rain.

W.T.Miller.

1155p

CREDIT: FRANKLIN D. ROOSEVELT LIBRARY

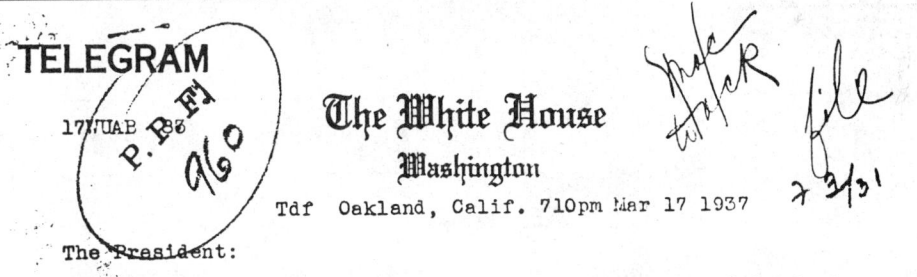

Telegram to the White House notifying The President of Amelia's take off.

CREDIT: THE OAKLAND TRIBUNE

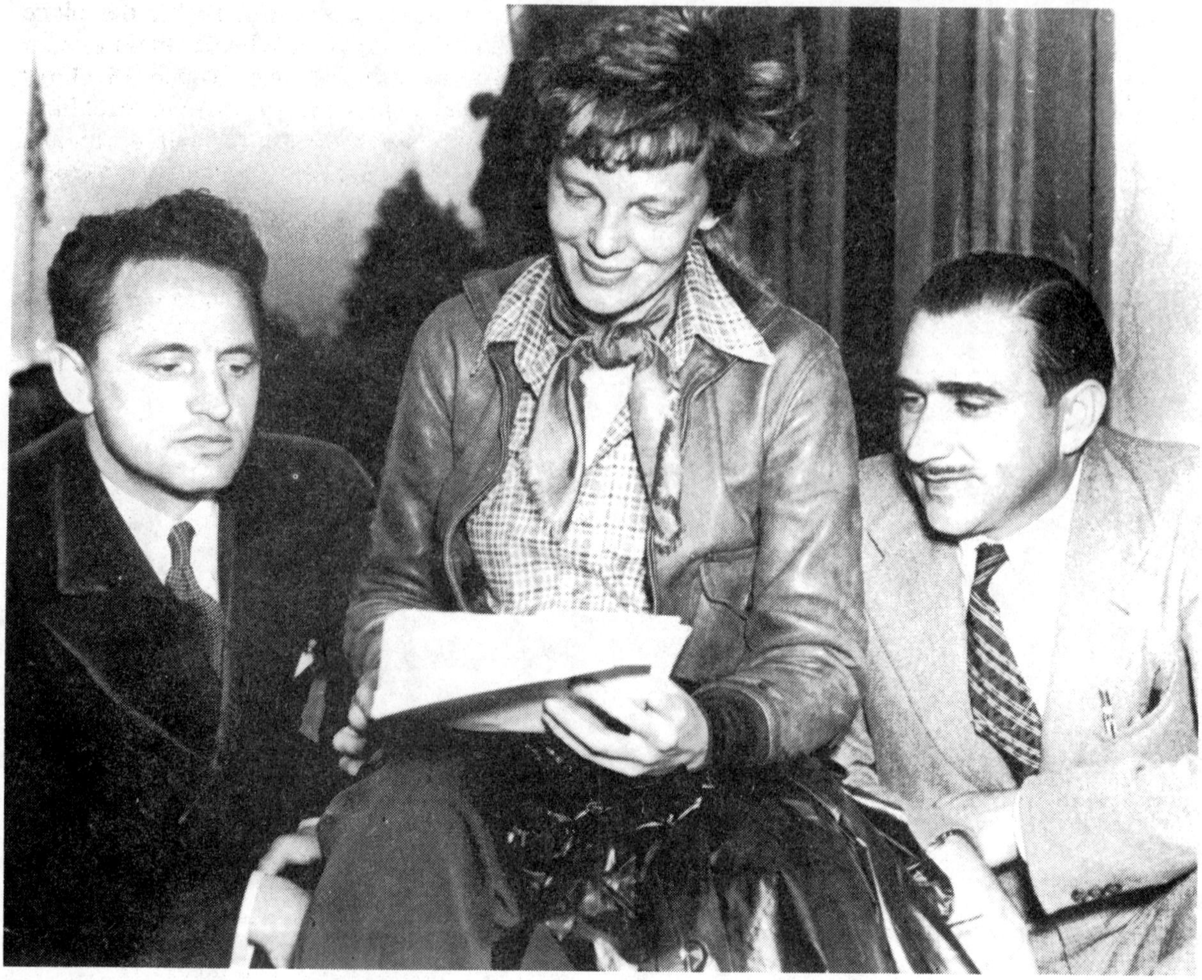

Captain Harry Manning, left, Amelia and Paul Mantz before taking off. Photo March 13, 1937.

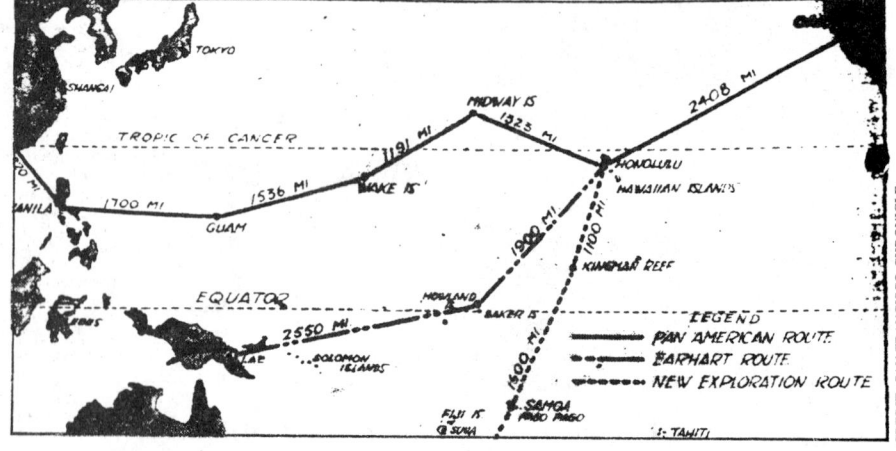

New Routes Over Pacific

New courses to be taken by American flyers across the Pacific. Top—The present Pan American route to Manila. Center—The projected hop of Amelia Earhart on Monday. Lower—The new Pan American route to New Zealand.

CREDIT: SAN FRANCISCO CHRONICLE

Fred Noonan had navigated this Pan American route before.

Throughout the flight, Fred Noonan navigated by celestial navigation, while Captain Manning worked the radio. Amelia reported in her log book:

"Paul and I have some cocoa 3 hrs. out. There is still a glow in the west. I have been flying most of the time. Now Paul does and I watch instruments. Stars about. The navigators are working like mad. Harry has just had a long radio discourse . . . "

"6–7 hours out. The stars are brillant but with the moon they can't be seen on horizon. Harry comes up to work the radio. Paul flies while Harry works over my head."

". . . Daylight comes at last . . . The generator just went out. Harry has held the key down so long it grew tired. Whats a gen. if he got his bearings? . . . "

After a nearly uneventful flight, the plane successfully set down at Wheeler Field at 8:25 a.m., Pacific standard time, March 18. Terry Miner, Mantz' fianceé, was there to meet him. Amelia and crew had set a 15 hour, 43 minute record and had established an east-west crossing record. Mantz, technical advisor for the flight, reported there were problems with the right-hand, constant-speed Hamilton-Standard propeller blades that became inoperative about six-hours before the plane reached Hawaii. Just prior to the propeller difficulty, the fliers experienced icing conditions. While at Wheeler Field, the propeller was repaired and the plane made ready for the long flight ahead. Mantz test flew the plane and reported that the propellers worked perfectly and functioned better than they had before. On this test flight the plane

Amelia and Captain Harry Manning checking his pelorus, March 6, 1937.

MARCH 18, 1937

4:38 p. m.—Took off from Oakland airport.

4:45 p. m.—Passed over the San Francisco-Oakland and Golden Gate bridges and headed out to sea.

6:04 p. m.—In air 1 hour, 26 minutes. All's well. Received report from S. S. Lurline that 35-mile northwest wind ahead, somewhat equally, visibility 10 miles. Now approximately 250 miles from San Francisco. Latitude 36 north, longitude 127 west.

6:53 p. m.—"Everything okeh." She radioed that she had climbed to an altitude of 8000 feet.

7 p. m.—Captain Edwin Musick of the PanAmerican Sikorsky bound for Australia reported Miss Earhart passed his plane at 5:40 p. m. (Musick left Oakland airport 24 minutes before her.)

7:13 p. m.—Plane 365 miles out. A code message from the plane gave the position as latitude 36:15 north, longitude 126:28 west.

8:15 p. m.—Passed the Pan American Hawaii Clipper, en route on routine flight to Hawaii-Manila; the clipper left Alameda at 3:35 p. m.

8:35 p. m.—Plane reported 569 miles out. Position given as latitude 39:42 north, longitude 131:05 west. Ship averaging speed of about 170 miles an hour. Favorable winds ahead.

10:31 p. m.—The Pan-American Airways received a message from Amelia Earhart saying: "We cannot hear you. All is well."

THURSDAY

12:02 a. m.—Miss Earhart radioed: "Everything okeh."

From Amelia's log on flight to Hawaii.

was flown from Wheeler Field to Luke Field, now Ford Island, also on Oahu. Amelia wanted to take off from Luke Field because it had a paved runway.

Commander Henry M. Anthony, who was then Communication Officer of the Hawaiian Section, San Francisco Division of the U.S. Coast Guard, in 1937, has provided some background information on the Electra's communication system. In a videotaped interview on April 18, 1984, he explained that he was present at a meeting in Hawaii, at Chris Holmes's estate, where he first met Amelia. Commander Anthony said that for two and one-half hours:

> " . . . there was Admiral Kenner, Dick Black, Paul Mantz, Manning, Fred Noonan, and Anthony . . . I was interested in her [Amelia's] communication plans, that was the major factor . . . He [the navigator] didn't have any voice communications back aft in the Electra, where he was located. The day before the flight, I went out to the plane, at Luke [Field], to look at her Electra . . . I was interested only in the radio equipment. She had a DF [direction finder], voice communication, in the cockpit and Noonan had CW [continuous wave/Morse code], back aft . . . His communication with her was by bamboo pole. They would tie on a note and pass it back and forth. He [Noonan] would answer the note and push it up to her: that was their communication."

The Hawaiian weather proved as inhospitable to Amelia's Electra as it was to her Vega nearly two years before. Adverse conditions were reported over the Pacific to Howland Island, the tiny dot in the ocean, where the Coast Guard had supervised the hurried completion of a crude landing strip for the Electra.

The next leg was to have carried Captain Manning and Fred Noonan, two navigators with excellent credentials. This time Amelia was not aiming for a large continent or chain of islands such as Hawaii. She was aiming for a dot in the ocean, a mile and a half long and a half mile wide. There was no room for error.

The Luke Field runway was paved and therefore not muddy as had been the case when Amelia made her solo flight to Oakland from Wheeler Field, but the plane was heavily

Amelia in 1936, before her world flight.

loaded with fuel and was carrying three people. Less than half way down the runway, disaster struck: a tire blew out and the plane ground looped, damaging the landing gear and a wing. Amelia instantly cut off the ignition, preventing the plane from catching fire.

First Lieutenant Donald D. Arnold, Depot Engineering Officer, Hawaiian Air Depot, Luke Field, now Ford Island, filed the accident report. It states that the Electra was topped off with 590 gallons of fuel on the morning of March 20, 1937. The report continues:

> "At 5:00 A.M. Mr. Mantz thoroughly inspected the airplane, tested the engines, and shut them off. The flood lights were turned on and Mrs. Putnam inspected the runway from the cockpit of the airplane. A light rain during the night had wet the runway. The lights were turned off and Mr. Noonan and Mr. Manning boarded the airplane. Mrs. Putnam started the engines at 5:30 A.M. and at 5:40 taxied north-

Commander Henry M. Anthony and Carol Osborne at the Amelia Earhart symposium, Smithsonian Institution on June 18, 1982.

CREDIT: KATHLEEN BROOKS-PIZMANY, SMITHSONIAN INSTITUTION PHOTO NO. 82-7358-19A

east down the Navy side of the runway to the lower end . . . the tee indicated a wind direction exactly on the center line of the runway from the direction of Barbers Point."

The officer explained that Amelia made a 180 degree left turn at the far end of the runway and momentarily halted the airplane on the center line. As soon as the airplane moved forward, he heard the steady, synchronous roar characteristic of full throttle application.

"The airplane appeared to assume the normal initial attitude for the take-off and slowly gained speed. Before the airplane had reached the halfway mark on the field the right wing seemed to drop slightly lower than the left and the airplane made a slow even forty-five degree turn to the left." Lieutenant Arnold continued:

"I saw a long streak of flying sparks under the airplane, followed instantly by the sound of grinding metal. The airplane instantly dropped on its belly and slid to a stop, right side up, but headed in the direction from which it had come."

Luckily, there was no fire. Lieutenant Arnold grabbed Chris Holmes by the arm and they sped to the scene of the crash. Amelia was standing upright in the cockpit and Noonan and Manning were not yet out. Mr. Holmes helped Amelia. The Luke Field crash truck was already on the scene, and a crowd formed around the plane. Lieutenant Arnold escorted Amelia, Holmes, Noonan, and Captain Manning to his car, and they slowly drove down the runway while Amelia reconstructed the accident. She declared:

"The ship functioned perfectly at the start. As it gained speed the right wing dropped down and the ship seemed to pull to the right. I eased off the left engine and the ship started a long persistent left turn and ended up where it is now. It was all over instantly. The first thing I thought of was the right oleo [strut] or the right tire letting go. The way the ship pulled it was probably a flat tire."*

---

*Paul Mantz said that Amelia had a tendency to hold run way alignment by jockying the throttles, rather than using the rudder. This throttle usage is an invitiation to a ground loop. Noted in Hollywood Pilot, The Biography of Paul Mantz by Don Dwiggins.

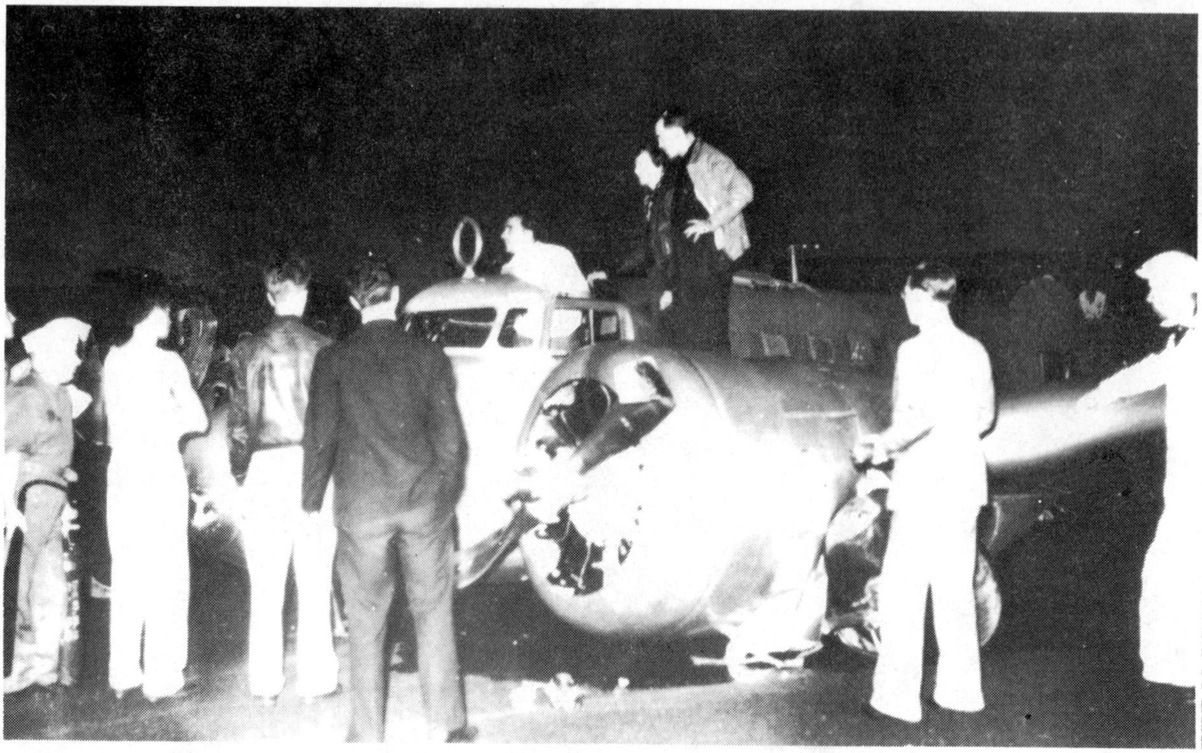

CREDIT: D.D. HATFIELD AVIATION COLLECTION

Amelia's flying laboratory after the tire blew out.

CREDIT: MAJOR SUSAN NEUGEBAUER, U.S.A.F. PHOTO

Amelia's tire tracks, March 20, 1937.

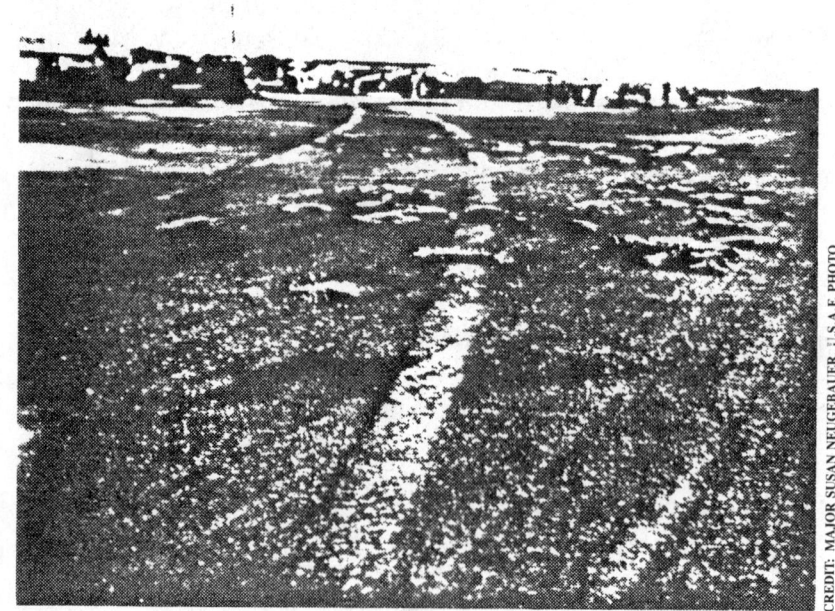

TIRE BLAMED FOR AMELIA PLANE CRASH

HONOLULU, T. H., March 21 (UP)—Army aviation experts tonight expressed unofficial opinions that a landing gear failure wrecked Amelia Earhart's $90,000 plane and led to abandonment temporarily of her dream of being the first woman to fly around the world.

Members of the Army Air Corps staff stationed at Luke Field, an island in the Pearl Harbor reservation, told the United Press they believed that part of the landing gear failed just before the right tire of her plane burst and threw the ship off its course in an attempted take-off Saturday morning.

CREDIT: SAN FRANCISCO CHRONICLE

Newspaper account of the accident, Monday, March 22, 1937.

FILE
R.F.G.

U. S. COAST GUARD
OFFICIAL DISPATCH DATE 2Ø MARCH 1937
UNIT HEADQUARTERS
INCOMING HEADING
CG28KD Z F5L MUSK QUAH TORY V QUAC P GR 37

FROM
SANFRANCISCO DIVISION

	ACKNOWLEDGE
X	PRIORITY
	ROUTINE
	NITE

TO (FOR ACTION)
CINCUS
CHIEF OF NAVAL OPERATIONS
HEADQUARTERS
COMDT 14TH NAVAL DISTRICT

TEXT
8Ø2Ø MISS EARHARTS RKN PLANE CRASHED ON TAKE OFF ON LUKE FIELD PEARL
HARBOR ACCOUNT OF LEFT TIRE BLOWING OUT ALL OCCUPANTS X SAFE PERIOD
MISS EARHART CALM AD COLLECTIVE REPORT FURTHER SITUATION LATER
SIGNED W T MILLER Ø95Ø

CREDIT: NATIONAL ARCHIVES

The damaged Electra is shipped back to Lockheed for repair.

CREDIT: SAN FRANCISCO CHRONICLE

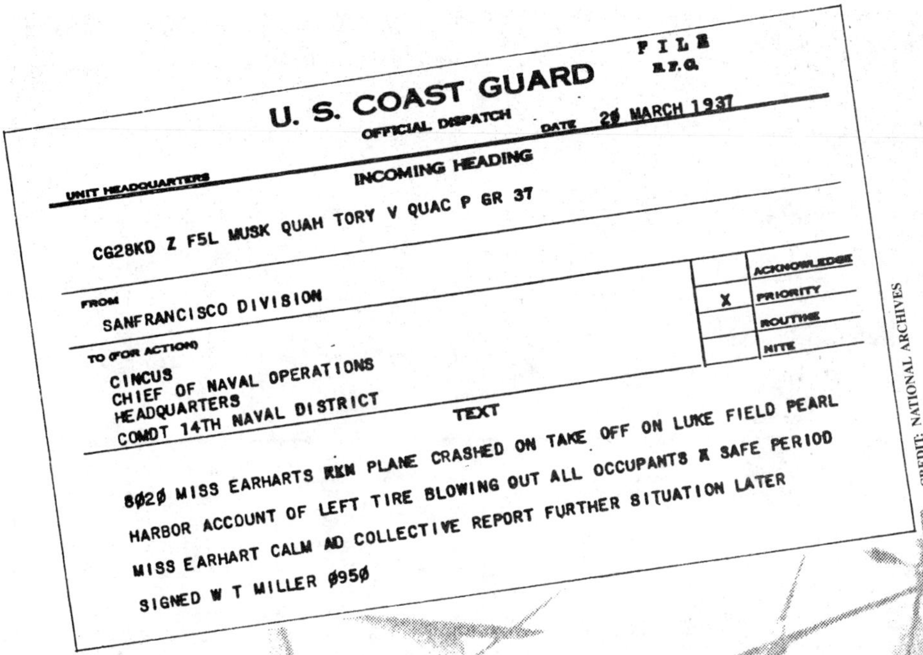

(above) U.S. Coast Guard account of the accident.

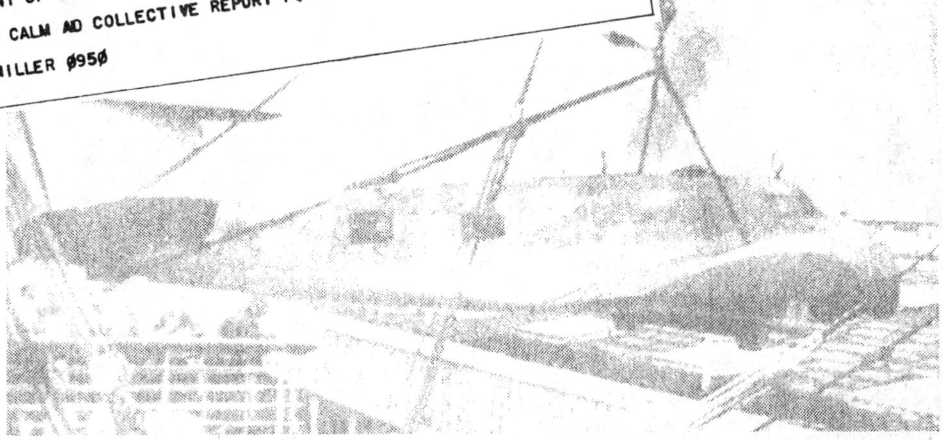

They stopped at intervals and Amelia examined the marks of the tires on the runway. She noted the right track was much wider than the left.

A ship wrecked on a reef is a tragic sight to her captain; as Amelia saw the crippled Electra, she had difficulty keeping back the tears. GP, in Oakland, received the news flash of the accident and within minutes sent a reassuring radiogram:

"So long as you and the boys are okay, the rest doesn't matter. Whether you want to call it a day or to keep going is equally Jake with me."

Reporters, restrained from rushing out to the wrecked plane, crowded around the fliers as they made their way toward the hangar. They clamored for the answer to one question, "Will you give up the flight now?"

Amelia, characteristically, said firmly, "Of course not. I shall certainly try again."

The Electra was shipped back to Lockheed Aircraft Corporation for repair. Lockheed issued a series of repair orders. Among them were orders to install an 18″ mast and a "V" antenna between the mast, and the connections on both fins on top of the airplane and another, similar antenna, on its belly.

Another repair order read, "Make up and install a table and catwalk over the top of the cabin gas tanks. This is for use of the navigator." All these repair orders were dated May, 1937. The cabin had been arranged so that Amelia sat in the left seat and the right seat was empty. The navigator was in the right rear, behind the fuel tanks, seated next to the windows, and in back of the wing, to take his sightings. Over Amelia's head was a knob for the

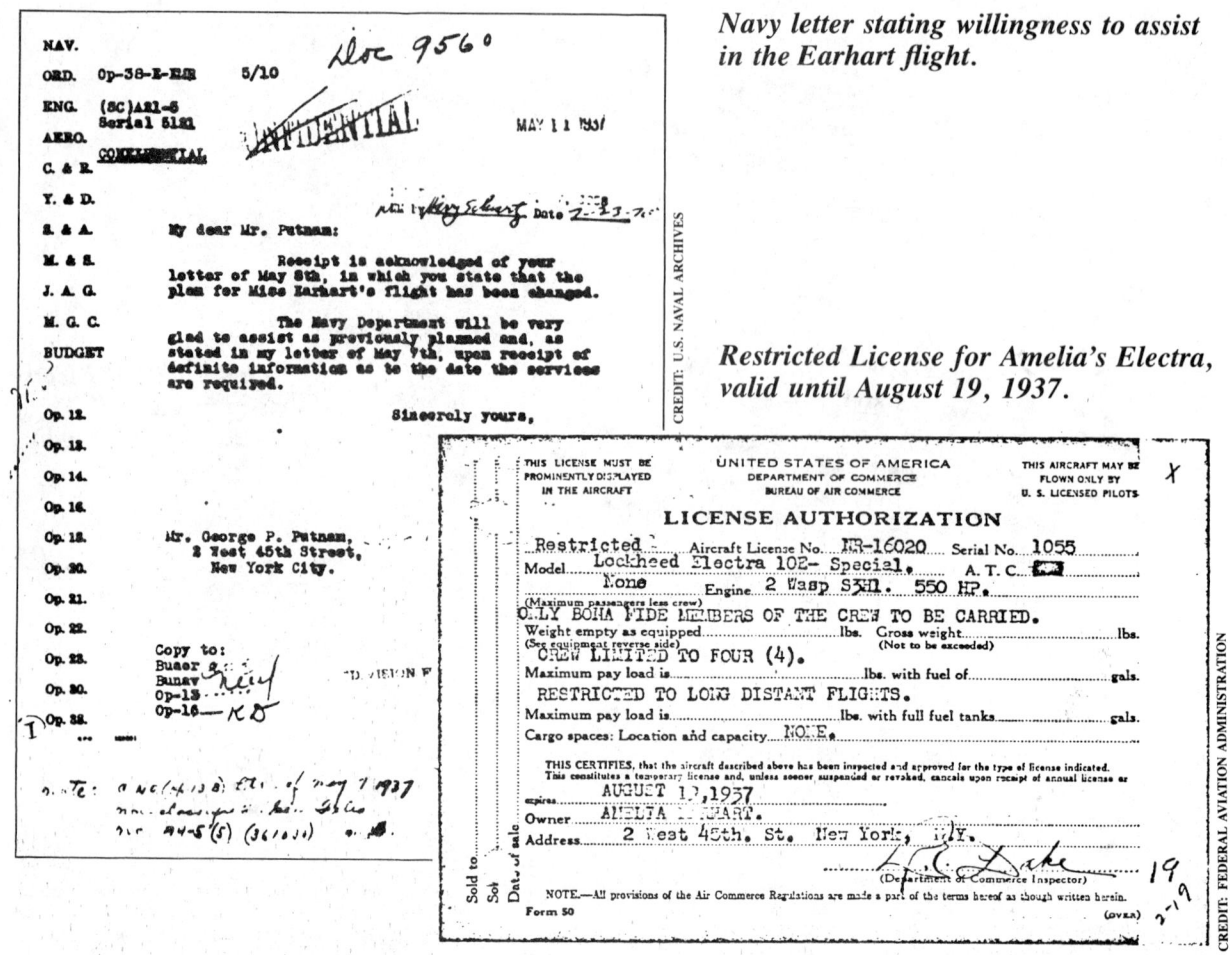

Navy letter stating willingness to assist in the Earhart flight.

Restricted License for Amelia's Electra, valid until August 19, 1937.

home in on any active radio transmitter.

Lockheed Repair Order dated 1-26-37 described work of "PAINT N ON WING & RUDDER TO MAKE LICENCE [sic] READ 'NR-16020' INSTEAD OF 'R-16020'." The "R" indicated that this was a restricted aircraft.

Finances presented a major problem. Had the original westerly flight plan been followed, the entire expense would have been met by the sale of the stamps and letters Amelia was carrying. Payments from the news and photo services and her lecture fees would balance the books on the $75,000 enterprise. Repair of the Electra cost approximately $14,000. An equal amount was needed to assure oil, fuel and mechanics' services along the route two months later. It was a staggering sum to raise. Amelia was loath to ask her friends for financial help, but many generous checks came in. Bernard Baruch wired her $2,500, "Because I like your everlasting guts!" Floyd and Jacqueline Cochran Odlum advanced a substantial sum; Admiral Byrd sent a check for $1,500, accompanied by a note reminding Amelia of time she had sent him a like amount for his antarctic expedition. One of the most heart-warming gifts was that of the mechanics at the Lockheed plant who worked an entire Sunday to meet the repair deadline but declined pay for it.

Steadily the fund grew until on May 17, 1937, when the plane was ready to leave the factory, Amelia wired President Elliott of Purdue University, "Our second attempt is assured. We are solvent. Future is mortgaged, but what else are futures for?"

While the experts repaired the plane, Amelia and GP had rescheduled and rerouted the flight.

Ann Bohrer, coeditor and publisher of Tail Spins *magazine, met Amelia when she was lecturing in 1937 at Lake Erie College of Painesville, Ohio. Amelia was wearing a black velvet dress with stiff white linen collar and sleeves. Ann presented her new* Tail Spins *magazine, a popular magazine with aviators like Admiral Byrd, who took many to the South Pole.*

Marshall Headle's flight test report.

Amelia and unidentified friend at Palo Alto Airport, circa 1937.

Cartoon from March 19, 1937

Amelia and W. C. Tinus, Bell Laboratories engineer, while he installs remote control for the planes Western Electric radio equipment, February, 1937.

Lockheed Repair Order to ready Amelia's Electra for her flight around the world, dated "4-29-37."

Amelia and E. Jay Quinby of the Western Electric Company. "The radio equipment is installed 'out-of-the-way,' but may be conveniently controlled from the pilot's position by means of this compact little unit [remote control unit]." Circa February, 1937.

Since it was considered unwise to fly over the Caribbean and African areas later than early June, Amelia planned to take off from Miami, heading east, the long way round the world, for Oakland.

GP corresponded with Admiral Leahy, Chief of Naval Operations in Washington, D.C., many times. In his letter of May 8, 1937, GP wrote, "So Miss Earhart has decided to reverse the route and to proceed from west to east. Also she will eliminate the Central American stage where increasing rains make the outlook dubious."

GP went on to say that Amelia would fly from Oakland to El Paso, New Orleans and Miami and there would be no announcements. He said that this flight across the country would simply be a "trial flight," and "the journey across the country will give her a chance for final testing of the refitted plane. If anything went sour she could return to the Lockheed plant. But if all goes well when she reaches Miami, we will there make the announcement of the revised plan."

Captain Manning reluctantly relinquished his post as navigator to Fred Noonan as his leave of absence from his ship was over. Amelia had every confidence in Fred's navigational skill, and Fred, for his part, was ready to make the entire voyage with her. With the departure of Manning, Amelia's project lost a valuable capability. As the Western Electric Company news release on March 10, 1937, stated:

"Captain Harry Manning, veteran skipper of the United States Lines . . . knows how to operate the key, and over the vast expanses of the Pacific the radio equipment may be used for either telephone conversations or telegraph code. Communication with vessels at sea and with marine shore stations may be established on the 500 kilocycle [kc] crystal-controlled frequency which the Western Electric Company has added to its standard aviation type-13 transmitter installed on the plane, making this frequency available in addition to those normally employed for aviation service . . ."
Noonan did not know how to operate the key.

The operation of the 500 KC emergency band required the use of an extremely long antenna. This was provided by a 250-foot trailing antenna, which had a streamlined weight on the end, and which could be reeled into and out of the bottom of the Electra by a switch in the cockpit. The antenna, when deployed, slightly increased the drag on the aircraft and had to be reeled in prior to landing. Amelia did not like the trailing antenna. At her request, the trailing antenna had been shortened significantly in Miami. The effect of this modification reduced the range of the 500 KC radio transmissions.

Amelia's 'Flying Laboratory' Stops in Oakland on Test Flight

Mrs. Amelia Earhart Putnam, "Lady Lindy" of the air, arrived in Oakland from Burbank yesterday on the first distance test flight of her $90,000 repaired "flying laboratory," in which she plans a second attempt to fly the world from San Francisco bay.

She arrived at 2:20 and took off again at 3:50 in the ship which cracked up two months ago in Honolulu on the second leg of her initial globe-girdling attempt. With her was Paul Mantz, her technical adviser. Her only comment on the repaired plane was that it was "working perfectly."

Before she took off she arranged with the airport signal tower to check her radio apparatus aboard and planned on keeping in constant touch all the way back. She is expected to return next week for the start of the second flight, on which she will be accompanied by Frederick Nunan, former Pan-American pilot.

Except through a possible alteration in the South seas route, she said the original itinerary would be followed on the second flight.

CREDIT: SAN FRANCISCO CHRONICLE

1967 article about W. H. "Walt" Grosselfinger.

Worked on Earhart Radio

Thirty years ago Amelia Earhart vanished somewhere over the Pacific Ocean on her attempt to fly around the world. Since that time numerous theories have been advanced to explain what happened and why. Walter H. Grosselfinger, now an assistant manager in Government Communications Projects at Headquarters, was asked for help by author Don Dwiggins, who devotes a portion of his new book, "Hollywood Pilot," to the Earhart mystery.

At the time Amelia Earhart was preparing for her flight Grosselfinger was working for the company in the marine radio/telephone field. He had previously worked with airlines and was interested in aviation radio.

WE Equipment Used

Amelia Earhart used radio equipment built by Western Electric which included a 250-foot trailing wire antenna. This antenna was not needed for routine HF voice communication but it was necessary for her to transmit an LF distress signal for the then existent radio direction finding equipment to fix her position in event of an emergency.

Grosselfinger performed adjustments on her radio set at Roosevelt Field on Long Island. Dwiggins' book suggests that her crew later shortened the wire antenna, perhaps because she objected to the effect of "drag" on the aircraft.

Walt Grosselfinger and wall chart showing his travels abroad.

Grosselfinger explained what would then have happened: "If the antenna was cut and the radio was not readjusted to this shorter length, then the set would not have transmitted properly. If the set was readjusted correctly the same effect would have resulted if she did not unreel the entire length of the antenna."

Amelia Earhart did not reach her destination. The Navy and Coast Guard ships in the area heard her HF calls for help but could not fix her position.

In his office, Grosselfinger keeps a chart of his own extensive travels. He was director of communications systems for Westrex for 12 years and has circled the globe several times, visiting 59 countries.

CREDIT: WESTERN ELECTRIC

Amelia begins her second world flight attempt. She flew to Miami prior to announcing to the press that she had begun her world flight.

MAY 22, 1937

FIRE DELAYS WORLD HOP BY EARHART

Bad luck overcame Amelia Earhart Putnam again last night. Her second projected hop from Oakland on a globe-circling flight tomorrow was delayed by damage to her plane by fire at Tucson, Arizona.

According to Associated Press, fire broke out in one of the motors a few minutes after the aviatrix had landed the craft at the Municipal Airport there on a flight from Burbank.

On June first, Amelia and Fred climbed aboard the Electra at the Municipal Airport at Miami, Florida. Amelia waved to GP and his tall son, David. They taxied out to the end of the runway, Amelia turned and gunned the engines. The Electra was in the air, and Amelia and Fred were off to girdle the globe.

JUST ONE MORE LONG FLIGHT | 215

Letter Amelia sent to our mother, from Miami.

Curtis H. Bliss, Amelia, Fred Noonan, and Gerald Bliss, at the Miami Airport, on May 31, 1937.

San Francisco Chronicle
THE CITY'S ONLY HOME-OWNED NEWSPAPER

JUNE 2, 1937

Amelia Ends First Leg of Hop

Aviatrix Lands in Puerto Rico Safely

(Wolo Caricature on Page 3)

SAN JUAN, P. R., June 1 (UP)—Amelia Earhart Putnam, queen of the airways, tonight set her $80,000 "flying laboratory" down on the sandy runways of the airport here after a 1161-mile hope from Miami, completing the first leg of an eastbound flight around the world.

She landed at 2:30 p. m. (E.D.T.) after a smooth, uneventful flight from the Florida coast, seven hours and 34 minutes out of Miami.

Tomorrow Miss Earhart plans to take off for Paramaribo, in Dutch Guiana, 1378 miles away, and the third leg will be eastward to Natal, Brazil, a distance of 1915 miles down the eastern coast of South America.

She was accompanied by Captain Fred J. Noonan, former Pan American Airways clipper pilot who also flew with her on the ill fated start of her west bound globe circling flight, which ended when she cracked up her big twin motored Lockheed at Pearl Harbor, Oahu, Hawaii.

JUNE 3, 1937

Amelia Hops 750 Miles to Venezuela

MIAMI, Fla., June 2 (P)—An easy jump of 750 miles, the second leg of her world-girdling aerial adventure, put Amelia Earhart in South America today with no more water to cross until she starts the hazardous flight across the South Atlantic from Natal, Brazil, to Africa.

Pan-American Airways over whose route the aviatrix has flown since she left Miami yesterday, reported she landed at Caripito, a little oil town in Venezuela this morning after a four-hour flight from San Juan, Puerto Rico.

Miss Earhart probably will hop to Paramaribo tomorrow and make a 1200-mile cruise to Fortaleza, Brazil, the next day.

JUNE 4, 1937

Amelia Arrives In Dutch Guiana

PARAMARIBO, Dutch Guiana, June 3 (P)—Amelia Earhart made a 750-mile hop over South American jungles today to get to Dutch Guiana, and then had to ride 25 miles on a trolley car.

She brought her silvery monoplane down at the Zandery airfield, 25 miles from Paramaribo, at 12:50 p. m. (11:50 a. m., E. S. T.) at the end of the third leg of her round-the-world jaunt from the United States.

Her next stop is to Natal, on Brazil's easternmost tip. She hopes to make the flight tomorrow.

JUNE 5, 1937

Fortaleza, Brazil, Welcomes Amelia

FORTALEZA, Brazil, June 4 (P)—Amelia Earhart landed at this Northeast Brazil seaport today at 4:31 p. m. (11:31 a. m., P.S.T.), after a flight from Paramaribo, Dutch Guiana on another leg of her hop around the world.

She had flown approximately 1300 miles since her takeoff at 5:10 a. m., but was 300 miles short of her previously announced goal, Natal, Brazil.

JUNE 6, 1937

Amelia Sets Hop For Africa Today

FORTALEZA, Brazil, June 5 (P)—Amelia Earhart paused at this northeast Brazil seaport to have the control apparatus of her round-the-world monoplane adjusted. She planned to leave about 5 a m tomorrow on a 287-mile hop to Natal, near South America's easternmost point.

If weather reports are favorable, she said, she will take off tomorrow from Natal on her 1900-miles transatlantic crossing, to Dakar.

JUNE 7, 1937

Amelia Will Start Atlantic Hop Today

NATAL, Brazil, June 6 (P)—Amelia Earhart, at the jump-off point for her crossing of the Atlantic on her world flight, announced tonight she would take off early tomorrow for Dakar, French Senegal.

Weather permitting, she said she planned to leave on the 1900-mile hop between 4 a. m. and 5 a. m.

She reached Natal at 8:53 a. m. today from Fortaleza, on Brazil's northeastern coast.

JUNE 8, 1937

Amelia Makes Atlantic Hop to African Coast

DAKAR, French Senegal, June 7 (P)—Amelia Earhart, en route around the world on a flight "just for fun," took the Atlantic ocean in her stride today.

The woman who double-dared the North Atlantic in 1928 and 1932 crossed the South Atlantic from Natal, Brazil, to St. Louis, Capital of Senegal, in approximately 13 hours and 19 minutes.

She landed in St. Louis, 163 miles from here, at 7:35 p. m. Greenwich mean time.

There was no immediate explanation of her landing in St. Louis, northeast of here along the west coast of Africa, instead of at Dakar, her scheduled objective.

The 38-year-old flyer, accompanied by her navigator, Captain Fred Noonan, left Parnamirio airport, Natal, at 1:16 a. m. eastern standard time.

She headed over the ocean in a light rain, and more than four hours later flashed a message by radio that "everything is going fine."

Today's flight carried her approximately 1900 miles.

Miss Earhart left the United States June 1 when she flew her big twin-motored monoplane from Miami, Fla., to San Juan, Puerto Rico.

Her plan in the flight is to stay as near the equator as possible.

JUNE 10, 1937

Amelia on Flight Across Africa

DAKAR, French Senegal, June 10 (P)—Amelia Earhart took off at 6:55 a. m. Greenwich mean time today on the Trans-African stage of her "just for fun" flight around the world.

JUNE 11, 1937

Amelia Arrives In French Africa

GAO, French West Africa, June 10 (P)—Amelia Earhart Putnam, completing the seventh leg of her round-the-world flight over 1140 miles of jungles and desert, slept here tonight amidst the noises of jungle beasts. Tomorrow she announced, she will fly 900 miles down the Niger river to Niamey. Miss Earhart and Fred J. Noonan, her navigator arrived at this outpost at 2:40 p. m. after a seven hours and 45-minute flight from Dakar.

JUNE 12, 1937

Earhart Crosses Sahara Desert

FORT LAMY, French Equatorial Africa, June 11 (P)—Amelia Earhart sped over 1000 miles of Sahara desert today, completing the second hop across Africa in her round the world flight.

She took off from Gao, French West Africa, at 6:15 a. m. G.M.T. (10:15 p. m. P.S.T. Thursday), and arrived here after a flight of 6 hours 40 minutes.

Her next and probably last transafrican hop will be to Khartoum, Anglo-Egyptian Sudan, 1200 miles from here, across desert and jungle.

JUNE 13, 1937

Amelia on Final Hop Across Africa

EL FASHER, ANGLO-EGYPTIAN SUDAN, June 13 (P)—(Sunday)—Amelia Earhart hopped off at 4:05 a. m. (10:05 p. m., Saturday, E. D. T.) today for Khartoum, Anglo-Egyptian Sudan, and Massawa, Eritrea, her last stops in Africa.

The famed aviatrix arrived here yesterday after a 900-mile flight from Fort Lamy, French West Africa.

Just for Fun

Amelia Earhart, blonde boyish American woman flyer, continued last week on her just-for-fun flight around the globe.

In easy hops, she flew from Paramibo, Dutch Guiana to Fortaleza Brazil thence to Natal completing the fifth leg of her globe-girdling flight. From Natal she took off across the South Atlantic landing at St Louis on the African coast after a 13-hour flight. From St Louis she flew on to Dakar, Senegal, where she tuned the motor of her $80,000 "flying laboratory" for a flight across the heart of wildest Africa in spite of the danger of extreme heat, sand-storms, monsoons. She took off from Dakar at dawn Wednesday and headed across the expanse of jungles.

CREDIT: SAN FRANCISCO CHRONICLE

San Francisco Chronicle
The City's Only Home-Owned Newspaper

SAN FRANCISCO, CAL., SUNDAY, JUNE 13, 1937

Mrs. Amelia Earhart Putnam and Acting Governor Rafael Menendez Ramoz of Puerto Rico At San Juan, in this picture; last week she was flying over Africa

CREDIT: SAN FRANCISCO CHRONICLE

JUNE 14, 1937
Amelia Starts Hop From Sudan to Asia

KHARTOUM, Anglo-Egyptian Sudan, June 13 (P)—Amelia Earhart paused only briefly at this historic capital of the Sudan today on her flight around the middle of the earth.

She set her monoplane down here at 7:23 a.m. Greenwich mean time (2:28 a.m. E.S.T.) after a 500-mile flight from El Fasher in the Western Sudan.

An hour and 14 minutes later she was in the air again winging her way toward Asia. She hoped to reach Aden, Arabia, on this hop.

JUNE 15, 1937
Amelia Unreported On Hop to India

ADEN, Arabia (Tuesday), June 15 (P)—An unidentified airplane, possibly that in which Amelia Earhart is making a leisurely flight around the world passed over here at 4:30 a.m. (8.30 p.m. E.S.T. Monday night) heading east.

Miss Earhart has not been reported since she took off at 7:30 a.m. (11.30 p.m. E.S.T. Sunday night) yesterday from Massawa, Italian Eritrea, for Aden. It was later understood, however, she would fly direct to Karachi, India, if weather permitted.

JUNE 16, 1937
Amelia Flies Over Desert on Hop to India

KARACHI, India, June 15 (AP)—Amelia Earhart arrived here tonight at 7:05 p.m. (9:05 a.m. E.S.T.) completing a long and interrupted hop from Massawa, Eritrea, on her "just for fun" aerial flight around the world.

She had been unreported for more than 29 hours on a leg of her flight that lay over Arabian desert and mountains and for about 1000 miles across the Arabian sea.

Miss Earhart said she would stay here probably a day, but that her tentative plans to take off Thursday depended on the weather.

Her itinerary, on the globe-circling flight as close as practicable to the equator, calls for stops at Darwin, Australia, then across the Pacific to Oakland, Cal., by way of the Pacific Island route of Pan-American Airways.

JUNE 17, 1937
Amelia on Non-Stop Hop to Calcutta

KARACHI, India, Thursday, June 17 (UP)—Amelia Earhart resumed her globe-girdling flight today after a two-day rest, taking off for a non-stop flight to Calcutta.

(continued on next page)

San Francisco Chronicle
THE CITY'S ONLY HOME-OWNED NEWSPAPER

Captain Fred J. Noonan, her navigator, accompanied her in the "Flying Laboratory" which was overhauled here after a 1900-mile flight from Assab, Eritrea.

JUNE 18, 1937

Amelia's Hop Nears Half - Way Marker

CALCUTTA, India, Friday, June 18 (UP)—Amelia Earhart Putnam, accompanied by her navigator, Captain Fred J. Noonan, took off at 11:11 a. m. G. M. T. (9:11 p. m. Thursday E. D. T.) today for Bangkok, Siam, the halfway point in her flight around the world.

She arrived here last night completing a 1:00-mile nonstop flight across India from Karachi in eight hours 24 minutes.

JUNE 19, 1937

Amelia Gets Away for Hop to Siam

RANGOON, Burma (Saturday), June 19 (UP) — Amelia Earhart took off in her $80,000 "Flying Laboratory" at 4:42 a. m. today from Akyab, Burma, for her third attempt in two days to complete the Calcutta-Bangkok, Siam, leg of her around-the-world flight.

Bad weather, which first caused her to stop at Akyab Thursday, made her turn back after a start for Bangkok yesterday and after another start earlier today.

HONOLULU, T. H., June 18 (UP) —The Coast Guard cutter Itasca today departed from Pearl Harbor bound for Howland island, where it will meet Amelia Earhart, woman flyer on a globe-circling airplane flight across the Pacific to Oakland, Cal.

JUNE 20, 1937

Amelia in Burma, Hops for Bangkok

RANGOON, Burma (Sunday) June 20 (UP) Amelia Earhart took off at 6:30 a. m. today (7 p. m. E. S. T. Saturday) on the next leg of her flight around the world.

It was believed her destination was Bangkok, Siam, about 400 miles southeast of here.

She arrived here yesterday from Arkab after a flight through a Burmese monsoon, which she described as the worst experience of her journey.

Half-Way

Flashing across the deserts and jungles of Africa and Asia toasel-hatted Amelia Earhart last week continued her just-for-fun flight around the globe, completing half her journey.

She shot her twin-engine monoplane "Electra" across Africa at a 172-mile-an-hour pace landing at Fort Lamay in West French Africa. From there she flew on to El Fasher, Anglo-Egyptian Sudan, to Massawa, Italian Eritrea, to Karachi, India.

JUNE 21, 1937

Amelia at Java: To Overhaul Plane

BANDOENG, Java (Monday), June 21 (UP) — Amelia Earhart, American flyer, landed her $80,000 "flying laboratory" here at 3:11 a. m. (Greenwich time) on a flight from Singapore to have her plane overhauled at the Netherlands airline base.

U.S. Coast Guard dispatch to headquarters requesting GP provide better communications with them.

TREASURY DEPARTMENT U. S. Coast Guard Ed. Sept. 1929	

U. S. COAST GUARD
OFFICIAL DISPATCH   10 JUNE 1937
UNIT HEADQUARTERS
INCOMING HEADING

CG 42 C Z QUAH V QUAC GR 17

FROM
SANFRANCISCO DIVISION

TO (FOR ACTION)
HEADQUARTERS

ACKNOWLEDGE	
PRIORITY	
ROUTINE	X
NITE	

TO (FOR INFORMATION)

ACKNOWLEDGE	
PRIORITY	
ROUTINE	
NITE	

TEXT

6010 REQUEST THAT PUTNAM BE REQUIRED KEEP THIS DIVISION ADVISED DAILY OF PROGRESS OF EARHART FLIGHT 1053

TOR 1449 RW NAVY # 42

Operator's Record.   Initials of "ACTION" officer.

Amelia's dispatches, sent back to GP to be relayed to the newspaper syndicate, were infused with a spirit of adventure, pleasure and reward. She kept careful records of the Electra's performance and of the reactions of Fred and herself to climatic changes, altitude, fatigue, and diet. A chore which never failed to amuse Fred, but which Amelia performed conscientiously, was the collecting of microorganisms in the upper air by means of a sky hook, a metal rod about the size and length of a broomstick, on whose end a metal cylinder was inserted. This was fastened outside the slightly-opened window. The time of day, altitude, and location were recorded when the cylinder was pulled in, sealed, and tucked away in the rear of the fuselage. She collected these samples for Fred C. Meier of the Department of Agriculture.

At the request of Admiral R. R. Waesche, Commandant of the U.S. Coast Guard, GP informed them of the Electra's progress. Unfortunately, GP did not provide sufficiently frequent reports, and this hampered communications. In a telegram dated June 10, 1937, the San Francisco Division requested:

"PUTNAM BE REQUIRED KEEP THIS DIVISION ADVISED DAILY OF PROGRESS OF EARHART FLIGHT."

By leisurely stages the Electra flew from Miami to Lae, New Guinea. The Atlantic crossing was easy because Amelia was flying toward the African continent and could easily locate land. But when she made landfall, the fliers did not recognize where they were. Noonan recommended that she fly south. Instead she opted to fly north. After flying about 50 miles up the coast, she landed in St. Louis,

A note Fred sent up to Amelia just before they reached the African Continent. Amelia commented, "What put us north" They were indeed north of their objective.

```
SX143...
      RIO DE JANEIRO, JUNE 7.--(UP)--AN AIR FRANCE RADIO MESSAGE TODAY
SAID AMELIA EARHART, AMERICAN WOMAN ROUND THE WORLD FLYER,
TOOK OFF AT 3:13 A. M. (12:13 A. M. CST) FROM NATAL FOR A
1900 MILE FLIGHT TO DAKAR, ON THE SENEGAL COAST OF AFRICA.
      MISS EARHART FLEW OVER THE ROUTE WHICH MAIL AVIATORS AND OTHER
FLIERS USE, THE SHORTEST DISTANCE FROM COAST TO COAST --APPROXIMATELY
1900 STATUTE MILES.
      MISS EARHART FLEW YESTERDAY FROM FORTALEZA, BRAZIL, TO NATAL
AFTER SOME DELAY BECAUSE OF MINOR MOTOR TROUBLE. THE DISTANCE FROM
FORTALEZA TO DAKAR IS 60 MILES LESS THAN FROM NATAL TO DAKAR,
BUT MISS EARHART THOUGHT IT BETTER TO GO TO NATAL WHERE FLYING
FACILITIES ARE BETTER.
      THE AIR FRANCE DISPATCH SAID THAT WEATHER CONDITIONS ALONG HER
COURSE WERE FAIR.
                          GF 823A
```

Senegal, on June 7. Amelia wrote that if she had turned south as Noonan recommended, a half hour flight would have brought them to Dakar, her objective. It is 163 miles from St. Louis to Dakar. Amelia had made landfall 113 miles north of her intended objective, after a flight of about 1,900 miles.

In *Last Flight*, which GP had published in 1937, Amelia commented that during their crossing of the South Atlantic, she and Fred passed a west-bound Air France mail plane, but unfortunately she could "not talk" to it. Amelia believed that the mail plane's radio equipment was telegraphic, that is, Morse code, while her radio equipment was "exclusively voice telephone."

In early June, Amelia had passed through Fort Lamy, now N'Djamena, El Flasher and Khartoum in the Sudan before heading for India. At Akyab, Burma, Amelia was greatly tempted by lengths of beautiful sari cloth she saw in the bazaar, but, of course, souvenirs were excess baggage, strictly denied aboard the spartan Electra. She did buy some colorful bracelets which she mailed to my daughter, Amy, for her sixth birthday. The only exceptions they allowed themselves were a handwrought sheath knife for the knife collection of Amelia's friend of the National Geographic Society, John Oliver La Gorce, and Fred's purchase of a graceful silver bowl for his wife, patiently waiting for his return in Oakland. The gifts weighed less than a pound all together.

One of the last stops before Lae, New Guinea, was Bandoeng, now Bandung, Java, a city about 75 miles southeast of Jakarta. In Bandoeng at the time was a young man named Francis "Fuzz" Furman, who between 1937 and 1939 was a field service representative for the Glenn L. Martin Company, under contract with the Dutch East Indies Air Force. He was responsible for keeping over 100 Martin B-10 bombers flying. Fuzz, now a retired 37-year employee of the Martin Company, began in 1932 as a licensed mechanic and worked his way up to manufacturing manager of various programs. Known as a diagnostician and problem-solver, he was an excellent mechanic. He had the opportunity to observe Amelia and Fred's reactions to the stresses of mechanical troubles suffered while trying to maintain their time schedule. Fuzz wrote that Amelia and Fred landed on Bandoeng where KLM and KNILM, a local organization and sister company to KLM, had a maintenance base. While the Standard Oil people were servicing Amelia's plane, Fuzz went over and offered his help.

When Amelia arrived in Bandoeng, she had reported having had some difficulties with the engine instruments while crossing Africa. Fuzz was familiar with the problem, for as he explained, "When I was in the Navy, I had overhauled that type engine." Her problems were with the exhaust gas analyzer, the generator and its fuel flow meter, but none were so serious as to interfere with flying the airplane.

Article from Martin Company newspaper on January 2, 1959.

THEY KEPT THE MARTIN B-10s FLYING. In 1937-39, F. O. (Fuzz) Furman was Martin field service representative in Bandoeng, Java. He is shown above (center) with his ground crew, some Dutch, some Javanese, who kept the B-10s flying.

JUST ONE MORE LONG FLIGHT | 221

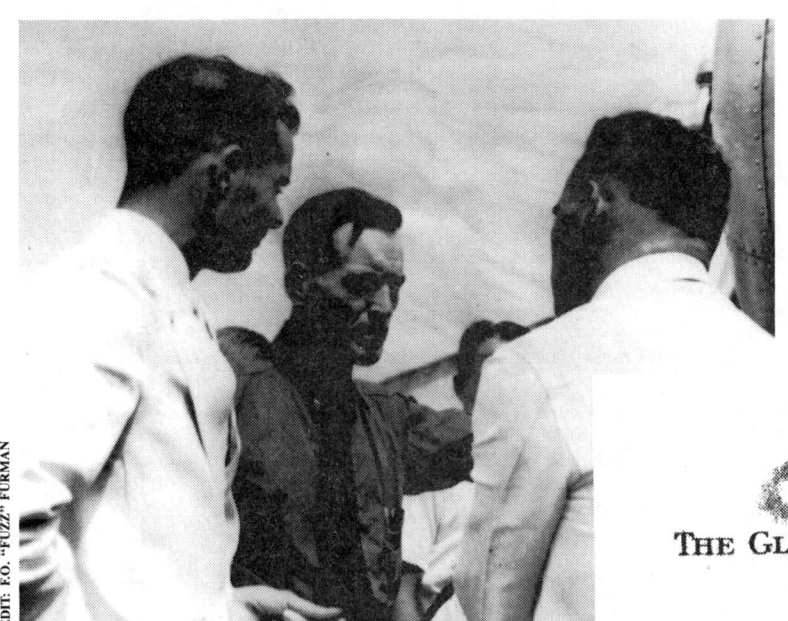

Fuzz Furman, Fred Noonan and Mr. Hanlow, Standard Oil Company representative at Bandoeng.

Fred, left, Amelia and Fuzz taken in Bandoeng, Java between June 21 and June 26, 1937.

Tribnews, London

My plans for leaving Bandoeng today can not be carried out. KNILM engineers and mechanics pleaded for two hours more to complete their work. That two hours is difference making next step and not so now ~~hop~~ plan hop ~~77 sometime after~~ midnight ~~Al~~ trying reach Sourabaya ~~before~~ my nightfall. Delay ~~but~~ will worth while as only here *doing where work* could find ~~it~~ ~~instrument~~ work be accomplished. Dutch use ~~many parts~~ American planes and accessories and excellent mechanics *where they made* My sightseeing ~~has extension~~ extended itself to Batavia

Notes from Amelia on her round-the-world flight—in Amelia's hand. She sent these back before taking off from Lae.

Fuzz, far left, Mr. Hanlow and KNILM maintenance personnel with Amelia and Fred in Bandoeng, June, 1937.

Amelia in front of her Electra while Fuzz worked on her plane, under the wheel well on starboard side.

According to Fuzz, Amelia's engines used 80 octane fuel except for take-off and initial climb when 100 octane was used, all supplied by Standard Oil Company. A 100 gallon tank carried 50 gallons of the 100 octane fuel, to be used only during periods of high power requirements. He continued:

> "We fixed the exhaust analyzer by replacing the exhaust sampling tube located in the exhaust manifold tail pipe. The exhaust analyzer evaluates the fuel-air mixture and tells if it is too rich, too lean, or just right. With constant speed propellers, it was almost impossible to fully lean out the mixture without getting into trouble—it would be easy to burn a piston or valve. Amelia's airplane also had a problem with the fuel flow meter. The meter told her how many gallons she was burning per hour."

Fuzz fixed the exhaust analyzer at Amelia's first stop in Bandoeng by replacing a worn drive gear on the engine. From Bandoeng, Amelia flew on to Surabaya, now Surabaja, Fuzz noted, "but called back to say she was still having trouble with the instruments." He recommended that she return to Bandoeng, the nearest place where there was someone familiar with that type aircraft equipment. Amelia and Noonan flew back, and Fuzz succeeded in getting the instruments fixed. This time the trouble was with the wiring in the generator used to operate the fuel flow meter, not the main generator for the plane. The KNILM instrument shop repaired the problem. Fuzz explained, "The two problems were on the same engine; the other engine did not cause any trouble."

Several days after arriving in Bandoeng, Amelia and Noonan left for the second time, and after a successful flight to Surabaya, Amelia wired Fuzz: "GREAT FLIGHT TO SURABAYA ACCOMPLISHED WITHOUT INCIDENT. EVERY THING STILL OK THANKS SINCERELY FOR ALL YOU DID." It was signed, "AMELIA EARHART."

Telegram Amelia sent to Fuzz, thanking him for his help in Bandoeng.

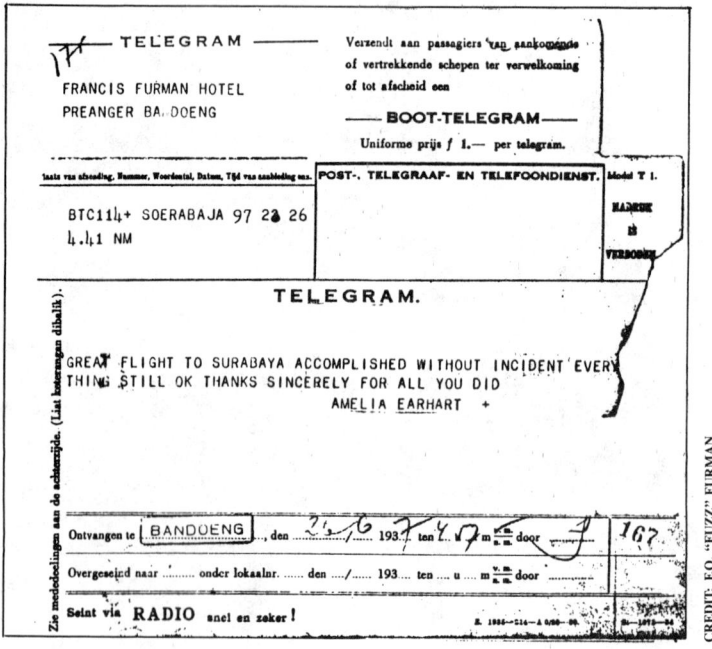

San Francisco Chronicle
THE CITY'S ONLY HOME-OWNED NEWSPAPER

FRIDAY, JUNE 25, 1937

Putnam Here to Prepare For Amelia's Return

George Palmer Putnam arrived in Oakland yesterday to make preparations for the reception of his globe-circling wife, Amelia Earhart, who is due at Oakland Airport on the last leg of her 'round-the-world flight, Wednesday or Thursday. Putnam said he talked with his wife on the telephone from Cheyenne, Wyo., at midnight. Wednesday. At that time she was in Sourabaya, Java, he said. She said that she and her navigator, Frederick Noonan, were in "good shape" and expected to be "in on schedule."

Her present program calls for her arrival at Howland Island Sunday, a hop from that point to Hawaii Tuesday and arrival here Wednesday or Thursday. Fuel, supplies and repair equipment have been parked at Howland Island in case of need.

Putnam said the most dangerous part of Miss Earhart's flight was between Java and Howland Island. The place is a mere sand spit thrust above water for a distance of two miles and is hard to find. The plane has no advance information of either air or weather conditions and must go it blind.

Almost coincidentally with the arrival of Putnam in Oakland is the coming of Jimmy Mattern, noted derby and 'round-the-world flyer, who arrives here today with his new $100,000 plane, which he plans to use in an Oakland-Moscow hop within a few days. Mattern was putting final touches on his plans at Burbank yesterday preparatory to the local takeoff. He is confident he can better the performance of the three Russian musketeers who dropped down at Vancouver, Wash., after an epochal flight over the Pole.

BACK FOR REPAIRS

BANDOENG, Dutch East Indies, Friday, June 25 (UP)— Amelia Earhart returned here today when the electric equipment of her plane developed trouble while flying to Soerabaya.

After making the 375-mile flight to Soerabaya, Miss Earhart decided to return here so that Dutch engineers might check over her plane.

start on the hazardous flight across the Pacific.

"I'll be in the United States in four days," she grinned as she climbed into the plane.

The jump to Lae is about 1200 miles.

JULY 1, 1937.

Amelia Hop Delayed by Radio Break

LAE, New Guinea, July 1 (Thursday) (UP)—Amelia Earhart today delayed her departure from here for Howland Island on her flight around the world until Friday because a line breakdown at the Malabar Radio station made it impossible to obtain time signals to test the chronometer on her plane.

She had planned to take off early today on the 2550-mile hop over the Pacific to tiny Howland Island.

Ahead of the famed flyer and her navigator, Fred J. Noonan, lay the hardest and most hazardous leg of the flight around the world. No plane ever has flown the course Miss Earhart must traverse to reach the island.

JUNE 26, 1937

Taking It Easy

Almost leisurely, Amelia Earhart continued her flight around the world. Her trip more than half completed, she left Calcutta for Bangkok, Siam, and finding the weather unfit for the flight, landed at Akyab. Next day, she piloted her flying laboratory through a Burmese monsoon to reach Rangoon, Burma. She described the flight as the worst experience of her journey. Leaving Rangoon, she proceeded leisurely to Bandoeng, Dutch East Indies, and announced she was going to take a three-day rest and have her plane overhauled before taking off on the next leg of her flight.

Amelia Hop Delayed By Motor Trouble

BANDOENG, Netherlands East Indies, June 25 (UP)—Amelia Earhart, American woman aviator flying around the world, returned here today from Soerabaya, farther east on Java Island, because of motor trouble. She tried to repair the damage herself, but failed.

JUNE 28, 1937

Earhart Arrives At Port Darwin

PORT DARWIN, Australia (Monday), June 28 (UP)—Amelia Earhart arrived here today from Koepang, Timor Island, Netherlands East Indies, in the $80,000 "flying laboratory" in which she is making a flight around the world.

The hop was of 500 miles across the Timor sea.

JUNE 29, 1937

AMELIA OFF ON HOP FOR NEW GUINEA

PORT DARWIN, Australia (Tuesday), June 29 (UP)—Amelia Earhart took off at 6:50 a.m. today, local time, in her big twin-motored Lockheed Electra, headed for Lae, New Guinea.

It is the last jump on her flight around the world before she will

---

Fuzz Furman explained, "Fred Noonan had that island [Howland] on his mind when he was in Bandoeng. It was a hard target to hit, for it was only a mile long by a half mile wide, and only a few feet above sea-level. If a cloud got in the way one might miss it, and they didn't have enough fuel reserve to fly around long if they missed the island."

Fuzz also denied the rumors about Fred Noonan's drinking habit, rumors which persist to this day. Fuzz observed:

"Noonan told me if he could hit that island all right, the rest would be easy. I saw a lot of Noonan," during the stopover at Bandoeng. In fact, "Noonan spent most of his time at the airport or the Preanger Hotel. I never noticed any drinking problem when I was with him."

Fuzz continued, "Noonan stayed four or five nights in the same hotel I was in." Noonan and Fuzz would go out to the airport together in the morning and Fuzz declared, "Noonan never once appeared to have any drinking problem . . . I knew many Standard Oil people. I was in Bandoeng, Java, until 1939, long enough after this incident to have met some of the Standard Oil people who were involved in servicing Amelia's airplane, giving her fuel in Bandoeng, etc., and I am sure that if Fred Noonan had been intoxicated in Lae, somebody would have told me about it, at least, through the grapevine."

Fuzz mentioned that every night, no matter where Amelia and Fred Noonan were, except during all-night flights, at a specified time she would faithfully telephone home. GP knew every day just where Amelia was on her round-the-world flight.

Another person who had the opportunity to observe Fred Noonan was R.D. "Bo" McKneely, Amelia's mechanic and later a Lockheed field service representative. He was the only other person who flew with Amelia and Fred on the first part of their round-the-world flight. In an interview on June 7, 1987, Bo said, ". . . we felt pretty confident with Noonan as a navigator . . . Now I am a man, a tee-totaler, I don't drink, and I never remember smelling any liquor on him or anything like that. Never have I seen him intoxicated so I can't believe it . . ."

After Bandoeng, Amelia's next scheduled landing was Koepang, on the south east tip of Timor, about 525 miles northwest of Port Darwin, Australia. The next stop was Port Darwin, where Amelia reported that they left parachutes to be shipped home as they believed a parachute would be of little value over the Pacific.

After Amelia and Fred left Port Darwin, they flew 7 hours and 43 minutes on to Lae, New Guinea, landing on June 29th at 3:00 p.m., local time. They spent the next two days packing the plane and discarding every unnecessary item.

A Lae, New Guinea notice to airmen available in 1937. It notes that the runway runs north and south, 3,000 feet long. The current air strip guide states: "CAUTION: Down drafts on approach to Rwy 32 [end of runway over cliff]."

When Amelia and Fred had some free time, they did some exploring around Lae, awaiting a break in the weather. The last weather report she received via Lae was a Radiogram from Fleet Air Base, Pearl Harbor, dated July 1, 1937 (Thursday):

" . . . lae to ontario [on station long. 165° E, half way to Howland] partly clouded rain squalls 250 miles east lae wind east south east twelve to fifteen period ontario eo [to] Long [longitude] one seven five partly cloudy cumulus clouds about ten thousand feet mostly unlimited wind east north east eighteen thence to howland partly cloudy scattered heavy showers wind east north east fifteen period avoid towering cumulus and squalls by detours as centres frequently dangerous"

Telegram from Amelia speaking to the one day delay.

(above)
Amelia climbs from cockpit of Lockheed Electra after taxying into one of Guinea Airways huge hangars.

The next nine photographs were taken by T. F. "Tommie" O'Dea of Perth, Western Australia, who was the General Manager of Guinea Airways in 1937. He took a series of photographs, perhaps the last photographs ever taken of Amelia and Fred Noonan.

Amelia on the wing of her Lockheed Electra.

Last telegram Amelia sent from Lae.

According to Fuzz Furman, Noonan had four watches and was constantly checking them with the chronometers at Bandoeng. Instruments were not as reliable in those days, and accurate time is essential to a celestial navigator.

On July first, winds and rain squalls, the forerunners of the dreaded monsoons, and Fred Noonan's inability to obtain an accurate time check, kept the plane grounded for 24 hours. A line breakdown at the Malabar Radio station made it impossible for Fred to obtain the time signals, essential to set his chronometer.

From Left, Mr. and Mrs. Joubert, Mrs. Jacobs, Amelia, Mr. Jacobs, Captain Fred Noonan. L.J. Joubert was manager of Bulolo Gold Dredging Ltd., and F.C. Jacobs was manager of New Guinea Goldfields Ltd. They were flown to Lae by Tommie O'Dea to meet Amelia and Fred.

Amelia on her arrival at New Guinea.

Amelia's last written message from Lae, New Guinea, was a Western Union telegram to the Press Tribune, Oakland, California, dated July 2, 1937 (Lae time):

"QUOTE DENMARKS A PRISON UNQUOTE AND LAE ATTRACTIVE AND UNUSUAL AS IT IS APPEARS TO TWO FLIERS JUST AS CONFINING LOCKHEED STANDS READY FOR LONGEST HOP WEIGHTED WITH GASOLINE AND OIL TO CAPACITY HOWEVER CLOUDS AND WIND BLOWING WRONG WAY CONSPIRED KEEP HER ON GROUND TODAY IN ADDITION FN HAS BEEN UNABLE ACCOUNT RADIO DIFFICULTIES TO SET HIS CHRONOMETERS LACK KNOWLEDGE THEIR FASTNESS OR SLOWNESS WE SHALL TRY TO GET OFF TOMORROW THOUGH NOW WE CAN NOT BE HOME BY FOURTH OF JULY AS HAD HOPED = EARHART"

In this telegram there were no fatalistic forebodings and no suggestion that she would do other than fly the Electra home with the same skill and confidence which she had displayed during her thousands of hours in the air.

At Lae, New Guinea, the Electra was refuelled for the longest non-stop flight of its life and that of its pilot—2,550 miles. The hazard lay not only in the distance to be traveled, but in the necessity of making a landfall on tiny Howland Island.

Howland is a flat coral island, shaped like a huge kidney bean. Its land area is .64 square miles, or 410 acres. The barren land has an elevation of only 18 to 20 feet. The Interior Department had constructed a runway down the length of the island and two cross runways.

If Amelia were to miss Howland, her fuel would give out long before she could reach the next land, Hawaii, 1,600 miles to the east. Fred's navigating instruments had been checked by Dutch experts at Bandoeng, Java, three days before the Lae take-off. Amelia talked by telephone with GP in Wyoming, assuring him that plane and crew were in top condition and that she expected to be home as soon after the "Glorious Fourth" as possible.

The radio was the only feature not entirely satisfactory, a consequence of the shortened trailing antenna. The Coast Guard Cutter *Itasca* was directed to cruise in the vicinity of Howland Island in order to send homing directional signals on 500 KCs, and Amelia felt this was sufficient coverage.

The report of the captain of the Coast Guard Cutter *Itasca*, Commander Warner K. Thompson, has revealed the tragic lack of communication with the fliers. The *Itasca* had been ordered to leave San Pedro, California, for Howland Island to make a routine inspection trip of the United States "line possessions," so called because they lie almost in line with the Equator. It was not until the *Itasca* had reached Pearl Harbor and picked up Mr. Richard Black, then an official in the Department of the Interior, that Commander Thompson realized that he had a date with Amelia. His first orders were simply to see that the flocks of birds were chased off the newly constructed runway on Howland Island.

Just prior to departure, the aircraft which had been safely stored in one of Guinea's hangars is pushed onto the tarmac by New Guinea natives.

Commander Thompson was surprised when Mr. Black loaded a Navy high frequency "emergency direction finder" on board because he considered the gear untried and erratic. Commander Thompson preferred to rely on the solid, low and medium frequency, direction finder which had proven dependable since its installation two years before. As Mr. Black was appointed GP's representative, however, Commander Thompson agreed to carry the equipment to Howland.

On the morning of July 2, Amelia and Fred climbed aboard, checked their instruments, signaled, "Ready!" and waved to the crowd which never failed to gather to watch their plane take to the air or come in for a landing.

Governor of Samoa sent a priority message to U.S. Coast Guard San Francisco Division:

"EARHART LEFT LAE TEN AM LOCAL TIME JULY 2ND DUE HOWLAND ISLAND 18 HOURS TIME."

Her flight was to carry her across the International Date line so that the day of her arrival would also be July second.

According to a first-hand report from J. A. Collopy, District Superintendent of Civil Aviation Board, dated August 28, 1937,

"The take-off was hair-raising as after taking every inch of the 1000 yard runway from the north west end of the aerodrome toward the sea, the aircraft had not left the ground 50 yards from the end of the runway [ending abruptly on a cliff, at the waters edge] . . . When it did leave it sank away but was by this time over the sea. It continued to sink to about five or six feet above the water and had not climbed to more than 100 feet before it disappeared from sight . . . In spite of this however, it was obvious that the aircraft was well handled and pilots of Guinea Airways who have flown Lockheed aircraft were loud in their praise of the take-off with such an overload."

All aboard and ready to go.

(above)
Last weather report Amelia received in Lae, dated July 1, 1937.

Opening up her throttles and away on her long last flight to Howland Island.

According to H. J. Balfour in a letter of December 31, 1969,

" . . . contact was made with her flight hourly from 10 am until 6 pm local time and at each sked position reports and height were received from her and as far as I can remember her last position report was somewhere in the vicinity of Ocean Island and at that time she was on course for Howland at 12000 feet and would have been 9 hours flying time since take off from Lae. The reason that she did not contact me after six pm was that she changed frequency of her transmission and this frequency was unsuitable for conditions at Lae account of the heavy static locally, but at every other time twoway contact was perfect and we requested her to remain on her present frequency but she told me that she wished to contact the American Coast Guard Cutter *"Itasca"* so there was nothing we could do about it but pass the last terminal forecast to her and the upper air report from Ocean Island." Mr. Balfour ended by saying, "Miss Earhart could not send or receive Morse and neither could her Navigator Mr. Noonan, she told me this during her visits to the radio station and I know this would have helped her quite a lot if either of them were competent radio operators as well as flying and navigation and all her messages to me was on voice."

There were three logs that covered the communication with Amelia during the last hours of her flight. Two of these were in the *Itasca* radio room and one was by the radio operator on Howland Island. The following is a combination of the information from these three logs:

Time	Itasca Log 1
0245	ABLE HEAR EARHART AT (ON 3105)
0345	HRD EARHART PLANE ON 3105
0455	... EARHART BROKE IN ON FONE 3105 / NW ???? UNREADABLE
0612	EARHART ON 3105 NW / WANTS BEARING 3105 ETC
0613	"200 MILES OUT"
0642	EARHART ON NW RECEPTION FAIRLY CLR NW..WANT BEARING ES [and] WNTS REPT [report] IN ½ HR
0730	CALLING CONSTANTLY ON 3105 ON FOE ES KEY / THOMPSON RM3C [Radioman, Third Class Thompson] ON D/F [direction finder]
0740	EARHART ON NW SEZ RUNNING OUT OF GAS ONLY ½ HR LEFT CANT HR [hear] US AT ALL / WE HR HER AND ARE SENDING ON 3105 ES 500 SAME TIME CONSTANTLY AND LISTENING IN FER HER FREQUENTLY
0757	AMELIA ON AGN AT 0800 SEZ HRS US ON 7.5 MEGS GA

Naval message regarding the last message received from Amelia while she was on her flight.

```
NPG 602
MUSK V KATY Z QUAX V NRUI Q QUAC P GR 88
    FROM  USCG ITASCA
    ACTION  COMDR SANFRANCISCO DIV CG
    INFO  COMDR HAWAIIAN SECT SANFRANCISCO DIV HONOLULU

PASSED TO OPNAV BY COMTWELVE FOR APPROPRIATE ACTION


6002 YOUR 6002 1401 WE HAVE HAD NO POSITIONS COMMA SPEED COMMA OR
COURSES FROM EARHARTS PLANE EXCEPT SO CALLED LINE OF POSITION AT
0843 WHICH HAD NO REFERENCE POINT PERIOD SHE GAVE US NONE OF HER
BEARINGS PERIOD BELIEVE SHE PASSED TO NORTH AND WEST OF ISLAND
ABOUT 0900 AND MISSED IT IN THE GLARE OF RISING SUN THOUGH WE
WERE SMOKING HEAVILY AT THAT TIME PERIOD JUDGE SHE CAME DOWN BETWEEN
337 AND 90 FROM HOWLAND AND WITHIN 100 MILES PERIOD HAVE BROADCAST
AS INDICATED 1402

                              13  ACTION
2139 AC 2 JUL MX/    05  10A  11  16  18  20  38  BUAER
SEE  NPG 679 FOR ACTION TAKEN
```

CREDIT: U.S. NAVAL ARCHIVES

Time	Itasca Log 2
0236	"ITASCA TO EARHART" / fone 3105
0245	HEARD EARHART PLANE BUT UNREADABLE THRU STATIC
0300	SENT WEATHER TO KHAQQ
0345	EARHART HEARD FONE "WILL LISSEN [sic] ON HOUR AND HALF ON 3105"—SEZ SHE
0453	HEARD EARHART "—PART CLDY"
0614	WANTS BEARING ON 3105 KCS ON HOUR "WILL WHISTLE IN MIC"
0615	"ABOUT TWO HUNDRED MILES OUT APPX WHISTLING NW [now]"
0645	"PSE [please] TAKE BEARING ON US AND REPORT IN HALF HOUR"
0646	"I WILL MAKE NOISE IN MIC ABT 100 MILES OUT"
0718	FONE TO EARHART "CANNOT TAKE BEARING ON 3105 VY GOOD PLEASE SEND ON 500 or DU [do you] WISH TAKE BEARING ON US GA [go ahead] PSE" NO ANSWER
0742	"KHAQQ CLING ITASCA WE MUST BE ON YOU BUT CANNOT SEE U BUT GAS IS RUNNING LOW BEEN UNABLE TO REACH YOU BY RADIO WE ARE FLYING AT A 1000 FEET"
0758	"KHAQQ CLNG ITASCA WE ARE CIRCLING BUT CANNOT HR [hear] U GA ON 7500 WID [with] A LNG [long] COUNT EITHER NW [now] OR ON THE SKD [skeduled] TIME ON ½ HOUR" (KHAQQ S5 A 3)
0800	"KHAQQ CLNG ITASCA WE RECD UR SIGS BUT UNABLE TO GET A MINIMUM PSE TAKE BEARING ON US AND ANS 3105 WID VOICE . . ."
0805	"KHAQQ FM ITASCA UR SIGS RECD OK WE ARE UNABLE TO HEAR U TO TAKE A BEARING IT IMPRACTICAL TO TAKE A BEARING ON 3105 UR VOICE HW DO U GET IT GA" UNASWD
0844	"KHAQQ TO ITASCA WE ARE ON LINE 157 337 WL REPT MSG WE WL REPT [report] N ES S THIS ON 6210 KCS WAIT, 3105"/ A3 AS (?/ KHAQQ TSMISION "WE ARE RUNNING ON LINE LSNIN [listen] 6210 KCS"/ KHAQQ DE NRUI [Itasca] "HRD U OK ON 3105 KCS 7500"
0847	"KHAQQ DE [from] NRUI PLS STAY ON 3105 KCS DO NOT HR U ON 6210 MAINTAIN QSO ON 3105, 7500"/ UNANSWD

Time	Howland Log
0015:	WEAK FONE ON 3105 (I AM USING A LONG VERTICAL ANTENNA FOR RECEPTION OF SIGNALS ONLY) UNABLE TO GET BEARING S
0440:	[From Itasca] . . . U HR EARHART ON 3105 / YES BUT CANT MAKE HER OUT/TUNED TO EARHART / NO HR
0715:	PICKED UP EARHART (USING LONG ANTENNA, S3, HARDLY ANY CARRIER, SEEMED OVERMODULATED, SWITCHED OVER TO LOOP FOR BEARING, S1 TO 0. SHE STOPPED TRANSMISSION) BEARING NIL——3105
0747:	(AM USING THE D/F AND RECEIVING SET SPARINGLY DUE TO HEAVY DRAINAGE ON BATTERIES) (THE BATTERIES ARE OF LOW AM-HOUR CAPACITY) EARHART ON THE AIR, S4, "GIVE ME A BEARING". EARHART DID NOT TEST FOR BEARING. HER TRANSMISSION TOO SHORT FOR BEARING, STATIC X5, HER CARRIER IS COMPLETELY MODULATED. COULD NOT GET A BEARING DUE TO ABOVE REASONS. ——3105
0859:	BATTERIES WEAK VOICE ON 3105. CAME IN AT END OF TRANSMISSION. —3105
0920:	ITASCA CALLING EARHART TO ANSWER ON 500 KCS STEADLY TILL—
0926:	RECEIVED INFORMATION THAT ITASCA BELIEVED EARHART DOWN. LANDING PARTY RECALLED BACK TO VESSEL.
1000:	ALL BATTERIES ON THE ISLAND ARE DISCHARGED. COMMENCED TO CHARGE THEM.

On July 19, 1937, after being relieved of the search mission, and prior to arrival in Hawaii, the *Itasca* summarized all radio communications in conjunction with Amelia's flight. In this summary were copies of the radio logs and comments that explain and expand upon the data shown. Significant entries are shown below:

TREASURY DEPARTMENT

UNITED STATES COAST GUARD

COAST GUARD CUTTER
ITASCA

At Sea, Pacific Ocean,
19 July, 1937.

From: Commanding Officer, ITASCA.
To : Commander, San Francisco Division.

Subject: Radio transcripts Earhart Flight.

Reference: (a) DcT 8018-2200, July, 1937.

Inclosures: 1. Excerpts from ITASCA radio log June and July, 1937.

1. For purposes of clarity, this report will trace the Earhart flight from the communications angle from the time the ITASCA was first ordered in connection with the flight on 9 June until the ITASCA was released by Navy on 18 July, 1937. The report is divided into three sections; (a) Before Flight; (b) The Flight; (c) The Search. Comments are made directly as events occur. Summary of opinion is made at the end of each section and at the end of the report. This report has been made "confidential" due to the fact that it contains a large number of personal messages and that further it discusses, frankly, certain matters which might be considered as controversial. This has been done in an effort to present an accurate picture of ITASCA opinion.

June 26th:

From: Com SF Div.
To : ITASCA.
Inf.: Governor GUAM. ; Commandant 12th Naval Distr.; ONTARIO; SWAN ComHawSec. Comdt. 14th Nav. Distr.
8026 FOLLOWING INFORMATION FROM EARHART THIS DATE QUOTE HOMING DEVICE COVERS FROM 200 TO 1500 AND 2400 TO 4800 KILOCYCLES ANY FREQUENCIES NOT REPEAT NOT NEAR ENDS BANDS SUITABLE UNQUOTE SUGGEST USING SUITABLE FREQUENCIES HAVING IN MIND UNCERTAIN CHARACTERISTICS OF HIGH FREQUENCIES PERIOD USE 333 KILOCYCLES OR FREQUENCY IN THAT VICINITY AND TRY 545 KILOCYCLES AFTER TEST WITH STATIONS YOUR LOCALITY TO DETERMINE WHICH IS BEST PERIOD ADVISE IF IMPOSSIBLE TO PLACE YOUR TEN TRANSMITTER ON 3105 KILOCYCLES PERIOD ADVISE EARHART AT LAE VIA TUTUILA THAT FREQUENCIES SELECTED AND CONTINUOUS SIGNALS AFTER ASSUMING HER DIRECTION FINDER IN RANGE PERIOD SEE BROADCAST ON QUARTER AFTER AND QUARTER BEFORE HOUR ON 6210 AND 3105 KILOCYCLES PERIOD AM ADVISING EARHART THAT ITASCA WILL VOICE RADIO ON 3105 ON HOUR AND HALF HOUR AS SHE APPROACHES HOWLAND PERIOD REPAIRS MADE AND EARHART NOW AT SOURABAJA EXPECTS LEAVE DAWN THIS DATE FOR PORT DARWIN AND NEXT DAY FOR LAE PERIOD ADVISE PRIORITY IF ADJUSTMENTS FOR TEN TRANSMITTER SATISFACTORY FOR USE ON 3105 1150.

From: NPM. (Naval Radio Honolulu).
To : ITASCA.
SUGGEST ONTARIO STAND BY ON 400 KILOCYCLES TO TRANSMIT LETTER N FIVE MINUTES ON REQUEST WITH STATION CALL LETTERS REPEATED TWICE END OF EVERY MINUTE STOP SWAN TRANSMIT VOICE NINE MEGACYCLES OR IF I UNABLE RECEIVE READY ON 900 KILOCYCLES STOP ITASCA TRANSMIT LETTER A POSITION OWN CALL LETTERS AS ABOVE ON HALF HOUR 7.5 MEGACYCLES STOP POSITION SHIPS AND OUR LEAVING WILL DETERMINE BROADCAST TIMES SPECIFICALLY STOP IF FREQUENCIES MENTIONED UNSUITABLE NIGHT WORK INFORM ME LAE STOP I WILL GIVE LONG CALL BY VOICE THREE ONE NOUGHT FIVE KCS QUARTER AFTER HOUR POSSIBLE QUARTER TO
 . EARHART.

The above message is the first direct contact that the ITASCA has had with Earhart previous to the anticipated flight. The ITASCA bases this message as the key message of the flight. It will be noted that the frequencies requested were high frequencies with the exception of ONTARIO. This is contradictory to the last message received from Commander San Francisco Division suggesting 333 and 545 kilocycles. It will also be noted that the requested 7.5 megacycles is beyond the frequency range, that at least to our knowledge, of the plane direction finder.

June 27th:
From: Earhart via RCA Radio Manila.
To : ITASCA (Black).
BLACK ITASCA KAA
SUGGEST ONTARIO STAND BY ON 400 KCS TO TRANSMIT LETTER N FIVE MINUTES ON REQUEST WITH STATION CALL LETTERS REPEATED TWICE END EVERY MINUTE STOP SWAN TRANSMIT VOICE 9 MEGACYCLES OR IF I UNABLE RECEIVE BE READY ON 900 KCS STOP ITASCA TRANSMIT LETTER A POSITION OWN CALLLETTERS AS ABOVE ON HALF HOUR 7.5 MEGACYCLES STOP POSITION SHIPS AND OUR LEAVING WILL DETERMINE BROADCAST TIMES SPECIFICIALLY STOP IF FREQUENCIES MENTIONED UNSUITABLE NIGHT WORK INFORM ME LAE STOP I WILL GIVE LONG CALL BY VOICE 3105 KCS QUARTER AFTER HOUR POSSIBLY QUARTER TO EARHART.

From: Com SF Div.
To : ITASCA (Black).
8027 FOR BLACK QUOTE IF ARRANGEABLE PLEASE SEND ME BY EARHART SET NEGATIVES HOWLAND ARRIVAL ETC STILL PICTURES PERIOD IF MOTION PICTURE CAMERA ON BOARD PERIOD EARHART'S STORY TO BE SENT DIRECT TRIBUNE OAKLAND APPRECIATE YOUR COOPERATION PERIOD SUGGEST YOU EMPHASIZE DESIRE SHE SECURE AIR VIEWS OF ISLAND PERIOD IF POSSIBLE REMIND HER BRING AVAILABLE PHOTOS FROM LAE SIGNED PUTNAM UNQUOTE 0940.

From: ITASCA.
To : Governor Samoa.
Inf.: ComHawSec. Com SF Div. SWAN ONTARIO.
8028 FOLLOWING FOR AMELIA EARHART PUTNAM LAE QUOTE ITASCA TRANSMITTERS CALIBRATED 7500 6210 3105 500 425 KCS CW AND LAST THREE EITHER CW OR MCW PERIOD ITASCA DIRECTION FINDER FREQUENCY RANGE 550 TO 270 KCS PERIOD REQUEST WE BE ADVISED AS TO TIME OF DEPARTURE AND ZONE TIME TO BE USED ON RADIO SCHEDULES PERIOD ITASCA AT HOWLAND ISLAND DURING FLIGHT 0910.

The above is the only information that Earhart received relative to available direction finder frequency range on board ITASCA.

June 29th:

    From: Naval Radio Tutuila.
    To : ITASCA.
COMMANDER USS ITASCA.
PLAN MIDDAY TAKE OFF HERE PLEASE HAVE METEROLOGIST SEND FORCAST LAE HOWLAND SOON AS POSSIBLE IF REACHES ME IN TIME WILL TRY L......Y OTHERWISE JULY FIRST REPORTIØ/ IN ENGLISH NOT CODE SPECIALLY WHILE FLYING STOP WILL BROADCAST HOURLY QUARTER PAST HOUR GCT FURTHER INFORMATION LATER.

    From: Lae.
    To : ITASCA. (Black.)
BLACK ITASCA VIA TUTUILA.
ACCOUNT LOCAL CONDITIONS PLAN START JULY 1ST 2530 GCT IF WEATHER OKEH STOP WILL ITASCA TRY CONTACT LAE DIRECT ON 25 METERS LAE ON 46 SO CAN GET FORECAST IN TIME PARTICULARLY INTERESTED PROBABLE TYPE PERCENTAGE CLOUDS NEAR HOWLAND ISLAND STOP NOW UNDERSTOOD ITASCA VOICING THREE ONE NOUGHT FIVE WITH LONG CONTINUOUS SIGNAL ON APPROACH CONFIRM AND APPOINT TIME FOR OPERATOR HERE TO STAND WATCH FOR DIRECT CONTACT.

    It will be noted that the above is contrary to the information received from Earhart at Port Darwin which stated that the ITASCA was to use 7.5 megacycles. The ITASCA has thus far given no indication of intention to broadcast on this frequency, although preparations have been made.

June 30th:

    From: ComHawSec.
    To : ITASCA.
MSG HONOLULU BLACK NOTIFY SOON POSSIBLE WHETHER AMELIA LANDS LUKE OR WHEELER PERIOD INFORM HER PUTNAM WIRES SHE TO BROADCAST GREETINGS NBC HOOKUP THROUGH KGU IMMEDIATELY UPON ARRIVAL HONOLULU SIGNED COGSWELL 1225.

    From: Fleet Air Base, Pearl Harbor,
    To : ITASCA, Naval Radio Samoa.
2530 FOR EARHART FORECAST THURSDAY LAE TO ONTARIO PARTLY CLOUDY HEAVY RAIN SQUALLS TWO HUNDRED FIFTY MILES EAST OF LAE WIND EAST SOUTHEAST TWELVE TO FIFTEEN PERIOD ONTARIO TO LONGITUDE ONE SEVEN FIVE PARTLY CLOUDY CUMULUS CLOUDS ABOUT TEN THOUSAND FEET MOSTLY UNLIMITED WIND EAST NORTHEAST EIGHTEEN PERIOD THENCE TO HOWLAND PARTLY CLOUDY SCATTERED HEAVY SHOWERS WINDS EAST NORTHEAST FIFTEEN PERIOD AVOID TOWERING CUMULUS AND SQUALLS BY DETOURS AS CENTERS FREQUENTLY DANGEROUS 1220.

From: EARHART.
To : ITASCA (Black) Naval Radio Tutuila.
BLACK ITASCA TUTUILA RADIO
ASK ONTARIO BROADCAST LETTER N FOR FIVE MINUTES TEN MINUTES AFTER HOUR
GMT FOUR HUNDRED KCS WITH OWN CALL LETTERS REPEATED TWICE END EVERY
MINUTE STOP PLAN LEAVE BY TEN THIS MORNING NEW GUINEA TIME EARHART.

From: EARHART via NPU VIA LAE.
To : ITASCA (Black.)
BLACK ITASCA - TUTUILA RADIO.
DUE LOCAL CONDITIONS TAKE OFF DELAYED UNTIL TWENTY ONE THIRTY GMT
JULY SECOND STOP ANY FORECAST LAE HOWLAND BEFORE THEN APPRECIATED NOTIFY
ONTARIO CHANGE BT EARHART.

July 1st:

From: Fleet Air Base, Pearl Harbor.
To : Naval Radio Tutuila; ITASCA.
2501 FOR EARHART LAE ACCURATE FORECAST DIFFICULT ACCOUNT LACK OF REPORTS
YOUR VICINITY PERIOD CONDITIONS APPEAR GENERALLY AVERAGE OVER ROUTE NO
MAJOR STORMS APPARENT PERIOD PARTLY CLOUDY SKIES WITH DANGEROUS LOCAL
RAIN SQUALLS ABOUT THREE HUNDRED MILES EAST OF LAE AND SCATTERED HEAVY
SHOWERS RAMAINDER OF ROUTE PERIOD WINDS EAST SOUTHEAST ABOUT TWENTY FIVE
KNOTS TO ONTARIO AND THEN EAST TO EAST NORTHEAST ABOUT TWENTY KNOTS TO
HOWLAND 0735.

"BEFORE THE FLIGHT"

SUMMARY:

1. The ITASCA was on station.

2. The ITASCA's equipment was correctly calibrated.

3. The ITASCA furnished Earhart weather reports and the best available forecasts.

4. Earhart had full information in clear form as to ITASCA frequencies and as to limits of ITASCA direction finder.

5. Messages list Earhart direction finder limits from 200 to 1500 kilocycles. Another message lists it as 200 to 1500 and 2400 to 4800. The last message was assumed to be correct.

6. The ITASCA's technical opinion as to Earhart's radio desires was never consulted. The Commanding Officer only contacted Earhart once directly by radio as to the arrangements. This was done because the Commanding Officer fore-saw the chance of disaster and desired personal and special precautions on the Earhart departure and final radio plans.

7. The Commanding Officer communicated with the San Francisco Division on two occasions as to the potential radio dangers of this flight. The Division cooperated fully and gave the ITASCA complete communication freedom. The Division likewise furnished the ITASCA all reliable data which could be obtained.

8. The Coast Guard had no intention of navigating Earhart to Howland. The high frequency direction finder obtained from the Navy by Mr. Black was set up on Howland and manned by an ITASCA radioman. <u>This was in accordance with Mr. Black's request.</u> Records show that Earhart was not advised by this vessel of the high frequency direction finder's existence. Mr. Black <u>states</u> that he did not inform Earhart. <u>This fact is very important as shown in Section (b).</u>

9. Mr. Black, from a telegram from Mr. Putnam, was Earhart's representative and handled all Earhart plans. Black was coordinating communications in accordance with Earhart's and Putnam's desires.

10. The Coast Guard in accordance with written orders cooperated with Mr. Black and met all Earhart requests as expressed through Mr. Black and one direct message to the Commanding Officer.

11. The ITASCA's radio personnel in the beginning were inexperienced. The operators were interested and proved capable in the heavy load which they carried. The ship's communication organization was sound and well administered.

(b)   "THE FLIGHT"

Definite information that Earhart was in the air was received from the San Francisco Division at 1830, Howland time. A radioman second class was sent ashore to Howland Island to man the high frequency direction finder.

The ITASCA with a double watch took up the work of attempting to contact the plane.

During the evening tests were made to check ITASCA signal strength key and voice with San Francisco radio.

The transcript of the radio logs from 0200 until 0930 is necessarily not complete due to the rapidity of events and also due to the Earhart exclusive use of voice, only partially received. At these times tuning was so essential that parts of the actual messages may not be given. Officers of appropriate rank and experience were present and where the parenthesis sections are entered corrections to the radio log are given. The radio log stands as it was written at the time and has not been changed or corrected. The transcript inclosed is an actual transcript. The portions included in this section form a true representation of the picture.

Excerpts from ITASCA radio log 1 July:

(This record contains explanatory material which is not contained in the radio log. This is particularly true of the complete ITASCA transmissions. The entire day of 1 July was devoted to trying to ascertain whether Earhart had hopped.)

1830   (Received following).

   From: Com SF Div.
   To : ITASCA.
   Inf.: NPM NPU NIDX SJAN ONTARIO.
8012 UNITED PRESS REPORTS EARHART TOOK OFF AT NOON LAE TIME 2130.

1900   (Started second watch. Two (2) logs from this point. Also at this time manned high frequency direction finder on Howland which kept 3rd log.)

1955   From: Lae.
       To : Mr. Black.
URGENT BLACK ITASCA TUTUILA RADIO:
AMELIA EARHART LEFT LAE TEN AM LOCAL TIME JULY 2ND DUE HOWLAND ISLAND 18 HOURS TIME BT VACUUM.

   During the period from 1900 to midnight the two radio logs form an accurate record of happenings.

   The ITASCA checked signal strength and frequency with San Francisco Radio.

   Key and voice were checked. No reply as to voice strength was received. The Howland Island log also forms a check. Signals were sent as agreed. San Francisco radio was obviously monitoring closely as told ITASCA to slow to 10 words when ITASCA sending at 15 as Earhart indicated desire. All signals thereafter were sent at 10 words.

0015-0018
   KHAQQ Unhrd.

   *(Earhart was supposed to send each silent period at fifteen after and at forty-five after. ITASCA never heard her at fifteen after but always at forty-five after, except at 0615, until towards end flight when she apparently abandoned schedules. ITASCA never left Earhart frequency, 3105, from 1900 1 July on.)

0025-28.
   Sent WX to KHAQQ on 7500 and 3105. (Actual transmission - ITASCA to Earhart (by key and voice) ITASCA TO Earhart - ITASCA at Howland to Earhart - Weather wind direction east wind direction east force eleven miles wind force eleven miles partly cloudy partly cloudy barometer twenty nine point nine two barometer twenty nine point nine two visibility twenty miles visibility twenty miles air temperature 82 air temperature 82 calm calm swell direction east swell direction east - this taken from actual weather sheet on file ITASCA.)

0030-34
   KHAQQ DE NRUI AAA (etc.) NRUI HOWLAND AAAA.

0036.
   (Asked Samoa if ONTARIO had heard Earhart, answer negative.)

0112.
(Commanding Officer in radio room sent following to ComFranDiv.) 6002 HAVE NOT HEARD EARHART SIGNALS UP TO THIS TIME BUT SEE NO CAUSE FOR CONCERN ES PLANE IS STILL ABOUT 1000 MILES AWAY PERIOD HAVE THREE OPERATORS ON WATCH *(2-On ship 1-On Howland) AND WILL REPORT ANY CONTACT WITH PLANE PROMPTLY TO DIVISION FOR FURTHER RELEASE TO PRESS COMMA PUTNAM COMMA HEADQUARTERS AND GRUENING INTERIOR WASHINGTON PERIOD DIVISION MAY EXPECT ITASCA CODE MESSAGE FORENOON HOWLAND TIME 0112.

*(Code message would have indicated safe or crash arrival. Precaution necessary due commercial interception all ITASCA official traffic. In summary will consider subject flagrant law violation intercepted traffic by commercial stations particularly during search.)

0215-0220.
Nothing heard on 3105 kcs.

(Entries are widely spaced due to work. The watch was continuous with three (3) receivers (2 on ship, 1 on Howland) and lack of entries is not indicative of irregularity. Everything in radioroom fully supervised. All schedules except Earhart omitted since 2000. Three (3) routine weather reports were handled between 0100 and 0143.)

0245-0248.
Heard Earhart plane on 3105 but unreadable through static.

(Comment - Bellarts caught Earhart's voice and it came in through loud speaker, very low monotone "cloudy and overcast". Mr. Carey, Associated Press representative, was present. Also Mr. Hanzlik of United Press, both gentlemen recognized voice from previous flights to and from Hawaii. There was no question as to hearing Earhart. Commanding Officer was notified. Mr. Black was called. Message was drafted for San Francisco Division by Commanding Officer. Message was purposely terse due necessity report between Earhart schedules.)

0255: From: ITASCA.
     To : Com SF Div.
     Inf.: HUNT.
6002 ITASCA HEARD EARHART PLANE AT 0248 0255.
(San Francisco Radio gave a prompt acknowledgement and ITASCA went off air.)

(The ITASCA having heard Earhart the next logical step was to attempt to establish communication. ITASCA was hearing Earhart messages (incompletely) and ITASCA broadcasts were heard throughout the Pacific - For safety, therefore, inter communication was the vital factor.)

0330. Sent WX.
(Wind direction east force 8 miles per hour clear visibility 20 miles calm swell direction east coiling unlimited .) (Repeated key and voice twice 7500 and 3105.)

(By voice repeated twice on 3105)
What is your position? When do you expect to reach Howland? ITASCA has heard your phone go ahead on key. Acknowledge this broadcast next schedule.

0345. Heard Earhart on phone.
(ITASCA from Earhart - ITASCA from Earhart - - - OVERCAST - WILL LISTEN ON HOUR AND HALF HOUR ON 3105 - - - - WILL LISTEN ON HOUR AND HALF HOUR ON 3105.)

0400-03.
Broadcast weather phone 3105.
Repeated weather on key 3105.
(Also "What is your position?" "When do you expect arrive Howland?" We are receiving your signals please acknowledge this message on your next schedule.)

0453. Sent weather /code/phone/ 3105 kcs. (Heard Earhart - partly cloudy.) Volume S-1.
0455. Earhart broke in on phone - unreadable.

0614. Wants bearing on 3105 kcs/on hour/ will whistle in mic.
0615. About two hundred miles out//appx//whistling//NW. (Volume S-3.)

0642. KHAQQ came on air with fairly clear signals calling ITASCA (voice).
0645. (KHAQQ REQUESTED) Please take bearing on us and report in half hour I will make noise in microphone - about 100 miles out (Earhart signal strength -4 but on air so briefly bearings impossible.)

0718. (To Earhart by phone) Cannot take bearing on 3105 very good/please send on 500 or do you wish to take bearing on us/ go ahead please/ (No answer).

0730. KHAQQ FROM ITASCA PLEASE ACKNOWLEDGE OUR SIGNALS ON KEY PLEASE/ UNANSWERED/

0742. KHAQQ CALLING ITASCA WE MUST BE ON YOU BUT CANNOT SEE YOU BUT GAS IS RUNNING LOW BEEN UNABLE REACH YOU BY RADIO WE ARE FLYING AT ALTITUDE 1000 FEET.----
(Other Log) Earhart on now says running out of gas only 1/2 hour left/(unverified as heard by other witnesses)/cant hear us at all/ we hear her and are sending on 3105 and 500 same time constantly and listening in for her frequently.

0743-46.
> KHAQQ DE NRUI RECEIVED YOUR MESSAGE SIGNAL STRENGTH 5 (sent AAA's etc. on 500 and 3105 told Earhart) GO AHEAD.

0747-48.
> KHAQQ DE NRUI RECEIVED YOUR MESSAGE SIGNAL STRENGTH 5 (ITASCA sent A's on 3105).

0749-51-/57.
> KHAQQ FROM ITASCA YOUR MESSAGE OKAY PLEASE ACKNOWLEDGE WITH PHONE ON 3105 (ITASCA then keyed A's.)

0758.
> KHAQQ CALLING ITASCA WE ARE CIRCLING BUT CANNOT HEAR YOU GO AHEAD ON 7500 EITHER NOW OR ON THE SCHEDULE TIME ON HALF HOUR.
> (Earhart signal strength 5 on radiophone.)

(In view of signal strength it is believed Earhart was closest to Howland at this time. It was about the time ITASCA expected her to arrive.)

0759-0800.
> KHAQQ DE NRUI AAAAAA (etc.) (On 7500) GO AHEAD ON 3105.

(The following is the only direct reply received from Earhart and tends to indicate that she was closest to Howland and flying away)

0800-03.
> KHAQQ CALLING ITASCA WE RECEIVED YOUR SIGNALS BUT UNABLE TO GET A MINIMUM PLEASE TAKE BEARING ON US AND ANSWER 3105 WITH VOICE. NRUI DE KHAQQ (sent long dashes on 3105 for 5 seconds or so.)

0804.
> NRUI2 DE NRUI P AR
> (ITASCA CALLING HOWLAND FOR CUT. HOWLAND REPORTED IMPOSSIBLE SECURE MINIMUM AND COULD NOT PICK UP SIGNALS ON 3105)

0805.
> KHAQQ FROM ITASCA YOUR SIGNALS RECEIVED OKAY WE ARE UNABLE TO HEAR YOU TO TAKE A BEARING IT IS IMPRACTICAL TO TAKE A BEARING ON 3105 ON YOUR VOICE/HOW DO YOU GET THAT/GO AHEAD.

0806.
> KHAQQ DE NRUI GO AHEAD ON 3105 OR 500 KILOCYCLES (ITASCA sending on 7500 as her only acknowledgement was for signals sent on 7500)

(The operator on Howland with Navy emergency direction finder had heard most of conversation on 3105 kcs after 0600 and tried to cut Earhart in but was unable due to Earhart's continued use of voice and brevity of Earhart transmissions. The direction finder on the island was driven by ITASCA gun batteries and during the night their power ran down. During the period from 0600 to the last Earhart transmission experienced officers were on Howland.
Earhart's maximum transmission probably never exceeded 7 or 8 seconds. Toward the end Earhart talked so rapidly as to be almost incoherent. The ship's direction finder was manned from 0725 on. No signal was ever received on 500 kcs in spite repeated requests.)

0807.
> (ITASCA to Earhart on 3105, 500, 7500 kcs.) GO AHEAD.

(The ITASCA fully recognized the emergency as Earhart now overdue at Howland and her 1/2 hour of gas now exhausted. Vital therefore to bring her in or to obtain cut for search in case she went down at sea. Observers agree that Earhart signal strength remained about same from 8 to 9 oclock and that her last transmission had nearly same strength as her 0758. ITASCA was laying down smoke screen stretching for ten miles. Smoke remained concentrated and did not thin out greatly.)

0811. ITASCA TO EARHART.
DID YOU GET TRANSMISSION ON 7500 KCS/ GO AHEAD ON 500 KCS SO THAT WE MAY TAKE A BEARING ON YOU/ IT IS IMPOSSIBLE TO TAKE A BEARING ON 3105 KILOCYCLES/ PLEASE ACKNOWLEDGE.

(Operator on Howland notified ITASCA that he was unable to secure bearing on 3105.)

0812-14.
(The above transmission repeated on 7500 - no answer. It is to be noted that Earhart's only actual acknowledgement to ITASCA signals came at 0800 in response to ITASCA message on 7500)

0815. KHAQQ FROM ITASCA (3105)
DO YOU HEAR MY SIGNALS ON 7500 KCS OR 3105 PLEASE ACKNOWLEDGE RECEIPT ON 3105/GO AHEAD.
(This unanswered.)

0816-17.
(The above repeated on 7500)

0818. Following to KHAQQ.
WILL YOU PLEASE ACKNOWLEDGE OUR SIGNALS ON 7500 OR 3105/GO AHEAD WITH 3105. (Unanswered).

0820-23.
(Requested KHAQQ to go ahead on 3105 with report of our signals)
(Three (3) receivers, loud speaker, Howland loop and ship's direction finder covering Earhart frequencies throughout this whole entire period - no answers.)

0833. KHAQQ from ITASCA.
WILL YOU PLEASE COME IN AND ANSWER ON 3105 / WE ARE TRANSMITTING CONSTANYLY ON 7500 KCS/ WE DO NOT HEAR YOU ON 3105/ PLEASE ANSWER ON 3105/GO AHEAD.
(This unanswered.)

0834-41. To KHAQQ.
ANSWER ON 3105 KCS WITH PHONE/HOW ARE SIGNALS COMING IN/GO AHEAD.

0844-46.
KHAQQ called ITASCA and said:
WE ARE ON THE LINE OF POSITION 157-337, WILL REPEAT THIS MESSAGE, WE WILL REPEAT THIS MESSAGE ON 6210 KCS. WAIT LISTENING ON 6210 KCS. (Other persons in radio room heard this transmission the same) WE ARE RUNNING NORTH AND SOUTH.
(This transmission was by voice on 3105 with a signal strength 5. Nothing was heard on 6210 kcs.)

0847. The following sent to KHAQQ, on 3105 and 7500 KCS.
WE HEARD YOU OK ON 3105 KCS. PLEASE STAY ON 3105 DO NOT HEAR YOU ON 6210 MAINTAIN QSO ON 3105.
(This broadcast was by voice on 3105 and by key on 7500. Nothing was heard on either 3105 or 6210.)

0849-53. Called KHAQQ and told her to go ahead on 3105 KCS.

0854.   Repeatedly called KHAQQ on broadcast.
to   YOUR SIGNALS OK ON 3105 GO AHEAD WITH POSITION ON 3105 OR 500 KCS.
0907.   (Unanswered. Listened on 3105 6210 and 500 kcs.)

0942-46.
    Called KHAQQ. Called on various frequencies and requested answers. Informed plane "WE CAN HEAR YOU FINE ON 3105 PLEASE GO AHEAD ON 3105". (This transmitted on 7500 kcs. Unanswered. Operators continued to listen in on frequencies 3105, 6210, 500 and direction finder at 500.)

Nothing was heard from KHAQQ up to 1000.

"FLIGHT SUMMARY"

1. The communication personnel was adequate and assigned as follows:

    2 - Radiomen high frequency receivers.

    2 - Radiomen on direction finders.

    2 - Commissioned officers in radio room.

    2200 to 0600:
        Lieut. Comdr. Baker.
        Ensign Sutter.

    0600 to 1000:
        Lieut. Comdr. Kenner.
        Ensign Sutter.

    Shore Station:
        1 - Radioman from 1900 on.

        0600 to 0900:
            Lieut. Comdr. Baker.

2. Ship's direction finder manned at 0725.

3. ITASCA transmitters were accurately calibrated.

4. ITASCA signals clearly received throughout by other units.

5. ITASCA fully followed all Earhart schedules 7500, 3105, etc.

6. Earhart requested ITASCA use 3105 at 0345. This was done on key and phone, but 7500 was also used for safety.

7. The ITASCA homing signals and weather were never omitted. They were sent by key, by voice on 3105 and keyed on 7500.

8. Earhart never answered any ITASCA questions and never gave a position. Communication was never really established.

9. Earhart acknowledged receiving ITASCA signals at 0800. This formed the only case and was apparently for signals sent by ITASCA on 7500.

10. Earhart messages lacked any useful position information and consisted of generalities.

11. Earhart could not secure null on ITASCA signals.

12. Earhart's last message was hurried, frantic and apparently not complete. Earhart did not return to air on 6210.

13. Earhart was on air very briefly and apparently over modulated. The attempts of the radioman on Howland to secure cut failed.

14. Judging from signal strength Earhart was closest between 0730 and 0844-46, when her signal strength was 5 with a 50 watt transmitter.

15. Earhart probably had receiver trouble.

16. Earhart apparently did not know position.

17. Earhart asked ITASCA to take bearings on her. This was never planned. Earhart knew that ITASCA could give her accurate bearings on 500 and yet never transmitted on 500 in order for ITASCA to assist her. ITASCA had continuous direction finder watch on 500 from 0725 on.

18. Earhart knew that she could use 500 when close in if necessary.

19. The signals which Earhart acknowledged were transmitted on 7500. Her direction finder loop could not handle this frequency. It is possible that she was referring to other signals.

20. The weather conditions were clear and a sun line was possible. Weather conditions in the early morning were excellent with stars out and a fix should have been possible. Apparently Earhart's last message referred to a sun line. (No reference point was given.)

(c) "THE SEARCH"

After the last Earhart message radio concentrated on contacting the plane further. This work is covered in the log.

There was still a definite feeling that Earhart would make Howland or that if she was down she would send an SOS with some sort of position.

ITASCA was purposely conservative in assuming Earhart down. Every indication from radio was that there was something wrong with her receiving equipment but that with Noonan's navigating ability the plane would secure a fix and tell ITASCA or yet make Howland.

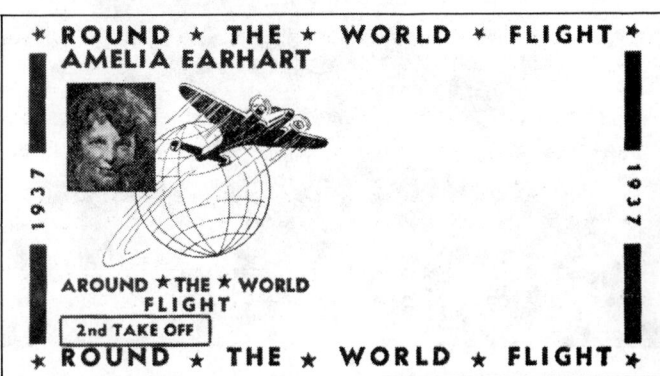

One of the last first day covers that exists. This is one of several given our mother prior to departure. There were 5,000 autographed first day covers on the Electra.

No further transmissions were received from Amelia and Fred, although a continuous watch was maintained for several weeks.

Close up study of Amelia taken on her arrival at New Guinea.

Chapter Nineteen

The Search

UPON realizing that the plane must be down, Commander Thompson wasted no time in plotting his rescue job. The report that the Commanding Officer, ITASCA, sent to the Commandant, 14th Naval District, Pearl Harbor, T.H. states:

" . . . 2 July, 1937:
Made preparation during night for landing task groups in connection with plane flight. Vessel in contact with Earhart plane at 0245 and intermittently thereafter. Early reception poor. At 0610 sent task group ashore to take stations for landing of plane. 0614 Earhart reported position 200 miles out of Howland. Commenced laying heavy smoke screen at daylight. 0645 Earhart plane reported position 100 miles out. 0742 plane reported apparently over the island and gas running low but no land fall. 0758, plane reported circling and requested transmission on 7500 kcs for bearings. 0800, plane reported reception of our signals but unable to obtain a minimum for bearing. 0843, plane reported as being on line 157-337 and running north and south, no reference point given, reception excellent. 0900, signalled shore party to return to ship as by this time fears were felt that the Earhart plane had probably landed wide of the island. Landing party returned at 0912.

Commander W. K. Thompson of the Coast Guard cutter Itasca who is directing the search for Amelia Earhart.

CREDIT: SAN FRANCISCO CHRONICLE

As soon as the plane had indicated that it was still aloft at 0843 and possibly on a line which would provide a land fall it was deemed advisable to retain homing position at Howland with the vessel for sometime on the possibility that the plane might still come in.

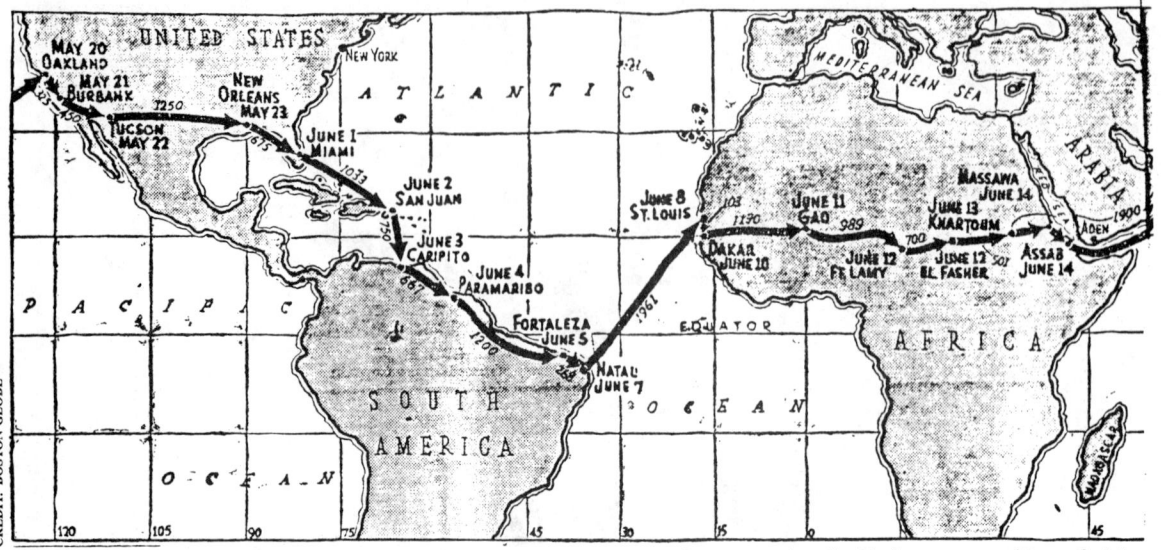

ROUTE OF AMELIA'S FLIGHT SHOWING AREA

Hand points to desolate Howland Island in mid-Pacific, which Amelia Earhart was unable to find in

AMELIA'S SISTER NOT WORRYING, SHE SAYS

Mrs Henry Morrissey of Medford Says Flyer Always Took Every Precaution

MEDFORD, July 3—"Amelia always took every precaution on her flights. I'm not worrying about her. I just know everything will come out all right."

Thus Mrs Henry Albert Morrissey, sister of Amelia Earhart, expressed her confidence today that her flying sister, lost somewhere on the Pacific, would be safely rescued.

Mrs Morrissey, who lives at 118 Traincroft st, refused to be upset this morning.

Mrs Morrissey pointed out that Amelia had taken a rubber life boat with her, among other equipment to meet just such an emergency as has occurred on her long flight over the Pacific to Howland Island, a tiny dot in the middle of the vast Pacific.

Amelia and her sister, Muriel, were both born and spent their childhoods in this town. Mrs Morrissey had been a school teacher here until her marriage in June, 1928. She has two children. She sat up late last night with her husband, awaiting word of her sister's safety. The word didn't come but she and her husband went to bed only a couple of hours later than their usual time, confident that "everything will come out all right."

Mrs Morrissey has been in touch with her mother, Mrs Amy O. Earhart. Mrs Earhart left Gloucester, where she now makes her home, on May 1 to go to California. There she witnessed Amelia's two starts on her round-the-world trip. The first start had ended in trouble at Honolulu and Miss Earhart had returned to California for a new start but on a different course. Mrs Earhart has not yet returned East after her daughter's take-off on this trip.

Article on 7-year old David Morrissey, Monday, July 5, 1937.

Amelia Earhart's 7-Year-Old Nephew Worries in Medford at Letter's Fate

Seven-year-old David Morrissey yesterday burst into tears and found it hard to understand why a letter which his aunt, Amelia Earhart, was carrying for him on her world-girdling flight and which he "promised to show to all the kids" might be lost at sea.

Unable to realize the entire seriousness of the situation, David, son of Amelia's sister, Mrs. Muriel Morrissey, of 45 Crocker road, Medford, pleaded with his mother to find out just why his letter might be lost.

"I promised to show it to all the kids," he said as tears filled his big brown eyes. "And Aunt Amelia said she would give me a ride in her airplane when she got back."

His mother, a younger sister of Amelia, anxiously awaited word from searchers for her sister, believed forced down with her navigator, Capt. Fred Noonan, in the Pacific ocean.

"I just refuse to believe that everything won't turn out all right," Mrs. Morrissey told reporters and friends who had met her famous sister on numerous visits here.

"I last saw Amelia in March and she outlined plans for the flight and told me 'It will be lots of fun.' It seems a pity that Amelia and Capt. Noonan should encounter a tropical storm so close to the end of their world journey."

Mrs. Morrissey said Amelia had her son's letter postmarked at every one of her stopping points.

"Both David and his sister, Amy, are eager to receive the letter." Amy is 5½ years old.

Mrs. Morrissey, who resembles her sister considerably, said her mother, Mrs. Amy Earhart, who is in North Hollywood, Calif., was "bearing up well."

THE SEARCH | 251

WHERE NAVY IS MAKING FRANTIC SEARCH

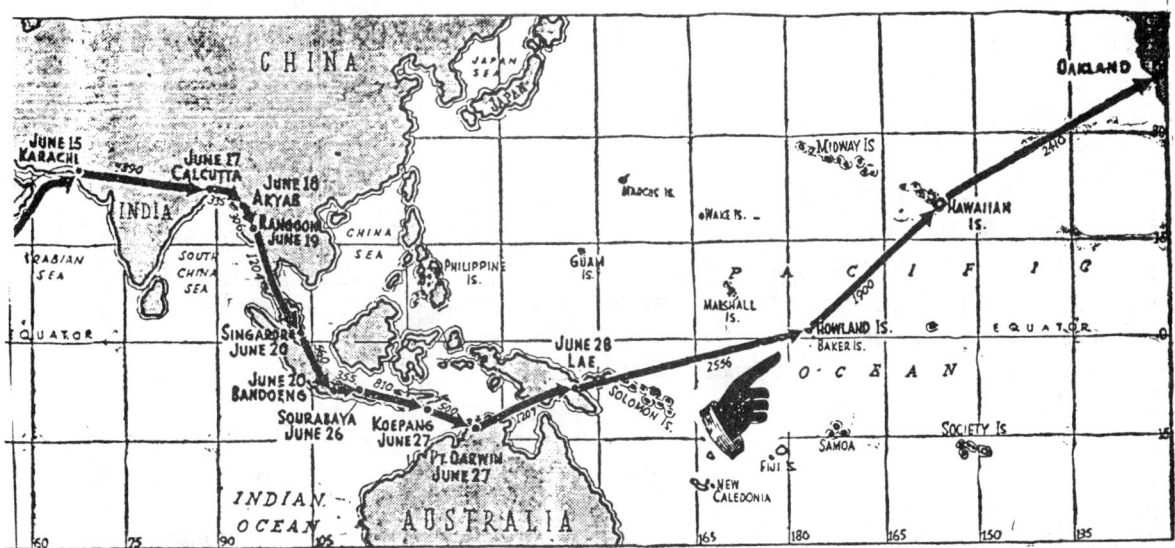

dngerous 2556-mile hop from Lae. Her plane is believed to be on the sea within 100 miles of this tiny isle.

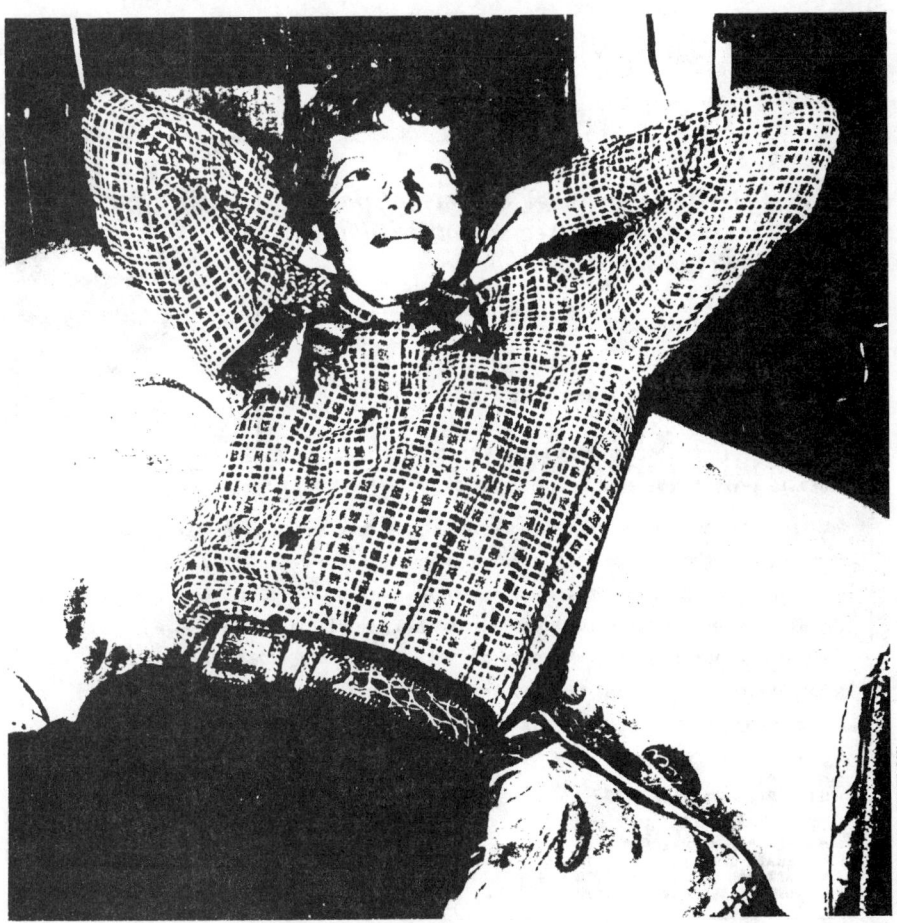

Amelia on March 11, 1937, prior to her first take off.

CREDIT: CARL BIGELOW

Message to all ships and stations that Amelia is believed down at sea.

```
NPG 831          NAVAL MESSAGE                ACTION COPY
        RECEIVED AT NAVY DEPARTMENT
T BLOT V NPG NITE RADIO SANFRANCISCO CK 63 GOVT HYDRO SECOND


GOVT HYDRO ALL SHIPS AND STATIONS
US COASTGUARD SHIP ITASCA BELIEVES MISS AMELIA EARHART DOWN BETWEEN
THREE THREE SEVEN AND NINE ZERO DEGREES FROM HOWLAND ISLAND AND
WITHIN ONE HUNDRED MILES OF ISLAND POSSIBILITY PLANE MAY USE RADIO
ON EITHER 3105 6210 OR 500 KCS VOICE REQUEST ANY VESSEL THAT UNKNOWN
VICINITY LISTEN FOR CALLS MADE CONTACT ITASCA CALL NRUI ON 500 KCS
                    HYDRO

2311 AC 2 JUL MX/
```

July 2, 1937 Itasca *message of Amelia's last reported position. " . . . sea smooth visibility nine cieling (sic) unlimited . . . "*

PLANES POISED FOR HUNT
Colorado to Catapult Trio in Search

The U.S.S. Colorado, speeding south to Howland from Honolulu, with the above three seaplanes aboard, yesterday altered course to head for Phoenix Islands. It will launch its planes about 6:30 tonight when 600 miles off the islands.

At 1040, it was definitely assumed that the plane was down so got underway at full speed and commenced the search in the area which at that time seemed most logical.

During the last half hour prior to getting underway an estimate of the situation was made based upon the following facts and assumptions:

"FACTS"

(a) Flying conditions within a radius of 40 miles of Howland excellent, wind east 8 to 13 miles, ceiling unlimited, sea smooth.

(b) Visibility south and east of Howland excellent and unlimited as far as could be observed. Sun rising clear and bright and island, ship and smoke screen in the glare thereof.

(c) Visibility north and west of Howland excellent to horizon but beyond that continuous banks of heavy cumulus clouds.

(d) Plane transmissions had indicated flight through cloudy and overcast skies throughout the night and morning.

(e) Plane transmissions had indicated that dead reckoning distance had been accomplished.

(f) Plane signal strength high and unchanged during last hour of transmission.

(g) Plane's line (of position?) indicated dead reckoning run correct.

(h) Stellar navigating possibilities, south and east of Howland and close to Howland, were excellent throughout the night.

"ASSUMPTIONS"

(a) That plane obtained no fix during latter part of flight due to visibility and assumed further this due to flying in cloudy weather and conditions which did not exist south and east of Howland but did exist north and west.

(b) That line of position obtained was a "sun" line obtained when they emerged from the cloudy area north and west of Howland and presumably the only observation made during the latter part of the flight. Further assumed that this line was correct.

(c) Assume that plane may have missed smoke screen, ship or island visually due to their lying in the glare of the rising sun.

(d) Assumed further that plane passed within 200 miles of Howland Island and north of it.

(e) Assumed that plane may have carried line of position found along line of flight for the period necessary for navigator to work and plot line of position not in excess of 100 miles.

(f) Assume plane did not come down within a radius of 40 miles of Howland.

Upon foregoing facts and assumptions it was decided that the most logical area of search lay in a sector of a circle between 40 miles and 200 miles off of Howland Island and between bearings 337 and 45 true, from that island. Search was accordingly laid down in accordance with this estimate."

" . . . At 2145 received definite instructions from Commandant, 14th Naval District, to be at Howland Island at daybreak Saturday, 3 July, 1937 to provide tender service for plane which had left Pearl Harbor at 1923. In view of the fact that the plane was already in the air enroute to Howland Island there was no alternative other than to abandon the search temporarily for the Earhart plane and proceed as indicated in the above noted orders; course was accordingly changed for Howland Island. Search was still maintained with searchlights."

3 July 1937:

"Arrived off Howland at 0710 in accordance with instructions. 0719, received information that Navy plane was turning back to base on account of extremely bad flying weather so resumed search to the northward which continued throughout the day . . . "

The search was continued on July fourth and fifth. On the evening of July 5:

" . . . At 2100 lights which had the appearance of flares were sighted to the northward and stood up to investigate. These reported lights had every indication of a bursting green rocket but were finally determined to be attributed to meteorological shower which was reported both by the Howland Island Station and U.S.S. SWAN . . . . "

6 July, 1937:

"Proceeded south and east during the night to effect rendezvous with U.S.S. COLORADO on the morning of the 7th for fuel purposes . . . "

As noted in the report of the Commanding Officer, U.S.S. Colorado, to Commandant, Fourteenth Naval District, dated July 13, 1937:

"While at Pearl Harbor the Commanding Officer of the U.S.S. COLORADO received

U.S.S. COLORADO

instructions from the Commandant, Fourteenth Naval District, Rear Admiral Orin G. Murfin, U.S. Navy, and conferred with the Commanding Officer, Fleet Air Base, Captain Kenneth Whiting, U.S. Navy, and other officers of the District and Air Base relative to the probable path and location of the Earhart Plane in the event of a forced landing. This information seemed to indicate that the most probable reason for missing Howland Island would be that of stronger winds than normally expected in the region, and that the plane had probably been carried southeast of Howland, a greater distance than that from which Howland could be sighted. These opinions lead the Commanding Officer of the U.S.S. COLORADO, at this time to believe that southeast of Howland was the most likely area."

On July 6, 1937, from Washington, D.C., Admiral William D. Leahy started the machinery for a Naval search of approximately 220,000 square miles of ocean. With emphatic support by President Franklin D. Roosevelt, Admiral Leahy ordered the *Lexington*, the Navy's largest aircraft carrier, several destroyers, and other available craft stationed on the west coast to criss-cross the area south and east of Howland Island. Literally thousands of tiny atolls were visited by the ships or scanned from low-flying planes sent out from the great carrier.

According to, *Get Underway!*, compiled from data taken on board the *U.S.S. Colorado*, and edited for crew members by Gust Nichandros and Lyle F. Richards during the summer of 1937,

" . . . It was at this time that we had any indication of where to commence our search.

Based upon all immediate information, the southeast quadrant seemed the most likely and accordingly, the Commanding Officer of the U.S.S. Colorado, Captain Friedell, planned to steam east along the equator. Planes would take off from the ship searching sixty miles north, then twelve miles east, then sixty miles south, and then moving on to the next rectangle as soon as the first had been well covered. The planes would return to the ship to refuel and relieve the aviators whenever necessary. In this manner, with four flights of planes for each day, an area of twelve thousand square miles would be completely searched. Each of the three planes carried an experienced observer to insure a more complete search . . . "

" . . . A report was received stating that Mrs. Mary Noonan, one month bride of Captain Noonan, was near collapse. She wept when she received a package of pictures taken during an earlier stage of the trip . . . One of the letters read in part, 'Amelia is a grand person on such a trip, a fine companion, takes hardships as well as a man. She also works like one.' . . . "

After 16 days of exhaustive search, the Navy sadly admitted defeat and cancelled the search on July 18, 1937.

The second day after Amelia's disappearance, GP talked with Jacqueline Cochran Odlum, who had frequently exhibited an uncanny ability to "find" lost people or planes. Jackie declared she "saw" Amelia floating on the water and gave him an exact bearing, which he radioed to the *Itasca*. The cutter raced to the location and zig-zagged over the area but found nothing. The massive sea and air search did not discover a trace of wreckage from the Electra.

Muriel's children, David and Amy Morrissey, aged seven and five, listen for news of their aunt in West Medford, 1937.

After Amelia's disappearance, letters of condolence from people all over the world poured in. There were also communications from spiritualists which caused Mother acute distress. We understood and appreciated the efforts of Jackie Cochran and others, who were genuinely trying to establish extrasensory contact with Amelia, either in this world or the next; it was, however, harrowing to read vivid descriptions of Amelia's body recognizable only by Gordon Selfridge's watch still clasped around her wrist, or of an emaciated, slightly crazed woman calling for help from a tiny coral reef.

GP was subjected to a cruel extortion hoax. An ex-seaman had found one of Amelia's bright scarfs left in the hangar at Wheeler Field in Hawaii, probably at the time of the Electra's ill-fated crash. Using the scarf, which GP recognized as belonging to Amelia, as a token of the authenticity of his information, the man demanded five thousand dollars for disclosing the name of the island in the Caroline cluster where Amelia was marooned and held prisoner by smugglers. Under the astute questioning of Mr. Richard Black, who had observed the Navy's prodigious search efforts from the cutter *Itasca*, the fake informer was caught in such a maze of contradictions that he soon admitted he had no information to sell, but was looking for "easy money." Mr. Black urged GP to have the man indited for extortion, but GP refused. GP gave the man $50 for his wife's scarf and then told him to get out of his sight and to try and go straight, "For Amelia's sake."

Soon after the *Lexington* ended her search for Amelia and Fred, GP asked the Japanese consul at San Francisco to relay to Tokyo the request that all fishing boats or tramp steamers plying among the island groups be alerted to watch for and report the presence of any American fliers in the area. He hoped that the Electra's crew might have been rescued by a small fishing boat which might have escaped notice during the search. None of the fishing and turtle-hunting pirogues would have any means of contact with the outside world until they returned home. The consul transmitted GP's request, but the silence remained unbroken. At this time, Japan was becoming involved in a war with China. On July 7, 1937, at the Marco Polo Bridge, near Peking, an incident between Japanese forces and Chinese forces initated the Sino-Japanese war.

The following is an essentially complete copy of the summary report to the Commander Lexington Group, to The Commandant, Fourteenth Naval District, dated 20 July 1937:

> "1. Annexes and appendices are submitted herewith as forming as complete a report as possible on operations of the Lexington group, consisting of Lexington with Aircraft Squadrons VS-2, VS-23, VS-4, VS-41, VT-2 and VB-4 embarked, of Commander Destroyer Division Three in Drayton, and Lamson and Cushing, during the period 4 to 18 July, 1937, inclusive, and of search operations of the U.S.S. Swan and U.S.C.G. Itasca while serving under Commander Lexington Group during the period 11–16 July 1937."

U.S.S. Lexington

CREDIT: ANONA HANSEN BROWN

"2. An effort has been made to confine the substance of this report to matters of fact rather than opinion."

"3. Track charts tracings are being forwarded under separate cover."

"4. The performance of duty by all units concerned was excellent . . ."

The mission of the Lexington was, "To make the most effective search possible in order to locate Earhart plane, or rubber boat, and personnel . . . All times used herein are Greenwich Civil [GCT or CMT]."

"A. *KNOWN FACTS*:

1. That Standard Lockheed Electra low wing land monoplane, No. X-16020, took off from Lae, New Guinea, latitude 146°55'E, longitude 6°45'S at 0000 GCT 2 July, 1937, bound for Howland Island, latitude 0°50'N, longitude 176°41'W. Pilot: Amelia Earhart Putnam; navigator: Fred Noonan, expecting to arrive in 18 hours.
2. That the plane's color was dural, with orange trim.
3. That a two man rubber life boat, life belts, flares and emergency water and rations were carried.
4. Rubber boat had a pair of oars and could be kept afloat by patching material and hand pump.
5. That the plane was equipped with radio capable of transmission and reception on 500 KCS, 3105 KCS, and 6210 KCS; assigned call letters "KHAQQ."
6. That the take-off from Lae was delayed awaiting a time tick and repairing broken fuel line.
7. That the plane was equipped with an orange box kite to be flown as distress signal, and by means of which an emergency antenna might be carried to a moderate height.
8. That the distance from Lae to Howland is 2227 nautical miles.
9. That the plane was filled with 1100 gallons of gasoline prior to departure.
10. That the planes's economical air speed was 130 knots.
11. That it's range in still air at this speed, with optimum carburetor adjustment was 3120 nautical miles, or an endurance of 24 hours at 45.8 gallons per hour.
12. That the plane's range in still air at 53 gallons per hour for 20.5 hours was 2719 nautical miles.
13. That the distance covered at average ground speed 105 knots in 20.5 hours would be 2152 nautical miles.
14. That the distance covered at average ground speed 120 knots in 20.5 hours would be 2460 nautical miles.
15. That the plane's position at 0720 GCT was given as 4°33'S, 159°06'east, putting it on it's course at 111 knots ground speed. This was the only complete position report received.
16. That the following weather forecast was received by the navigator prior departure Lae: "Lae to 165° E:winds ESE 12–15; 165° to 175°: ENE 18; 175° E to Howland; ENE 15 and squalls to be detoured."
17. That the following messages were received from the plane:
0720, to Lae: Position report lat. 04–33.5 S, long. 159° 07' W. [E.]
1030 Nauru Island heard "A ship in sight ahead."
1418 Itasca began receiving incomplete messages on agreed schedules. No answers to questions put to Earhart. No positions given. No success in attempted radio bearings by Itasca, and no apparent success by Earhart.
1745 "200 miles out."
1816 "100 miles out, coming up (fast)."
1912 "one-half hour fuel and no landfall (position doubtful)."
1928 "Circling trying to pick up Island."
2013 "Line of position 157-337" (no reference point given).
2025 "157-337 heading north and south."
18. That the Ontario was stationed in latitude 3° S, longitude 165° E.
19. That the SS Myrtlebank was in approximate latitude 1°40' S, longitude 166°45' E.
20. That the Itasca was stationed immediately to north-eastward of Howland.
21. That morning of 2 July Itasca was

laying a heavy smoke screen which hung for hours.

22. That the strength of radio signals in Itasca was greatest at 1928.
23. GCT sunrise, Howland, on 2 July was 1745.
24. That the plane would float with empty gas tanks, if undamaged.
25. That the plane's normal radio power supply was so located that it could not have been used with plane on the water.
26. Morning of 2 July visibility to south of Howland was excellent. Heavy clouds were about 20 miles northwest. Surface winds ENE 6, shifting to ESE 16."

B. *PROBABILITIES ARISING FROM RUMOR OR REASONABLE ASSUMPTIONS*

1. That the plane was equipped with an emergency radio set that could be operated from battery power supply.
2. That life saving equipment was stowed in the tail.
3. That the color of the lifeboat was yellow.
4. That the plane had one side door and no escape hatch in top.
5. That gasoline stowage was in tanks in the passenger compartment, and that gasoline was pumped by hand to two 50 gallon gravity tanks in the wings.
6. That the following summarized weather forecast, received at Lae, as the plane was taking off, and later transmitted to the plane three times, was received: "Accurate forecast difficult account lack of reports: conditions average—no major storms; dangerous local rain squalls 300 miles east of Lae and scattered heavy showers remainder of route; winds ESE 25 to Ontario then E to ENE 20 to Howland." . . .
8. That the altitude at which the plane flew would have depended upon weather conditions and the desire to estimate drift or pick up a landfall, and cannot be judged.
9. That the navigator was competent and experienced.
10. That at about 1030 the plane passed the Ontario giving a ground speed of 106 *or* the Myrtlebank giving a ground speed of 118 knots.
11. That at 1928 the plane passed closest to the Itasca and within 100 miles, after a run of 2050 to 2350 miles.
12. That at 53 gallons per hour the plane made 140 knots in still air.
13. That the plane landed on an uncharted reef or island, or on the water, within 300 miles of Howland.
14. That the plane would float with engines nearly submerged, with wings nearly submerged, with fuselage partly submerged, and with tail surfaces out of the water.
15. That the Itasca first reported to Howland by semaphore that plane was NW of island and had evidently missed it (res gestae) [deed accomplished].
16. That at 2030 the plane landed northwest of Howland.

C. *CONDITIONS DETERMINED FROM SAILING DIRECTIONS OR BY EXPERIENCE:*

1. That the prevailing winds are easterly, 10 knots.
2. That the average current in the area to north and west of Howland Island is northwest, ½ knot (experienced by Lexington) . . .
7. That about latitude 4° north is the boundary between the southern equatorial current, flowing westerly, and the counter-equatorial current, which begins to form near the Gilberts, flowing easterly.
8. That along this boundary there are apt to be circular currents and areas in which floating objects would accumulate.
9. That with the plane nearly submerged and tailing with the wind, the wind resistance would be small and the underwater drag great, so that the current effect would be great . . .
11. That a rubber boat would be most greatly affected in its drift by the surface wind, regardless of water current.

Amelia in 1937. Photo taken by W. Stanley Hicks.

12. That with a rubber boat, the chances of rowing across wind sufficiently to make land would be excellent for a boat starting 100 miles or more to the eastward of the Gilberts, *provided navigational equipment was available* ...

III *EARHART PLANE'S MISSION:* To land safely on Howland Island before exhaustion of fuel supply.

IV *COURSES OF ACTION OPEN TO EARHART PLANE:*

A. *ALTITUDE:*
1. To fly close to the water in order to take advantage of reduced headwinds and to obtain frequent drift observations and correct course accordingly.
2. To fly at a moderate altitude, descending as necessary to sight station ships and landfalls.
3. To fly at high altitudes, correcting course by frequent celestial observations, to increase fuel economy.
Number 3 is the most likely method.

B. *COURSE:*
1. To correct course according to drift observations at low altitude.
2. To head to southward of course as far as longitude 165° E, then to head for objective in accordance with weather forecast received.
3. To deliberately over-correct to southward with the intention of running up a morning longitude line of position through the objective.
4. To deliberately over-correct to northward with the intention of running down a morning longitude line of position through the objective.

In view of the difficulty in sighting Howland toward the eastward in the early morning, of which Noonan must have been well aware, it seems most probable that he took either the course of action specified in 3 or in 4 above. Of those the former had the advantage of bringing the plane close to the Phoenix group in case of early shortage of gas, but the disadvantage of winding up over the open sea if Howland was missed. The latter had the advantage of bringing the plane over the Phoenix group if Howland was missed, but the disadvantage of being over the open sea in case of premature gas shortage.

The following indications point to adoption of the former course:
1. The plane was evidently in position to obtain observations during the early morning.
2. Visibility to the southward was excellent and the Itasca's smoke plume could have been seen 40 miles or more, whereas heavy clouds lay to the northward.
3. The Itasca's first estimate of position was northwest.

C. *SPEED*
1. To run at speed higher than the economical speed, 130 knots, in order to arrive expeditiously and reduce the chances of bad judgement induced by fatigue.
2. To run at the economical speed, 130 knots, to provide a maximum factor of safety.
3. To run below the economical speed in order not to approach the objective until well after sunrise.

Of these, the second is considered far the most probable.

The plane evidently turned between 1900 and 1930 and at 110 knots these times would give runs of 2090 and 2145 nautical miles along the course—somewhat short of objective.

V. *MOST PROBABLE ACTION OF PLANE*
It is most probable that:
1. The plane cruised at economical speed at a moderate altitude laying course between Howland and the Phoenix Islands.
2. That navigational fixes were reasonable frequent but somewhat in error.
3. That radio bearings were inaccurate or impossible due to atmospherics and to the recognized inherent limitations of high frequency direction finders.
4. That the plane's gas supply was slightly diminished either by a leak or by non-economical adjustment of the carburetor.
5. That headwinds stronger than expected were experienced.
6. That at about 1900, while somewhat short of its objective, the plane turned

and headed northward on a line of position run forward from celestial observation about 1700, passing nearest Howland Island at 1928 after a 65 mile run, and, at about this time, began to circle looking for the island.
7. That at about 2000 the pilot announced the direction but not the reference point for a line of position she was running on, evidently believing it to run through the island, and began running north and south across this line near the point at which her navigator believed the island to be.
8. That at about 2030 the plane landed on the sea to the northwest of Howland Island, within 120 miles of the Island.

VI OTHER COURSES OF ACTION OF PLANE:

It is possible also that:
1. The plane flew beyond the Island.
2. The plane headed south past the Island.
3. The plane landed on a reef or island either charted or uncharted.

TOTAL REASONABLE AREA IN WHICH PLANE MIGHT BE

DATE	PROBABLE	MOST PROBABLE
2 July	360,000 Sq. Mi.	57,600 Sq. Mi.
13 July	720,000 Sq. Mi.	163,200 Sq. Mi.
18 July	864,000 Sq. Mi.	211,200 Sq. Mi.

VII OWN LIMITATIONS:

1. Number limitations:
   Available: Carrier Group, Swan and Itasca.
   (Colorado ordered detached immediately upon our arrival).
2. Fuel limitations:
   Set by Navy Department. The Lexington is the controlling factor, as it was directed she should return to San Diego from search area without refueling. This necessarily limits her speed and that of the entire Earhart Search Group, as the plane guards Drayton, Lamson and Cushing and the Swan and Itasca will have to fuel from her if they do not practice strict fuel economy.
3. Area per day possible consistently under fuel limitations.
   (a) Carrier Group 28,800 square miles.
   (b) Itasca (assuming 10 mile front) 1320 square miles.
   (c) Swan (assuming 10 mile front) 1000 square miles.
4. Total number of days possible:
   (a) Carrier Group 13th to 19th—seven (201,600 sq.mi).
   (b) Itasca 11th to 17th—seven (9,240 sq.mi).
   (c) Swan 11th to 20th—ten (10,000 sq.mi).
5. Total number of square miles under imposed limitations 220,840.
6. Weather limitations: Frequent squalls which reduce visibility and at times make carrier aircraft operations overhazardous.

VIII ASSUMPTIONS:

1. That the plane landed on water or on an uncharted reef within 120 miles of the most probable landing point, 23 miles northwest of Howland Island.
2. That, if on the water, the plane drifted between the limits northwest 3/4 knot and due west 1½ knots.

IX COURSES OF ACTION OPEN TO US:

1. To systematically search the most probable area in a westerly direction so as to overtake a drifting plane, and so fit our potential search area as to best cover this area, considering its southern sector as having been adequately covered by Colorado and her aircraft and by Itasca and Swan.
2. To cover the most probable area including its southern sector, considering earlier search to the southward ineffective, and thus necessarily sacrifice some of the northerly or westerly area.
3. To search to the best of our ability the widely separated and remote areas mentioned in many conflicting reports.

X DECISION:

To make the most effective possible search with all available forces by:
1. Requesting that Colorado complete search to southeastward, including Phoenix group, prior 11 July, then fuel destroyers on 12 July;
2. Using Swan and Itasca for westward sweep, including thorough search of Gilbert group and maximum probable drift limit;

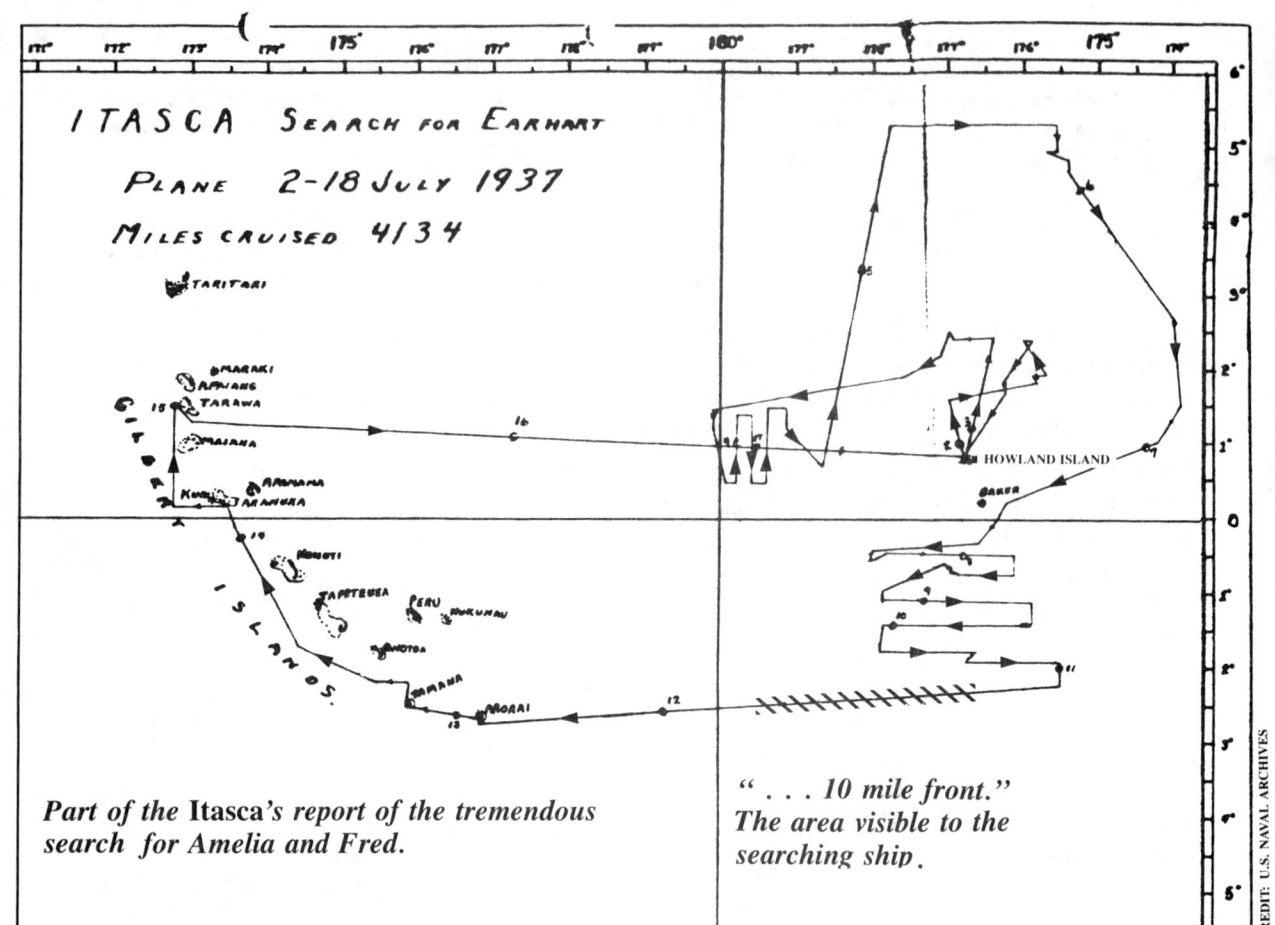

Part of the Itasca's report of the tremendous search for Amelia and Fred.

"... 10 mile front." The area visible to the searching ship.

3. Using Lexington group to its maximum sustained capacity for an intensive search from east to west covering the above defined most probable area except the southeastern sector;

in order to locate the Earhart plane, or rubber boat, and personnel.

During the search there had been official mutterings about the cost to the Navy of the search for Amelia and Fred. In Press Conference #382, in the Executive Offices of the White House, on Tuesday, July 20, 1937, one of the questions put to President Franklin D. Roosevelt was:

"Any comment on the House mutterings on the cost of the Earhart search?"

The President asked, "What was that?"

The question again: "On the House mutterings on the Earhart search.— request for investigation and what not."

President Roosevelt answered: "I did not know there was any mutterings. I saw a U.P. dispatch from Honolulu yesterday which said that the cost of the search has been $4,000,000 to the Government.

"Of course, a thing like that is just plain prevarication. That is the politest term to call it, a so-called news dispatch.

"Actually, as you probably know, every Navy plane on a ship like the Lexington or a ship like the Colorado has to do so many hours in the air during the course of a year. Well, this counts towards the number of hours in the air. Therefore there is no additional cost because of the cost of keeping the plane in the air because the money would be spent whether they were doing a search problem of this kind or whether they were doing a maneuver.

"It is the same way on the fuel oil. The

THE SEARCH | 263

Three of the hundreds of Naval and Coast Guard telegrams reporting on the search.

Southern Gilberts searched with negative results.

Phoenix group searched with negative results.

Northern Gilberts searched with negative results.

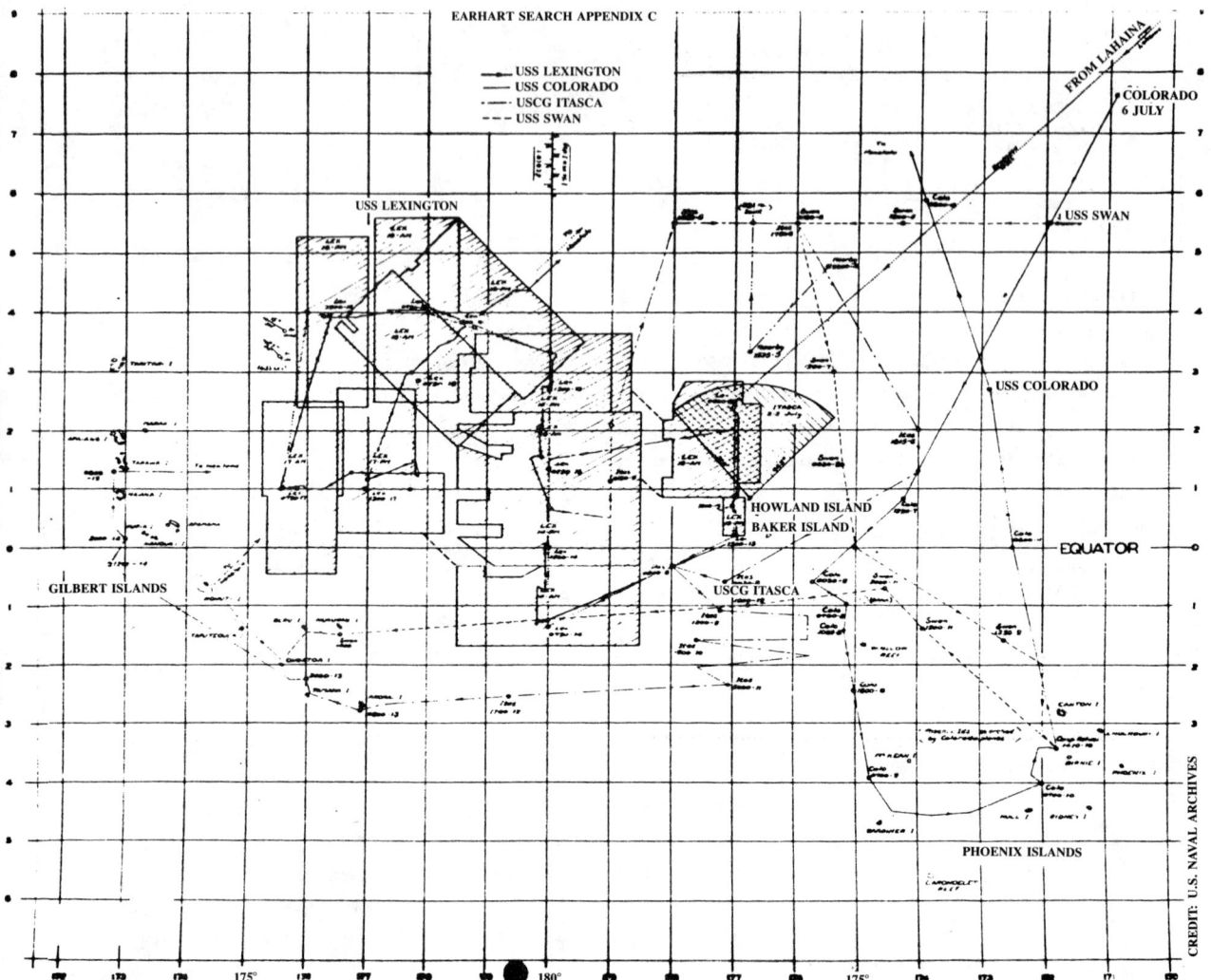

*Copy of the original map from the **Itasca**'s report showing the pattern of the four vessels involved in the search.*

Navy had a very skimpy—from the point of view of efficiency—a skimpy allowance for fuel oil. They have to be very careful how they spend it and they have to stay within the allowance of fuel oil in the course of a year. Each ship, as a general proposition, is limited to the amount of fuel oil she is supposed to use—within its quota of the appropriation from the Congress. While the search entailed a slightly faster use of fuel oil than they would use on ordinary cruising, it is not any faster use of it than they would use on the annual maneuvers where the Lexington has to proceed at full speed, where a whole battleship squadron has to move at 19 or 20 or 21 knots in regular maneuvers. So the cost to the Government is absolutely no greater on the use of fuel oil than it would have been had they not made any search.

"There are two other points, of course. A mission of this particular kind is a sad mission to have to go on, especially when it results in not finding Miss Earhart. But, at the same time, it is pretty valuable experience and training for the Navy. The Lexington did a perfectly amazing job in getting away, the way she did from Los Angeles. It was quite a feat. It was practice, very excellent practice, and it was a good thing. She took all of her planes on board and took on all of her officers and men and got under way in sixteen hours from the time the order was given. It was a good job.

```
NAVAL MESSAGE                           ACTION COM
NPG 5513      RECEIVED AT NAVY DEPARTMENT      1937
FROM:    COM FOURTEEN                        PRIORITY
TO:      NAVY DEPARTMENT                     RESTRICTED
INFO:    COMDESCOFOR COMAIRBATFOR CINCUS COMDESBATFOR COMDESRON TWO
```

RESTRICTED

0017 LEXINGTON GROUP ORDERED DISCONTINUE SEARCH EVENING EIGHTEENTH
IF FLYING CONDITIONS PRACTICABLE SEVENTEENTH AND EIGHTEENTH OTHERWISE
DISCONTINUE EVENING NINETEENTH PERIOD FOLLOWING COMPLETION UNLESS
OTHERWISE DIRECTED LEXINGTON WILL PROCEED DIRECT SAN DIEGO SPEED
FIFTEEN DESTROYERS PROCEED PEARLHARBOR FUEL THEN TO SAN FRANCISCO
OR SAN DIEGO SPEED FIFTEEN 0955

TOR IN CODE ROOM 1715 17 JULY 1937

The message that ordered the search for Amelia and Fred discontinued.

CREDIT: U.S. NAVAL ARCHIVES

CREDIT: SAN FRANCISCO CHRONICLE

Navy Gives Up Its Hunt For Amelia

Lost Pair Declared Officially Dead by Authorities

HONOLULU, T. H., July 18 (UP) —All hope for the safety of Amelia Earhart, the world's No 1 woman flyer, was abandoned tonight as the U. S. S. Lexington, mighty airplane carrier of the U. S. Navy, gave up search for her in the South Pacific.

The flyers are now given up officially for dead, navy officials said.

Announcement of the end of the hunt for the tousle-haired conqueror of both the Pacific and the Atlantic was made in Honolulu by Admiral Orrin G. Murfin, commander of the Fourteenth Naval district.

The Admiral directed the search from the time Miss Earhart and her navigator, Frederick J. Noonan, disappeared July 2 on a flight from Lae, New Guinea, to Howland Island.

HUSBAND GRIEVES!

LOS ANGELES, July 18 (AP)—Grief-stricken, George Palmer Putnam, husband of Amelia Earhart, had little to say tonight when told the navy had given up the noted flyer as dead and was abandoning its search.

"I am deeply appreciative of what the navy has done," he said. "That is all I can say."

"We have covered all possible territory," the Admiral said, "some of it we have been over as much as three times. I could not conceive of any other place where we might direct our search, and obviously we can't keep it up indefinitely. We feel that we've done everything possible now."

The Coast Guard cutter Itasca and the mine sweeper Swan already had given up the search for the missing flyers.

Announcement that the navy had abandoned the search for the world's No. 1 woman flyer and Noonan was made after 62 of the Lexington's planes hunted the pair for almost four days over the South Pacific in the vicinity of Howland Island.

FLASH LAUNCHES SEARCH

The Earhart search was started by the Itasca July 2 after the Coast Guard cutter, stationed at Howland Island for the purpose of aiding the woman flyer, intercepted a message from her plane saying she was running short of fuel.

"The only other point to make is that the Navy would do this in the case of any American, rich or poor, where there was some chance of saving life and they knew where to go. In this instance we all thought we knew where to go. We would have done it for the poorest citizen.

"So much for that and the U.P. dispatch."

In December, 1941, Pearl Harbor was attacked, plunging the United States into World War II. GP, who served as a Major in the U.S. Army Air Corps in the Burma-Chinese sector in 1944, flew in B-29's, and spent much of his off-duty time following clues and listening to often harrowing tales. Toward the end of WWII when the collapse of the Japanese resistance was imminent, a woman's voice was sometimes heard, broadcasting false information to the American forces. Could this "Tokyo Rose"* possibly be Amelia, brainwashed to the point of leading her country-men into enemy traps? Every fiber of GP's being denied the possibility, but he alone in all that vast area could without question identify Amelia's voice,

*Tokyo Rose was active from early 1943 onward.

even though weakened and tense from psychological mistreatment. He made a dangerous three-day trek through Japanese-held territory to reach a Marine Corps radio station near the coast where the broadcast reception was loud and clear. After listening to the voice for less than a minute, GP said decisively, "I'll stake my life that that is not Amelia's voice. It sounds to me as if the woman might have lived in New York, and of course she has been fiendishly well coached, but Amelia—never."

During the South Pacific campaign of World War II, Navy and Air Corps personnel were alerted to the possibility of rescuing prisoners held by the Japanese in the beleaguered island fortresses. When the Marshall Islands were captured by American forces in February, 1944, a directive, issued by the United States Government, urged that any clues to the possible seizure of the two American fliers, Amelia and Fred, be investigated and reported. Later the same year when the island of Saipan was occupied, a search was conducted and Japanese and native prisoners interrogated.

The theory that Amelia and Fred had been captured and held by the Japanese authorities during the hostilities was not abandoned until after the Japanese had capitulated and were occupied by General Douglas MacArthur in 1945. At that time Jacqueline Cochran Odlum, who had done heroic service in organizing American women fliers to ferry new planes from the United States to the European air bases, was given a final mission by General "Hap" Arnold: to make an official investigation of the activities of Japanese women in the Imperial Air Force. In doing this research Miss Cochran, the first American woman to land in Japan after the surrender, had access to many government files which were later taken to Washington for microfilming. Jacqueline's friendship for Amelia led her to delve into a folder when she saw pictures of Amelia and newspaper clippings presumably about her. There she found data about other American fliers including Colonel (later General) James Doolittle and Jacqueline herself. There was nothing that indicated that Amelia had been a prisoner, and the Japanese government has repeatedly disclaimed any involvement in the capture and imprisonment of the fliers.

LAST GIFT FROM AMELIA ARRIVES

Sent From New Guinea as Birthday Present to Niece Three Days Before She Disappeared

OUT OF THE PAST
Amy Morrissey, 5, niece of the lost Amelia Earhart, shown with six oriental bracelets mailed to her from Bombay June 25, with the note in Miss Earhart's writing expressing the hope that they would arrive in time for Amy's birthday, July 30. They arrived but the donor did not.

Chapter Twenty

History Not Mystery

THAT the Electra simply ran out of fuel when it was unable to make its scheduled landing on Howland Island is not a spectacular solution to the mystery, but it is the one that is surely most plausible.

Of the recurrent rumor that Amelia and Fred Noonan were on a spy mission, Fuzz Furman wrote, "Why would Amelia be spying anyway? Everybody knew what was going on in the Pacific. I was out there [Bandoeng, Java] putting bombers together for the Dutch in case the Japanese attacked Java. We knew what the Japanese were doing."

Fuzz observed that people in the United States did not pay any attention to the Japanese because they didn't think the Japanese had the technical ability to build airplanes to compete with the United States. According to Fuzz, the Japanese set up a radio station on Java to spy and to intercept the Dutch East Indies messages. The Dutch, instead of chasing them out, let them go ahead. The Dutch decoded their messages and were well aware of the activities of the Japanese. Fuzz maintains that Amelia and Fred were interested only in getting around the world and were worried about successfully reaching Howland Island. Howland was the smallest target they had aimed for and just a small error could have cost them their lives.

Another of the many rumors that persists is that President Roosevelt had requested that Amelia report any signs of Japanese fortifications of the mandated islands in the three large groups, the Carolines, the Marianas, and the Marshalls. No word of such a mission can be found in the writings of either the former President or Amelia, or even in the United States government records. In answer to inquiry, the late Mrs. Franklin D. Roosevelt wrote that her husband never mentioned any request to Amelia that she observe any fortifying of mandated islands during her flight.

To produce a sensational conclusion to Amelia's story, some biographers have mingled hearsay, rumor and total fabrication. Now that the fiftieth anniversary of Amelia's disappearance is at hand, additional theories are surfacing as many writers attempt to cash in on the inevitable publicity that will accompany this event. What continues to be striking about many of these theories is the total lack of convincing evidence which would substantiate them.

Some, for example, are variations on the old spy mission theory, which one can trace to the fictional movie of 1943, *Flight for Freedom*. Between 1937 and 1942, the belief that Amelia and Noonan were on a spying mission for the United States government had little currency. But a series of events resulted in a feature film starring Rosalind Russell and Fred McMurray which left an indelible impression on the public, still apparent nearly fifty years later.

Sensational publicity for the new 1942 movie, Flight for Freedom.

"THAT STORY'S DYNAMITE.. DON'T DARE TELL IT!"

Before Pearl Harbor, They Said: "THAT STORY'S DYNAMITE ..DON'T DARE TELL IT!"

SOUTH PACIFIC MYSTERY

The heads of Rosalind Russell and Fred MacMurray, co-stars in RKO Radio's "Flight for Freedom," are seen, inset against a map of the South Pacific area in which this romantic drama of pre-war aviation has its climax. This is the story about which it is said, "it could not have been told before Pearl Harbor," and which, in addition to its endearing romance and suspenseful adventure tells a story of United States Navy awareness of illegal acts by Japan in the area of mandated islands which they had sworn not to fortify.

CREDIT: RKO PICTURES

This movie originated in 1937 with George Palmer Putnam's submission to RKO of a story entitled, *LADY WITH WINGS: The Life Story of My Wife, Amelia Earhart*. It was Amelia's biography as seen through his eyes; Evelyn Hammitt of RKO read it in April, 1939. On February 1, 1940, Harry Edington wrote to GP, explaining that the studio had considered the story but had "definitely decided it wasn't for our coming program. We are staying away from all airplane pictures in the immediate future." RKO rejected the story.

In 1940 or early 1941, however, the well-known movie writer Horace McCoy submitted to RKO an eighty-three page story entitled, *STAND BY TO DIE*. According to RKO documents, the theme was as follows: "A world-famed woman flyer is asked to cooperate with the U.S. Government. On a round-the-world flight, she and her navigator will pretend to be forced down. The navy will search for them—and thus be able to photograph all Japanese-held islands. Meanwhile the girl and her navigator will be safe on a certain island. The scheme works as planned, except that the Japs get suspicious and capture girl and navigator. However, they escape. They will marry . . . ."

A GIRL MUST KNOW HER MOTOR!
Rosalind Russell works on her racing plane, in this scene from "Flight for Freedom," in which she is co-starred with Fred MacMurray by RKO Radio. The picture tells of the romance and adventure of a daring aviatrix who performs a service for her country under the seal of secrecy. It is based on an historic event of a few years back.

CREDIT: RKO PICTURES

William Nutt read the story prior to Pearl Harbor. On April 4, 1941 Nutt wrote an inter-department communication to Jacqueline Cochran, wife of the owner and president of RKO Studio's, Floyd Odlum, in which he made the following comment:

> "Though this is based on a rather exciting and novel idea, I do not think it is a good idea for the screen—at least, not at present . . . I do not think the United States Government would care very much for the idea, for the story suggests some pretty underhanded methods on the part of the U.S."

On April 29, 1942, however, RKO had prepared an agreement between the author, Horace McCoy, several individuals at RKO, and GP. The agreement was to assign all rights of the story to Horace McCoy as author and to grant RKO all rights in and to the original, unpublished and uncopyrighted story entitled *Stand By To Die*. GP signed for himself and as executor of her estate, for Amelia.

By August, 1942, the movie had become a screenplay by Oliver H.P. Garrett, and by October 15, 1942, the final script had grown to one hundred eighty three pages and the title had been changed to *Flight For Freedom*. This is the film which movie-goers saw in 1943. Its release coincided with the publication of a "long short story," by the same title in *Women's Home Companion* in January of that year.

Although the *Companion* frankly presents *Flight for Freedom* as "magazine fiction," it is clear that the popular imagination viewed neither the film nor the story as fictitious. On the contrary, the famous female flier of *Flight for Freedom* was invariably associated with Amelia Earhart, and one of the most enduring theories regarding her disappearance was thus born. The promotion material for this "sensational" film did nothing to allay this misapprehension.

Another element which perhaps contributed to the spy theory was the fact that Amelia and GP repeatedly requested confidentiality in their correspondence with suppliers like Lockheed and Western Electric, and with President and Mrs. Roosevelt, the State Department and the

GEORGE PALMER PUTNAM

2 West 45th Street,
New York City.

May 8, 1937.

Dear Admiral Leahy:

Thank you for your courteous note of the 7th in reference to Miss Earhart's flight.

This note is to lay before you the exact situation. It is for the moment very confidential. Aside from Miss Earhart and myself only two people know the revised plan.

The delay from the chosen mid-March date has resulted in changed weather conditions on several stretches of the proposed route. In a couple of instances these are drastic. Specifically, the weather probabilities in the stretch from Natal north are increasingly bad as June advances. The same is true of the Dakar-Aden-Karachi route. Obviously it is therefore desirable to get to Natal and across the South Atlantic and Africa as promptly as possible.

So Miss Earhart has decided to reverse the route and to proceed _from_ _west_ _to_ _east_. Also she will eliminate the Central American stage where increasing rains make the outlook dubious. She will fly from Oakland probably to El Paso, New Orleans and Miami. There will be no announcement. So far as Oakland is concerned, it will be simply the commencement of another "trial flight". As a matter of fact, the journey across the country will give her a chance for final testing of the refitted plane. If anything went sour she could return to the Lockheed plant. But if all goes well when she reaches Miami, we will there make the announcement of the revised plan.

As matters stand, this "sneak" take-off from Oakland will occur probably between May 18th and May 24th. What most concerns you, of course, is the approximate time when she is probably due at Howland. It just isn't possible to state that with any definity now. It is a fair guess that it might be somewhere between twenty-five and thirty days from the date of take-off. However, by the time she reaches say Karachi, which is approximately half way around, we should be able to estimate fairly accurately. That should also make possible adequate "warning".

May I, therefore, proceed on the assumption that it is satisfactory to know the Howland probability about a fortnight in advance?

I will appreciate it if you will keep this information quite to yourself until the Miami announcement is made. I will, of course, be at the Miami take-off and thereafter will headquarter at my office here in New York, probably until A.E. reaches Darwin or New Guinea, when I will move out to the airport at Oakland.

Thanking you again for your courtesy, I am,

Sincerely yours,

G P Putnam

Admiral W. D. Leahy,
Chief of Naval Operations,
Navy Department,
Washington, D. C.

One of many letters from Amelia and her husband that asked for "confidentiality." They soon became classified by mistake.

Navy. Knowing full well the hazards of her undertaking, Amelia had no desire that each take-off and landing become a media event. She hoped to accomplish the goals of her flight with a minimum of publicity, and she wanted to be able to change her plans suddenly, if necessary, without sending out dozens of press releases. The secrecy which surrounded the planning for this endeavor had nothing to do with espionage. It was typical of many of her actions throughout her life, beginning with her first altitude record in 1922. As GP pointed out, the realization of Amelia's plans "depends upon so many factors."

The classification system of the Department of Defense also contributed to the mystery that seemed to surround Amelia's disappearance.

Government papers were classified as far back as the Civil War, but there was no formal classification procedure until 1921 when Army Regulation 330-5 came into being. This regulation, however, did not provide any systematic declassification mechanics. It was not until November 9, 1953, during President Eisenhower's administration, that the first declassification order was written into the directive.

Amelia's personal wish to keep her plans "confidential" caused some government personnel to classify her information Confidential. Mrs. Roosevelt had requested that Southgate, Chief of Division of Protocol, "keep this matter confidential." It was understandable that no one wanted to challenge the President on this matter.

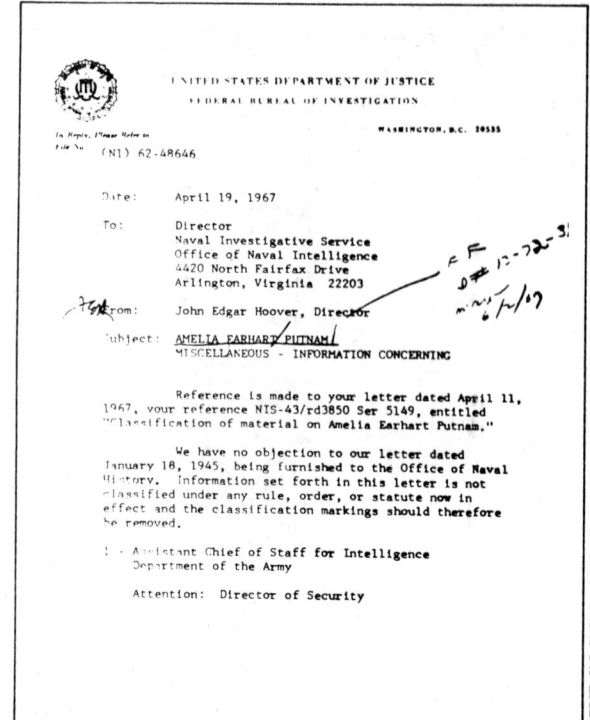

Memo from J. Edgar Hoover, F.B.I., Amelia Earhart file is no longer classified.

Letter to Malvina Scheider from Richard Southgate, offering to be of assistance on the Earhart flight.

Memo to file of Naval Investigative Service discussing Amelia Earhart materials to be declassified.

NAVAL INVESTIGATIVE SERVICE
FAIRMONT BUILDING
4420 NORTH FAIRFAX DRIVE
ARLINGTON, VIRGINIA 22203

IN REPLY REFER TO
NIS-43/jeg
3890
1 June 1967

MEMORANDUM FOR THE RECORD

Subj: Declassification and disposition of Amelia Earhart PUTNAM file

1. The Naval Investigative Service dossier (number 13-72-31) on Amelia Earhart PUTNAM bears an overall classification of Confidential. This is based on the inclusion in the file of confidential material from other Government agencies and the use of this material as enclosures, references, appendices, etc. to other documentation prepared by various Navy components or offices.

2. The other Government agencies which originated confidential material included in this file are the Department of State and the Federal Bureau of Investigation. By letter of 19 May 1967 to the Secretary of the Navy, the Assistant Secretary of State advised that the State Department material in question had been regraded to unclassified (this specifically refers to the letter of 10 September 1960 to Admiral Arleigh A. BURKE, Chief of Naval Operations, from Assistant Secretary of State J. Graham PARSONS, with enclosures). By letter of 19 April 1967, the Director, Federal Bureau of Investigation advised this Service that the FBI material in question was not now classified (this specifically refers to FBI letter of 18 January 1945).

3. The Director, Naval Investigative Service, by letter of 21 March 1967 to the Director of Naval Intelligence, stated that this file contains nothing that could be construed as defense information or material, the unauthorized disclosure of which could be prejudicial to the national defense. The Director of Naval Intelligence, by letter of 27 March 1967 in reply, advised that there was no objection to the declassification of this file from an intelligence point of view. Sufficient authority having therefore been obtained, all classified material in this file may now be declassified.

4. In accordance with SECNAV approval (ltr 2506P92 of 1 May 1967), this dossier is to be transferred to the Office of Naval History for retention following declassification. Mr. ALLARD, Head, Operational Archives Branch, Naval History Division, advised the writer by phone on 31 May 1967 that the transfer should be accomplished by memorandum addressed to the Director, Naval History Division (OP-09B92), Building 210 (4th deck), Washington Navy Yard, Washington, D.C., 20390.

5. The above has been made a matter of record at the request and for the use of LTJG WILLIAMS, NIS-33B.

D. R. PASCHAL
Head, Special Projects Division
S.E.C. Department

Letter from Paul Mantz asking to obtain a copy of the **Itasca** *official report.*

```
                UNITED AIR SERVICES, Ltd.
                     BURBANK, CALIFORNIA

EXECUTIVE OFFICES
                                        April 26th 1938.


        Mrs. Franklin D. Roosevelt,
        The White House,
        Washington, D.C.

        Dear Mrs. Roosevelt:
                    The writer acted as technical advisor
        to Miss Earhart and made the flight with her to
        Honolulu which was climaxed by her accident on the
        take-off.
                    I received a letter from Miss Jacqueline
        Cochran the other day requesting that I answer a
        great many questions regarding my opinion and actual
        messages that were received and tied together with
        the times in relation to the take-off.
                    I have often wanted to make up a
        complete report in detail on this situation in
        order to determine whether or not a search would be
        practical, even at this late date. In order to do
        so would like to have a copy of the official report
        of the "Itasca" which is on file at the Coast Guard
        Headquarters in Washington. I saw this report in
        San Francisco at the time Miss Earhart was first re-
        ported missing but made no notes and if you could
        arrange to have a copy sent to me I would in turn
        furnish you a detailed report and theories for your
        own personal use - but not for publication.
                    I have attempted to draw up this
        information ever since last August but just this
        morning I was advised by Mr. F. K. Johnson of the
        U.S. Coast Guard, San Francisco, that the official
        report was on file in Washington and could not be
        released except through certain channels.
```

```
        Mrs. F. D. Roosevelt                 -2-

                    I feel that all of us who were so
        close to Miss Earhart should at least make a
        certain amount of effort along the lines I know she
        would follow if the situation were reversed.
                    Would deeply appreciate it if you could
        have the above information forwarded and in turn you
        will receive a report which I am sure will answer any
        question of doubt that may be in your mind.

                              Yours very truly,
                              UNITED AIR SERVICES, LTD.

        APM:S                 A. Paul Mantz, President
```

Even Henry Morgenthau, Jr., Secretary of the Treasury, was unsure of the proper classification of the Amelia Earhart materials, as the letter from Paul Mantz to Eleanor Roosevelt on April 26, 1938, makes clear. In his letter he asked for "a copy of the official report of the 'Itasca' which is on file at the Coast Guard Headquarters in Washington."

On May 10, 1938, Mrs. Roosevelt wrote a note to Henry Morgenthau saying,

" . . . Now comes this letter . . . I do not know whether you can send the man these records, but, in any case, I am sending you the letter and let me know whatever your decision may be.
Affectionately, 'E.R.'"

Three days later, on May 13, 1938, in a conversation Secretary Morgenthau had with Malvina Scheider, the Morgenthau diaries recorded:

" . . . I've been given a verbal report. If we're going to release this, it's just going to smear the whole reputation of Amelia Earhart . . . Yes, but I mean if we give it to this one man we've got to make it public . . . And if we ever release the report of the Itasca on Amelia Earhart, any reputation she's got is gone . . . I know how Amelia Earhart absolutely disregarded all orders, and if we ever release this thing, goodbye Amelia Earhart's reputation . . . if the President ever heard that somebody questioned that the Navy hadn't made the proper search . . . Well, still if she wants it, I'll tell her [Eleanor]—I mean what happened . . . "

Henry Morgenthau sent a note to Mrs. Roosevelt on July 5, 1938, telling her that Paul Mantz had been sent a copy of the *Itasca* log and they [the Navy] would cooperate with answering any of Paul Mantz' questions regarding the search for Amelia.

Morgenthau's conviction that the release of this information would destroy forever Amelia's reputation is curious, to say the least. The available documents strongly suggest some malfunction in the radio equipment; they also reveal that the failure of both pilot and navigator to learn Morse code and the use of the CW key was a serious deficiency.

Two pages from Henry Morganthau Jr.'s, "Morganthau Diaries," transcription of a telephone call with Malvina Scheider, in reference to Paul Mantz's request.

May 13, 1938.
9:30 a.m.

GROUP MEETING

Present: Mr. Magill
Mr. Bell
Mr. Gaston
Mr. Gibbons
Mr. Haas
Mr. White
Mr. McReynolds
Mr. Upham
Mr. Lochhead
Miss Chauncey
Miss Lonigan
Mr. Foley

412

-16-

H.M.Jr: And I'm not going to keep quiet.

(On White House phone) Oh, hello. - Oh, thanks. Hello, Tommy (Malvina Scheider). How are you? This letter that Mrs. Roosevelt wrote me about trying to get the report on Amelia Earhart. Now, I've been given a verbal report. If we're going to release this, it's just going to smear the whole reputation of Amelia Earhart, and my ..... - Yes, but I mean if we give it to this one man we've got to make it public; we can't let one man see it. And if we ever release the report of the Itasca on Amelia Earhart, any reputation she's got is gone, because - and I'd like to - I'd really like to return this to you.

(Continuing) Now, I know what Navy did, I know what the Itasca did, and I know how Amelia Earhart absolutely disregarded all orders, and if we ever release this thing, goodbye Amelia Earhart's reputation. Now, really - because if we give the access to one, we have to give it to all. And my advice is that - and if the President ever heard that somebody questioned that the Navy hadn't made the proper search, after what those boys went through - I think they searched, as I remember it, 50,000 square miles, and every one of those planes was out, and the boys just burnt themselves out physically and every other way searching for her. And if - I mean I think he'd get terribly angry if somebody - because they just went the limit, and so did the Coast Guard. And we have the report of all those wireless messages and everything else, what that woman - happened to her the last few minutes. I hope I've just got to never make it public, I mean. - O.K. - Well, still if she wants it, I'll tell her - I mean what happened. It isn't a very nice story. - Well, yes. There isn't anything additional to something like that. You think up a good one. - Thank you. (Conversation ends)

(To Chauncey) Just send it back.

Chauncey: Sure.

H.M.Jr: I mean we tried - people want us to search again

413

-17-

those islands, after what we have gone through. You (Gibbons) know the story, don't you?

Gibbons: We have evidence that the thing is all over, sure. Terrible. It would be awful to make it public.

H.M.Jr: Well, the only thing that out of this - I want you (Lonigan) to check up with Social Security. Archie, give this (photostat of WPA figures) to her and let her check, and Ed, you check the legislation, will you please?

Foley: Yes. Here's an unsigned memorandum.

H.M.Jr: Excuse me?

Furthermore, one cannot reasonably attribute the communication failure between the *Itasca* and the crew of the Electra solely to Amelia's "disregard of all orders." She would hardly have *deliberately* used an unreliable high frequency for direction finder purposes, contrary to the advice of the San Francisco Division. Her requests that the *Itasca* transmit homing signals on 6210 kcs could have resulted from misinformation, improper transmission of information, or a memory lapse; it hardly seems to support the charge of deliberate disobedience. That there was a definite lack of coordination between the civilians who were in charge of the flight and the assisting vessels also undoubtedly contributed to the failure of the flight.

Earlier, on August 28, 1937, District Superintendent Collopy submitted the following report to the Civil Aviation Board, Salamaua, Territory of New Guinea:

". . . I was present during the whole of the time they [Amelia and Fred Noonan] were at Lae to assist them in any way I could. They arrived at Lae at 3 p.m. on 29th June, and left at 10 a.m. on 2nd July. Practically the whole time the aircraft was at Lae, Guinea Airways Engineers were carrying out maintenance work on the aircraft, engines, and instruments . . . The main cause of her delay at Lae was because they awaited a satisfactory weather report and an accurate check on time signals for setting the chronometer . . . according to Captain Noonan the total fuel capacity of the aircraft was 1150 U.S. Gallons and oil 64 U.S. Gallons. They left Lae with a total of 1100 U.S. Gallons of fuel and 64 U.S. Gallons of oil. One tank contained only 50 gallons of its total capacity of 100 gallons. This tank contained 100 octane fuel and they considered the 50 gallons of this fuel sufficient for the take-off from Lae . . .

"As the result of a talk with Mr. E. Chater and Mr. Balfour the Lae radio operator it is very apparent that the weak link in the combination was the crews lack of expert knowledge of radio. Their morse was very slow and they preferred to use telephony as much as possible. Balfour stated that they advised him they would change the wave length at nightfall. Balfour advised them just before nightfall not to change as their signals were coming through quite strong. They apparently changed however as Balfour never heard them again."

"At about three p.m. a message came through to the effect that they were at 10,000 feet but were going to reduce altitude because of thick banks of cumulus clouds. The next

Mr. and Mrs. E. H. Chater, then Manager of Guinea Airways, with Amelia and Fred. Photo is dated June 30, 1937. Chater and Harry Balfour were the last to talk to Amelia on the radio as she flew from Lae on July 2, 1937.

Western Electric Co., "Close-up view in the control compartment . . . The circular dial seen through the lower part of the steering wheel is the 9A remote frequency control for the 13C radio transmitter, and the rectangular panel with the circular dial just to the left of the wheel is the 27A remote control unit for the 20B radio receiver. At the right of the seat may be seen the key controlling the transmitter when used for telegraph and also the type 1019 headphones," photograph, September 1936.

and last message was to the effect that they were at 7,000 feet and making 150 knots, this message was received at approx. 5 p.m."

"Mr. Noonan told me that he was not a bit anxious about the flight to Howland Island and was quite confident that he would have little difficulty in locating it. One can only have opinions as to what actually happened to them, but in the light of the foregoing regarding radio, and the confusion which arose during the search in connection with all the radio messages which were suppose to have emanated from the aircraft I do think that had an expert radio operator been included in the crew the conclusion may have been different . . ."

W. C. Tinus, retired Vice President of Bell Telephone Laboratories, wrote in a letter in 1962:

"I was the radio engineer who was responsible for the design and installation of her radio communications equipment, [at the Newark Airport, New Jersey in February, 1937] and since there is apparently still some doubt as to what her equipment consisted of, perhaps I can clear up one or two points . . ."

"I had been a radio operator aboard ship in my younger days and knew the importance of being able to communicate at 500 kc over the oceans. I persuaded Miss Earhart and Mr. Putnam on this point and modified a standard three-channel Western Electric equipment of the type then being used by the airlines to provide one channel at 500 kc and the other two at around 3000 and 6000 kc . . . A simple modification also enabled transmission to be made on CW or MCW, as well as voice, and a telegraph key was provided which could be plugged in, in addition to a microphone for voice communication. It was my thought that many ships throughout the world had 500 kc radio compasses and could probably better obtain bearings if the key were held down for an extended period while radiating modulated CW (MCW)."

"I was less successful in persuading Miss Earhart of the importance of having a qualified radio operator in her crew. I had only a short period one afternoon at Newark Airport to show her and Captain Manning (of the United States Lines Sea Rescue fame) how to operate the equipment."

" . . . I did not see her equipment during the period between the first and second starts, but had no reason at the time to believe it had been changed."

"Several months after her disappearance we received a small package from Pan American Airways at Miami containing her telegraph key, cord and plug, which she had left in their hanger there. Without these items she could have communicated on 500 kc by voice and could have sent out a suitable signal for direction finding by simply holding the microphone button down for a time. The remainder of her equipment peculiar to the low frequency 500 kc channel probably weighed five or ten pounds, but apparently she did not leave it in Miami or it, too, would have been returned to us." He ended, " . . . She was equipped for 500 kc communication originally and she did leave one item, her telegraph key, behind when she departed from Miami."

Earlier in the month, Mr. Tinus gave an interview in which he said the following:

" . . . I remember explaining to Amelia how radio operators who did not speak the same language talked to each other with the International Que Signals, and urged her to get a copy of the International Radio Telegraph Conventions Bible . . ."

"The Laboratories urged me to write an article on her [Amelia's] installation, but I urged

---

LOCKHEED AIRCRAFT CORPORATION
INTER-DEPARTMENTAL COMMUNICATION

AIR MAIL

Date July 30, 1937

To   Courtlandt S. Gross:

Subject: RADIO EQUIPMENT ON EARHART ELECTRA.

Remarks: At the time this ship was built, we installed the following equipment:

Western Electric 13C 50 Watt Transmitter, equipped with crystals to operate on the following frequencies: 3105, 6210, and 500 kilocycles.

Western Electric 4-Band 20B Type Receiver. The 4 bands cover the following range of frequencies:

200-400
550-1500
1500-4000
4000-10,000 kilocycles.

The source of power for both the transmitter and receiver was from a dual battery installation which was also made here at the factory. Batteries were kept charged by one engine-driven generator. The radio compass, which was installed elsewhere, was manufactured by the Bendix people. I have been unable to ascertain whether an auxiliary or hand operated generator was installed. However, we have good reason to believe that additional equipment was installed by Miss Earhart at the time her ship was in Miami.

J. W. Cross

JWC:M

Letter about radio equipment on the Electra.

they await her return. Consequently, all that was published was one picture of me and Amelia at Newark Airport when I was showing her how to use her equipment."

" . . . This is one of the most interesting stories of my career, that is the only reason I am relating it to you. . . at Newark Airport I showed him [Manning] how to plug in the key, how to switch to CW to MCW, and in particular, how to set the equipment to 500 Kilocycles on the three-position lever; two high frequencies and one low . . . This story has never been told because it isn't very favorable to some people's judgment and that's the reason the Navy suppressed that when it was told this year . . . "

Further support for the claim that Amelia had removed the trailing antenna comes from Commander Anthony, who during WWII was a Lieutenant Commander in the U.S. Coast Guard and a skilled cryptanalyst, one of three credited with breaking the Japanese maru code,

Fliers Crashed Within Sight of Goal Because Unable to Hear Itasca's Signals, Newly Revealed U. S. Records Declare

TRIB C MAY 8 1938

(This is the first of a series of articles telling for the first time the real story of what happened to Amelia Earhart when she was lost in the South Pacific while on an around-the-world flight last year.)

By ALFRED P. RECK
(Copyright 1938, for The Tribune)

The confidential files of the Coast Guard cutter Itasca disclosed today for the first time the real story of what happened when Amelia Earhart went down to death in the South Pacific.

Written in the routine report is the story of a dramatic fight for life and a gamble of human ability against mechanical handicaps.

A year ago this month Miss Earhart and her navigator, Frederick J. Noonan, were winging their way eastward from Oakland on what was to have been the first circling of the globe at the equator.

They reached Lae, New Guinea, and were coasting across the Pacific at the end of their longest over-water hop—2550 miles to Howland Island—within a few minutes of their destination when disaster struck them.

For a year the world has wondered what happened after Miss Earhart sent her first radio flash of impending tragedy. Are Earhart and Noonan alive?

FACTS REVEALED

The answers are written in the log of the Itasca and are made public for the first time in The Oakland Tribune, upon authorization from Coast Guard headquarters in Washington, D. C.

Miss Earhart did not miss Howland Island.

As far as practicable air navigation is concerned for such a long over-water flight, she and her Oakland navigator hit the island "square on the nose."

Earhart's failure was not due to any lack of ability of her own or her navigator's, but was due solely to lack of proper equipment and preparation.

These facts and others, telling the true story of what happened on the much publicized world flight, were obtained from the files of the Itasca, which attempted to monitor Earhart on the hop from Lae to Howland.

PREPARATIONS FAULTY

There is more tragedy in the last over-water flight than the public ever has realized, for two brave and able fliers were sacrificed on the altar of unpreparedness.

They reached their objective after more than 20 hours in the air from the tip of New Guinea. They piloted the so-called "flying laboratory" straight and true to the tiny speck of coral in the mid-Pacific and then they went down to a courageous death only a few miles away.

The Earhart plane crashed into the ocean, with probably instant death for both the pilot and the navigator, not through any fault of theirs, but because their radio equipment was valueless.

Long after the last publicly announced message from the Earhart plane was received, the world's most famous woman pilot and her navigator were cruising north and south in the vicinity of Howland, in the glare of the rising sun, hoping to sight what they could not locate by radio.

NOT INFORMED

On the island was a high frequency direction finder, borrowed by the Department of Interior from the Navy Department at Honolulu, but Earhart did not know it was there.

Richard B. Black of the Department of Interior, who was in charge of Government cooperation in the flight, failed to notify Earhart of the existence of the direction finder, according to the Coast Guard official report.

The commander of the Itasca, who furnished a radioman from his ship to man the direction finder, also said he didn't notify Earhart that the instrument which might or might not have meant success, had been set up.

Anyway, the high frequency direction finder did not function when Earhart needed it most because Black, who ordered the equipment placed aboard the Itasca for transportation to Howland, did not borrow from the Navy electrical equipment to operate it.

GUN BATTERIES USED

The high frequency direction finder was operated on Howland Island solely on gun batteries borrowed from the gun turret of the Itasca's 3-inch gun. The batteries were strong enough to run the direction finder only a short time, and in the still hours of the dawn, when Earhart and Noonan were flying hopefully toward Howland Island, the batteries failed. They were worn out.

Quoting the exact words of Commander W. K. Thompson of the Itasca, in his official report:

"The Coast Guard had no intention of navigating Earhart to Howland Island. The high frequency direction finder obtained from the Navy by Mr. Black was set up on Howland Island and manned by a Coast Guard radioman.

"This was in accordance with Mr. Black's request.

Records show that Earhart was not advised by this vessel of the high frequency direction finder's existence. Mr. Black states he did not inform Earhart."

KNEW OF HAZARD

There is little question that Miss Earhart and Noonan knew that they might experience radio difficulty on the hazardous hop across the Pacific, as they had flown the South Atlantic without a radio, which had failed to function.

Messages directed to them emphasized the importance of speeding up the trip at the last stages, and they gambled—and lost—on the human ability to overcome mechanical handicaps.

It was a brave gamble, but useless.

Just before the departure from Lae the takeoff was delayed because of the failure of radio receiving equipment, which prevented Noonan from calibrating his chronometer. But messages sent to them from the United States urged a speedy return.

A few days' delay to insure proper functioning of the faulty radio might have saved two courageous persons. But anyone who is brave enough to attempt such a flight also is a gambler, and they shook the dice of fate and lost.

"It is my considered judgment that any want of batteries for the direction finder temporarily mounted at Howland Island at the time of the Earhart flight had no bearing on the fate of the plane and its crew and no blame can or should be imputed to anyone on such a basis."

This was the statement issued today by Captain Stanley V. Parker, commander of the U. S. Coast Guard headquarters in San Francisco.

The Coast Guard cutter Itasca was given eight hours notice to proceed to Howland Island to take up a position to aid Amelia Earhart on the flight which carried her to death in the South Pacific.

This is revealed in Coast Guard records made public today.

With scanty information available, the cutter went ahead and made every preparation possible to safeguard the flight.

When Miss Earhart and her Oakland navigator, Frederick J. Noonan, left Lae for Howland Island, it was hours before the Itasca learned that the plane had taken off and then the information came from a press association broadcast.

INFORMATION ASKED

On June 21 the Itasca transmitted the following message from Washington to Earhart:

"Advise Earhart from Darwin she will communicate with the Itasca via Samoa the desired frequency, time and type of signal best for her homing device. She will advise fully via Samoa before leaving Lae."

The message went unanswered and was repeated the next day.

On June 23 the Itasca again radioed Miss Earhart, requesting her to designate the time and type of radio signals desired. The cutter also informed her that "we will give smoke by day and searchlight by night."

The next day the Itasca received a message from San Francisco, transmitted at the request of George Palmer Putnam, Miss Earhart's husband, asking the cutter to adjust its radio transmitter "for possible use of 3105 kilocycles for voice." Putnam also informed the Itasca that the direction finder on the plane covered a range of about "200 to 1400 kilocycles."

Then, from Sourabaya, Miss Earhart radioed the Itasca that her direction finder or homing device "covers 200 to 1500 and 2400 to 4800 kilocycles but not near the end bands."

She then asked the Itasca to transmit the letter "A," the cutter's positions and its call letters every half-hour on 7500 kilocycles, a frequency far beyond the range of the Earhart plane's direction finder.

DISCREPANCY NOTED

On June 27 Miss Earhart again requested the Itasca to call her on 7500 kilocycles and added: "I will give long calls by voice on 3105 kilocycles at a quarter after and a quarter to the hour."

The Itasca informed Miss Earhart that her direction finder would operate best at from 270 to 550 kilocycles, but she insisted on 7500 kilocycles.

Familiar with radio conditions in the South Pacific, the Itasca noted that the frequency requested would be good in that area only within a radius of 30 to 35 miles.

No one could learn just what equipment was left on the plane. Various pieces had been discarded from time to time as the flight neared the end. Putnam could give the Itasca no accurate information and Miss Earhart either was too busy or neglected to answer inquiries.

It was then that Commander Thompson sent two messages to Washington, D. C., warning of the potential radio dangers of the flight.

If Amelia Earhart's radio-sending equipment was not faulty she failed to keep her broadcast schedule to the Coast Guard cutter Itasca on her tragic flight from Lae, New Guinea.

Records of the Coast Guard disclose that her calls never were heard at the quarter past the hour time she had designated.

The only signals from her plane picked up by the Itasca were at the quarter of the hour, and toward the end of the flight, which ended in a South Pacific crash and death, Miss Earhart abandoned her schedules altogether.

At 2:45 a. m. on July 2, last year, the Itasca heard Earhart's voice for the first time.

"Cloudy and overcast," she reported in a very low monotone.

RECEIVER OUT

Apparently Miss Earhart's radio receiving equipment was completely out. Only once during the entire flight did she acknowledge receiving the Itasca's signals, and that was on a frequency good only for 30 to 35 miles.

The cutter hung off Howland Island, the tiny speck of coral in the Pacific which meant safety and fame to the brave woman flier, if she reached it.

Great billows of black smoke poured from the cutter's funnel to act as a guide to the speeding plane. In all directions except to the northwest, the weather was clear. About 40 miles to the northwest there were low hanging, dark clouds.

Keeping its schedule, the Itasca called Earhart every half hour, as requested before the start of the flight. The calls went unanswered.

SIGNALS HEARD

The Itasca broadcast signals on 7500 kilocycles. Then came the first and only response, reporting that the cutter's radio calls had been heard.

At 8 a. m. came this message from the plane:

"KHAQQ calling Itasca. We received your signals but unable to get a minimum. Please take bearing on us and answer 3105 with voice."

For an hour signals came in from the Earhart plane at the same strength, indicating it was circling for a sight of a landfall.

The Itasca's smoke screen stretched for 10 miles, the commander noted.

He commented in the log that the reply at 8 a. m. to the signals sent on 7500 kilocycles, good only for from 30 to 35 miles, indicated she was closest to the island at that time and then started flying away.

GROPED FOR ISLAND

At 8:44 a. m., an hour after Miss Earhart reported her fuel was running low, the plane was in the air and she sent this frantic message by voice:

"KHAQQ to Itasca. We are on line of position 157-337. Will repeat this message. We will repeat this message on 6210 kilocycles. Wait. Listening in on 6210 kilocycles. We are running north and south."

Miss Earhart's voice for the first time sounded frightened, the Itasca radio operators reported. For some reason she decided to change to a different radio frequency. Her voice was broken and choked.

That was the last message ever received from her. It was the last signal heard from her plane.

Desperately, the Itasca called her and not even an echo came back.

All of the supposed messages and signals reported later proved to be false, Commander Thompson said.

"I believe that Miss Earhart passed north and west of Howland Island and missed it in the glare of the rising sun," he wrote. "She probably had receiver trouble. The only signals which Miss Earhart acknowledged were on 7500 kilocycles. Her direction finder could not handle this frequency."

Because of the cloud banks to the northwest and her reference to flying through clouds, the Itasca commander believes she went down in that direction.

What would have been a record-breaking and triumphal flight was defeated at the last moment by a faulty radio, lack of adequate preparation and the every day occurence of a rising sun.

which allowed us to read much of the Japanese message traffic. During July, 1937, Henry M. Anthony was Communication Officer of the Hawaiian Section of the San Francisco Division of the U.S. Coast Guard. Commander Anthony stated during his 1984 interview:

> "On July second, we tried to get her [Amelia] onto 500 KCS, to take bearings on her, but she didn't answer. I don't think she could. From Miami, on her eastern flight, Amelia had off-loaded her 500 medium-frequency [500 KCS], antenna because of a weight factor. We only had one communication in that whole flight, when she acknowledged receiving the *Itasca* and we could read her, and her transmission never lasted over 8 seconds, 8 to 10 seconds . . . During the Prohibition era I used a DF, which I helped design, in locating rumrunners on land and sea—with 4.0 results. However, signals of more than 8 seconds duration are needed for accuracy—something which AE NEVER DID!"
>
> ". . . She only answered one communication from the *Itasca*. She didn't use her DF [direction finder], whether the DF was defective, we'll never know. She didn't use it, because if she had, she couldn't have missed Howland . . ."

Commander Anthony was in Hawaii, copying every transmission from the *Itasca* between July second and July seventh.

A highly critical summary of the last leg of Amelia's flight is contained in the U. S. Coast Guard response to a Pan American System Report on Proposed Joint Rescue Procedure, dated August 26, 1937. In this response of March 22, 1938, Stanley V. Parker, Commander, San Francisco Division states:

> " . . . it has never been learned definitely just what radio equipment the Earhart plane carried . . . From all indications, there is some basis for the belief that the receiving equipment on the plane was not functioning properly, as no acknowledgements were received from the plane to any dispatch sent by the ITASCA. It has been established that neither Miss Earhart or Noonan knew how to use CW key, at least at normal operating speeds, and complete dependence was placed on radiophone. The ITASCA was to be used as a homing beacon *only* as no C.G. direction finder equipment capable of operating on the higher frequencies was available on the ITASCA. From all experience so far with high frequency direction finders, the results obtained on loops are subject to many indeterminate errors and are considered unreliable.

Letter of Commendation to Henry M. Anthony, U.S. Coast Guard, for his participation in connection with the search for Amelia and Fred.

```
                                                    22 September, 1937.

From:       Commandant.
To  :       Radio Electrician Henry M. Anthony, Hawaiian Section

Subject:    Recognition of duty performed.

Reference:  (a) Letter, Commanding Officer, ITASCA, 31 August, 1937.
                (73-800), with 1st Indorsement, Commander, San Francisco
                Division, 3 September, 1937 (73-800).

      1.    Headquarters is gratified with the interest, ability
and devotion to duty displayed by you as Communication Officer of the
Hawaiian Section of the San Francisco Division in connection with the
search for the Earhart plane from 2 to 7 July, 1937.

            By direction.


                                            L. C. COVELL,
                                            Assistant Commandant.
```

CREDIT: U.S. NAVAL ARCHIVES

Miss Earhart was specifically warned by the San Francisco Division against attempting to use the high frequencies for direction finder purposes, and to confine all attempts at direction finding to the intermediate frequencies. This advice was not followed by Miss Earhart as her requests for homing signals were for the ITASCA to transmit on 6210 kc. She did not choose to make known whether she could not or would not use the intermediate frequencies. The information received from the plane was very meager and of little or no value to assisting forces. It can be stated that every arrangement entered into by the Coast Guard in connection with the Earhart flight was carried out, all in spite of the fact that the ITASCA was given only a few hours notice prior to leaving the States, and that all instructions were issued by dispatch. It was very evident after the flight started that the entire flight was badly managed, and that Mr. Putman, [sic] at San Francisco, was not aware of all facts, and that the information which he furnished was often at variance with that received from Miss Earhart. The Coast Guard was not asked to take bearings on the plane and did not do so, although an effort was made to take bearings on a direction finder located on Howland Island. No accurate bearings were obtained . . . "

" . . . All radio controls were available only to the pilot. The means of communication between pilot and navigator were extremely unsatisfactory and this one factor would make it possible for garbled dispatches in the plane itself . . . There was one position report sent out from the plane about 700 miles out from Lae. It was about this time that the first communications from the plane were received on board the ITASCA. Continued communications received from the plane indicates that the transmitter was functioning properly, but that there was considerable doubt as to whether the receiver was functioning properly. Only one acknowledgement was received from the plane, this about one hour before the crash . . . The Coast Guard was not ordered or designated to safeguard the flight. Messrs. Miller and Black of the Department of the Interior had more information on the flight and were representing Mr. Putman [sic] on board the ITASCA. The ITASCA was ordered to Howland Island for the purpose of acting as a radio homing beacon and plane guard at Howland Island. It is apparent that Mr. Black obtained the assistance of the Navy, as the U. S. S. ONTARIO was stationed midway between Lae and Howland. The Army also was represented at Howland Island . . . An official dispatch was filed by the San Francisco Division for and delivered without delay to the ITASCA immediately upon receipt of word at San Francisco that the flight had started. A dispatch was also filed for the Navy, but no information is available to indicate that the ONTARIO ever received the information before the plane had passed over her. Definite schedules had been arranged as to times and frequencies for use between the ITASCA and the plane, but unfortunately the plane failed to observe either times or frequencies. It was never intended that the ITASCA would take bearings unless they were on intermediate frequencies. As stated before, the purpose of the ITASCA at Howland Island was to act as a homing beacon and guard ship *AT* that place— and nothing else . . . it is apparent that the entire flight lacked coordination between assisting vessels and Miss Earhart, and that this was due, in a large measure, to the fact that the Coast Guard was not consulted by the civilians in charge of the flight . . . "

" . . . The use of the radio amateurs is questionable, due to the fact that much information received from that source is very unreliable and results in a needless waste of time when time is the important element in any search. The above statement is made with regard to facts alone, and is not meant to imply that amateur radio is untrustworthy. Great credit is due the amateur, but in cases where searches are made hundreds or thousands of miles distance from shore, it must be seen that the agencies best equipped for any radio intercept watches are those of the military and commercial organizations near the scene of the search and ashore. *Not one* of the amateur reports received during the Earhart search was accurate, and all reports of receipt of signals from the Earhart plane were definitely known to be false, as the San Francisco Division had a continuous intercept watch at three separate locations guarding 3105 and 6210 kc using beam receiving antennas, with better equipment than is available to amateurs, and no signals were heard other than those of the ITASCA on 3105 kc . . . "

In addition to the many reports and investigations that sought to explain Amelia and Fred's disappearance, the theory that they were captured and executed by the Japanese has persisted. It has been impossible to lay this theory to rest entirely. In response to my request for information from Mike Mansfield, American Ambassador in Tokyo, he wrote on May 12, 1986,

" . . . I am immediately looking into your request and will let you know what the results are."

With the help of Ambassador Mansfield, I received a report from:

" . . . the archives of the National Institute for Defense Studies, which holds the extant military archives of Japan. Saipan, of course, was under Japanese military administration when Miss Earhart's plane disappeared . . ."

The report, by Fumihiko Nakajima, provides a detailed account of the author's experiences and opinions during his residence in Saipan during the 1930's. It is, however, merely the personal report of one individual, and not an official position paper from the Japanese government.

Nakajima, in 1981 an Adjunct Professor at the University of Guam, wrote a series of reports in which he responded to news reports concerning the alleged crash of the Earhart plane in Saipan on July 2, 1937. At that time Nakajima was a chemical engineer who had been stationed in Saipan since 1935 as an employee of the South Sea Development Company, Incorporated. He began writing these reports in 1960 at the request of Dr. T. Steel Newman, whom he identifies as "the superintendent of War in the Pacific National Historical Park on Guam and American Memorial Park on Saipan in National Park Service of the U.S. Department of the Interior."

Nakajima disputes the theories proposed by Paul Briand in his book *Daughter of the Sky* and later advanced by Fred Goerner of CBS that the Electra crash-landed in Saipan, that Earhart and Noonan were taken prisoner by the Japanese and were later imprisoned and/or executed. He maintains that in 1937 the Japanese had not fortified Saipan, that there were no

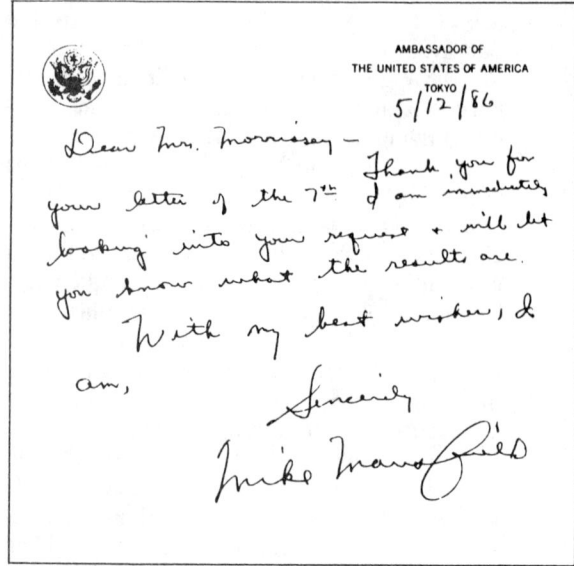

Letter from Mike Mansfield, U.S. Ambassador to Japan

Letter from Eleanor Roosevelt in 1961, telling Muriel that the President never told her that Amelia was on any special mission.

DEPARTMENT OF STATE
WASHINGTON

August 19, 1960

Dear Mr. Younger:

I refer to your interest in the Amelia Earhart case as expressed in your letter of June 9, 1960, and to my letter of June 29, 1960.

Our Ambassador at Tokyo has informed me that the Government of Japan has now completed an exhaustive investigation which revealed no basis whatever for the rumor, given recent currency by speculative articles in the press, that Miss Earhart was executed by Japanese officials on Saipan in 1937. The investigation included a search of all available Japanese records, and interrogation of a number of Japanese officials who had served in the Saipan area in 1937.

Since the facts surrounding Miss Earhart's disappearance still remain a mystery, I should like to assure you that any avenues which seem promising of additional information will be explored as they arise. I shall write to you again as a matter of course whenever significant information is received.

Sincerely yours,

William B. Macomber, Jr.
Assistant Secretary

CREDIT: STANFORD UNIVERSITY ARCHIVES

A 1960 letter to House of Representative Younger denying Amelia's death was on Saipan.

The most recent letter from the Japanese government denying any involvement in Amelia's death.

Former Hirohito Officials Deny Miss Earhart Was Jap Captive

TOKYO, Aug. 26 (UP)—A survey of former Japanese officials made it appear fairly certain today that Amelia Earhart did not land on a Japanese-mandated island when she disappeared in 1937, as had been earlier reported.

Miss Earhart was on a flight around the world and was flying over the Pacific at the time.

The survey was conducted by the United Press after Alvan Pitak, 33, a former Marine lieutenant, said he had gathered evidence that Miss Earhart might have landed on the Marshall Islands and been taken to Japan as a prisoner.

Pitak said he got his information from a Marshall Island.

The governor of the islands in 1937, Kenjiro Kitajima, said he had "absolutely no knowledge" of any woman landing there during his term of office. Other results of the survey:

Former Vice Adm. Sehichiro Fujimori, who had jurisdiction over the islands, said he knew of no American flier who landed on them. The Japanese navy took part in the search for Miss Earhart, he recalled.

Tsuneo Kudo, a Japanese trader who was active in the islands, said: "I don't think the Japanese would have been so foolish as to mistreat an American of such fame had she been forced down."

CREDIT: U.S. NAVAL ARCHIVES

An August, 1949 newspaper denial by former Emperor Hirohito officials.

CONSULATE GENERAL OF JAPAN
Federal Reserve Plaza, 14th Floor
600 Atlantic Avenue
Boston, Massachusetts 02210
(617) 973-9772

December 15, 1986

Dear Mrs. Morrissey:

With regard to your letter dated October 20, 1986 addressed to His Majesty the Emperor of Japan, your enquiry was referred to the Defense Agency. Unfortunately, as a result of extended research, we have concluded that no record has been fournd on Ms. Amelia Earhart nor on the Lockeheed 10 airplane, s/n NR16020 at the Agency.

I hope that future endeavors will prov to be more fruitful.

With kindest regards,

Yours sincerely,

Minoru Tamba
Consul General

Japanese soldiers stationed on Saipan at the time, and that it is unlikely that such an event could have happened without his, that is, Nakajima's, knowing it. He argues further that thousands of Japanese who had lived on Saipan and subsequently returned to Japan "did not know of Miss Earhart incident." The Japanese, he claims, in later years searched for the plane in Saipan and found no trace of it. No Japanese or Okinawan eye-witness of the alleged crash could be found.

Concerning any execution of spies, Nakajima writes:

> "The execution of foreigner was very importantly international affair. It was impossible that the governor of civil administrator did it. There was no military in Saipan at the time, and Saipan had not been fortified."

Nakajima maintains that there may have been executions after the war broke out, but he believes that there were no secret executions prior to that time.

He points out further that during the war a number of U.S. fighter planes crashed in the harbor of Saipan, making it likely that any wreckage recovered from that area was from military aircraft and not from the Electra. He also cites records and reports which suggest strongly that the Electra was at least 2,000 miles from Saipan when the flight ended, probably within 150 miles of Howland Island.

There has been a story for many years that the U. S. Navy pathology department has the remains of Amelia and Fred. In reply, the Navy wrote:

> "I am responding on behalf of the Secretary of the Navy to your letter . . . There is no truth to the rumor you mentioned that the Navy holds the remains of Miss Earhart and Mr. Noonan."

Correspondence with the Department of Defense further states:

> "A thorough search for Amelia Earhart Putnam was conducted by the U.S. Navy at the time of her disappearance. As a result of various published allegations, additional investigations were conducted. These disclosed nothing of accurate substance to support the belief that Ms. Earhart was engaged in any type of espionage or reconnaissance activity for the United States . . . .There is nothing to indicate that the Japanese considered Ms. Earhart a foreign agent or spy, or that they ever held her prisoner. According to the records, their [Japan] interest in locating her plane stemmed from the same humanitarian impulses that inspired the other searchers."

The Japanese government continues to deny any knowledge of the Earhart disappearance. On December 15, 1986, Minoru Tamba, Consul General of the Consulate of Japan wrote:

> "With regard to your letter dated October 20, 1986 addressed to His Majesty the Emperor of Japan, your enquiry was referred to the Defense Agency. Unfortunately, as a result of extended research, we have concluded that no record has been fournd [sic] on Ms. Amelia Earhart nor on the Lockeheed [sic] 10 airplane, s/n NR16020 at the Agency."

Believing Amelia was lost, within a year of her disappearance, Judge Advocate General of the Navy wrote to GP in response to his letter of September 7, 1938:

> ". . . requesting an affidavit for use in establishing proof of death in the case of your wife, Amelia Earhart . . . inclosed herewith an affidavit made by Captain Leigh Noyes, U.S. Navy, who was the Commanding Officer of the U.S.S. LEXINGTON at all times during the period covered by the search . . . "

This was filed in probate court in 1938.

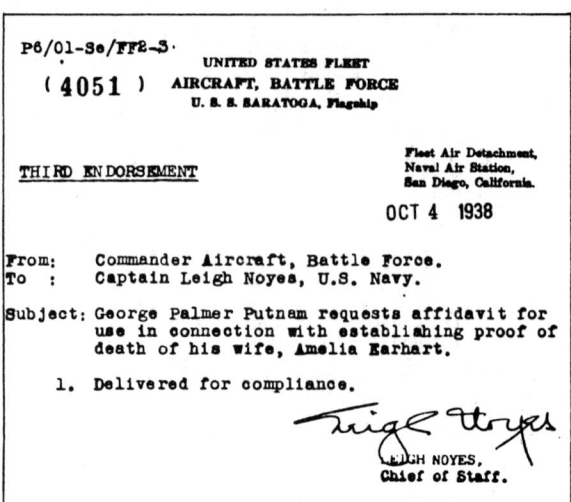

HISTORY NOT MYSTERY | 285

A page including Amelia's death from the Earhart family Bible.

Cover letter (facing page) and document GP submitted to probate to settle the estate.

Deaths.

Grace Otis, daughter of Alfred G. and Amelia Otis died September 3rd AD 1864

Harrison Gray Otis, Son of Alfred and Amelia Otis died July 14th AD 1867

Grace H. Otis wife of William Alfred Otis died June 2nd 1898

William Alfred Otis died [...]

Mrs Maria Harres mother of Amelia Otis born Aug 2nd 1797 died Sept 16th 1896 —

Mark Edwin Otis died April 16, 1917

Edwin Stanton Earhart September 22, 1930

Amelia Earhart Putnam lost at Sea about July 4-5-6-1937, in the Pacific.

Amy Otis Earhart on October 29, 1962, in West Medford. Rest in peace.

David Allayne Morrissey Dec 3, 1978 in Lynn

Henry Albert Morrissey May 20, 1979 at Veterans Hospital, Bedford, M[A]

State of California)
County of San Diego) ss.

Leigh Noyes of Coronado, California, being duly sworn, deposes and says, that he is a Captain in the U.S. Navy, and was the Commanding Officer of the U.S.S. LEXINGTON at all times during the period covered by the search conducted by the U.S. Navy for Amelia Earhart; that

The U.S.S. LEXINGTON, accompanied by the destroyers CUSHING, LAMSON and DRAYTON, said vessels composing the "LEXINGTON Group", sailed from LAHAINA ROADS, MAUI, TERRITORY OF HAWAII, for the HOWLAND ISLAND AREA at 5.15 p.m., July 9, 1937; that

On the morning of July 13, 1937, the LEXINGTON Group arrived at a point about one hundred (100) miles North of HOWLAND ISLAND and began the search; that the U.S.S. LEXINGTON had on board sixty-three (63) airplanes which were employed in this search; that the search conducted by the LEXINGTON Group was confined to the sea area; that on July 13, 1937, and the following day, the search was conducted to the Westward, and was continued in the sea area in which it was considered most probable that the lost Earhart plane would be found; that the search conducted by the LEXINGTON Group continued until July 18, 1937, on which date orders were received to discontinue the search; that

The statistics below indicate the extent of the air operations during the search period, July 13 to July 18, 1937, inclusive:

Area searched	151,556 square miles.
Miles flown	143,842 miles.
Plane hours in the air	1,591 hours; that

In addition to the search conducted by the LEXINGTON Group, the U.S.S. COLORADO, U.S.S. SWAN and the U.S.C.G. ITASCA also searched for the missing Earhart plane including islands of the PHOENIX and GILBERT groups; and that

No trace of either the Amelia Earhart plane or of its occupants was found.

                                                  Affiant.

LEIGH NOYES, Captain, U.S. Navy.

Subscribed and sworn to before me this fourth day of October, 1938.

CREDIT: U.S. NAVAL ARCHIVES

Court Asked to Declare Amelia Earhart Dead

LOS ANGELES, Oct. 19.—(UP)— A petition to have Amelia Earhart declared legally dead was on file in probate court today.

The woman flier's husband, George Palmer Putnam, asked for appointment as trustee of Miss Earhart's estate, which was listed as $25,000 worth of personal effects and real estate of unestimated value.

Putnam explained that his wife had communicated with him on each stop of her ill-fated world flight, but had failed to reach Howland island and was still missing despite an exhaustive search of the South Pacific.

Lost with Miss Earhart was Fred Noonan, navigator of her world flight. Their "flying laboratory" apparently fell into the Pacific last July.

CREDIT: SAN FRANCISCO CHRONICLE

Newspaper accounts of Amelia's being declared legally dead.

Amelia had every intention of returning after her flight. This is supported in a letter GP wrote to my mother, while settling Amelia's estate:

" . . . You see she spent all her money on aviation and on this last flight. You must realize that she expected, properly, to make a great deal of money out of the results of the flight after her return. For instance, she owned the ship entirely, which was worth $70,000 or more. Some of its purchase came from her and some from me, as well as the other larger contributors . . . "

GEORGE PALMER PUTNAM

10042 VALLEY SPRING LANE
NORTH HOLLYWOOD, CALIFORNIA
PHONE: STANLEY 7-1040

December 3, 1940

Dear Mother Earhart:

...... you had to say,
...... and cooperative you have been.
...... you would be.

On the finances there is just one understanding on your part which needs to be corrected. I dont know where it came from. Miss Berger has the impression you thought there was about $25,000 or more in cash in the Estate at the time of AE's disappearance. Actually the cash in the bank at that time was almost exactly $8000. There was owing from Paul Mantz a note for $5000 and that was just about all the cash. In addition, we thought the Estate owned a half interest in the property bought by AE jointly with Paul Mantz. $1500 went into that and the Estate's share should have been worth not less than $3000. However, as I have told you, Paul fought that and because AE had signed certain papers we had to settle for $500, although Paul understood perfectly that what he was doing was taking the money away from the Estate, which meant you. Technically I think there is no doubt he was within his rights, although the whole thing was a great puzzle to me. So Paul has paid into the Estate the $5000 covered by the note and the $500 as above.

The only stock that AE owned was one bond. You see she spent all her money on aviation and on this last flight. You must realize that she expected, properly, to make a great deal of money out of the results of the flight after her return. For instance, she owned the ship entirely, which was worth $70,000 or more. Some of its purchase came from her and some from me, as well as the other larger contributors. The outstanding debts totalled many thousands. We got some cancelled, and others we made settlements at considerable discount. Anyway, they all had to be paid or settled and they were.

It was nice of you to sugg---
sake you would come ba-----
work from ----

Affectionately,

G P P

Earhart Estate Trustee Plea Filed

Appointment as trustee of an estate of some $25,000 left by Amelia Earhart, aviatrix, who was lost near Howland Island in the South Seas while on a flight around the world, was requested yesterday by her husband, George Palmer Putnam, publisher.

The request was made in a petition filed in Superior Court, the document stating that the property consists mostly of securities and real estate. Putnam lives at 10042 Valley Springs Lane.

AMELIA EARHART NOW LEGALLY DEAD

LOS ANGELES, Jan. 5 (AP)— Amelia Earhart, noted woman flier who disappeared on a round-the-world flight in the summer of 1937, was declared legally dead today. The action was taken at the request of the flier's husband, George Palmer Putnam.

Putnam Is Sued

LOS ANGELES, March 6. (U.P.)— Paul Mantz, who was Amelia Earhart's technical adviser, Tuesday filed suit against George Putnam, seeking title to two parcels of property he said were given jointly to him and Miss Earhart when they were associated in business and which should revert to him at her death. Mr. Putnam is the executor of his late wife's estate.

GP's letter to Amelia's mother, explaining the financial situation following the disappearance of the Electra.

Captain Clarence S. Williams, known to Amelia as Commander Williams, served as navigator on board several destroyers, and acted as the head of the Navigation Department of the U.S. Navy Reserve Midshipmen's School, Northwestern University, Chicago. Between WWI and WWII Captain Williams taught air navigation, compensated airplane compasses and laid out the courses for many famous flyers, including Amelia.

In 1932 Captain Williams began a five-year consultation to Amelia, plotting two transcontinental record breaking courses—her Los Angeles to Mexico City to New York flight between April to May, 1935 and her Hawaiian flight to Oakland in January, 1935. He also prepared the charts and navigation data for Amelia's round-the-world flight. They were successful over other routes and there was no reason to suspect they should not have been on this flight too.

During an interview on April 23, 1984, with Harvey Christen, retired Lockheed executive, he mentioned his 1938 conversation about Amelia with a Pan American Clipper pilot. The pilot stated that Howland Island wasn't where it was suppose to be on the maps. Various reports in 1937 list different coordinates.

VARIOUS HOWLAND COORDINATES

	Latitude	Longitude
Commander Williams (AE flight plan)	0° 49′N	176° 43′W
USS Colorado report 13 July '37	0° 47′N	176° 43′W
USS Lexington report 20 July '37	0° 50′N	176° 41′W
The Times Index-Gazetteer of the World	0° 48′N	176° 38′W

One must realize that a minute (1/60 of one degree) is equivalent to one nautical mile, 6,076.1 feet. On July 2, 1937, the morning was clear, and according to the *Itasca* report, visibility was 20-40 miles, the *Itasca* was "smoking heavily," and the smoke hung for hours. Although it does not seem likely that the

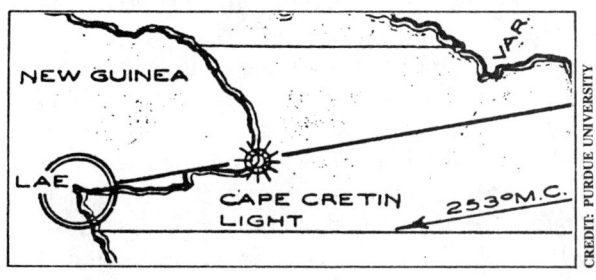

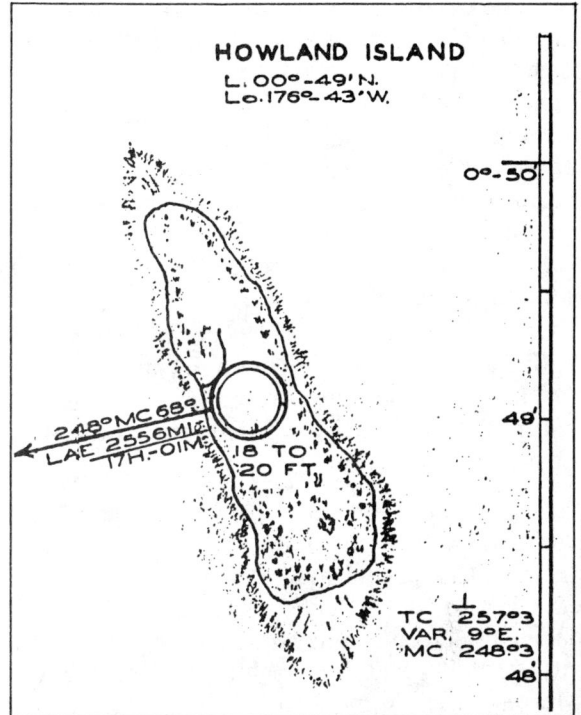

Howland Island logistics Amelia had when she planned her western flight.

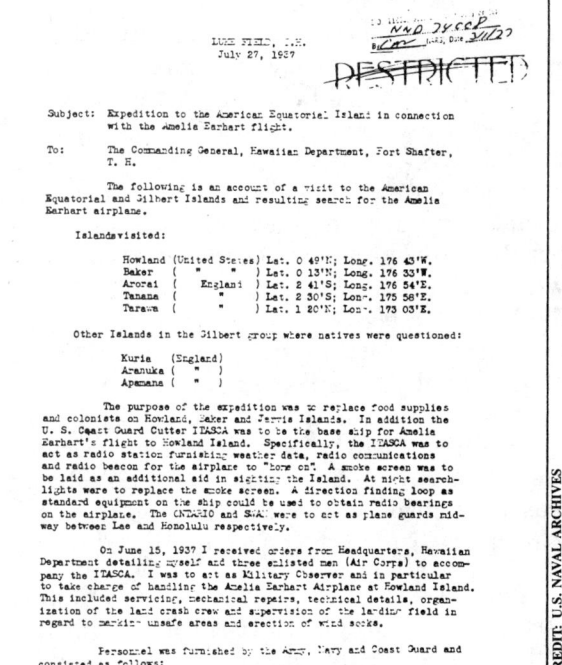

Luke Report gave one of various coordinates used for Howland Island.

five mile coordinate error was the major reason for Amelia's disappearance, it was perhaps one of the many factors which contributed to the flight's failure.

As many of the ships' logs and investigative reports indicate, Amelia's inability to communicate with the *Itasca* seems to emerge as a dominant causal factor in her disappearance. The following summary describes her radio equipment and its capabilities.

One of the significant aspects of Amelia's flight was her inability to communicate with the *Itasca*. The following summary will help describe the radio equipment and its capabilities.

Transmitter—Amelia had a Western Electric type 13C, 50 watt, three crystal controlled channels (500, 3105 and 6210 KCs) transmitter. The 500 KC frequency was unique and intended as an emergency transmitting channel only. She also had the capability of using CW (Morse code) or modulated CW (MCW). A CW key or a microphone could be plugged into a jack box which enabled Amelia to transmit in either CW or voice.

Receiver—Amelia had a Western Electric type 20B, four band, variable frequency receiver with 200 to 400 KCs, 550 to 1,500 KCs, 1,500 to 4,000 KCs and 4,000 to 10,000 KCs. The receiver was located in the cabin and above the gasoline tanks, and it was operated by a control box on the instrument panel. The control box consisted of a large dial with two frequencies on the top half and two on the bottom. There were four control knobs on the corners and several switches. The triangular pointer on the control box identified which of the receiving bands were in use.

Direction Finding (DF) Antenna—Amelia first had an RCA Loop-type RD2093D, but it was later changed to a Bendix loop DF. This was operated from the cockpit over her head.

Antenna—One "V" antenna was from a mast on top of the plane to each of the tail fins, and a similar one on the bottom of the plane. These were the high frequency antennas for the 3105 and 6210 KC frequencies. The 500 KC frequency required an antenna at least 250 feet long. That is one quarter of the 500 KC wave length and the minimum effective length. This antenna consisted of a 250 foot wire with a streamlined weight on the end. The wire was wound onto an electrically driven reel located in the tail of the airplane. The reel could be operated by a switch located in the cockpit.

R.D. "Bo" McKneely, a graduate electrical engineer and the one who traveled the first several thousand miles with Amelia and Fred, emphasized the tremendous confidence that they had in Noonan. Bo said Amelia " . . . sat in the left hand seat where all the important instruments on the panel are . . . "

Bo was Amelia's mechanic and rode as copilot with her. He mentioned, "I was with her when she got her Lockheed 10 [1936] and we made quite a few flights across the country shaking the airplane down and working on the autopilot . . . we made a few more flights across the country before we went to Miami where she jumped off for her around the world flight . . . We had built up a lot of confidence in the navigator [Noonan]. When we flew over the gulf, Noonan estimated the time we would have landfall and it fell almost to the second. He was doing that with just calculations, he didn't have any instruments . . . He was just calculating the distance including–and the winds that we got reporting on . . . "

In reference to the trailing antenna, Bo said, "I don't know why she would do that [remove the trailing antenna] because she had a transmitter on board that used that and it was a long range antenna . . . The only thing that comes to mind is an HT transmitter . . . "

Bo remembered, "She had a transmitter on board and a trailing antenna . . . it was in the tail of the airplane . . . I know she had, I can see the black box [perhaps a transceiver] right now. This was in the tail of the airplane . . . "

" . . . we were having trouble with the autopilot, going back and forth across the country . . . the Sperry people would work on it . . . when we flew to Miami, we went to Pan American. Pan American had autopilots in their fleet of flying boats. They came over, took the unit out of the airplane, brought it over to their hanger . . . and took a lot of equipment out of it. Pan American put it back in and tested it and

the darn thing worked better than at any other time."

Bo said Amelia was a "fine gal, I'm just sorry that that happened . . . the only thing I am sorry about is that I didn't go with her." It was never decided that Bo would go with them prior to the Miami take off but, " . . . I just feel that another pair of eyes would have been all they needed and I could have been up there controlling the fuel flow to the engines to get the most range out of the aircraft and probably gotten more time out of it . . . "

When Amelia left Miami for her round the world flight, she left a telegraph key and plug. Several people involved with the radio equipment believe that she also shortened or cut off the entire trailing antenna.

It is impossible to put an end to speculation about how Amelia's last flight actually ended. One can, however, reconstruct the last portion of the flight on the basis of Naval and other government documents.

- Paul Mantz once explained to Amelia how to ditch her Vega if needed, prior to the Hawaiian to Oakland flight.
- During Amelia's flight from Hawaii to California in 1935, she established a record as the first civilian to make a long-distance flight with a two-way radio telephone. Even at this time Amelia used only the radio telephone on frequencies 3105 KCS and 6210 KCS.
- Fred Noonan was a veteran Pan American Airways navigator. According to First Lieutenant Daniel A. Cooper, Air Corps, in the Luke Field, T.H. Report dated July 27, 1937, "HE INSTRUCTED ALL PAN AMERICAN AIRLINE NAVIGATORS ON THE TRANS PACIFIC RUN AND NAVIGATED ON ALL THE P.A.A. PIONEER TRIPS IN THE PACIFIC."
- The transmitter frequencies (preset frequencies) were crystal controlled.
- The plane had a Western Electric 4-Band 20B Type Receiver. The 4 bands covered a range of frequencies: 200–400, 550–1500, 1500–4000, 4000–10,000 kilocycles.
- The plane had a radio direction finder covering 200 to 1430 KCS with all wave receiver for telegraphy.
- All radio controls were available only to the pilot.
- Neither Amelia nor Fred Noonan were able to use CW/Morse Code effectively.
- Amelia left a CW Telegraph Key, Cord and Plug in Miami.

SUMMARY MATRIX OF AMELIA'S KNOWN RADIO TRANSMISSIONS

Time GMT	Time Local	Altitude	Radio Strength*	Action/Communication
0000	10:00 a	10 K		Departed Lae/Climbed
0500	3:00 p	10 K		Reported descent to 7K'
0720	5:20 p	7 K 740.7 n.m.		Reported position called the FIX
1030	8:30 p			"A Ship in sight ahead."
1418	2:48 a		S-1	"Cloudy and overcast" (very faint)
1515	3:45 a			"Overcast-Will Listen on Hour and Half Hour on 3105 . . ."
1623	4:53 a		S-1	"Partly Cloudy"
1742	6:12 a			"Will Whistle in Mic"
1745	6:15 a		S-3	"About two hundred Miles out . . ."
1816	6:46 a		S-4	". . . about 100 Miles Out . . ."
1912	7:42 a	1 K		". . . We Must Be On You, But Cannot not See You . . . Only 1/2 hour left . . . Altitude 1000 Feet."
1928	7:58 a		S-5	". . . 'We Are Circling But Cannot Hear You . . .' In view of signal strength, it is believed Earhart was closest to Howland." About now, Itasca expected her.
2014	8:44 a		S-5	"We Are On The Line Of Position 157-337 . . ."
2025	8:55 a		S-5	". . . Are Running North and South."

*S-1 = Very Faint   S-2 = Faint   S-3 = Fair   S-4 = Good
 S-5 = Very Loud

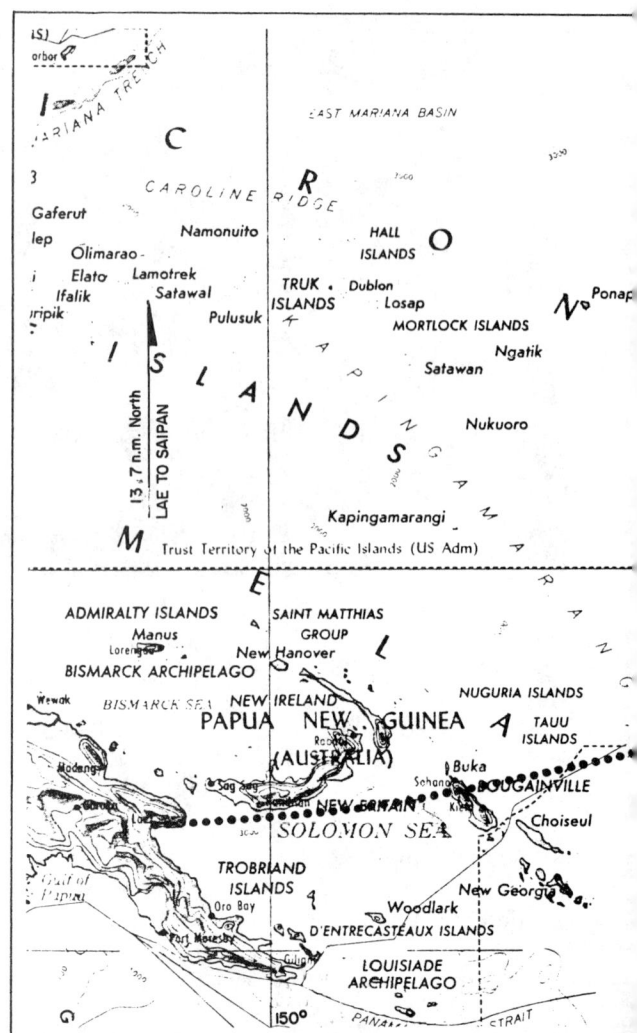

- Amelia carried 1,100 gallons of gasoline.
- Amelia's ideal fuel consumption would have been 45.53 gallons per hour (gph).
  - 1 hour at 100 gph
  - 3 hours at 60 gph
  - 3 hours at 51 gph
  - 3 hours at 43 gph
  - remainder at 38 gph
- Amelia's economical airspeed was 130 knots (150 mph).
- When Amelia crossed the Atlantic, she hit Africa 113 miles north of her objective.
- The last weather report given to Amelia before the flight:
  - Lae to Ontario wind ESE 12–15.
  - Ontario to longitude 175°, ENE 18.
  - Hence to Howland, winds ENE 15.
- Amelia left Lae, New Guinea, on the morning of July 2, 1937, at 10:00 a.m. local time (0000 GMT time).
- The plane's takeoff did not end at the end of the runway, it continued to sink to about five or six feet above the water and had not climbed to more than 100 feet before it disappeared from sight.
- Amelia contacted Lae, New Guinea, hourly from 10 a.m. until 6 p.m. local time. At each contact, position reports and height were transmitted. Her last position report [FIX] was latitude 4° 33.5'S, longitude 159° 7'E.
- GCT (GMT) sunrise, Howland, on July 2 was 1745.
- The morning of July 2, visibility to the southward was excellent and the *Itasca*'s smoke plume could have been seen 40 miles.

The Great Circle route of Amelia's flight.

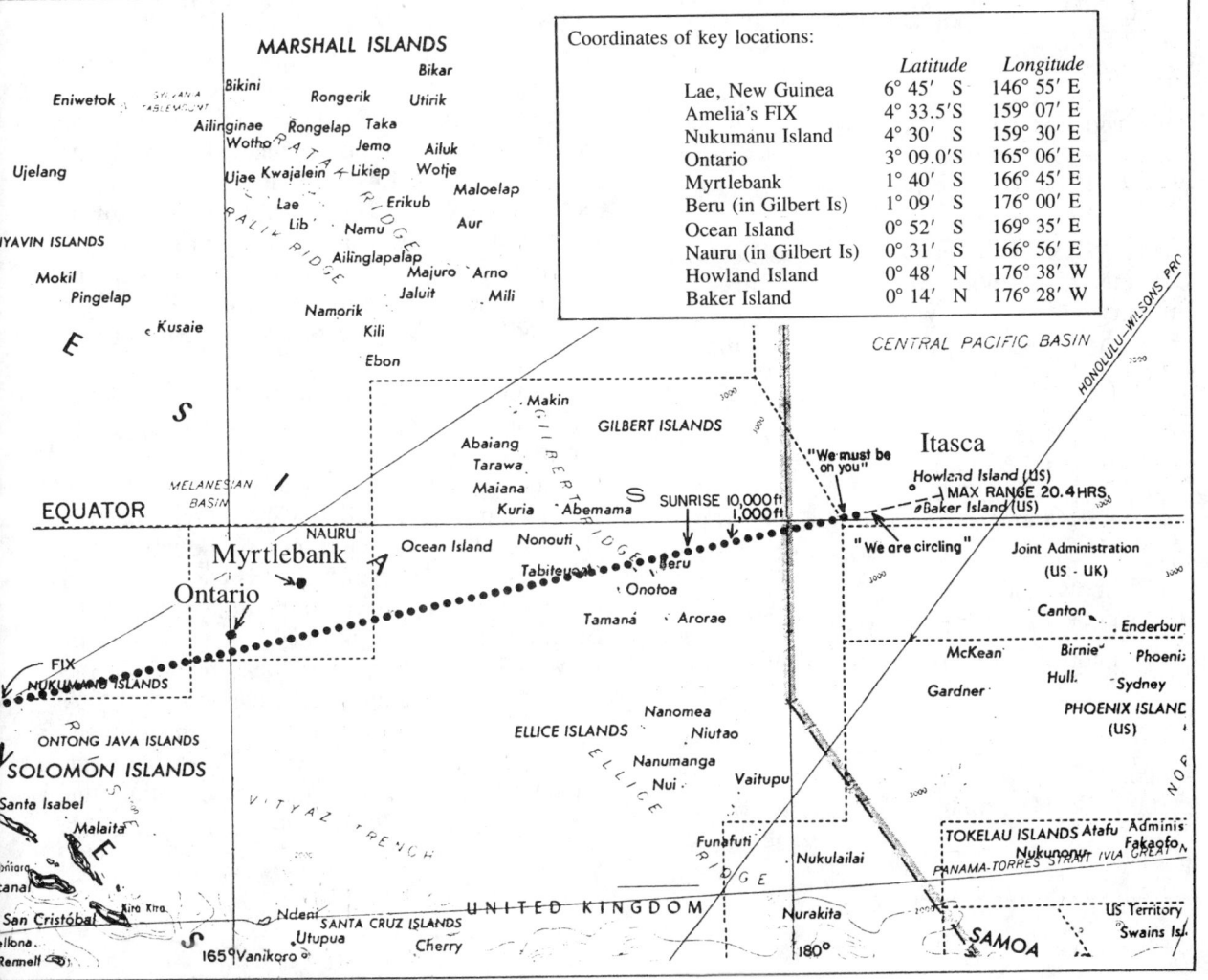

The following observations seem justified, based on the fore-going summary. Amelia had on board the maximum fuel load that she could carry. Although this caused some difficulty during her takeoff from Lae, it would have provided, barring unforeseen problems, the capacity to reach her intended destination. She had demonstrated her skill as a pilot on many occasions, and there is no reason to believe that her performance in handling the plane and in maintaining her course on this part of the flight was subpar.

Similarly, Fred Noonan had shown himself to be a superior navigator, skillful at both celestial navigation and dead reckoning. Furthermore, there is no evidence that suggests that Amelia and Fred had any intention other than to fly to Howland Island.

Amelia's last fix was reported at 5:20 p.m. Lae time, 7 hours, 20 minutes into flight {740.7 NAUTICAL MILES (NM) FROM LAE}

$$\frac{740.7 \text{ nm}}{7\text{hr. } 20 \text{ min.}} = 101 \text{ knots (116 mph) average ground speed}$$

Considering the fuel overload, the climb to 10,000 feet, and the 12–15 mph ESE headwind, the calculated 101 knot average ground speed is reasonable.

The "ship" must have been the *Ontario*. It was only 15 nm north of Amelia's course, and the ground speed was reasonable. The *Myrtlebank* was 84 nm north of Amelia's course.

$$\frac{364.1 \text{ nm}}{3.16 \text{ hr.}} = 115 \text{ knots ground speed from fix (132 mph) to } Ontario$$

$$\frac{466.0 \text{ nm}}{3.16 \text{ hr.}} = 147 \text{ knots ground speed from fix (169 mph) to } Myrtlebank$$

```
  115 knots ground speed
+  13 knots (15 mph) headwinds
  128 knots (147 mph) airspeed from fix
                     to Ontario

  147 knots ground speed
+  13 knots (15 mph) headwinds
  160 knots (184 mph) airspeed from fix
                     to Myrtlebank
```

Amelia would not fly at an airspeed greater than her economic airspeed, which was 150 mph (130 knots).

When Amelia gave her fix, she would have been 24 nm off the ideal course over a distance of 740 nm travelled. Considering the navigation techniques available at the time, that is, the absence of satellites and computers, this would be considered good navigation.

Amelia understood that locating Howland Island would be difficult, but she did not fully appreciate how difficult.

Unfortunately, it is now clear that Amelia did not understand adequately the operation of her radio. She wanted to talk on 3105 KCS and 6210 KCS. She did not understand the significance of the 500 KCS frequency, she cut off at least a major portion of the trailing antenna, if not all, thereby seriously degrading the radio's performance on 500 KCS. All ships including the *Itasca* and the *Ontario* were set up to communicate on 500 KCS, and even more important, their radio direction finders were limited to low frequencies. From the radio message strength of S-5, it is clear that she was in the area of Howland Island. Although one can ascertain her approximate location at the time she began to circle, it is impossible to determine exactly where the plane went down.

One must wonder at the apparent lack of position data on the plane toward the end of the flight. Amelia's time to the Fix was slower than she had expected. She reported, "We must be on you but cannot see you," an hour later than her anticipated flight plan of 18 hours. After flying an additional 16 minutes, she began to circle.

Amelia apparently was under clouds during at least part of the night but should have been in the clear during the latter part of the flight. The statement, "We should be on you..." would seem to be based more on the time of flight (19 hours) than on position, 124 nm west of Howland. The only navigational data from the plane was the statement, "Line 157–337." A line of position is one half the information necessary to determine position. A second line which crosses the first is required as a minimum for making this determination.

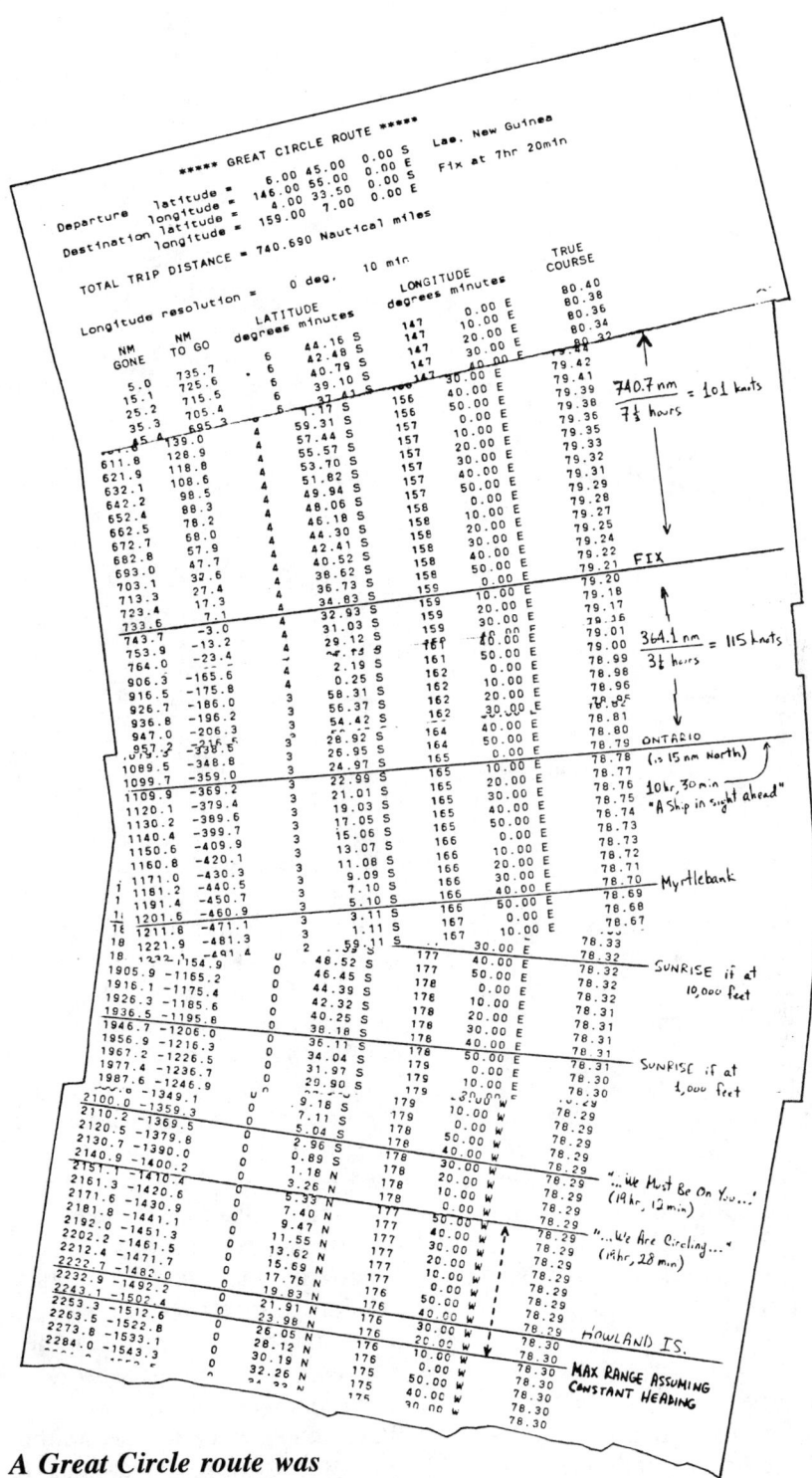

A Great Circle route was constructed between Lae and the Fix, utilizing a computer program provided by Paul Mennen. This line was extrapolated, based on the assumption that Amelia continued on course. After she began to circle, it is impossible to determine from the known facts, exactly where the plane went down.

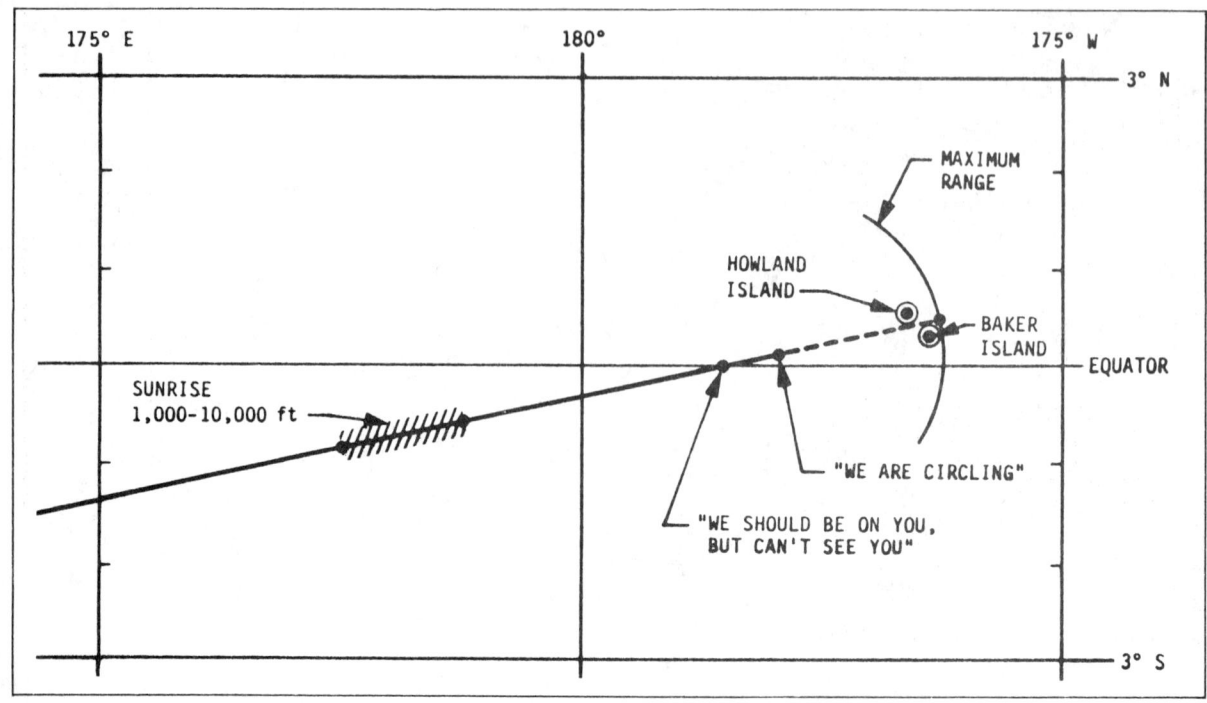

Computer analysis of the last leg of Amelia's flight.

There is no record of planned navigational fixes. The only record is the data provided by Clarence Williams for her planned flight from Howland to Lae, consisting of time and course only. Fred Noonan must have had a course planned but one fan only speculate as to what it might have been.

According to the calculations, Amelia began to circle about 85 nm west of Howland. She continued to fly for another 57 minutes. If she had continued on course at the ground speed of 115 knots, she could have continued for another 109 nm. Her Great Circle course would have taken her 28 nm south of Howland Island and only 8 nm north of Baker Islands.

From the radio message strength given in the *Itasca* log, S-5, it is clear that Amelia was in the area of Howland Island.

One must bear in mind that ditching an airplane is a dangerous maneuver. The difficulty is in flairing out at the proper altitude. If the plane is flared too high, it will stall and fall into the ocean. The probability of misjudging altitude is great if the surface of the ocean is smooth and even greater if the pilot is under stress.

There is no basis for faulting the performance of the Coast Guard support vessel. Commander Thompson, Captain of the *Itasca*, and his crew handled their assignment in an exemplary fashion.

On the basis of the information available at the present time, it is impossible to say with certainty what happened to Amelia, Fred and the Electra. The area in which they appeared is vast and the Pacific Ocean extremely deep. Perhaps someday, as a result of technological advances in underwater exploration, it may be possible to locate and recover the plane, but for now, its resting place and the exact circumstances of its disappearance remain a mystery.

We like to have our mysteries solved; I wish that I could produce an unimpeachable solution. But I believe that at this point, no one can. It seems to me most likely that Commander Thompson's conjecture is correct, and that Amelia's plane was submerged within minutes after her last radio message and probably within one hundred miles of Howland Island.

HOWLAND I. TO LAE						
2556 MI. 17H-01M.						
NO.	TIME ON CRSE.	TIME TO CHGE.	TIME TO GO AT ST.	TOTAL TIME AT ST.	DIST. ON CRSE.	MAG. CRSE
1	:22	00:00	17:01	00:00	56	248°
2	1:11	00:22	16:39	00:22	177	248°
3	1:11	1:33	15:28	1:33	177	248°
4	1:11	2:44	14:17	2:44	177	248°
5	1:11	3:55	13:06	3:55	177	249°
6	1:11	5:06	11:55	5:06	177	249°
7	1:10	6:17	10:44	6:17	176	250°
8	1:10	7:27	9:34	7:27	176	250°
9	1:10	8:37	8:24	8:37	176	250°
10	1:10	9:47	7:14	9:47	176	251°
11	1:10	10:57	6:04	10:57	176	251°
12	1:10	12:07	4:54	12:07	175	251°
13	1:10	13:17	3:44	13:17	175	252°
14	1:10	14:27	2:34	14:27	175	253°
15	1:24	15:37	1:24	15:37	210	253°
1	17:01	TOTALS			2556	

FLIGHT DATA BY Clarence S. Williams
CONSULTANT IN NAVIGATION
LOS ANGELES, CALIFORNIA

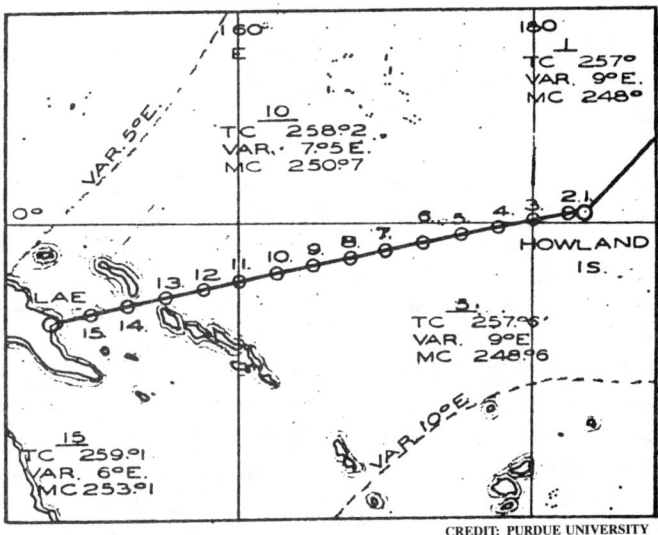

CREDIT: PURDUE UNIVERSITY

CREDIT: PURDUE UNIVERSITY

Commander Williams calculation for the original westbound flight using a speed of 150 mph, and NO wind. Amelia would be using the reciprocals for her Lae to Howland flight.

CREDIT: F.O. "FUZZ" FURMAN

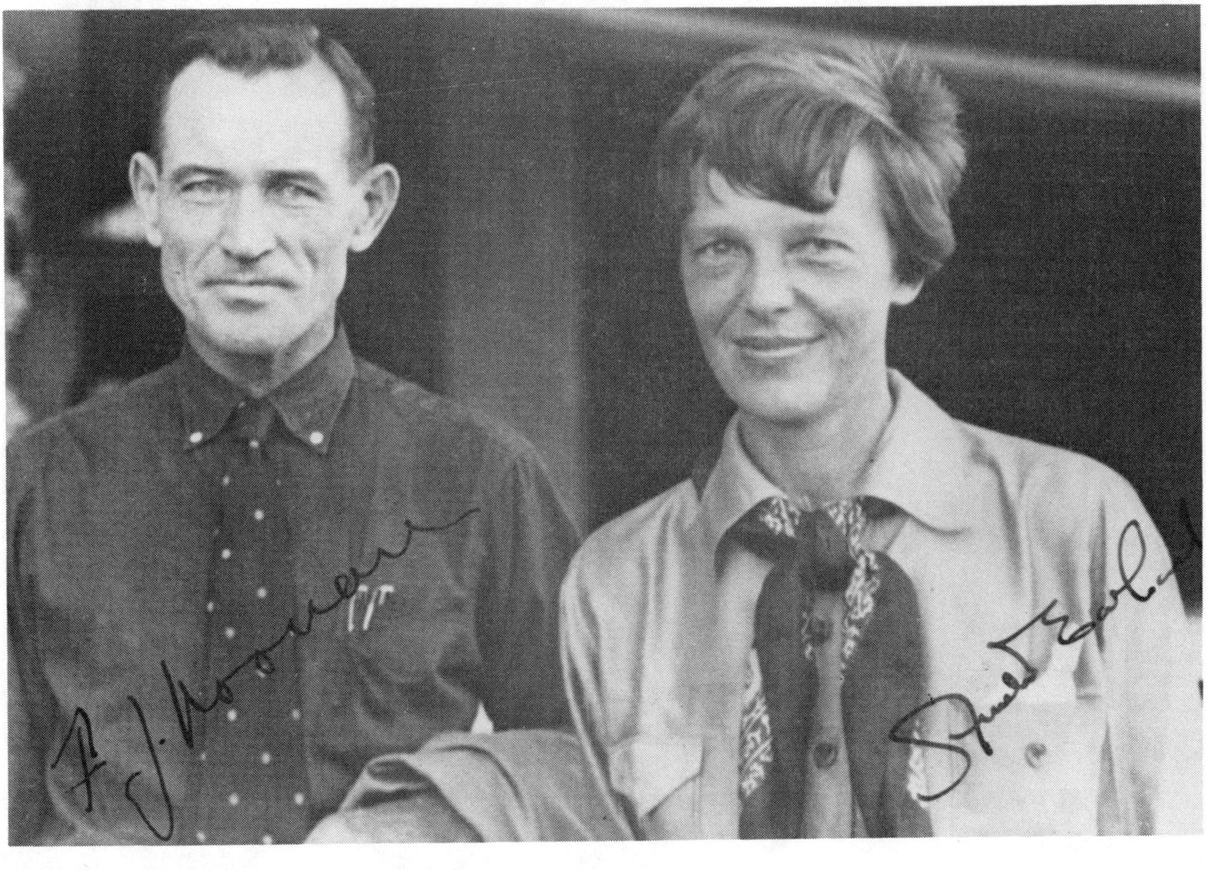

The *Navy Times* reporter Macon Reed wrote that he did not consider the ending altogether unhappy. "For," he said, "agreement upon a set of procedures for future emergencies was worked out. For example, it was determined that in the future air-sea rescue cases, all dates should be given in Greenwich Mean Time. And gradually the mistakes of this flight and the search have become the basis of improved techniques that have saved many lives since then and are still evolving more effective measures. Amelia Earhart flew to advance the interests of aviation. That was her mission. She may not have accomplished what she set out to do in this last flight, but advance aviation she did."

The manner of Amelia's death is not of great importance to me now. That she did not live to have a child of her own and to enjoy the honors she had earned is sad. She escaped what she dreaded, the advancing years, demanding that she relinquish her vital activities and inevitably bow to physical disabilities. Amelia lived life each day from the time she slid down the slippery home-made roller coaster as a pig-tailed bundle of energy to the day in July, 1937, when she climbed aboard her beloved Electra in Lae, well knowing the hazards, but resolutely facing the odds and playing for greater stakes than ever before.

Many tributes in prose and poetry have come to Amelia during the past fifty years. There are countless memorials, from the simple plaque in front of our house in West Medford and the plaque on the old homestead in Atchison to the enduring annual scholarships given by Zonta International and the Ninety-Nines. The inspiration that her life and courage gave to many of us who are earth-bound can never be measured.

"We need to know such deeds of useless courage . . ." said one writer.

"Your blithe spirit lives forever!" sang a poet.

"However she came down," declared the practical Navy man who reported the Itasca's frustrating hours of searching the waters around Howland Island, "Amelia was not a failure."

> Please know I am quite aware of the hazards. I want to do it because I want to do it. Women must try to do things as men have tried. When they fail, their failure must be but a challenge to others.

Appendix

RECORD FLIGHTS

1922, October: Altitude Record at the Los Angeles meet.

1928, June 17–18: First woman to fly the Atlantic as a passenger; pilot Wilmer Stultz and mechanic Lou Gordon flew the Friendship from Trepassey, Newfoundland, to Burryport, Wales, 20 hours, 40 minutes.

1929, August 18–22: Third place in the first Women's Transcontinental Air Derby race from Santa Monica to Cleveland, Ohio.

1930, July 6: Women's speed record; three-kilometer course; at 181.18 mph.

1931, April 8: Pitcairn autogiro World's altitude record at 18,451 feet.

1932, May 20–21: First woman to fly solo across the Atlantic; from Harbor Grace, Newfoundland, to Londonderry, Ireland, 14 hours, 56 minutes.

1932, August 24–25: Women's non-stop transcontinental speed record from Los Angeles, California to Newark, New Jersey; 2,447.8 miles; 19 hours, 5 minutes.

1933, July 7–8: Broke her own transcontinental speed record of the year from Los Angeles, California, to Newark, New Jersey: 17 hours, 7 minutes, 30 seconds.

1935, January 11–12: First person to fly solo from Honolulu to Oakland, California; 2,408 miles; 17 hours, 7 minutes.

1935, April 19–20: First person to fly solo from Los Angeles, California to Mexico City, Mexico; 13 hours, 23 minutes.

1935, May 8: Solo flight from Mexico City to Newark, New Jersey, 14 hours, 19 minutes.

1937, March 17–18: Flight from Oakland, California to Honolulu, Hawaii; 15 hours, 43 minutes.

1937, July 2: Record flight around the world at the equator before disappearing with her navigator Fred J. Noonan; covered a distance of 22,000 miles.

CITATIONS, MEMBERSHIPS, AWARDS, GIFTS

Much as Amelia appreciated the medals, scrolls, awards, and honorary membership cards which came to her in ever-increasing numbers after 1932, she steadfastly refused to have them on display in either her New York or her California home. I append this list, "not in boastful guise," but because I feel this record is part of Amelia's story—the tangible recognition of her achievements, given to her with sincere affection and esteem, and accepted with humility and pleasure.

Medal from the City of Philadelphia dated October 5, 1932 and Honorary Membership in Poor Richard's Club of that city

Medal of Honor of 1932, from the City of Chicago, Illinois

Medal from the American Society of Mechanical Engineers

Medal from the Breakfast Club of the City of Glendale, California

Silver wings and scroll giving rank of Honorary Major of 381st Observation Squadron, United States Army Reserve

The Lindbergh Medal from the Wings Club of New York, New York

Mayor's medal from the City of New York, New York

Distinguished Flying Cross with miniature lapel bar, awarded by the Congress of the United States, Washington, D. C.

Harmon Trophy of 1937, shared with Jean Batten of Melbourne, Australia

Gold medal and citation from the National Geographic Society, Washington, D. C., 1932

Achievement trophy from the Zonta International Club of New York, New York

Medal of Valor and Achievement and Scroll from the Society of Women Geographers, New York, New York, May 21, 1932

Certificate of Honorary Membership from the International Shrine of Birdmen of Mission Inn, Riverside, California

Gimbel Award as the "Most Outstanding Woman of America in 1932"

Honorary Degree of Doctor of Science from Thiel College, Greenville, Pennsylvania

Honorary Degree of Doctor of Public Service from Oglethorpe University, Atlanta, Georgia

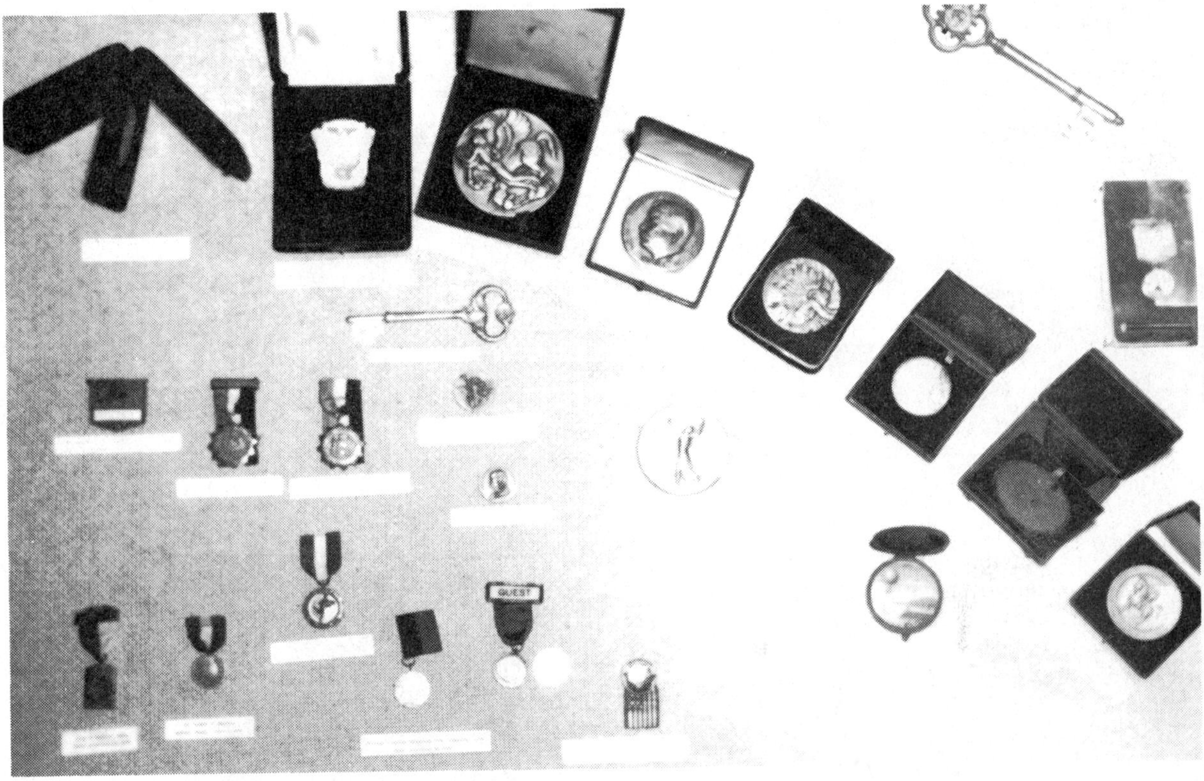

CREDIT: CLAUDIA OAKES, SMITHSONIAN INSTITUTION

Citation and license as a one-trip Airmail pilot for the United States Post Office Department on the flight from Los Angeles to Mexico City

Gold Medal, gift of Sra. Aida S. de Rodriguez, wife of the ex-president, and presented in behalf of the international council of the union of American women, April 1935

Platinum Medal from Sra. Amalia S. de Cárdenas, Mexico's first lady of the land, April 20, 1935

Gold medal by the Mexican Society of Geography and Statistics

Medal from the Lafayette Flying Corps of France

Citation from the French Aero Club

Jeanne d'Arc Medal from Le Lyceum-Societé des Femmes de France a New York, May 20–21, 1932

Decoration Medal from the Kingdom of Rumania, 1930

The Ninety-Nines, Inc. Annual Amelia Earhart Scholarship for women students in any branch of aeronautics.

The Zonta International Annual Amelia Earhart Memorial Scholarship for women graduate students in the field of aeronautical science.

Annual Amelia Earhart Memorial Award presented to a graduate of the United States Air Force Academy for excellence in the social sciences.

CREDIT: WORLD WIDE PHOTOS

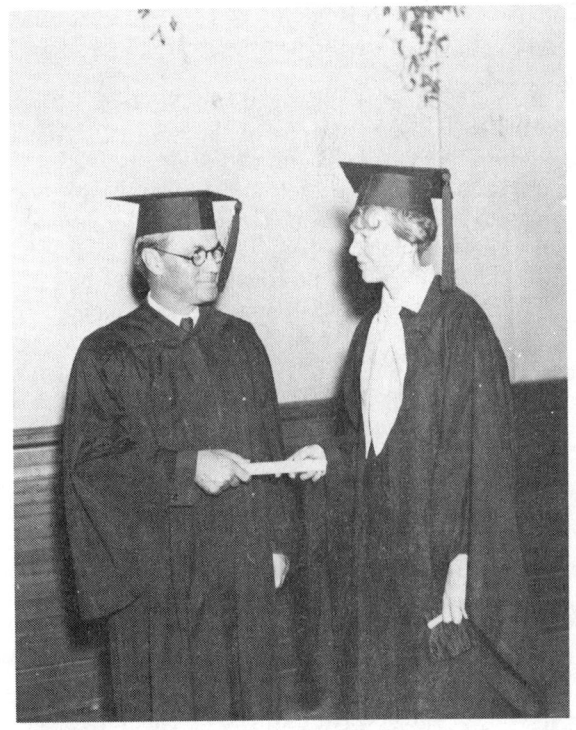

Amelia receives an honorary Doctorate from Oglethorpe University.

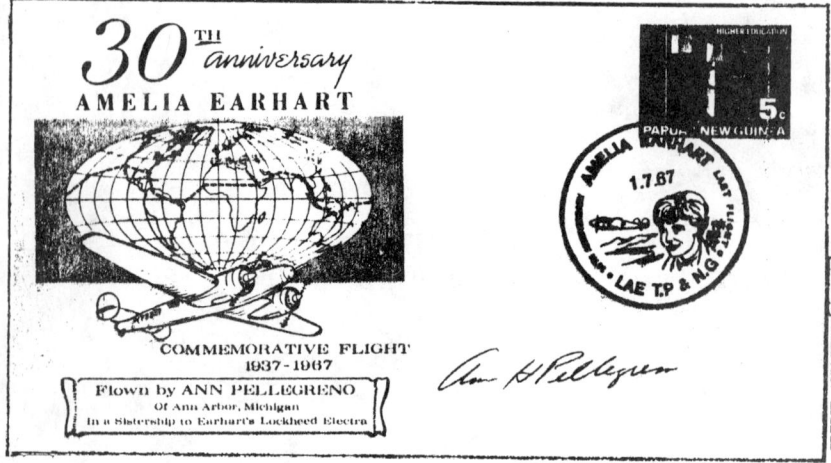

A first day cover from Ann Pellegreno's round-the-world flight.

- Ministry of Communications ordered 780 air-mail postage stamps of issue of December 1, 1934 (0.20 centavos denomination) be countermarked "Vuelo de Amelia Earhart, Mexico, 1935"
- Amelia Earhart Award for Civil Air Patrol Leadership, USAF Auxiliary, Ellington Air Force Base, Texas.
- The Amelia Earhart Elementary School of Alameda, California.
- The Amelia Earhart Hotel for Women under the auspices of the United States Air Force in Wiesbaden, Germany.
- A memorial marker placed on the grounds of the Atchison, Kansas, Airport by the Area VII, Zonta Clubs. Also a museum of mementoes and a bronze plaque in the Atchison Public Library, and a memorial marker on the former Otis homestead, Amelia's birthplace.
- A flashing beacon light on Howland Island, the Earhart Memorial Light. (Bombed December 18, 1941, but now restored.)
- An exhibit of medals, pictures, and books in the National Air and Space Museum, Smithsonian Institution, Washington D. C.
- Earhart and Otis family documents and photographs, mementoes and writings in the Women's Archives of Schlesinger Library, Radcliffe College, Cambridge, Massachusetts.
- An exhibit of medals in the library of Purdue University, Lafayette, Indiana.
- A memorial plaque given by the Fraternal Order of Airmail Pilots in Miami, Florida, International Airport.
- A memorial plaque on the hangar and jet repair facility given by Northeast Air Lines at Logan International Airport, Boston, Massachusetts.

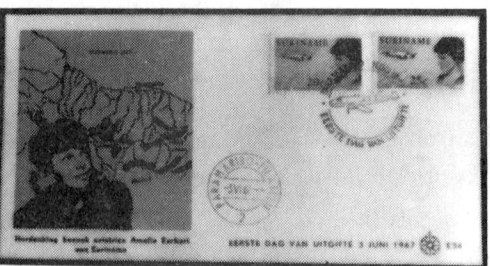

AMELIA EARHART, transatlantic flyer, with new dahlia named in her honor. — *Photo by Dick Whittington.*

DAHLIA HONORS MISS EARHART

Honoring America's great transatlantic woman flyer, Amelia Earhart Putnam, a new giant peach-colored dahlia, one of the most outstanding of the early season blooms, has been named Amelia Earhart.

The flower has been perfected by J F Cordes of Santa Monica, and will be presented to the public for the first time at the Los Angeles thirteenth annual Dahlia Show, to be held in the Biltmore Hotel September 1 and 2.

"This is the first thing ever named for me," Miss Earhart said as she granted the use of her name for the beautiful flower.

Ann Pellegreno, in her Lockheed Model 10 Electra, recreated Amelia's flight on the thirtieth anniversary.

A memorial painting donated by the Zonta Club of Washington, D. C., in the meeting rooms of the Y.W.C.A. Building.

A granite pillar commemorating the Friendship landing, given by the citizens of Burryport, Wales.

A hybrid yellow rose and a giant buff dahlia named for Amelia.

A Commemorative Airmail stamp issued by the United States Post Office, July 24, 1963.

A memorial plaque on a rock on Diamond Head, Hawaii, placed there by a group of her Hawaiian friends in 1940.

A golden hybrid iris.

A mountain peak in the Yosemite National Park, named by the Rocketdyne Mountaineering Club.

A tidewater dam across the Mystic River at Somerville, Massachusetts, constructed by the Metropolitan District Commission of Massachusetts.

Amelia Earhart Airport, Atchison, Kansas, the only airport in the United States named after Amelia.

Bronze statue of Amelia in the International Forest of Friendship Atchison, Kansas.

Bronze statue by Ernest Shelton in North Hollywood Park, North Hollywood, California.

Song, "Amelia Earhart's Last Flight" by Dave McEnery, written in 1939.

Amy Earhart and Dr. Paul Garber of the Smithsonian Institution at ceremonies for Amelia in 1946.

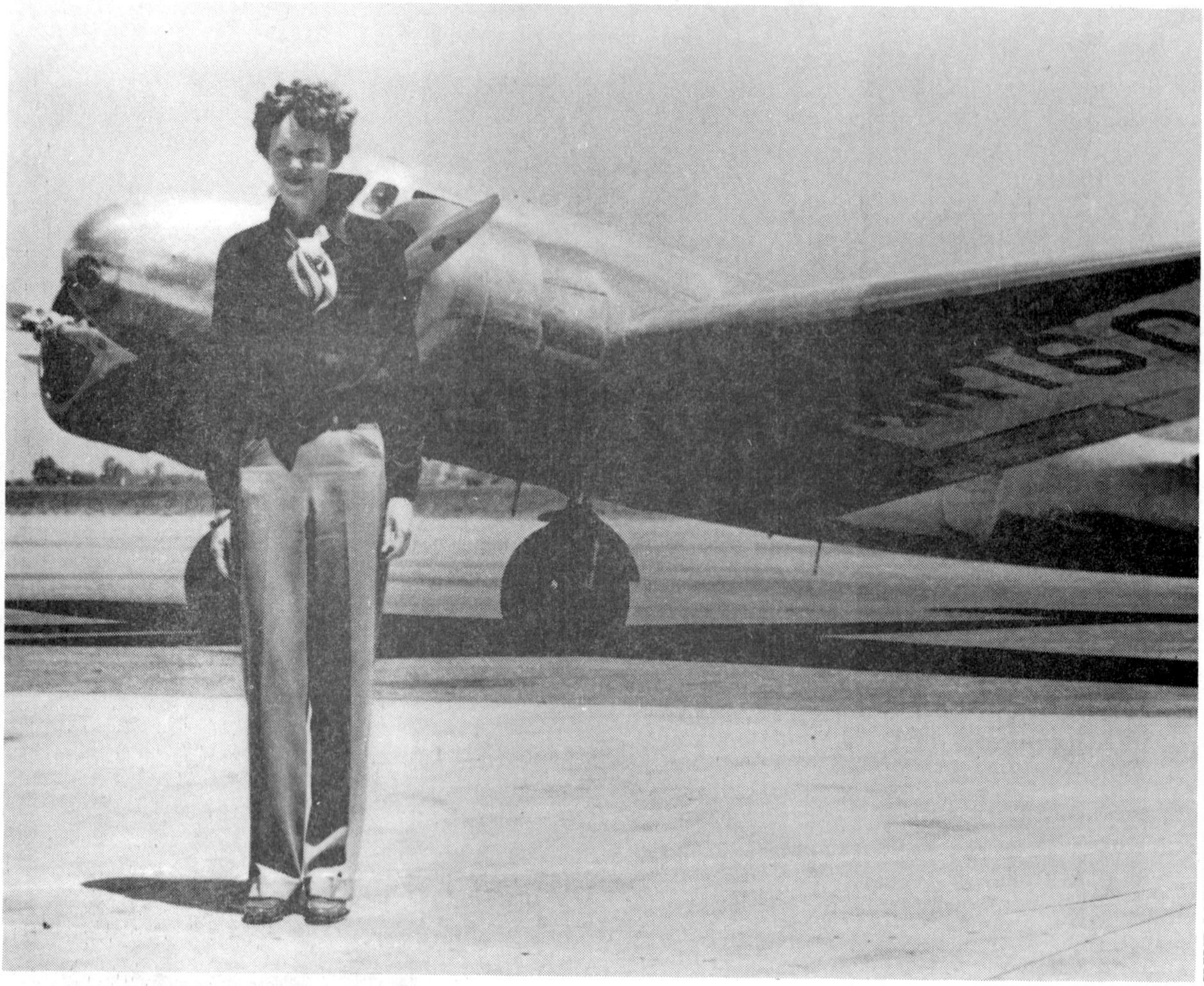

CREDIT: LOCKHEED-CALIFORNIA COMPANY

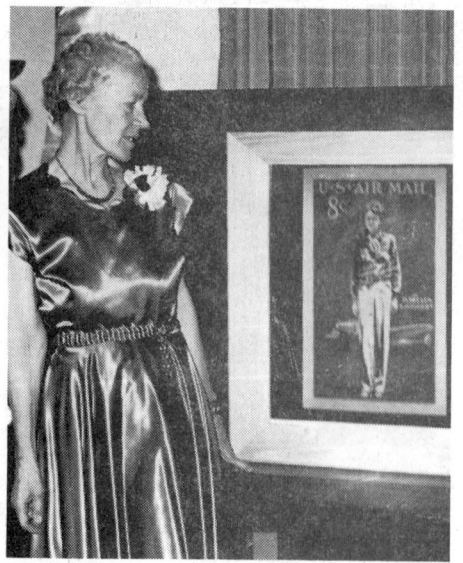

To A.E.

Earthbound, we watched, enthralled,
As unafraid you climbed the cloud strewn sky
Your flight a symbol of that great heart
That dared apathy and prejudice defy.
"Own your soul!" your voice rings clear.
So gaily began your last long flight
Circling the globe Electra's gallant crew
Through wind and fog missed finding Howland's light
For me, A. E., you'll never die
The world, fleetingly, became less sad and drear
For the courage and concern we saw
In your brief, joyous sojourn here.

Muriel Morrissey

Helped Build Howland Island's Lighthouse Dedicated To Amelia

Reading an article about Atchison's Bicentennial celebration program in the dedication of the International Forest of Friendship at Warnock Lake on July 22, 23 and 24, Samuel K. Kahalewai, Hutchinson, recalled an incident in which he was involved after Amelia Earhart vanished in the Pacific ocean during a flight around the world.

It was in relation with the building of a lighthouse on Howland Island, which was Amelia's destination when she and her navigator, Fred Noonan disappeared 39 years ago today.

Here is a letter in explanation of Kahalewai's interest in the Atchison event that was received by Joe Carrigan, general chairman of the Atchison American Revolution Bicentennial Committee, which was accompanied by the picture of the Howland Island lighthouse (incidentally the letter was addressed to Joe Kerrigan):

Dear Mr. Kerrigan:

I read an article and thought I can do my little part for a gallant lady, whom we were close to and dearly loved. I was only a teenager when I volunteered as a colonist in living on the equatorial islands so I became a member of the 13th expedition to the line islands, sailing from Honolulu on July 8, 1938. I was a replacement for one of the members on Howland island and our first duty was to complete the lighthouse, dedicated to Amelia Earhart. Fortunately, I had my little Argus camera with me and upon completion and painting of the lighthouse, I snapped this picture which would make it 38 years a few weeks from today.

While living on Howland island, it was always our duty to take surface observations in the hopes that they may still be alive or parts of the plane. Our hopes ran high one day when we sighted something afloat right off the northern shore so all four of us swam out but the sharks were too numerous and dangerous, even in 15 feet of water, that we abandoned the thought. It was just a huge log that was adrift for many years

THIS IS THE picture of the Howland Island Lighthouse built in 1938 and dedicated to Amelia Earhart. The accompanying story explains its origin and how Samuel K. Kahalewai, Hutchinson, forwarded it to Joe Carrigan, general chairman of the Atchison American Revolution Bicentennial Committee, after having read an article concerning the International Forest of Friendship.

CREDIT: SAM KAHALEWAI

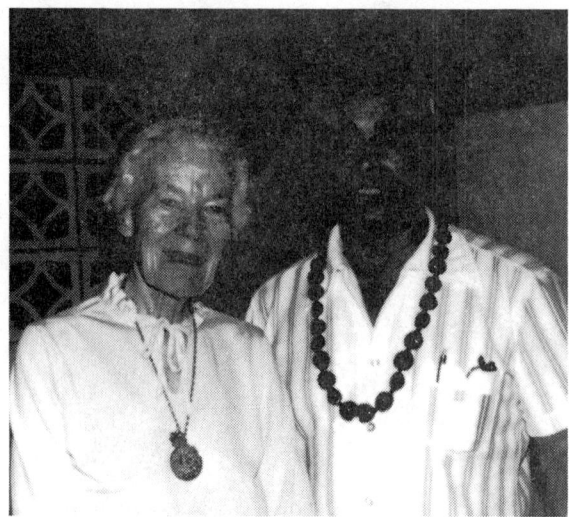

Muriel and Sam in Atchison, Kansas, at the Forest of Friendship celebrations, July 22, 1983.

TO: MURIEL EARHART MORRISSEY:

THIS PHOTO WAS TAKEN ON SEPTEMBER 22, 1938, RIGHT AFTER THE FINISHING TOUCHES THAT COMPLETED THE LIGHT HOUSE.

I WAS A MEMBER OF THE 13th CRUISE TO THE EQUATORIAL OR LINE ISLANDS, LEAVING HONOLULU ON JULY 18, 1938 AND ARRIVING AT HOWLAND ISLAND ON JULY 21, 1938.

I WAS A MEMBER AND RESIDENT OF HOWLAND ISLAND FOR FIVE MONTHS BEFORE BEING REMOVED AND RELOCATED ON CANTON ISLAND (Phoenix group).

I SPENT TWO YEARS IN THIS AREA BEFORE BEING RELIEVED OF MY DUTIES AND MY EMPLOYMENT WITH THE U.S. DEPT. OF INTERIOR WAS TERMINATED SO THAT WE CAN REGISTER FOR THE DRAFT OR JOIN ANY BRANCH OF THE ARMED SERVICES.

IT IS WITH ESTEEM PLEASURE, PRIVILEGE AND HONOR THAT I GIVE THIS PHOTO TO YOU, SISTER OF AMELIA EARHART WHOM THIS LIGHTHOUSE WAS DEDICATED TO AND WITH MY WARMEST REGARDS. Aloha Sam

The corner stone was laid on Nov. 16, 1937 with impressive ceremonies. In attendance was Dr. Ernest Gruening, director of terriotiral and island possessions, U.S Dept. of Interior, and son Peter, Mr. Richard B. Black, Mr. Warner and the staff from the USCG Cutter Roger B. Taney.

Samuel K. Kahalewai

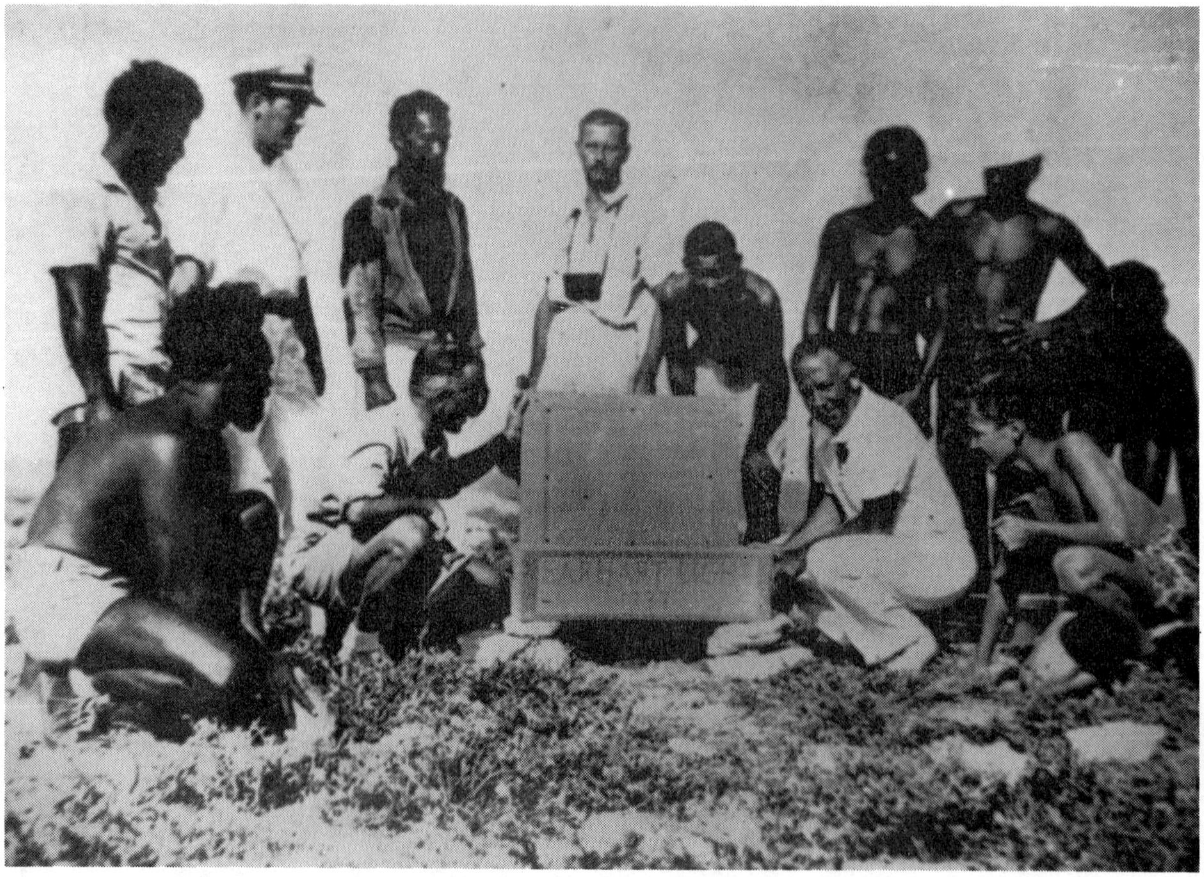

CREDIT: SAM KAHALEWAI

CREDIT: SAM KAHALEWAI

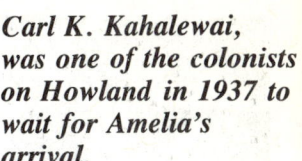

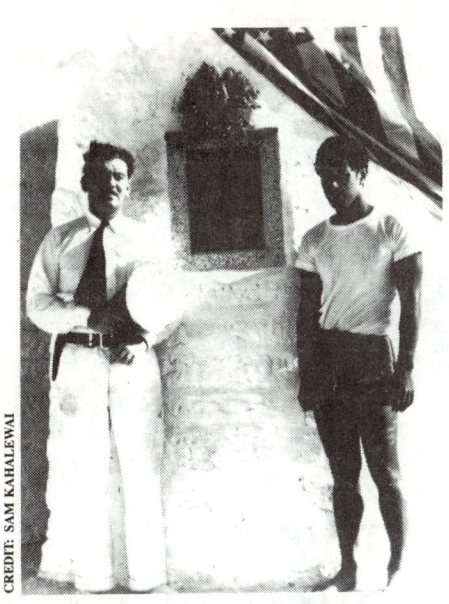

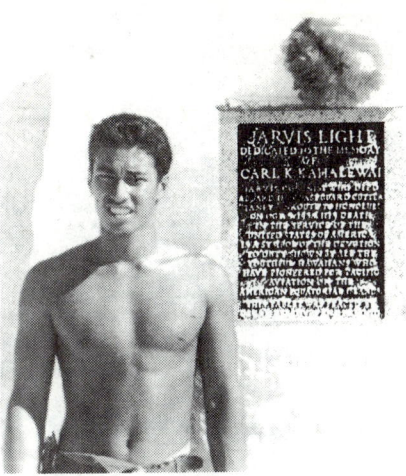

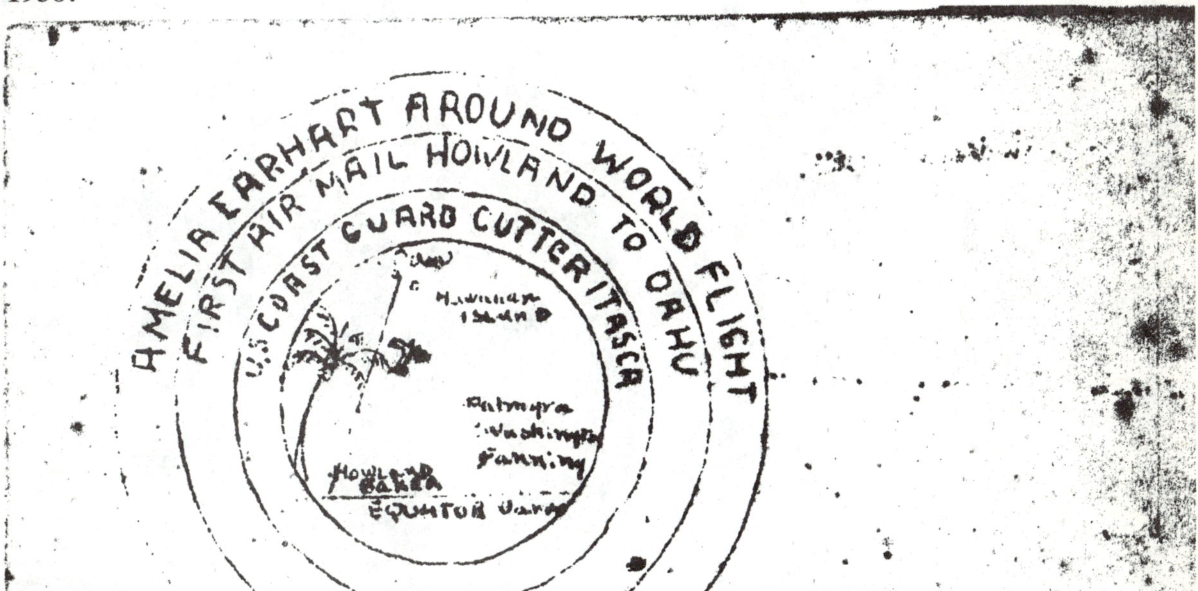

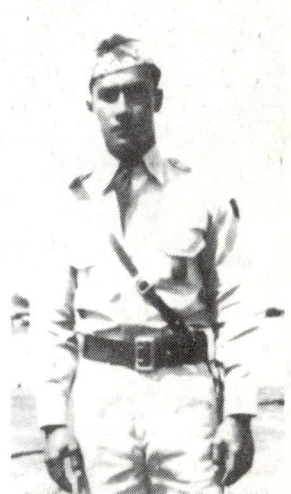

Richard Black and Sam Kahalewai, dedicating the light house on Jarvis Island to Sam's brother, Carl, in 1938.

Sam at the dedication plaque to his brother, Carl.

Carl K. Kahalewai, was one of the colonists on Howland in 1937 to wait for Amelia's arrival.

CREDIT: SAM KAHALEWAI

These first day covers were to have been picked up by Amelia and flown to Hawaii. The crew on Howland Island had made many preparations for Amelia and Fred's arrival.

September 17, 1938. THE ATCHISON DAILY GLOBE

ONE MORE CHAPTER
in the TRAGIC STORY
of MISSING FLYERS

By Charles J. Bauer

THE old-time sailors were superstitious. They had many salt-rimed sayings and one that held good pretty often was, "A ship with a woman ain't got no luck."

Twelve women have started out on airplane flights across the Atlantic and Pacific oceans. Seven of those women are missing.

Last of the seven and most famous of them all is Amelia Earhart, whose record in the air is equaled by few men pilots. She was the first woman to fly the Atlantic, first woman to fly that ocean non-stop, the first to fly from Hawaii to the United States, the first woman to make a non-stop flight across the United States.

What is Amelia Earhart's fate?

U. S. Naval and Coast Guard officers who led the far-flung search for her believe that the odds against her being alive are tremendous. Yet there is a remote chance that the plucky woman flyer is leading a fairy tale existence on some uncharted Pacific island, hoping that some lucky day she and her navigator, Fred Noonan, will be found.

Six other women met misadventure on trans-oceanic flights.

Soon after Lindbergh's epochal Paris flight in 1927, Mildred Doran, a school teacher, was lost over the Pacific. With J. A. Pedlar and V. R. Knope, Miss Doran was competing in the Dole prize race from Oakland, Calif., to Hawaii. Engine trouble forced their ship to return to Oakland. Repairs were made and the plane rose again, headed out over the Golden Gate and was heard from no more.

Christmas Eve, 1927, Mrs. Frances Grayson left Newfoundland with Lieut. Oskar Omdal, F. Koeler and Brice Goldborough on an attempted flight to Europe. They still are unaccounted for.

That same month a European princess disappeared on a flight from England to Canada. She was Princess Loewenstein-Wertheim and with her were Capt. Leslie Hamilton and Col. Frederick Minchin.

It was over a similar route that Elsie Mackay and Capt. W. G. R. Hinchcliffe were lost the following March.

The other two women lost on ocean flights were Beryl Hart and Edna Newcomer.

Miss Hart and Lieut. W. W. MacLaren vanished in January, 1931, on a flight from Bermuda to the Azores.

Rome was the destination of Miss Newcomer and Dr. L. M. Pisculli, but nothing was heard from them after they left America.

Two other women, Ruth Elder and Lilli Dillentz, were rescued with their crew after being forced down on the Atlantic in an attempted flight to Paris. Miss Elder is one of America's better known woman flyers and Miss Dillentz is one of Germany's better known actresses.

PAUL REDFERN is the central figure in the many recurring legends of a white man who exerts kingly rule over a tribe of savage Indians in an unexplored part of South America.

Three months after Lindbergh's flight, Redfern, who then was a young man, took off from Brunswick, Ga., in a land plane. Rio de Janeiro, 4300 miles distant, was the goal of his non-stop flight. His route lay over the Caribbean Sea and the jungles and mountains along the east coast of South America.

Last sighted by a ship several hundred miles north of the South American mainland, Redfern never was heard of again, except in the aforementioned legends. Rescue parties sought him as recently as last year, confident that he was forced down in Brazil, and that he still lives.

Less hope is held for the celebrated French aviators, Charles Nungesser and Francois Coli. After a decade of silence the wartime ace Nungesser and his companion are believed dead. It was May 8, 1927, when their "White Bird" was escorted over the Seine basin, and headed out into the mists of the Atlantic with New York the destination.

Last December, Jean Mermoz, ofttime conqueror of the South Pacific, tried to fly his French plane to South America once more. Mermoz was lost on this flight and still is unaccounted for.

The French nation is not discouraged by these losses. It had planned a great Atlantic Derby last summer to commemorate the 10th anniversary of Lindbergh's flight, but refusal of U. S. officials to permit takeoffs in the derby prevented the race.

Most of the missing flyers are believed dead. Yet history provides ample precedent for the solving of the Redfern and other mysteries.

THERE is the fiction-like adventure of Solomon Andree, Nils Strindberg and Hans Fraenkel.

Back in July, 1897, those three air pioneers soared from Spitzbergen in a balloon and headed for the North Pole. They were lost and their fate remained a complete mystery until 33 years later.

In August, 1930, a party of whalers landed on White Island. They found there the last camp of Andree, Strindberg and Fraenkel.

(Copyright, 1937, by EveryWeek Magazine)

Among the excellently preserved remains were a diary and many rolls of film which yielded a complete and illustrated story of the tragedy.

The three men had been forced down on the ice after their balloon had floated many miles. They fashioned a tent from their silk balloon. Then they made sledges and started back across the ice fields in an attempted return to civilization.

They had plenty of ammunition and so were not lacking for food. The journey became a race with winter. But the ice moved north faster than the men could travel south and when the ice broke up, they made camp on White Island.

There Andree, Strindberg and Fraenkel met death, victims probably of the cold. Evidence indicated that their end had come in the wake of a terrific blizzard.

One of the most miraculous rescues in the history of aviation was part of the London Daily Mail's 1919 prize flight to the United States.

First off in the race for the $50,000 offered by the newspaper were Harry Hawker and Lieut.-Comm. Kenneth MacKenzie Grieve. Previously Hawker had made a successful 1800-mile flight in his 2½-ton biplane, "At-

APPENDIX | 309

Solomon Andree (above), pioneer balloonist whose remains were found on White Island 33 years after he was lost on a flight to the North Pole.... Right—Ruth Elder. This famous aviatrix and her crew were rescued on the Atlantic ocean after disaster overtook their flight to Europe.

Amelia Earhart (sketch at left) is the most famous flyer ever to be lost at sea.

Left—Paul Redfern.

Mildred Doran joined the ranks of missing flyers on a flight to Honolulu in 1927.

lantic." Late in the afternoon of May 18, 1919, the "Atlantic" roared down the hill of a Newfoundland farm, 350 gallons of gas aboard. It nearly struck a fence. Then as it gained altitude, watchers saw the landing gear drop. The ship vanished in a fog.

Suspense soon became doubt and, within five days, hope for the flyers was abandoned. King George V even sent condolences to Mrs. Hawker.

But three days later the steamer Mary radioed from off the coast of Scotland that the flyers were safe aboard. They had picked up 1050 miles out of Newfoundland a week before.

THE flyers told this story of their trip: boiled away and after shutting off the motor, the flyers found that bits of solder had dropped cooling system. At 100 feet above the ocean Hawker switched the ignition on again, but the engine failed to start until the craft was about to plunge into the water. The plane gained altitude, but the radiator soon boiled again.

When a faint smudge the men had sighted ahead turned out to be a ship, they circled three times and landed directly in front of it.

King George decorated Hawker and Grieve, and the Daily Mail awarded them a $5000 consolation prize. A month later Capt. John Alcock and Lieut. Arthur Whitten Brown won the $50,000.

Just as thrilling and even more harrowing was the story of the crew of a U.S. Navy plane. Two of these planes had left San Francisco Aug. 31, 1925, on what the navy hoped would be the first non-stop flight to Hawaii. One plane landed on the water and was towed back. The other ship was forced down after making 1900 miles. It had exhausted its fuel supply. The crew members were Comm. John Rodgers, Lieut.-Comm. Byron Connell, Pilot S. R. Pope, William Bowlin and O. G. Stantz.

A cordon of navy vessels had been strung along the route but the distressed plane was not sighted. Day after day the plane drifted, with the aid of sails rigged from wing fabric. After zigzagging some 450 miles, it was sighted by a submarine off the Island of Kauai and towed into harbor. The flyers were near death from lack of water and 10 days' exposure.

THE patron saint of flyers lost at sea well might be the unsinkable Mr. Hausner. Stanley Hausner attempted a flight to Europe in 1932. His plane was forced down on the ocean and for eight days he drifted. He finally was picked up by a British tanker. He existed on sandwiches and coffee those eight days. Hausner's luck didn't hold, however, and he was killed in a plane crash in 1935.

The fate of Joaquin Collar and Mariano Barberan of Spain was anticlimax to triumph. They flew from Seville to Cuba in 1933 and were greeted with a great celebration. Then, only a few weeks later, they vanished over the Gulf of Mexico and never were found.

Similar disappearances claimed Lloyd Bertaud, J. D. Hill and Philip A. Payne, bound for Europe from Old Orchard, Me., in 1927; Sir John Carling, Captain Tully and Lieutenant Metcalf, westbound from England in 1927; Charles T. P. Ulm of Australia, en route from Oakland, Calif., to the Hawaiian Islands in 1934; and Sir Charles Kingsford-Smith, also of Australia, who with Ulm and two others made the first flight from California to Australia.

CREDIT: THE ATCHISON GLOBE and ATCHISON COUNTY HISTORICAL SOCIETY

One day after Amelia Earhart exchanged this bon voyage handclasp at Oakland Airport with Lieut. Charles T. P. Ulm, December 3, 1934, Ulm and two companions on a projected hop to Honolulu were down near Hawaii and the object of a sea and air search that proved fruitless. Yesterday was the ninth day of a similar search for Miss Earhart.—Tribune photo.

Index

Abernathy, Mrs. E. E.   48
Abraham, Robert W.   164
Adams, President John   1
Adams, Porter   101
Air League of the British Empire   88
Airway Pioneers, Society of   199
Alcoholics Anonymous   59
Allen, Lt. Governor   98
Altman, Catharine   30
Altman, Miriah Joseph   30
Amelia Earhart Day   164
Amelia Earhart Design   119, 120
Amelia Earhart Symposium   205
American Aeronautical Society   76
Andrews, Roy Chapman   118
Anthony, Commander Henry M.   204, 205, 277, 279
Ariyoshi, Governor George R.   164
Arnold, First Lieutenant Donald D.   204, 205
Arnold, General "Hap"   266
Atchison Daily Champion   35
Atchison Globe   169, 308–309
Atchison Trinity Church   6
Avro Avian   88, 102, 115
Baker Island   286, 291–294
Balbo, General Italo   132
Balchen, Bernt   122, 126, 133
Balfour, Harry J.   233, 275
Bandoeng, Java   220–226, 229, 231, 267
Barnes, Pancho   102
Barnes, Ralph   70
Baruch, Bernard   208
Beech-Nut Packing Company   109
Bell Telephone Laboratories   178, 211, 276
Bellarts, Leo G.   235, 242–247
Bendix Air Race (Trophy)   182
Bendix D.F. Homing Device   170, 191, 192, 236–247
Bendix, Vincent   170
Beverly Hills Speedway   64
Black, Admiral Richard   204, 231–232, 256, 305–307
Blackwell, Lucy Stone   17
Bliss, Curtis H. and Gerald   215
Bloomer, Amelia Jenks   17
Bohrer, Ann   209
Boll, Mabel (Diamond Queen)   79
Boston Edison Company   74
Boston Airport   95
Briand, Paul   286
British Guild of Airpilots and Navigators   131
Bruce, Anne   90, 98
Bryn Mawr College   44
Bulolo Gold Dredging Ltd.   229
Burlington Railroad   2, 40, 42
Byrd, Commander Richard Evelyn   78–79, 81, 83, 85, 96–97, 101, 126, 208, 209
Byrd, Marie   79
Campbell family   112
Cardenas, President Lazaro   165
Cardenas, Señora   165
Carter, Tonie   267–272

Castruccio, Dr. Giuseppe   132
Central High School   37
Cermak, Chicago Mayor Anton J.   43
Challiss, Lucy and Katherine   24, 26, 112
Challiss, Luther   5
Challiss, James   112
Challiss, Mary Otis   5
Challiss, Dr. Paul   5
Chapman, Samuel   59–61, 68, 70–71, 74, 79, 81, 100, 107
Chapman, William   79, 80
Chappellet, Cyril   178, 180, 188
Chater, E.H.   280
Chevalier, Lieutenant John B.   95, 100
Choy, Nelwyn   164
Christen, Harvey and Vera (Doane)   105, 143, 289
Christian Science Church   59, 112
Cipriani, Frank   235
Cleveland National Air Races   105, 141, 142
Coast Guard and Naval documentation   185–186, 200–201, 207–208, 218, 234, 236–247, 249–265, 271–272, 283–284, 286–287, 289–290
Cochran, Jacqueline (see Odlum)
Collopy, J. A., Report   232, 275–276
Columbia University   54–58, 70, 73, 116
Confidential   188, 276–277
Consolidated Airlines   183, 188
Coolidge, President and Mrs. Calvin   87, 95, 101
Copeland, Royal S.   172
Cosmopolitan magazine   101, 105–106, 113
Cross of the Legion of Honor   131–132
Cross of Chevalier of the Order of Leopold   132
Crosson, Marvel   104
Croydon Airport   88
Curtiss Canuck "Jenny"   61, 65
Curtiss Field   104–105
Curtiss Pusher   98
Curtiss School of Aviation   61
Darrow, Dr. Daniel   75–76
Darrow, Dr. Louise deSchweinitz   55–56, 75–76
Daughter of the Sky   286
Daughters of the American Revolution   136
Davila, Charles A.   146
De Jarnette, Miss Pearl   30, 32
Death, Proof of   283–284
DeCarrie, Margot   198
Denison House   69–70, 72–76, 78–79, 86, 88, 96, 100, 109, 116
Dennison Airport   76, 79
DeSchweinitz, Dr. Louise (see Darrow)
Dimity, E. H.   183, 199
Distinguished Flying Cross   136
Doctor of Science   138
Dole Race   164, 308–309
Donahey, Senator Vic   173
Donohoe, Mrs. Nellie G.   199
Doolittle, General James   265–266
Doran, Mildred   308–309
Douglas Cloudster   64

Douglas, Donald   64
Drake University   32
Dutch East Indies Air Force   220, 267
Dwiggins, Don   205, 213
Earhart, Amy Otis (mother)   1, 5–7, 14, 16, 17, 23–25, 28–38, 41–44, 50, 54, 57, 59, 68–69, 72, 79–82, 86, 93, 95–96, 98, 112, 114, 140, 215, 250, 256, 284–285
Earhart, Edwin Stanton (father)   4–5, 7, 14, 22–24, 28, 30, 32–43, 50, 54, 57, 59–60, 65, 68, 79, 112–113, 116, 138, 284
Earhart, Helen   112–113
Earhart, Martha   30
Earhart, Mary Wells Patton   4, 11–18
Earhart, Reverend David (grandfather)   4, 40
Eckener, Dr. Hugo   131
Edington, Harry   270
Elliott, President Edward   168, 170, 208
Fahy, Clara   102, 104
Faireys, C. R.   131
Federal Aviation Administration (Dept. of Commerce)   177
Federal Bureau of Investigation (FBI)   271
Federal Communications Commission   155
Fédération Aéronautique Internationale   65, 76
Flemming, Larry   199
Flight For Freedom   267–271
Floyd Bennett Airport   182
Fokker *Friendship*   78–92, 97, 100–101, 115, 118, 122, 124, 133, 159, 185
Forest of Friendship   305
Fox family   112
Frickers Metal Company office   86
Friedell, Captain   254
Furman, F.O. "Fuzz"   220–229, 267
Gallagher, James   127
Garber, Dr. Paul E.   303
Garrett, Oliver H.P.   272
Get Underway!   254
Gilbert Islands   258, 260–261, 263, 291
Golden Eagle   104
Goodyear Field   67
Gordon, Louis "Slim"   78–80, 84–86, 89, 90, 92, 94–96, 100, 115, 133
Gorgas, Dr.   32
Gorski, Eddie   122
Gower, Louis   78, 80, 84, 92, 98
Grace Episcopal Church   100, 107
Grand Central Air Terminal   112, 113
Great Northern Railway   36, 37
Great Circle Route   123, 293
Grieben, Walter   195
Gross, Robert   176
Gross, Cortland   177
Grosselfinger, W. H. "Walt"   178, 213
Grosvenor, Gilbert   134, 136
Guest, Raymond   76
Guest, Mrs. Frederick (Amy Phipps)   76, 78, 81, 83, 86–88, 116

INDEX

Guinea Airways 227, 232, 275
Hadley, Reverend Dwight 100, 106, 114
Hammitt, Evelyn 270
Hanlow, Mr. 221, 223
Harres, Gebhard 1, 32
Harres, Maria Grace 1, 5, 284
Hart, Beryl 308–309
Hart, Merwin K. 105
Harvard University Summer School 70
Hawks, Frank 139
Headle, Marshall 210
Heath, Lady Mary 88, 102
Henderson, Cliff 142
Hicks, W. Stanley 157, 196, 198, 259
Hirohito, Emperor 282–283
Holmes, Chris 152, 154, 204–205
Hoover, President Herbert 60, 133, 136–137
Hoover, J. Edgar 276
Hovde, Frederick L. 168
Howland Island 187, 189–190, 225, 230–247, 249–265, 272–295
Hoyt, Jean D. 104
Hubbell School 30
Hyde Park High School 42, 48, 70
Industrial Workers of the World (I.W.W.) 59–60
Ingalls, Sheffield 169
Ingalls, Senator John J. and Constance 5–6
Jacobs, F. C. 229
Japan, Consulate General of 281–283
Japanese servants 152
Japanese mandated islands 281–283
Jarvis Island 273
Jensen, Martin 164
Johns Hopkins Medical School 55, 76
Johnson, Dr. Charles 35, 44
Johnson, C.L. "Kelly" 193, 194
Joubert, L.C. 229
Kahalewai, Carl K. 305–307
Kahalewai, Samuel 305–307
Kansas Pacific Railroad 4
Kenner, Admiral 204, 246
Kent, Rockwell 118, 145
Kimball, Dr. James H. 79, 84, 122, 124–125, 159–160
King Albert and Queen of the Belgians 132, 136
King Carol of Rumania 146, 148
Kingsford-Smith, Sir Charles 308–309
Kinner Airster "Canary" 63–64, 67–68, 177
Kinner Airplane & Motor Corporation 67, 79
Kinner Airfield 61, 64, 67
Kinner, Bert 63, 65–67, 76–77, 106
Kissel Kar "Yellow Peril" 68, 72, 76, 79, 96
Kleppner, Mrs. Amy Morrissey 255, 266
KLM and KNILM 220, 222–224
Knope, V.R. 308–309
LADY WITH WINGS: The Life Story 270
Lady Astor 88
Lae, New Guinea 189, 219–220, 222, 225–230, 233, 250–251, 257, 265–266, 278–295

LaGorce, John Oliver 134, 220
Lake Erie College 209
Landon, Governor Alf M. 169
La Plante, General Thomas A. 164
Larkin, Mayor Edward H. 82, 97–98, 100
Last Flight 220
Layman, David T. 78
Leahy, Admiral William D. 212, 254
Lee, Anita King 192
Lincoln Junior High School 80–81, 107
Lincoln, President Abraham 2
Lindbergh, Colonel Charles 76, 78, 90, 100, 118, 124, 129, 131, 141, 146, 167, 178, 274
Lindbergh, Anne 118, 131
Lindsay, Vachel 21
Livingston, "customer" 176–178
Lockheed, Allan 143
Lockheed Vega 95, 99, 104–105, 115, 123, 127–128, 139, 143–144, 165, 167, 183
Lockheed Model 10E Electra "Flying Laboratory" 168–247, 254, 256, 267, 271–294
Lockheed Aircraft Corporation 143, 176–178, 180–181, 188, 193, 207, 211, 282
Long, Ray 107
Los Angeles Times Building 60
Los Angeles Municipal Airport 139
Ludington Lines 110
Luke Field (Ford Island) 204–206, 286
Luke Report 286–290
MacArthur, General Douglas 266
MacCaughan, George 23, 34–35
MacGregor, Professor James 56
MacLaren, Lieutenant W.W. 308–309
Mann, Grace and Genevieve 30
Mann, J.P. 30–31
Manning, Captain Harry 88, 92, 188, 191, 198–205, 212, 282
Mansfield, Ambassador Mike 286
Mantz, Paul 76, 151, 153, 154, 157, 176–177, 185, 191, 196, 198, 200–205, 213, 278, 290, 295
Mantz, Mrs. Mitzie 153–154
Marianas Islands 267
Marshall Islands 266–267, 291
Martin, Glenn L. Company 220, 221
Martin, John A. 2, 5
Martin, Ralphie 14, 16
Massachusetts General Hospital 96
Massachusetts University 69
Mather, Mr. 37
Matson ship *Maliko* 155
May, John S. 169
May, Oscar 169
McCall's magazine 101
McCarran, Senator Pat 173
McCoy, Horace 270
McKinley, President William 11
McKneely, R.D. "Bo" 182, 228, 288
McMurray, Fred 267–270
McQueen, Mrs. Ulysses Grant 94
Meier, Fred C. 219
Mexican Geographic Society 165
Miami Municipal Airport 214
Midway Island 185, 188, 189

Miller, W. T. 192, 200, 201, 280
Miner, Terry 203
Missing Flyers 308–309
Mission Inn 148
Molineaux, Reverend John H. 11
Montijo, John "Monty" 64, 67
Morgan Park High School 42
Morganthau Diaries 273–274
Morganthau, Henry Jr. 273–274
Morrissey, Amy (see Kleppner)
Morrissey, David 250, 255, 284
Morrissey, Henry Albert "The Chief" 75–76, 81, 106–107, 250, 289
Morse Code 199, 204, 220, 233, 281–282, 284, 295
Murfin, Rear Admiral Orin G. 254, 265
Musick, Captain Edwin 203
Nakajima, Professor Fumihiko 286–288
National Geographic Society Medal 134–135
National Aeronautic Association 101
National Geographic Magazine 124, 151
National Geographic Society 134–136, 220
National Air Races, Cleveland 105, 141–142
Naval Investigative service 273
New Guinea Goldfields Ltd. 229
Newcomer, Edna 308–309
Newman, Pauline Coleman 73
Newman, Dr. T. Steel 286
Nichandros, Gust 254
Nichols, Mayor Malcolm E. 97–98
Nichols, Ruth 65, 78, 102
Ninety-Nines 104–105, 113, 300
Noonan, Fred J. 188, 196, 200–205, 212, 214–216, 218–221, 224–227, 229, 232–233, 248, 250, 257, 260, 262, 265–267, 275, 278, 284–295
Noonan, Mrs. Mary 254, 265
Noyes, Blanche 105
Noyes, Leigh 283–284
Nukumanu Islands 290–291
O'Dea, T.F. "Tommie" 227, 229
Oakland Airport 157, 162–163, 194, 197, 225, 275
Oakland Tribune 195, 270
Odlum, Floyd and Jacqueline Cochran 208, 254, 256, 266, 278
Ogontz School 44–45, 47–50, 54, 56, 70, 81, 116
Oldham, Mr. 20–21
Omlie, Phoebe 102, 105
Otis, Mark 35, 43–44
Otis, Theodore 35, 44
Otis, Alfred Gideon (grandfather) 1–3, 5–6, 8, 14, 25–28, 30, 35, 60, 114, 289
Otis, Carl (Nicey) 16–17, 22, 30
Otis, Grace Hetherington 10, 11, 284
Otis, Harrison Gray 60, 284
Otis, James 1
Otis, Margaret 6, 10, 17
Otis, Mark (uncle) 7, 15–16, 18, 35, 43–44, 284
Otis, Amy (see Earhart, Amy Otis)

Otis, Amelia Josephine Harres (grandmother) 1–2, 11, 24–28, 32, 35–36, 43–44, 114, 284
Pacific Airmotive Corporation, Ltd. 158
Painlevé, M. Paul 131–132
Palo Alto Airport 210
Pan American Airways 188, 202–203, 213, 216–217, 282, 293, 295
Paris, Neva 102, 104
Park, Virginia 44
Parker, Commander Stanley V. 279–280
Parker, E. H. 175
Patton, Mary Wells 4
Payne, Hubert Scott 86
Pearl Harbor 161, 206, 218, 231, 265, 269
Pedlar, J.A. 308–309
Pennoyer, Commander 133
Perkins, Marion 72, 74, 78, 86, 88, 95, 109
Perkins Institute for the Blind 76
Perry, Margaret 142
Phipps, John S. 78
Phoenix Islands 260–261, 263, 291
Piccard, Auguste 132
Pinchot, Governor 32
Pisculli, Dr. L.M. 308–309
Pitcarin Autogiro 110, 113
Pollock, Lucille 107
Port Darwin, Australia 225–226
Porter, New York Mayor 140
Post, Wiley 159, 167
Powder Puff Derby 102
Pratt & Whitney "Wasp" 126, 155, 158, 170, 176–177, 194
Preanger Hotel 224–225
President Pierce 156
Press Tribune 227–228, 230
Pellegreno, Ann 302
Press Conference #382 262
Purdue University 168, 170, 183, 208
Purdue Research Foundation Board of Directors 168, 170
Purdue Airport 170
Putnam, George Palmer 78–80, 84, 86, 88, 90, 96, 100, 113–118, 120, 122–124, 129–132, 136, 139–141, 144–145, 148–149, 151, 154, 156, 167–168, 174–176, 178, 184–185, 188, 207–208, 214, 218–219, 225–226, 256, 265
Putnam, David 140, 214
Putnam's, G. P. Sons Publishing Company 78, 88
Quinby, E. Jay 212
Raiche, Dr. Bessica 48
Railey, Captain Hilton 78–80, 86–89
Rasche, Thea 102, 104
Raymond, Allen 86
Redfern, Paul 308–309
Richards, Lyle F. 254
Richey, Helen 182
Ringers, Thomas J. 227
RKO Radio Pictures 268–270
Robinson's Department Store 144
Rock Island Railroad 14, 23

Rock Island Claim Department 36
Rogers Air Field 65
Rogers Airport 60
Rogers, Will 102, 167
Roosevelt, Hall 175
Roosevelt, Eleanor (Mrs. Franklin D.) 174–175, 184–185, 267, 276, 278–279, 286
Roosevelt, President Franklin D. 60, 162, 184–185, 187, 189, 201, 254, 262, 264–265, 267
Root, Elihu 32
Royal Flying Corps 53
Russell, Rosalind 267–270
S. S. *American* 86
S. S. *Lurline* 151, 153, 203
S.S. *Myrtlebank* 257, 258, 290–293
U.S.C.G. *Ontario* 227, 233, 236–247, 257, 258, 285
S. S. *Roosevelt* 88
San Francisco Division, U.S.C.G. 204, 219, 232, 236–247
Santa Fe Railroads 2
Scheider, Malvina 271–273
Schofield, Helen 28
Selfridge, Gordon 88, 256
Senate Air Safety Committee 172
Seng, A.W. 169
Shedd family and Elizabeth 42
Short, Mary 107
Sino-Japanese War 256
Skinner, Cornelia Otis 118
Skyward 83
Smith College 49, 54, 59, 107
Smithsonian Institution 205, 303
Snowden, Robert P. 169
Southern, Neta Snook 60–61, 63–64, 67, 90
Southgate, Richard 185
Spadina Military Hospital 49, 54
Sparhawk, Katherine 158
Sparhawk, Lieutenant and Mrs. George 154
Spaulding, Captain 54
Squantum Air Base 76
Squier, Carl 120, 143
St. Margaret's College 49, 52
St. Clement's Episcopal Church 37
Stabler family 69
Stabler, Marian and Frank 54
Stand By To Die 270
Standard Oil Company 220–221, 224, 226
Stanton, Elizabeth Cady 17
Stearman, Lloyd 143
Stephens, Lieutenant E. W. 161–162
Stultz, Wilmer L. "Bill" 78–80, 84–90, 92, 94–96, 98, 100, 115
Sutherland, Abby A. 48–49
Tadgell, Richard 107
Tail Spins magazine 209
Teterboro Airport 123
Thaden, Louise 105
The Fun of It 144
Thiel College 5, 138
Thompson, Gilbert E. 234
Thompson, Commander Warner K. 231–232, 249, 278

Tinus, W. C. 211, 276–277
Tissot, Ernie 151, 153, 155
Tokimo 30, 36
Tokyo Rose 265–266
Torney, Dr. George H. 70
Toynbee Hall 88
Transport Pilot's License 114
Trinity Episcopal Church 8, 11
Trout, Bobbi Evelyn 102, 104–105, 146–147
Trufant, Katharyn 107
Turbyfill, Mark 54
20 HRS. 40 MIN., Our Flight In The Friendship 61, 64, 81, 94, 113
Twitchell, Mrs. 30
U. S. Navy pathology department 288
U.S.C.G. *Itasca* 190, 231, 233–247, 249–253, 261–262, 264–265, 278
U.S.S. *Lexington* 254–265, 287
U.S.S. *Colorado* 252–254, 261, 264, 286
U.S.S. *President Roosevelt* 188
U.S.S. *Ramapo* 155
U.S.S. *Swan* 253, 261, 264
U.S.C.G. *Rodger B. Taney* 270–271
Ulm, Lt. Charles T.P. 279, 308–309
Union Air Terminal 148, 167, 187
Union Oil 139
University of Kansas Law School 5
Valbuena Airport 165
Vanity Fair 108, 121
Vassar College 5
Vellasenor, Eduardo 165
Vidal, Eugene L. 162
Waesche, Admiral R. R. 219
Waggoner family 112
Waldron, Mrs. 52
Walton, Sarah 28, 112
Washington, General George 1
Washington Airport 171
Welch, Mrs. Foster 86–87
Wells, Fay Gillis 164
West High School 36
Western Electric Company 170, 178, 180–182, 200, 211–213, 271, 276–277, 287–291
Westinghouse 178
Westport High School 49
Wheeler Field 153, 158, 164, 200, 203–204, 256
White House documents 274
Whiting, Captain Kenneth 254
Williams, Clarence S. 159–161, 191–192, 289, 295
Women's Home Companion magazine 268–270
Women's Transcontinental Air Derby 102, 105
Women's Aeronautic Association 94
Women's Educational & Industrial Union 71
Woolley, Major Charles H. 80, 85
Works Progress Administration (WPA) 187, 189
World's Fair, St. Louis 14
Wright, Orville 145
Younger, House of Representative 287
Zonta International 109, 146, 295